GOD'S WIFE, GOD'S SERVANT

Drawing on textual, iconographic and archaeological evidence, this book highlights a historically documented (but often ignored) instance, where five single women were elevated to a position of supreme religious authority. The women were Libyan and Nubian royal princesses who, consecutively, held the title of God's Wife of Amun during the Egyptian Twenty-third to Twenty-sixth dynasties (c.754–525 BC). At a time of weakened royal authority, rulers turned to their daughters to establish and further their authority. Unmarried, the princess would be dispatched from her father's distant political and administrative capital to Thebes, where she would reign supreme as a God's Wife of Amun.

While her title implied a marital union between the supreme solar deity Amun and a mortal woman, the God's Wife was actively involved in temple ritual, where she participated in rituals that asserted the king's territorial authority as well as Amun's universal power. As the head of the Theban theocracy, the God's Wife controlled one of the largest economic centers in Egypt: the vast temple estate at Karnak. Economic independence and religious authority spawned considerable political influence: a God's Wife became instrumental in securing the loyalty of the Theban nobility for her father, the king.

Yet, despite the religious, economic and political authority of the God's Wives during this tumultuous period of Egyptian history, to date, these women have only received cursory attention from scholars of ancient Egypt. Tracing the evolution of the office of God's Wife from its obscure origins in the Middle Kingdom to its demise shortly after the Persian conquest of Egypt in 525 BC, this book places these five women within the broader context of the politically volatile, turbulent seventh and eighth centuries BC, and examines how the women, and the religious institution they served, were manipulated to achieve political gain.

Mariam F. Ayad was born in Cairo and studied Egyptology at the American University in Cairo and the University of Toronto before earning her doctorate in Egyptology at Brown University in 2003. She is currently the Assistant Director of the Institute of Egyptian Art & Archaeology in Memphis, Tennessee.

GOD'S WIFE, GOD'S SERVANT

The God's Wife of Amun (c. 740–525 BC)

Mariam F. Ayad

For Gwyn,
Hope you'll enjoy this book
and find it useful—
All the best,
Mariam Ayad

LONDON AND NEW YORK

First published 2009
by Routledge
2 Park Square, Milton Park, Abingdon, Oxon OX14 4RN

Simultaneously published in the USA and Canada
by Routledge
711 Third Avenue, New York, NY 10017

Routledge is an imprint of the Taylor & Francis Group, an informa business

First issued in paperback 2012

Typeset in Garamond by
HWA Text and Data Management Ltd, London

British Library Cataloguing in Publication Data
A catalogue record for this book is available from the British Library

Library of Congress Cataloging in Publication Data
Ayad, Mariam F.
God's wife, God's servant: the God's Wife of Amun (ca. 740–525 BC) /
Mariam F. Ayad.
p. cm.
"Simultaneously published in the USA and Canada" – T.p. verso.
Includes bibliographical references.
1. Amon (Egyptian deity) – Cult. 2. Mut (Egyptian deity) 3. Egypt – History – To 332 B.C. 4. Egypt – Religious life and customs. 5. Princesses – Egypt – History. 6. Titles of honor and nobility – Egypt – History. 7. Royal houses – Egypt – History. 8. Egypt – History – Eighteenth dynasty, ca. 1570–1320 B.C. 9. Temple of Amon (Karnak, Egypt) 10. Egypt – Antiquities. I. Title.
BL2450.A45A93 2009
299'.31211 – dc22 2008053560

ISBN 13: 978–0–415–41170–7 (hbk)
ISBN13: 978–0–203–87586–5 (ebk)
ISBN 13: 978–0–415–81950–3 (pbk)

It has not been possible to prove … that an Egyptian meant by "god" either the Only – without there being any other god – or the One and Highest of the gods.

Erik Hornung
Conceptions of God in Ancient Egypt: The One and the Many, 60

CONTENTS

List of figures ix
Preface and acknowledgments xiii
Map of Egypt and Nubia xv
Map of Luxor xvi
List of abbreviations xvii

Introduction 1

1 **The historical setting** 3
The God's Wife: historical development and associated titles 3
The God's Wife prior to the New Kingdom 4
The God's Wife during the New Kingdom 4
THE MYTHIC CONCEPTION I: ATUM AND THE HELIOPOLITAN CREATION MYTH 5
THE MYTHIC CONCEPTION II: THE KING'S DIVINE CONCEPTION 7
Egypt at the end of the New Kingdom 8
Egypt during the Libyan period 10
The Nubians in Egypt 11
The Libyan and Nubian God's Wives of Amun 15
Egypt under Saite rule 22
Nitocris 23
Ankhnesneferibre: the last God's Wife of Amun 27
Amun, Mut, and the "throne names" of the God's Wives 29

2 **Rites and rituals** 34
Entertaining the gods 35
Playing music: shaking the sistrum 35
THE SISTRUM, THE *MENAT*-NECKLACE AND OBJECTS SACRED TO HATHOR 37
Provisioning the gods: offerings to the gods 52
Wine 52
Food 55
Cool water/incense 57

"A boon which the king gives" 60
Maat 61
Building houses for the gods/dedicating shrines 70
Partnering with the king 1: Symmetrically opposed scenes 75
In providing for the gods 75
Rewarded by the gods 82
Partnering with the king 2: "For god, king, and country" 87
Protecting the gods 87
Rites of protection at the cenotaph 87
"Burning fans" 90
"Rites at Kom Djeme" 94
Rejuvenating the gods 96
The elevation of the tjest-*support* 96
Rites of divine re-entrance 99
Other rites of "royal and divine" dominion 103
"Driving four calves" 103
"Striking chests" or the presentation of *meret*-chests 108
Celebrating the sed *festival* 110

3 Avenues to legitimacy 116
Assumption of the priesthood 116
The gradual appropriation of priestly duties 116
Saite secularism 120
The God's Wife and initiation rites 120
Avenues to legitimacy 124
Shepenwepet I 124
Suckling scenes 125
Crowning scenes 127
Amenirdis I 129
Shepenwepet II 133
Divin marriage iconography 134
Nitocris 139
Ankhnesneferibre 140
Adoption, succession to office, and age at appointment 142
Sexuality, celibacy and the sexual role of the God's Wife 146

Epilogue 153
The end of the God's Wife as an institution 153
The legacy of the God's Wives of Amun 154

Notes 156
Bibliography 183
Index 199

FIGURES

(The plate section can be found between pages 110 and 111)

	Map of Egypt and Nubia	xv
	Map of Luxor	xvi
0.1	Chapels of the God's Wife of Amun, Karnak	2
1.1	Remains of Shepenwepet I's funerary chapel	17
1.2	Chapel of Osiris, Ruler of Eternity	17
1.3	Chapel of Osiris, Ruler of Eternity, façade	18
1.4	Façade of the funerary chapel of Amenirdis I	20
1.5	Doorway leading to the tomb chapel of Nitocris	26
2.1	Chapel of Osiris, Ruler of Eternity, room I, eastern wall, lower register	41
2.2	Chapel of Osiris, Ruler of Eternity, room I, eastern wall, lower register	42
2.3	Ramses II rattling the sistrum before Amun Ka-Mutef, Karnak Hypostyle Hall	44
2.4	King Ptolemy II shakes the sistrum before the goddess Mut, Temple of Mut at Karnak	46
2.5	Chapel of Osiris, Ruler of Eternity, room I, eastern wall	48
2.7	Shepenwepet II offering wine to Osiris, chapel of Osiris-Wennofer-who-is-in-the-midst-of-the-Persea-Tree, room I, western wall	54
2.9	God's Wife pours libations, chapel of Osiris-Wennofer-who-is-in-the-midst-of-the-Persea-Tree, room II, eastern wall	58
2.12	Nubian king presenting *Maat* to Amun-Re, chapel of Osiris, Ruler of Eternity, room I, north wall, eastern half, lower register	65
2.13	Shepenwepet II presents *Maat* to Aumn-Re, chapel of Osiris, Lord of Life, room I, western wall	68
2.15	Amenirdis partners with the goddess Seshat in the rite of "Stretching the Cord," chapel of Osiris, Ruler of Eternity, north wall, western half, lower register	73
2.16	Amenirdis offers an image of a temple to Amun-Re, chapel of Osiris, Ruler of Eternity, north wall, eastern half, upper register	74
2.17	Lintel, chapel of Osiris, Lord of Life	75

2.18	Chapel of Osiris-Wennofer-*Neb-djefa*a	79
2.22	Rites of protection at the cenotaph, Edifice of Taharqo by the Sacred Lake, subterranean room E, east wall, lintel	87
2.24	The elevation of the *tjest*-support, Edifice of Taharqo by the Sacred Lake, subterranean room E, south wall	97
2.26	Shepenwepet II drives four calves before Osiris, Re-Horakhty, and deified Amenirdis, funerary chapel of Amenirdis, courtyard, southern wall, eastern half, upper register	105
2.27	Hatshepsut drives four calves	105
2.28	Shepenwepet II's celebration of the *sed* festival	111
3.1	Chapel of Osiris, Ruler of Eternity, room II, western wall, lower register	117
3.3	Hatshepsut's *chapelle rouge*, inner sanctuary, north wall; Karnak Open Museum	122
3.4	Chapel of Osiris, Ruler of Eternity, façade of Libyan chapel, door jambs, upper register	125
3.5	Counterpoise of King Taharqo's *menat*-necklace	126
3.6	Chapel of Osiris, Ruler of Eternity, façade of Libyan chapel, door jambs, lower register	128
3.7	Amenirdis receives life, chapel of Osiris, Ruler of Eternity, east wall, lower register	131
3.10	Divine marriage: Mut embraces Amun-Re	136
3.11	Karnak Hypostyle Hall, east wall, southern half, lower register	138
3.12	Karnak Hypostyle Hall, east wall, southern half, lower register	138

Plates

2.6	Amenirdis offering wine to Amun-Re, chapel of Osiris, Ruler of Eternity, room I, north wall, upper register
2.8	Shepenwepet II offering wine to Osiris, chapel of Osiris-Wennofer-who-is-in-the-midst-of-the-Persea-Tree, room I, western wall
2.10	Shepwepet II offers a *hekenou*-jar to Ra-Horakhy, funerary chapel of Amenirdis at Medinet Habu, courtyard, south wall, eastern half, lower register
2.11	Shepwepet II offers a *hekenou*-jar to Ra-Horakhy, Isis and deified Amenirdis, funerary chapel of Amenirdis at Medinet Habu, courtyard, south wall, eastern half, lower register
2.14	Ankhnesneferibre offers *Maat* to Amun-Re, Mut, and Khonsu, chapel of Amasis and Nitocris, vestibule, southern wall
2.19a	Chapel of Osiris-Wennofer-*Neb-djefa*, southern door jamb
2.19b	Chapel of Osiris-Wennofer-*Neb-djefa*, northern door jamb
2.20a	Taharqo embraced by Osiris, chapel of Osiris, Lord of Life, southern door jamb

2.20b Shepenwepet embraced by Isis, chapel of Osiris, Lord of Life, northern door jamb
2.21a Ankhnesneferibre, who receives life from Isis, chapel of Amasis and Nitocris, room I, northern door jamb
2.21b Psametik (III) receives life from Harsiese, chapel of Amasis and Nitocris, room I, southern door jamb
2.23 God's Wife burning fans bearing the image of Egypt's enemies, Hatshepsut's *chapelle rouge*, inner sanctuary, north wall; Karnak Open Museum
2.25 Shepenwepet II, funerary chapel of Amenirdis, courtyard, southern wall, eastern half, upper register
3.2 Hatshepsut's *chapelle rouge*, inner sanctuary, north wall; Karnak Open Museum
3.8 Amenirdis I embraced by Amun-Re, chapel of Osiris-Wennofer-who-is-in-the-midst-of-the-Persea-Tree, eastern door jamb
3.9 Shepenwepet II embraced by Amun-Re, Chapel of Osiris-Wennofer-who-is-in-the-midst-of-the-Persea-Tree, western door jamb

PREFACE AND ACKNOWLEDGMENTS

A brief note on the book's title: *God's Wife, God's Servant*. While indivduals familiar with the Egyptian language will immediately realize that the Egyptian words for "wife" and "servant" have the same phonetic value, *hemet*, this book's title is not intended as a pun. In fact, it is inspired by the official titles of the last God's Wife of Amun, Ankhnesneferibre, who had the unprecedented distinction of becoming the High Priest of Amun (literally, "First Servant of God"), and as such, officiated on behalf of the king in temple ritual. Ankhnesneferibre's assumption of the High Priesthood of Amun defied culturally prescribed gender roles. The book's title thus closely reflects this study's aims as it attempts to define the role played by the God's Wives in ancient Egyptian temple ritual and contextualize Ankhnesneferibre's phenomenal rise to the High Priesthood.

This project could not have been completed without the help and support of many individuals and institutions. Preliminary field research for this book, carried out in 2003, was made possible through a generous post-doctoral fellowship funded by the National Endowment for the Humanities and administered through the American Research Center in Egypt. Special thanks go to Madame Amira Kathab and the staff of ARCE's Cairo office for providing logistical help in obtaining the requisite permits to visit various sites and museums in Egypt and for their overall support of my research. Thanks also to Dr. Raymond Johnson, Director of Chicago House in Luxor, for his hospitality and for allowing me access to Chicago House's wonderful library during my numerous visits to Luxor.

Much of the manuscript was written while on sabbatical in Cambridge and I would like to thank Mrs. Anne Lonsdale and the Fellows of New Hall College for their hospitality and for providing me with crucial access to the wonderful library and computer facilities available at the University of Cambridge. I would also like to thank Dr. Richard R. Ranta, Dean of the College of Communication and Fine Arts at the University of Memphis and members of the College Graduate Council for awarding me a much needed faculty development leave, without which I could not have finished this manuscript in a timely manner. Special thanks to Drs Lorelei H. Corcoran, Patricia V. Podzorski, and Nigel C. Strudwick for covering my teaching and administrative duties while on leave.

Special thanks must also go to Sandra Won Sohn and Mary-Kamal Eissa for proofreading early drafts of the manuscript and to Danielle Phelps for her help in producing the maps used in this book, for proofreading several drafts of the manuscript, and her overall cheerful attitude as she helped with numerous other tasks related to this project.

Several individuals and institutions have generously allowed me to reproduce their figures and drawings in this book. My heartfelt gratitude goes to Lyla Brock for allowing me to use her unpublished line-drawings of the God's Wife and to Drs Donald B. Redford and Jerry Kadish for their permission to include those figures in this book, which appear as Figs. 3.1, 3.4, and 3.6. I must also thank Éditions Dévy for the permission to reproduce plates from Schwaller du Lubicz's *Temples of Karnak*, pls. 233, 234, and 430; Dr. James P. Allen, Chairman of Brown University's Department of Egyptology and Ancient Western Asia, for permission to reproduce Parker *et al*, *Edifice of Taharqo*, plates 25 and 26; the Egypt Exploration Society for permission to use Edouard Naville's *The Temple of Deir el-Bahri* VI: *Lower Terrace*, clxi; the Institut français d'archéologie orientale in Cairo for permission to reproduce in part Barguet and Leclant, *Karnak Nord* IV, plate cvi.

Finally, my deepest appreciation goes to HG Bishop Angaelos, the spiritual leader of Coptic community in the UK and the parishioners of St. George's Cathedral in Stevenage, for their friendship, support, and encouragement. Last, but not least, I would like to thank my parents for enduring my obsession with the God's Wives of Amun and for nurturing my passion for all things Egyptian.

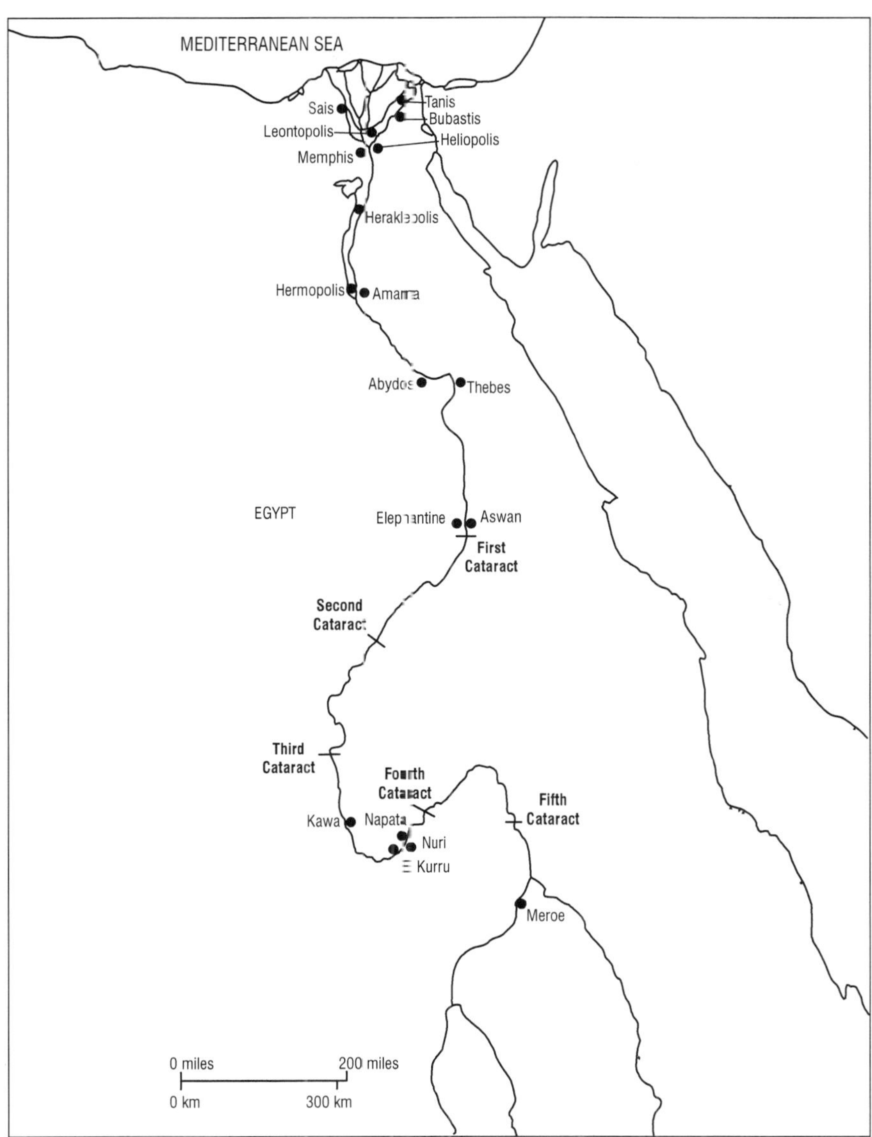
MEDITERRANEAN SEA
Sais
Tanis
Bubastis
Leontopolis
Heliopolis
Memphis
Herakleopolis
Hermopolis
Amarna
Abydos
Thebes
EGYPT
Elephantine
Aswan
First Cataract
Second Cataract
Third Cataract
Fourth Cataract
Fifth Cataract
Kawa
Napata
Nuri
Kurru
Meroe
0 miles
200 miles
0 km
300 km

Map of Egypt and Nubia

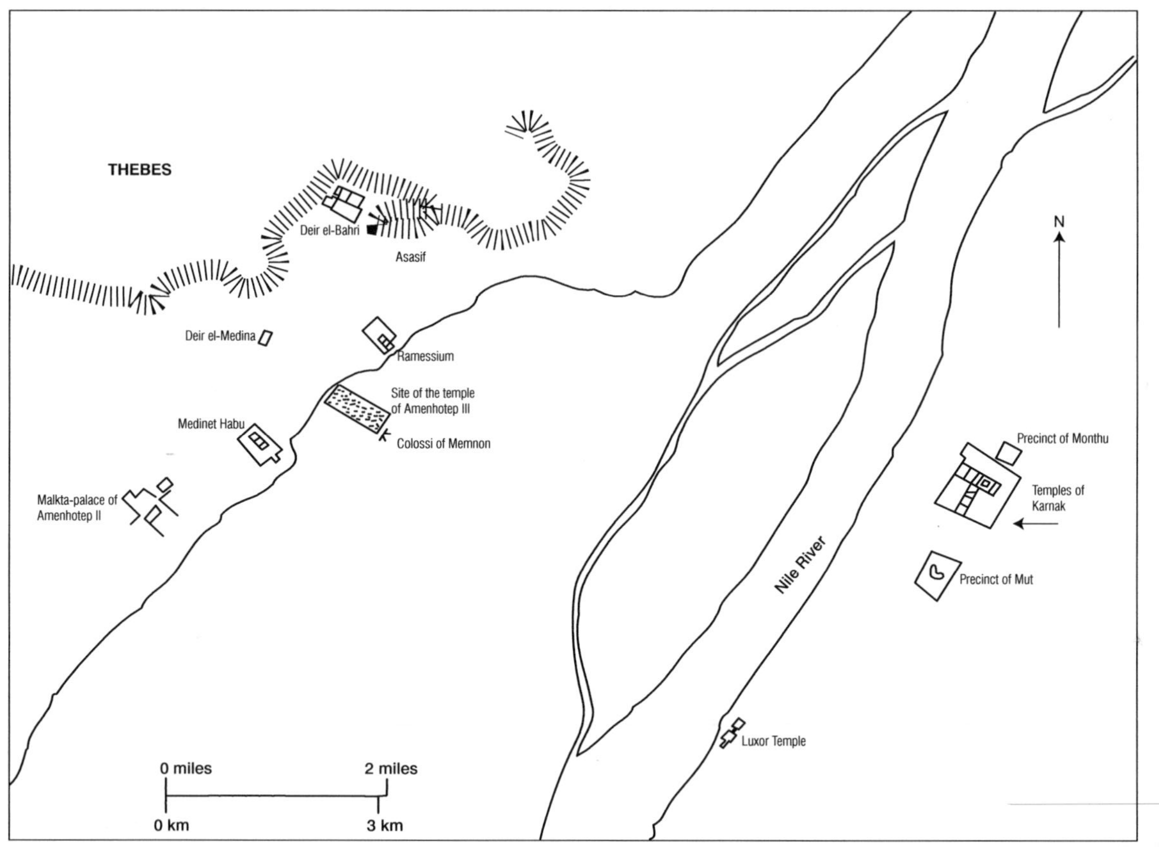
THEBES
Deir el-Bahri
Asasif
Deir el-Medina
Ramessium
Site of the temple
of Amenhotep III
Colossi of Memnon
Medinet Habu
Malkta-palace of
Amenhotep II
N
Precinct of Monthu
Temples of
Karnak
Precinct of Mut
Nile River
Luxor Temple
0 miles
2 miles
0 km
3 km

Map of Luxor

ABBREVIATIONS

AJA	*American Journal of Archaeology*, Baltimore
ANET	*Ancient Near Eastern Texts*
ASAE	*Annales du Service des Antiquités de l'Égypte*, Cairo
BdE	*Bibliothèque d'études, Institut français d'archéologie orientale*, Cairo
BIE	*Bulletin de l'institut d'Égypte*, Cairo
BIFAO	*Bulletin de l'institut français d'archéologie orientale*, Cairo
BSEG	*Bulletin de la Sociéte d'égyptologie de Genève*, Geneva
BSFE	*Bulletin de la Sociéte française d'égyptologie*, Paris
Cd'É	*Chronique d'Égypte*, Brussels
CG	*Catalogue général des antiquités égyptiennes du Musée du Caire*, Cairo
CRAIBL	*Comptes rendus des séances de l'Academie des inscriptions et belle lettres*, Paris
DE	*Discussions in Egyptology*
EEF	*Egypt Exploration Fund, London*
EES	*Egypt Exploration Society, London*
ET	*Études et travaux*
FHN	*Fontes Historiae Nubiorum: Textual Sources for the History of the Middle Nile Region between the Eighth Century* BC *and the Sixth Century* AD. Vol 1: *From the Eighth to the Mid-Fifth Century* BC, eds. T. Eide, T. Hägg, R. H. Pierce, and L. Török. Bergen: University of Bergen, Department of Classics, 1994
GM	*Göttinger Miszellen*, Göttingen
IFAO	*Institut français d'archéologie orientale*, Cairo
JAOS	*Journal of the American Oriental Society*
JARCE	*Journal of the American Research Center in Egypt*
JEA	*Journal of Egyptian Archaeology*
JEOL	*Jaarbericht van het Vooraziatisch-Egyptisch Genootschap "Ex Oriente Lux"*, Leiden
JESHO	*Journal of the Economic and Social History of the Orient*
JNES	*Journal of Near Eastern Studies*, Chicago
JSSEA	*Journal of the Society for the Study of Egyptian Antiquities*
LÄ	*Lexikon der Ägyptologie*, Wiesbaden
MÄS	*Münchner Ägyptologische Studien*, Berlin

MDAIK	*Mitteilungen des Deutschen Ärchäologischen Instituts, Abteilung Kairo*
MIFAO	Mémoires Publiés par les membres de l'institute francais d'archéologie orientale du Caire
MMA	*Metropolitan Museum of Art,* New York
MMAF	*Mémoires publiés par les members de la mission archéologique française au Caire,* Paris
OIP	*Oriental Institute Publications, The University of Chicago,* Chicago
PÄ	*Probleme der Ägyptologie,* Leiden
PM	Porter and Moss, *Topographical Bibliography*
PN	H. Ranke, *Die ägyptischen Personennamen.* 3 vols. Glückstadt: J.J. Augustin, 1935, 1949, 1977.
Rd'É	*Revue d'Égyptologie,* Cairo
RT	*Recueil de travaux rélatif à la philology et à l'archéologie égyptiennes et assyriennes,* Paris
SAK	*Studien zur Altägyptischen Kultur,* Hamburg
SAOC	Studies in Ancient Oriental Civilizations, The Oriental Institute of the University of Chicago, Chicago
WB	*Wörterbuch*
ZÄS	*Zeitschrift für Ägyptische Sprache und Altertumskunde,* Leipzig, Berlin

INTRODUCTION

This book revolves around a short Egyptian phrase, composed of just three hieroglyphic signs: . The signs spell the title *hemet netjer*, or "God's Wife." The Egyptians typically referred to a specific deity by name, only rarely using the generic, more general word for "god", *netjer*.[1] This book deals specifically with five royal women who bore the title *hemet netjet en imen*, or the "God's Wife *of Amun*," between 754 and 525 BC, a period when the title, and the institution, of God's Wife reached its zenith.

In the period spanning 754–525 BC, one Libyan, two Nubian, and two Saite women held the title of the God's Wife of Amun. Yet, despite their different ethnic backgrounds, all five women shared certain common features. Each was the daughter of a king. Almost invariably, each of the God's Wives placed the title *sat-nesou*, or "King's daughter," before the royal circle ("cartouche") enclosing her name, often using this, their most explicit link to the royal house, as their sole identifying title. Long after the title ceased to be held by queens, each of these royal princesses assumed queenly attire: the vulture headdress, surmounted by a rearing cobra (*uraeus*), or (in the case of the Nubian God's Wives), a double *uraeus*. But just like a king, a God's Wife assumed a *prenomen*, or "throne name," upon ascension to office and adopted feminine versions of several kingly titles. Thus, a God's Wife could also be a "(female) Horus," a "Mistress of the Two Lands," or a "Mistress of Diadems/ Appearances." Additionally, the Libyan, Nubian, and Saite God's Wives were often depicted presenting *Maat* to the gods, who, in return were regularly shown crowning, suckling, or protectively embracing a God's Wife. These were all aspects of temple ritual that had previously been the prerogative of the king only. Yet despite their obvious importance, outside a small circle of specialized academics, these women remain unknown. And even within academic circles, scholars who have previously dealt with this title have tended to view the office, particularly during the Third Intermediate and Saite periods, as a monolithic whole. In this study, I intend to show that this view is far from accurate. Indeed, the ever-expanding repertoire of the titles borne by the God's Wife and her increasingly sacred iconography indicate that the office of the God's Wife continued to change and evolve even within the relatively short span of this 200 year period.

Although it has long been recognized that the God's Wives of Amun of the Twenty-third to Twenty-sixth dynasties (*c.* 754–525 BC) assumed several aspects of

Figure 0.1 Chapels of the God's Wife of Amun, Karnak (Photo © M. Ayad)

the royal iconography and royal titulary, to date, a comprehensive study of the God's Wives of Amun is still lacking. This study attempts to define as accurately, and as comprehensively, as possible the duties of the God's Wife, both in the temple and beyond. Although this book primarily focuses on the Libyan, Nubian, and Saite God's Wives, their titles and roles must be seen, not only within the framework of the historical and social milieu in which they lived, but also as a product, if not a direct extension, of the title's Eighteenth dynasty origins.

Much of the evidence presented in this study derives from the iconographic scenes found on the walls of a few, small, little known, and poorly preserved chapels (Figure 0.1). The chapels, which lie to the east and north of the main temple of Amun-Re at Karnak, were constructed by the God's Wives of Amun. Compared to the plethora of texts and monuments documenting other individuals and other periods of Egyptian history, the evidence for these women is scanty, rather random, and understudied. The dearth and relatively poor state of preservation of the scenes showing these woman is nowhere more evident than at Karnak, where, just a hundred yards away from the chapels they erected for Osiris, lie the grand monuments of the New Kingdom Thutmoside and Ramesside rulers.

Regardless of the quality of its preservation, this kind of pictorial evidence is especially important when dealing with almost any aspect of the Libyan, Nubian, and Saite dynasties, a period from which no "historic documents survive" as Redford recently put it.[2] Much reliance will be placed on the evidence provided by the adoption decrees of the Saite princesses Nitocris and Ankhnesneferibre, and what little historic information that may be gleaned from the textual and iconographic evidence preserved in the tombs of their officials and the funerary and cultic chapels they erected at Medinet Habu and Karnak.

1

THE HISTORICAL SETTING

The God's Wife: historical development and associated titles

Three hieroglyphic signs spell the Egyptian title *hemet netjer*, a title commonly translated into English as "God's Wife." The short, straightforward phrase hides Egyptologists' vague understanding of the nature and role that the bearers of this title played in temple ritual. In modern scholarship, two other titles have been used interchangeably to refer to the women who bore this enigmatic title. These titles are *douwat netjer* (often translated as "Divine Adorer," "Divine Worshipper," "Divine Adoratrix," or "Divine Adoratrice") and *djeret netjer* (or, "God's Hand").

Placed at the beginning of each of the titles, in "honorific" transposition of the hieroglyphic signs, is the logographic sign (Gardiner sign list # R 8), which has the phonetic value of *netjer*. The sign represents a "cloth wound on a pole."[1] The "clothing" of this staff signifies its status as a sacred object, or fetish, "charged with (divine) power."[2] A secondary, derived interpretation of this sign is that it represented a cult flag. Entrances to Egyptian temples (Greek: *pylons*) were typically decorated with tall flagpoles.[3] Considered a fetish, or "an emblem of divinity,"[4] this sign may be viewed as an attribute of divinity, placed at the entrance of temples to mark them as places of divine residence. Whatever its origin may be, this sign became the "commonest Egyptian hieroglyph for 'god'."[5] The second part of the title *hemet netjer* spells the word for "wife" in Egyptian. The sign on top: (Gardiner sign list # N 41), represents a "well full of water," but came to represent a female's organ, or a vagina.[6]

Next to the staff symbolizing "god" in the title *douwat netjer*, or "Divine Adorer," is a star (Gardiner sign list # N 14).[7] This sign occurs in the Egyptian words for "morning," "rise early," "dawn," and "morning star," but also in the verbs "to praise, worship" and "'to adore' (in the morning)."[8] The hand in the title *djeret netjer* ("God's Hand") is a hieroglyphic ideogram, i.e. it literally conveys the idea of a hand, which here has the phonetic value of *djeret*. Each of the three titles ends with a short, flat hieroglyphic sign: . Representing a cross-section of a rounded loaf of bread, this sign has the phonetic value "*t*," and was added at the end of Egyptian words to render them grammatically feminine.

While the title *douwat netjer*, or "Divine Adorer," clearly relates to the God's Wife's role as the chief worshipper of Amun, the title *djeret netjer*, or

"God's Hand," seems to emphasize her sexual role in relation to the creator god, who, according to the Heliopolitan creation myth, used his hand to masturbate and thus set creation in motion[9]. Indeed, the title *djeret netjer* ("God's Hand") seems to emphasize its bearer's sexual role in relation to the creator god. How such a sexual role was enacted in temple ritual remains unknown. Although one or both of these titles were occasionally borne by the God's Wife, in ancient times, the three titles were not used interchangeably, and were, for the most part, held by different women. Indeed, during the reign of Hatshepsut, who was herself a God's Wife of Amun, the daughter of the high priest of Amun Hapuseneb, whose name was Seniseneb held the title of Divine Adorer.[10]

The God's Wife prior to the New Kingdom

Prior to the Eighteenth dynasty, the title of "God's Wife" is attested only in an abbreviated form, *hemet netjer*, without a reference to any particular deity. During the Middle Kingdom, two women, both non-royal, held this abbreviated form of the title. Their names were Iy-meret-nebes and Neferu, and it is possible that both were priestesses.[13] The absence of the name of a deity does not necessarily mean that these women did not have a particular god in mind. Hornung remarked that, for the most part, the Egyptians confined their interactions to a particular god of the pantheon, who then acted more or less as a patron deity. So that when ancient Egyptians referred to "a god," without specifying a particular deity, it was this personal patron deity that they had in mind.[14]

When a god was first mentioned as having a "wife," it is the ithyphallic god, Min.[15] This "Wife of Min" had a name that incorporated her divine consort's: Wenou-Min, and had a tomb hewn in the cliffs near the Middle Egyptian town of Akhmim. Although the exact date of the tomb's construction cannot be precisely known, Wenou-Min's tomb probably dates to the same time period as similar near-by tombs: the First Intermediate Period (*c.* 2181–2040 BC).[16] The fact that Wenou-Min owned her own tomb indicates that she was a woman of means. Indeed, her other two titles link her to the king. Wenou-Min was both a "Sole Lady-in-Waiting" (Egyptian: *khekeret nesout watet* literally: "the King's sole ornament") and a "King's noblewoman" (Egyptian: *Shepset-nesout*).[17] The latter title was an archaizing title, common in the Old Kingdom, but one that did not survive into the Middle Kingdom.[18] Both titles, but especially the former, place her securely within the ranks of the Egyptian "Aristocracy."[19]

The God's Wife during the New Kingdom

The earliest known association of a God's Wife with Amun occurs at the beginning of the New Kingdom, when the fuller, more complete form of this title *hemet netjer en imen*, or "God's Wife of Amun," appears on the Donation Stela of Ahmose-Nefertari.[20] Although the name of Queen Ahhotep, Ahmose-Nefertari's mother, occurs next to the title of God's Wife of Amun, the title was probably given to Ahhotep posthumously.[21] Shortly after expelling the Hyksos from Egypt, Ahmose (*c.* 1552–1527 BC) conferred

The mythic conception 1: Atum and the Heliopolitan creation myth

Ennead

Atum

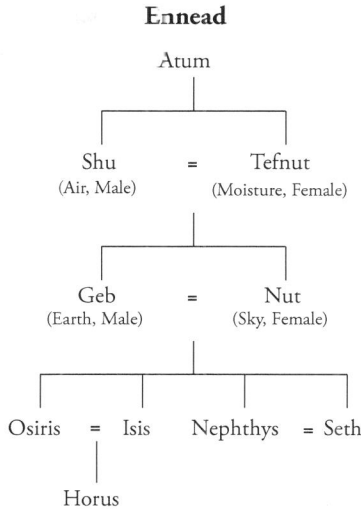

Shu = Tefnut
(Air, Male) (Moisture, Female)

Geb = Nut
(Earth, Male) (Sky, Female)

Osiris = Isis Nephthys = Seth

Horus

The Ancient Egyptians constructed several myths to account for the genesis of their world. It seems that each major cultic center developed its own account of creation. Sometimes, these myths converged. But when they did not, the multiplicity of approaches did not seem to bother the Egyptians. It is almost impossible to know whether these myths were propagated, and held in belief, simultaneously or in succession. But we know that some developed before others.

Known by its Greek name of Heliopolis, the ancient city of *Iounou* produced one of the oldest and most enduring Egyptian accounts of creation. According to the Heliopolitan creation myth, the creator god Atum, whose name means "the Complete One," "the Undifferentiated One," "Lord of all," or "the All," having no partner and existing all alone, set creation in motion by masturbating.[11] From his issuance came the first divine pair: Shu and Tefnut, the personifications of "air" (male) and "moisture" (female), respectively. In turn, this divine pair coupled and gave birth to Geb, the male personification of earth, and Tefnut, the female personification of the sky. Four children were produced from the union of Earth and Sky: two brothers (Osiris and Seth) and two sisters (Isis and Nephthys). Two brother-sister marriages ensued. Horus, "King of the Living," was born to Osiris and Isis, while the union of Seth and Nephthys remained childless. The group of nine gods preceding Horus became known as the "Ennead" (Chart above). Venerated as primeval gods, the Ennead, in a sense, formed a sort of a royal genealogy.[12] The king was the living image, the incarnation, of Horus on earth.

the title of God's Wife on Ahmose-Nefertari, his half sister and Chief Royal Wife. The Hyksos, a group of semi-nomadic western Asiatic herdsmen, had occupied part of the Egyptian Delta during the Second Intermediate Period (*c.* 1720–*c.* 1550 BC). The Donation Stela records Ahmose's decision to appoint his wife to two prominent religious positions: Ahmose-Nefertari was to become a Second Priest attached to the priesthood of Amun, as well as a God's Wife of Amun.[22] In creating the office of God's Wife of Amun, Ahmose took an obscure Middle Kingdom title and gave it national importance. Bolstering the cult of Amun served to establish his control over his newly unified country. Investing loyal members of his immediate family with power could only secure his own position. Ahmose's decree was monumentalized on a stela and publicly displayed near the third pylon at the temple of Amun at Karnak. The stela, whose three fragments were recovered over a period of twenty years, also recorded the establishment of a generously endowed estate of the God's Wife. Besty Bryan pointed out that the language of this decree was not particularly ecclesiastical, but contained distinct economic and administrative details, including the price paid by Ahmose to purchase the priesthood for his wife. The decree established the perpetual rights of the God's Wife and her successors to this newly-endowed estate, and specifically stated that the God's Wife's right to the estate's income was "independent of any kings who should arise in future generations."[23] From the time of Ahmose-Nefertari onward, the title, *and office*, of God's Wife of Amun became closely connected with the Egyptian ruling house. With Ahmose-Nefertari, the title of God's Wife became a royal prerogative held exclusively by a king's Chief Wife, or a king's daughter. Ahmose-Nefertari, Hatshepsut, and her daughter Neferure, all frequently used the title of God's Wife as their sole identifying title, which probably indicates that it was their favorite title.[24]

In the latter half of the Eighteenth dynasty, however, and for much of the rest of the New Kingdom, the title of God's Wife occurred only sporadically. This relative obscurity of the title has caused speculation that the title, once used to bolster Hatshepsut's claim to the Egyptian throne, was intentionally given less prominence as a reaction to her rule.[25] Indeed, linking the stela's condition ("broken in three sections"), to the place of its discovery, ("placed as fill" within the Third Pylon), suggested to Bryan a somewhat intentional demolition of this monument by Thutmosis III and his successors – possibly as part of a larger state-sponsored attempt to overhaul the conditions set forth in the Donation Stela. Certainly, hiding this decree from public view signaled an official reversal of its stipulations – particularly as these stipulations pertained to the God's Wife's right to, freely and independently, control the wealth of the second priesthood and her own estate.[26]

Remarkably, though, in the Nineteenth dynasty, Tausret, widow of Seti II, who ruled on her own as a queen regnant (*c.* 1209–1200 BC) after her husband's death, was also a God's Wife.[27] But it is the fact that the Chief Royal wives of the first three rulers of the Nineteenth dynasty were God's Wives that gives us an impression of the political importance attached to the title of God's Wife even at the beginning of the Nineteenth dynasty. In appointing their Chief Wives – Sat-re, Tuya, and Nefertari-Merymut – Ramses I, Seti I, and Ramses II were merely following the precedent set by Ahmose, founder of the Eighteenth dynasty and the New Kingdom.

The mythic conception II: the king's divine conception

The association of the title *hemet netjer en imen* with royal women, in particular with the king's Chief Wife, gave rise to the theory that this title reflected the idea of a marital union that took place between the supreme god Amun-Re and a mortal woman.[28] Along with receiving the milk of goddesses, a union between the king's mother and the supreme deity imbued the future king with his divine nature. It was precisely this divine nature that enabled an Egyptian king to serve as a mediator between mankind and the gods. This sacral function made the king irreplaceable and consequently provided him with the mythological and ideological underpinnings of his power.[29]

Temple scenes representing the king's divine conception and birth are known from the reigns of Queen Hatshepsut (*c.* 1473/73–1458/57 BC) and Amenhotep III (*c.* 1390–1352 BC). The former comes from the second terrace of Hatshepsut's funerary temple at Deir el-Bahri, while the latter is found in one of the side chambers at the back of Amenhotep III's temple at Luxor.[30] Both cycles show Amun sitting on a platform bed with the queen mother. But while Hatshepsut's relief cycle was "almost completely [erased] under Akhenaton," Amenhotep's copy was not as severely damaged.[31] Amenhotep III's birth cycle, engraved on the walls of the so-called Birth Room, depict queen Mutemwia sitting next to Amun. She is fully dressed in a tight sheath dress, a vulture-headdress, and a double-feathered crown (Figure 1.1). Her knees obscured from view by Amun's, the queen receives life from the god, who places the key of life (an *ankh*-sign) at her nose. Amun, wearing a long kilt, an upper body garment, a pectoral, and his customary double-feathered crown, holds the queen's hand. The couple's feet are supported by the goddesses Selket and Neith, both depicted as slender women sitting on another bed placed under the divine couple. Each goddess is identified through the emblematic symbol placed vertically on her head: Selket, the scorpion and Neith, the shield. The texts accompanying this scene narrate how Amun, hearing of the queen's surpassing beauty decided to take on the guise of her husband, the ruling king, in order to visit her at night. Inevitably, though, the queen recognizes Amun by virtue of the aroma of incense emanating from his divine body.[32]

Typically, the king's birth cycle would be narrated retroactively, i.e. after a king had already attained the throne. Represented most conservatively, the imagery of this union was never intended to convey an account of what actually took place between the queen and her nocturnal visitor. Rather, the imagery was used to propagate the king's right to rule by emphasizing his divine pedigree. Although earlier references to the king's divine parentage are alluded to in literary texts, for example in the prophetic account of the birth of three Fifth Dynasty kings,[33] Hatshepsut's cycle of scenes is the earliest known pictorial record of this narrative.[34] Hatshepsut's emphasis on her divine parentage, including her account of how both her earthly and divine fathers chose her to rule, probably stemmed from her need to solidify her claim to the Egyptian throne. "The motif of divine appointment [and birth] effectively negated the issue of usurpation."[35] Likewise, Amenhotep III's birth cycle, an almost verbatim copy of Hatshepsut's, was a part of an overall program designed to emphasize his "embodiment of creative divinity"[36] in a process that aimed to declare Amenhotep III's deification during his own lifetime.[37]

Scholars who would link the title of "God's Wife of Amun" to this imagery seem to ignore the fact that neither in the birth cycle of Hatshepsut nor in that of Amenhotep III, does the queen mother bear the title God's Wife of Amun – despite the explicit representation of Amun-Re's visit and the inclusion of birth scenes in both cycles.[38] They choose, instead, to derive support for this connection from the iconography of the Donation Stela of Ahmose-Nefertari, where Ahmose-Nefertari is depicted standing behind the figure of her son, who is represented there as a child. On that stela, Ahmose-Nefertari also bears the epithet "she who says all things and they are done for her," a title thought to have been borne exclusively by the royal mothers of the Old Kingdom.[39] Moreover, the idea that the title God's Wife is linked to the king's divine conception does not adequately explain the occurrence of this title in association with kings' daughters.

Egypt at the end of the New Kingdom

The last few reigns of the New Kingdom's Twentieth Dynasty witnessed much corruption, economic instability and political turmoil. It was during the long reign of Ramses IX (*c.* 1127–1108 BC), for instance, that tomb robbers violated the great tombs of earlier kings. Although the culprits were caught and tried, the investigation revealed extensive corruption and neglect "extending to the very top of the administration."[40] Matters did not improve much under Ramses X (*c.* 1108–1104 BC), whose reign witnessed the strike of the workmen and artisans responsible for excavating and decorating the royal tombs. Papyri from the workmen's settlement at Deir el-Medina reveal that delays in delivering the workmen's rations caused much resentment and discontent. To demand back pay, the workmen went on strike. Likewise, the king's influence and the power of his senior administrators – especially the vizier, his second in command – became increasingly weaker. Effective power shifted to the South, where the Viceroy of Kush (Nubia's main administrator) and the High Priest of Amun at Karnak acquired progressively expanding powers. The expanding influence of the holders of these two positions is best seen in the mode of transmission of their offices. Under earlier, more powerful kings, the Viceroy of Kush and the High Priest of Amun were both royal appointees. But by the end of the New Kingdom, both positions had become hereditary, their holders dispensing of them as they would personal property.

It was inevitable that such powerful and ambitious individuals would eventually vie for more power. During the reign of Ramses XI (*c.* 1104–1075 BC), a military conflict (read: civil war) erupted between the High Priest Amenhotep and the Viceroy of Kush Panehsy, who now controlled a sizeable portion of Egypt's military forces. Although Panehsy was initially successful, extending his forces into Middle Egypt, the conflict ended in his withdrawal to Nubia around 1087 BC, where shortly afterwards, he died. With Panehsy's death, the office of Viceroy of Kush became part of the responsibilities assumed by the High Priest of Amun at Thebes: Herihor. Combining his newly acquired military powers with his earlier religious responsibilities, Herihor became the *de facto* ruler of Upper Egypt. During Ramses XI's eleventh regnal year, Herihor inaugurated a new "Renaissance" era, which Herihor now used to date newly constructed or decorated monuments. (The Egyptian term "*wehem mesout*" used in the dates, literally translates as "repetition of births.") In addition to discarding the king's regnal years when dating new monuments, Herihor had monuments inscribed with his own titles instead of the king's. These titles, as seen on the walls of the temple of Khonsu at Karnak, included not only his regular priestly titles but also the royal title of "King of Upper and Lower Egypt."[41] In doing so, he outright challenged the authority of the last Ramesside ruler Ramses XI, who had already abdicated all effective power not only in the South, but also in Lower Egypt. It was a high official by the name of Smendes and his wife who greeted Herihor's emissary Wenamun at the Royal residence at Tanis. Wenamun had been dispatched from Thebes to purchase Lebanese cedar wood for the sacred barque of Amun and it was Smendes, not the king, who supplied him with the necessary documents for safe passage to the Levant.[42]

It was during the turbulent reigns marking the end of the New Kingdom that a much weakened king turned to his daughter to help consolidate his power at Thebes. Isis (also known by her Egyptian name Aset), daughter of Ramses VI, was dispatched from her father's residence in the Egyptian Delta to Thebes, where she became a God's Wife of Amun. Surviving into the reign of Ramses IX, Isis held office for at least 25 years.[43] Isis features prominently in the history of the God's Wives as she seems to have been the earliest known *single* God's Wife of Amun.[44] Prior to Isis' appointment, the office of the God's Wife of Amun was primarily held by the king's chief queen. Her immediate predecessor was another Isis, the wife of Ramses III.[45] And just as her namesake, Isis, the wife of Ramses III combined the titles God's Wife and Divine Worshipper, so did this daughter of Ramses VI. Furthermore, Isis was the only attested God's Wife since Ahmose-Nefertari to hold the title in its complete form: *hemet netjer en Amen*.[46] Recently, Luc Gosselin suggested that the appointment of Isis as God's Wife did not curb the influence of the Amun priesthood. Instead, he suggested that using an oracle to confirm her appointment was a concession of royal power that may be viewed as an acknowledgement of the "triumph of the High Priesthood of Amun."[47]

With Ramses XI's death, Egypt's Twentieth Dynasty came to an end, and with its end Egypt's New Kingdom gave way to a period known as the Third Intermediate Period. Kingship seems to have passed rather peacefully to Smendes (1075–1044 BC), who had been the effective ruler in Lower Egypt, even prior to Ramses XI's death. Of obscure origins, Smendes probably married into the royal family to further his political ambitions. His reign marked the beginning not only of the Twenty-first Dynasty, but it also ushered in a new era of increasing instability and fragmentation.

The scanty evidence of the early Third Intermediate Period coupled with the random chances of survival of what little evidence we do possess hinder our ability to formulate sweeping theories regarding the transmission of the title of "God's Wife," or the associated titles of "God's Hand" and "Divine Adorer" during this turbulent period. While other women may have held one or all three titles, only three women are known to have held the title of *douwat netjer*, or "Divine Adorer," during the early part of the Third Intermediate Period: Maatkare (I) Mutemhat, daughter of King Psusennes I of the Twenty-first dynasty and his wife Henuttawy; Henuttawy,[48] a daughter of the High Priest of Amun Pinudjem II and his wife Isetemkheb, also of the Twenty-first dynasty; and Karomama Merytmut of the Twenty-second dynasty.[49] Of these, only Maatkare (I) Mutemhat combined the two titles *douwat netjer* and *hemet netjer en imen*.[50] It thus seems that just as in the Eighteenth dynasty, different women held the titles *hemet netjer*, "God's Wife" and *douwat netjer*, "Divine Adorer," so also was the case in the early part of the Third Intermediate Period.

Whether taking on the title of God's Wife or identifying herself as a Divine Worshipper, Maatkare Mutemhat enclosed her name in the royal cartouche.[51]

Uniquely, Karomama of the Twenty-second dynasty bore the title "Divine Worshipper of Amenope" (Egyptian: *douwat netjer en Amen <en> ipet*).[52] Sometimes also known as Amun of Luxor, Amenope was an ithyphallic form of the god Amun. Karomama appears to have been the earliest known God's Wife to place feminine versions of the distinctly royal titles "Son of Re" and "Lord of Appearances/Diadems" before her cartouche-enclosed name, becoming a "Daughter of Re" and a "Mistress of Diadems."[53]

Egypt during the Libyan period

By the beginning of the Twenty-third dynasty, the stability that had characterized earlier periods of Egyptian history was long gone. The most characteristic aspect of this period is the total disintegration of central authority. Egypt was now divided into rivaling fiefdoms, with several competing dynasts ruling at the same time, each claiming royal authority. While each ruler claimed complete overlordship over all of Egypt, in reality, their influence may have extended only a few miles beyond their residence. Extensive inter-marriage between the various competing ruling houses and the rather limited pool of names shared among these rival dynasts, their spouses, and their offspring, further complicates the picture. Three names in particular were almost universally borne by the male members of the rival families: Osorkon, Sheshonq, and Takeloth. Likewise, their queens and princesses shared an almost equally limited number of names. This particular aspect makes the history of this period very difficult to write. The general trend of the period seems to be toward increasing fragmentation such that by the time of the Nubian invasion of Egypt in 730 BC, multiple dynasts ruled at Tanis, Leontopolis, Bubastis and Sais.[54] Along with several other "lesser"[55] chiefs, these dynasts rivaled for control over the Egyptian Delta. Anthony Leahy suggested that this set-up did not particularly bother the Libyan rulers themselves who preferred to rule alongside one another in "a loose confederation reinforced by family alliances."[56] Indeed, as Robert Ritner recently pointed out, the "natural tendency of such tribal units [was] to fragment."[57] In this chaotic time, two cities emerged as particularly important: Tanis and Leontopolis, while the peripheral city of Sais controlled more than a third of the Delta, extending west to the Libyan border and north to the shores of the Mediterranean. In Middle Egypt, Hermopolis and Heracleopolis each had their own king. Such was the situation when the Nubians started their northward march.

The Nubians in Egypt

Although the de-centralization of power under the Libyan rulers may be attributed to their feudalistic culture, it clearly represented a break from the Egyptian norm. The Nubian invaders of Egypt definitely thought so. Accordingly, they portrayed themselves as restorers of order (Egyptian: *Maat*). What exactly prompted the northward expansion of the Napatan kingdom remains a mystery. Similarly unknown (and unknowable) is the early history of the Napatan kingdom itself.[58] The Napatan Kingdom's rise to power may have started as early as the late tenth or early ninth century BC. Nubia's geographic location and its role as an intermediary in the trade of exotic goods and gold undoubtedly contributed to the rise of a complex state in Napata, and evidence from early grave goods at el-Kurru suggests "intense contacts with Thebes"[59] even at this early stage. Evidence from the cemetery of el-Kurru further suggests that the kingdom of Kush may have arisen five to six generations prior to the rule of Kashta,[60] the first Napatan ruler whose name is attested in Egypt.

On the Egyptian side of the border the evidence is equally scanty. After the tenure of Panehsy, a royal representative of the Egyptian King in Nubia (whose more traditional title was Viceroy of Kush), Nubia appears to have remained without a Viceroy for the duration of the Libyan Period.[61] Then appears one Pamiu, whose name means "The Tom Cat," and is consequently suggestive of his Delta origin, where the cat goddess Bastet was especially venerated in the city of Bubastis, a city named after her in the central Delta. In addition to his responsibilities south of the border, Pamiu kept busy at home, holding the titles of Priest of Amun, Scribe of the Temple in the Domains of Amun, Accounts Scribe, and Overseer of the City and Vizier. As Viceroy of Kush, Pamiu's tenure in office was probably sometime between 775 and 750 BC.[62] The extent of Pamiu's authority over Nubia has been questioned recently, with scholars arguing that it was limited to the oversight of Lower Nubian temples.[63]

It is around this time that a Napatan ruler by the name of Alara (*c.* 780–760 BC) appears on the scene. "Alara is the first member of the dynasty of the kings of Kush whose name is preserved to us. He is first mentioned in the text of the funerary stela of queen Tabiry, who was his daughter by Kasaqa, and wife of Piye."[64] There, his name is enclosed in the royal cartouche. Elsewhere though he is given the title of *wer*, or "tribal chief."[65] This title, coupled with the fact that Alara's name occurs in Egypt *only* on monuments belonging to his descendants, suggest that he never claimed kingship of Egypt.[66] Moreover, as Russmann pointed out, Alara's titles seem contrived, giving the impression that they were "partial (or pseudo-)Egyptian royal titles."[67]

Alara's successor was Kashta (*c.* 760–747 BC), who in all probability was also his brother. Kashta was apparently able to spread his influence over all of Lower Nubia

The 25th Dynasty genealogy

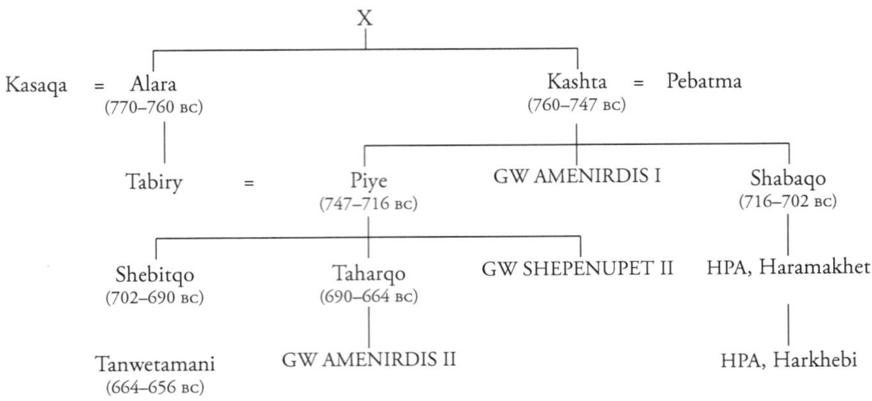

and down to Egypt's southern border at Aswan, where a stela bearing his name was recovered. Found by Maspero just outside the granite portal of Alexander II at the temple of Khnum on the Island of Elephantine at Aswan, the stela is currently housed at the Egyptian Museum in Cairo (JE 41013).[68] It gives Kashta's titles as: the "King of Upper and Lower Egypt *Maat-Re*," the "Son of Re, the Lord of the Two Lands, Kashta."[69] But it remains questionable whether Kashta actually extended his influence as far north as the Theban region.[70] Elsewhere in Egypt, Kashta's name, like Alara's, appears only in the filiation of his descendants.

Sometime around 747 BC, Kashta's son Piye (or Piankhy) was crowned in Napata. There, "he declared himself … ruler of Egypt and absolute overlord of all kings, chiefs and princes in his kingdom."[71] Piye's Egyptian policy was more aggressive than his father's, and in his fourth year (*c.* 744 BC), he marched his army into Thebes. His visit appears to have been peaceful with the primary purpose of attending the *Opet* festival and presenting Amun-Re with many gifts.[72] Piye's visit may have been motivated by political reasons as well as religious ones though.[73] By paying homage to Amun, Piye undoubtedly strengthened his ties with the Theban elite and promoted his image as a religious traditionalist. Remarkably, no Theban pontiff appears to greet Piye on this occasion, or some 15 years later (728 or 730 BC), when Piye launched his second military campaign.[74] It is possible that Piye was able to cash in on relationships that were established (or developed) during his first visit. The narrative preserved on his victory stela suggests that the success of his second campaign was largely due to the support and loyalty of the Theban community.[75] Once more, Piye timed his campaign so that he could participate in the religious festivities taking place at the time. After celebrating the *Opet* and Beautiful Valley festivals, Piye joined his army in its northward pursuit of the Egyptian/Libyan dynasts, or "rebels," as Piye called them on his great triumphal stela, where we read:

> I shall sail north myself, that I may overthrow what he has done, that I may cause him to leave off fighting forever. After the ceremonies of the New Year have been

> performed, I shall offer to my father Amun on his beautiful festival, when he makes his beautiful appearance of the New Year that he may send me in peace to see Amun in the beautiful festival of the Feast of Opet. I shall cause him to appear in his sacred image (on his way) to Harem-of-the-South (Luxor) in his beautiful festival of the "Feast of Opet by Night" and on the festival "abiding-in-Dominion (Thebes)," which Re made for him on the first occasion. I shall cause him to go in procession to his house resting on his throne on the day of "Making the God Enter," in the third month of the season of Inundation, day 2.[76]

Piye's Great Triumphal stela details how his army put Memphis under siege. Soon after Memphis fell into his grip, the rest of the Delta submitted. Eventually the Saite ruler Tefnakht, whose southern expansion may have triggered Piye's campaign in the first place, was captured and, reportedly, murdered.[77] The new epithets Piye acquired in Memphis ("Son of Bastet, beloved of Amun" and "Son of Isis, beloved of Amun") were clearly designed for propagandist purposes, and boldly declared his dominion over Lower Egypt.[78] Without making any provisions for a governor, viceroy, or deputy to hold the reins in his absence, Piye returned to Nubia shortly after his victory and remained there until his death in *c.* 716 BC.[79]

Possibly because Piye never appointed a deputy governor, the Saites, this time led by Tefnakht's son, Bakenrenef, revolted again. Sometime between 715 and 712 BC, Shabaqo (*c.* 716–702 BC), who had just ascended to his brother's throne, had to re-conquer Egypt.[80] Once more, this invasion, which took place in Shabaqo's second regnal year, did not eliminate the Nubians' Delta rivals, who seem to have survived under "Kushite overlordship."[81] Manetho, an Egyptian priest-turned-historian who lived in the third century BC, reports that after his capture, Bakenrenef was burned alive.[82] Manetho's vivid account of the Nubian victory, however, remains unsubstantiated. In fact, the only contemporaneous account of Shabaqo's victory survives on a scarab.[83] The scarab records that Shabaqo

> has slain those who rebelled against him in the South and the North, and in every foreign country. The Sand-dwellers who rebelled against him and fallen down through fear of him, that come of themselves as prisoners. Each one has seized his fellow among them, because he (the king) has performed the benefaction for <his> father (Amun), so greatly does he love him.[84]

Like his predecessor before him, Shabaqo may have been able to depend on Theban support to achieve his victory. Shabaqo moved his residence to Memphis, possibly to quench the expansionist efforts of the Delta rulers, especially of the Saite, Bakenrenef.[85]

Because Shabaqo was the first Nubian ruler to reside in Egypt, he is sometimes considered the true founder of the *Egyptian* Twenty-fifth dynasty. Shabaqo followed an Egypto-centric policy and set the stage for his successors to pursue a similar policy.[86] It was under Shabaqo that Nubian "administrative control, royal regalia, iconography, and artistic style were formulated …"[87] Evidence of his active building program in Egypt is attested from as far north as the Delta cities of Bubastis and

Athribis, all the way south to the Upper Egyptian cities of Esna and Edfu. Shabaqo also expanded or renovated temples at Memphis, Dendera, and at Thebes, where his activity is attested at the temples of Karnak, Luxor and Medinet Habu. Shabaqo's active building program all over Egypt may be viewed as a sign of his desire to be acknowledged as ruler of all the land.[88] Shabaqo also secured Egypt's eastern border in the Sinai peninsula, and attempted to put the dangerous western Delta under a governor: a policy which was later revoked under his successors Shebitqo and Taharqo.[89] Shabaqo's extensive building activity in Egypt contrasts sharply with his near neglect of Nubia, where he erected very few monuments. The scarce monuments he left in Kush suggest that "his principal aim was the consolidation of his dynasty in the Egyptian half of the double kingdom."[90]

It was during Shabaqo's reign that the high priesthood of Amun-Re was resurrected. Haremakhet, son of Shabaqo became the first High Priest of Amun to hold office at Karnak in some 40 or 50 years.[91] Haremakhet's appointment is sometimes interpreted as an attempt on Shabaqo's part to gain legitimacy in Egypt.[92] This appointment may be better understood, however, as part of Shabaqo's multi-faceted program to resurrect, or assume, older Egyptian traditions. Just as moving his residence to Memphis signaled his desire to be viewed as an Egyptian king, so could his appointment of a High Priest be considered an attempt to assert himself as a restorer of all things Egyptian. Shabaqo's Egypto-centric policy seems to have worked. It is Shabaqo who appears as the first king of the Twenty-fifth dynasty in Manetho's account of Egyptian history.[93]

Shabaqo was succeeded by his nephew Shebitqo, the son of Piye. Shebitqo's brief reign (*c.* 702–690 BC) is attested from a few remains found in Thebes and at Memphis where he resided.[94] He seems to have been more involved with foreign policy, intervening in Syro-Palestine against the Assyrians.[95]

In due course, Shebitqo was succeeded by his "field-director" Taharqo (690–664 BC), another son of Piye's. In a grand ceremony held at the city of Memphis, Taharqo was crowned King of Egypt.[96] Two stelae erected at the temple of Amun in Kawa (Temple T) commemorate the events surrounding Taharqo's ascension to the throne. Interestingly, a stela recording an exceptionally high flood level tells of his mother's journey north to attend the coronation at Memphis:

> Now my mother was in Bow-Land (Nubia); namely the king's sister, sweet of love, the king's mother, Abar, may she live. Moreover, I had departed from her as a recruit of twenty years when I came with his majesty to North-land. Then she came sailing north to see me after a period of years. She found me appearing on the Throne of Horus, after I had received the diadems of Re, and was wearing the *uraei* on my head, all the gods being the protection of my body. She was exceedingly joyful after seeing the beauty of His Majesty (just) as Isis saw her son Horus appearing on the throne of his father Osiris after he had been a youth in the nest of Khemmis.[97]

This stela probably records events related to Taharqo's coronation. Only such a momentous event would merit the arduous journey north.[98]

That the first decade and a half of Taharqo's reign was a period of prosperity is clear from the vast building activity undertaken during this period, both in Egypt and Nubia.[99] In Egypt, Taharqo constructed four gateways at Karnak's four cardinal points, of which only remnants of the one he constructed in the First Court survive.[100] Taharqo's building activity was not limited to the Theban area, but extended from Philae in the south to the Delta in the north.[101] In addition, he erected temples in his homeland: at Sanam, Gebel Barkal, and Kawa. In Nubia, his monuments were of a scale unknown since the New Kingdom, turning Napata into a "monumental complex of sanctuaries."[102] Furthermore, there is evidence that some of the work done in Nubia was carried out by craftsmen who were brought there all the way from Memphis.[103]

Taharqo is also known for his opposition to the Assyrians. He was the reigning king in Egypt when Esarhaddon's armies reached Memphis in 671 BC. While Taharqo seems to have survived this invasion, a second invasion drove him all the way back to Nubia.

In 664 BC, Taharqo was succeeded by Tanwetamani.[104] Soon after his coronation in Nubia, Tanwetamani went to Thebes, and from there marched northward to Memphis. For a brief while, he was able to defeat the Saites having eliminated their leader, Necho, an Assyrian vassal. The Assyrians, however, soon retaliated and in 663/64 BC re-invaded Egypt, captured Memphis, and installed Psametik I, a Delta ruler and a descendant of Tefnakht, as King of Egypt. That Tanwetamani's reign started in the year 664 BC is supported by Serapeum Stela no.192, in which Psametik I "counted his regnal years in direct continuation of those of Taharqo."[105] The two kings thus seem to have ruled concurrently.[106] Psametik I marshaled his troops south, bringing Middle Egypt under his control. Subsequently, Tanwetamani fled to Nubia, where he continued to rule for an unknown period of time. The evidence suggests that Tanwetamani was still recognized in Upper Egypt until 656 BC, when Nitocris, the daughter of Psametik I, was appointed a God's Wife of Amun.[107] His name survives on a small chapel dedicated to Osiris-Ptah in South Karnak.[108] With Tanwetamani's flight to Nubia, Kushite rule in Egypt came to an end.

The Libyan and Nubian God's Wives of Amun

On the eve of the Nubian invasion of Egypt, one of the most prominent individuals at Thebes was the God's Wife of Amun, Shepenwepet I. Shepenwepet was the daughter of Osorkon III (*c*. 777–749 BC), the penultimate ruler of the Twenty-third dynasty.[109] After a long hiatus, she was now the incumbent God's Wife of Amun. While other women of the Third Intermediate Period bore the title of Divine Worshiper, none seems to have held the title of God's Wife since the time of Isis, daughter of Ramses VI. While Isis's appointment may have marked the initial politicization of the office of God's Wife, it was not until the Twenty-third dynasty that the full political potential of the office was realized. Like her Ramesside predecessor, Shepenwepet I seems to have been a single woman.[110] There is no record of anyone claiming to be her husband. Likewise, the archaeological and textual records make no mention of any children that may be attributed to her.

Shepenwepet's genealogy is mentioned on the southern part of the east wall in room II in the chapel of Osiris, Ruler of Eternity. There, she is identified as "the Mistress of the Two Lands, *Khnemetibimen*, the Mistress of Diadems, Shepenwepet, King's Daughter of the Lord of the Two Lands, the Lord of Ritual, the Son of Re, the Lord of Diadems, Osorkon (III), son of Isis, whose mother is the Chief Royal Wife Karoatjet."[111] Karoatjet is the only woman named as Shepenwepet's mother in this inscription – and there is little reason to doubt that she was her biological mother.[112] In other words, no "adoptive mother" appears in that inscription. In fact, when Shepenwepet I was appointed as a God's Wife, there was no incumbent to "adopt" her.

Shepenwepet I was probably installed by her brother Takeloth III, shortly after his accession to the Egyptian throne as his father's co-regent (*c.* 754–734 BC).[113] But because no record of her installation survives, it is not quite clear whether it was her father's or brother's decision to appoint her as God's Wife. Either way, her appointment was probably timed to fill the gap caused by the elevation of Takeloth III to the Egyptian throne. Takeloth III, who had been a High Priest of Amun, probably relinquished his priestly duties upon ascension to the throne. Another individual was needed to fulfill the High Priest's ritualistic duties. In the aftermath of civil war, appointing a male member of the dynasty to the priesthood could potentially undermine the king's authority. Reviving a distinguished priestly title and bestowing it on the king's daughter/sister was less threatening. With no offspring of her own, she could not engender a rival dynasty; thus her loyalty to the reigning king was further ensured.

Shepenwepet's elevated status found expression in the location chosen for her funerary chapel: within the temple enclosure of the mortuary temple of Ramses III at Medinet Habu (Figure 1.1).[114] Shepenwepet's mud-brick chapel anticipated later use of the space by the God's Wives of the Nubian and Saite dynasties. Although destroyed in antiquity,[115] hers was the earliest of four funerary chapels that once stood in a row, their façades facing the small Eighteenth dynasty temple of Amun *djeser-set* constructed by Hatshepust (*c.* 1473–1458 BC) and Thutmosis III (*c.* 1479–1425 BC). But nowhere is Shepenwepet's status more visibly declared than in the reliefs surviving on the walls of a small chapel in East Karnak (Figure 1.2). The chapel, which was dedicated to Osiris, Ruler of Eternity, features several members of the Twenty-third dynasty: King Osorkon III, his son and co-regent, Takeloth III, and Shepenwepet, who despite the presence of her brother and father, is represented as the main cultic officiant in that monument[116] (see Chapter 2).

The Nubians were quick to recognize the political potential of the office of God's Wife, and immediately took advantage of this institution to establish their authority over Thebes. Before they had completed their invasion of Egypt, a Nubian woman, Amenirdis I, was appointed as a God's Wife.[117] Amenirdis I was the daughter of Kashta and his wife Pebatma, and the sister of kings Piye and Shabaqo (see chart on p. 12).[118] Upon assuming office, Amenirdis acquired a new "throne," or official name, *Khaneferoumout*, which translates as "May the Perfection/Beauty of Mut appear."[119] Extant evidence suggests that both Amenirdis' mother and her sister accompanied her from Napata to Thebes, which may indicate that she was a mere child when she was appointed God's Wife of Amun.[120]

Figure 1.1 Remains of Shepenwepet I's funerary chapel (Photo © M. Ayad)

Figure 1.2 Chapel of Osiris, Ruler of Eternity (Photo © M. Ayad)

Figure 1.3 Chapel of Osiris, Ruler of Eternity, façade (after Schwaller Du Lubicz, *Temples of Karnak*, pl. 233)

That Amenirdis survived into the reign of Shebitqo (702–690 BC) is clear from representations preserved on the walls of the chapel of Osiris, *Ruler-of-Eternity* in East Karnak (Figures 1.2 and 1.3). Shebitqo, whose Horus name, *Djed-khaou* (lit. "Stable of appearances"), is still clearly visible on the façade of this chapel, was responsible for the addition of a third, outer, room to the earlier, bi-partite Twenty-third dynasty structure.[121] The room, whose proportions were wider than those of the earlier chapel, was added to the north of the original structure and incorporated the façade of the earlier chapel as its southern wall. On the eastern half of the newly-constructed Nubian façade, Shebitqo receives symbols of the *sed* festival from Amun (Figure 1.3). Next to Shebitqo's gigantic representation is a series of four small vignettes, one atop the other, showing the God's Wife Amenirdis I standing before various deities.[122] The inscriptions accompanying these vignettes give Amenirdis' names and titles, where after the cartouche containing her name is the epithet *ankh.ti* "alive." Likewise, Amenirdis "who is alive" dominates the decorative scheme of the room added by the Nubians.

Amenirdis seems to have been the first known woman to combine the three titles: "God's Wife," "Divine Adorer," and "God's Hand."[123] Although the three epithets are now commonly associated with the office of God's Wife of Amun, and are used interchangeably in scholarship, in the late New Kingdom and early Third Intermediate Period, different women held the titles "God's Wife," and "Divine Adorer." In adding the title "God's Hand" to her predecessors' more customary titles, Amenirdis I "may have intentionally evoked a direct connection with Ahmose-Nefertari, the first God's Wife of Amun and the first to use the title ... ["God's Hand"]."[124] Indeed two inscribed statues of Ahmose-Nefertari were recovered from the chapel of Osiris *Heqa-Djet* at Karnak, a chapel in which Amenirdis I is extensively represented. Amenirdis also adopted a variant of Ahmose-Nefertari's epithet: "The one who speaks and everything is done for her because of the greatness of his love for her."[125]

Sometime during her long tenure, Amenirdis I adopted Shepenwepet II, daughter of Piye and Shebitqo's sister as her successor. As a God's Wife, Shepenwepet took on the official, or throne, name of *Henutneferoumout-iretre*, which may be translated as "Mistress of Perfection/Beauty is Mut, the Eye of Re."[126] Along with King Taharqo, Shepenwepet erected a small chapel in North Karnak. The chapel was dedicated to Osiris in his special function as "Lord of Life, Answerer of the Afflicted."[127] Shepenwepet II was also solely responsible for the construction of several chapels in East and North Karnak. To the west of the chapel of Osiris, Ruler of Eternity, she dedicated a chapel to Osiris: this time in his incarnation as "Osiris-Onnophris, who-is-in-the-midst-of-the-Persea-Tree."[128] In North Karnak, Shepenwepet built a chapel whose reliefs partially record Shepenwepet celebrating certain aspects of the *sed* festival.[129]

Significantly, Shepenwepet II made the decision to demolish a funerary chapel that Amenirdis had originally erected at Medinet Habu. The chapel had been constructed of unfired mud-brick and resembled the adjacent earlier chapel of Shepenwepet I in plan and construction. Shepenwepet II replaced Amenirdis's mud-brick funerary chapel with a stone chapel (Figure 1.4).[130] Shepenwepet II monumentalized her decision in an inscription that runs along the doorway leading into Amenirdis's newly constructed stone *cella* (inner chapel). It declares that Shepenwepet "built this monument for eternity for her mother."[131] The date of construction of Amenirdis's chapel may thus be assigned the latter part of Shebitqo's reign (702–690 BC), or more probably, the early years of Taharqo's reign (690–664 BC)..[132]

The new design chosen by Shepenwepet II differed completely from the earlier architectural plan. In fact, the architectural design Shepenwepet chose for her adoptive mother's chapel was quite unique, and unprecedented in Egyptian temple or funerary architecture.[133] A narrow doorway in its single-towered pylon-façade leads to a columned court. Currently, only the bases of the four columns that once stood in the court are preserved. In antiquity, the columns supported a roof that covered a colonnade that ran along the two sides of the court, but left the middle aisle open. The rectangular court is wider than it is deep. Doorways in its east and west walls led to the adjacent chapels of Shepenwepet I and II, respectively. A third door in the court's south wall leads to the cult chapel of Amenirdis I, also known as a *cella*.[134] In fact, the south wall of the court forms the façade of Amenirdis's cult chapel. A single chamber constitutes

Figure 1.4 Façade of the funerary chapel of Amenirdis I (Photo © M. Ayad)

the shrine that covers the tomb of Amenirdis I. This shrine is independently roofed with a stone barrel vault and is about 3 m. deep and 2 m. wide.[135] This chamber is set within a larger roofed building. The resulting corridor created in the space between the two structures is quite narrow and is about 4 m. high. The corridor surrounds Amenirdis's cella. The burial chamber of Amenirdis I lies underneath her cult chamber; and although Hölscher indicated that this crypt was accessible in 1954, currently it is not.[136] Both crypt and *cella* are (exceptionally) devoid of inscriptions, "[i]nstead, scenes and texts from Amenirdis's funerary service are found on the wall of the corridor surrounding the cella."[137] The exterior wall surfaces of the *cella* form the inner walls of the passage. These are engraved with offering lists and cult representations, while the outer walls of the passage depict scenes from the funerary cult of Amenirdis. Forty-five scenes from the Opening of the Mouth ritual are engraved on the upper register of these outer walls while the lower register includes excerpts from the Pyramid Texts and two sun hymns.[138] The choice of which texts to include in her mother's chapel undoubtedly fell to Shepenwepet and her scribal staff. These texts thus probably also reflect Shepenwepet II's religious beliefs. The texts preserved on the walls of this chapel are especially significant in light of the dearth of evidence documenting the funerary beliefs of the Nubian God's Wives.

Without easily identifiable prototypes, the funerary chapel of Amenirdis I constitutes a pivotal, albeit intriguing, link in the development of Egyptian mortuary and cultic architecture. Essentially, Shepenwepet, or her architect(s), combined older architectural elements in new and innovative ways. For instance, Shepenwepet II took an ancient architectural form, the so-called "Tent Shrine," which was already in use in the Third dynasty temple-complex of King Djoser at Saqqara, and placed it within another, but larger, tent shrine.[139] The corridor created around the inner shrine later became a standard feature of Greco-Roman temple architecture, but it appears for the first time in the chapel of Amenirdis I. Similarly, the use of stone masonry in constructing the chapel forms a break from earlier Third Intermediate Period practice.[140] In addition, the vault in Amenirdis's *cella*, while small, is possibly the earliest example of "a true [stone] vault in the Late Period."[141]

That Shepenwepet II decided to demolish Amenirdis I's mud-brick funerary chapel and erect another in stone further manifests the extent of resources available to the God's Wife under the Nubians.[142] Shepenwepet II was also responsible for a considerable amount of construction in the Theban area. Next to her predecessor's funerary chapel, Shepenwepet II started to erect a funerary chapel of her own. Her chapel seemed to copy the architectural design of Amenirdis: two tent shrines, set one inside the other. However, at some point, the plan of Shepenwepet II's chapel was altered to accommodate two extra side chapels (or *cellae*). These additions belonged to the Saite God's Wife of Amun, Nitocris and her biological mother Mehetnusekhet. These later additions replaced the corridor created between the two independently roofed shrines that would have surrounded Shepenwepet II's *cella*.[143]

Forty years after her own adoption, Shepenwepet II adopted Amenirdis II, daughter of Taharqo, as her "heiress apparent."[144] The evidence concerning Amenirdis II is quite scanty. Her name is hardly attested on any Theban monuments, appearing only next to her adoptive mother's on blocks recovered from the ramp in front of the Monthu temple in North Karnak.[145] It is not clear what became of Amenirdis II once the Saites controlled Thebes. She may have been bypassed in favor of Nitocris, daughter of Psametik I, when the latter was "adopted" into office in *c.* 656 BC. Subsequently, Amenirdis II may have had to return to her ancestral home with the retreating Nubian armies.[146] It should be noted though that the Nubian royal cemeteries at Kawa and el-Kurru have not yielded any direct evidence of Amenirdis II, nor for that matter her adoptive mother Shepenwepet II nor of Amenirdis I.[147] Similarly, none of the sarcophagi belonging to the Nubian God's Wives has been recovered.[148] The absence of evidence has not prevented theories concerning the fate of Amenirdis II from emerging. Habachi reconstructed the partially preserved name of the wife of the Vizier Mentuhotep as Amenirdis, suggesting that Amenirdis II married this vizier after she was ousted from her position as presumptive God's Wife of Amun.[149] This suggestion, however, was debunked by Morkot, who suggested that only a king, not "a mere vizier" would be a proper match for a prospective God's Wife.[150] Because Amenirdis II's name occurs on very few monuments, Leclant concluded that she never attained the status of a God's Wife.[151] More recently, Aidan Dodson suggested that while Amenirdis II never actually attained the position of God's Wife, she may have retained her status as a "God's Hand" even under Nitocris I. According to Dodson, Amenirdis II would have acquired this title at her appointment as Shepenwepet's successor.[152]

The idea that the title "God's Hand" may have been used for "the heiress apparent" was strongly opposed by the German scholar Erhart Graefe who has

Table 1.1 Dates and affiliation of the God's Wives of Amun of theTwenty-third to Twenty-fifth dynasties

God's Wife	*Father*	*Dynasty*	*Approximate dates (in office)*
Shepenwepet I	Osorkon III	XXIII (Libyan)	*c.* 754–714 BC
Amenirdis I	Kashta	XXV (Nubian)	*c.* 740–700 BC (installed between 747–735 BC)
Shepenwepet II	Pi(ankh)y	XXV (Nubian)	*c.* 710–650 BC
Nitocris	Psametik I	XXVI (Saite)	*c.* 656–586 BC
Ankhnesneferibre	Psametik II	XXVI (Saite)	*c.*595–525 BC

conducted extensive research on the staff associated with the God's Wives.[153] Supporting Graefe's argument are several scenes dedicated by Amenirdis I and Shepenwepet II. At the chapels of Osiris, Ruler of Eternity and Osiris, Lord of Life, Amenirdis I bears the titles of God's Wife as well as God's Hand. In the chapel of Osiris, Ruler of Eternity, the title "God's Hand" occurs as part of a longer dedicatory inscription, in which Amenirdis I announced that she had erected the chapel "for her father, Osiris, Ruler of Eternity" (Figures 2.12, 2.15).[154] The title also occurs in the scenes inscribed on the south, north, and west walls of Room E in the Edifice of Taharqo by the Sacred Lake in Karnak and in Hatshepsut's *chapelle rouge* (Figures 2.23, 2.24). There, the "God's Wife, God's Hand" engages in highly charged cultic activities: she ignites fans bearing the image of Egypt's enemies in the Hatshepsut's Red Chapel and performs various rites aimed at proclaiming divine and royal dominion in the Edifice of Taharqo.[155] Just as in the chapel of Osiris, Ruler of Eternity, the bearer of this title is the incumbent God's Wife, not her "heiress apparent." But perhaps most significantly, the title "God's Hand" appears in the filiation of Shepenwepet II in the chapel of Osiris, Lord of Life and on the blocks depicting her *sed*-celebration (Figures 2.20b and 2.28). In both instances, the title is borne by "Amenirdis (I), the justified."[156] Indicating her decease, Amenirdis's cartouche-enclosed name is followed by the epithet "*maa-kherou*" (literally, "True-of-Voice") in both instances.

Egypt under Saite rule

Descended from the Twenty-fourth dynasty rulers whom Piye and later Shabaqo encountered during their northward expansion, the Twenty-sixth dynasty rulers are designated Saite after their city of origin: Sais, in the western delta. From the outset, the Saite rulers were "trying desperately to shore up their position, both at home and abroad."[157] This they achieved through a series of alliances. The dynasty did not officially commence until Psametik I (664–610 BC), aided and supported by the Assyrians, was crowned King of Egypt. Psametik seems to have succeeded his father Necho as ruler of Sais.[158] And just like his father, he ruled as a vassal-king, loyal to the Assyrians. Indeed, Psametik's alliance with the Assyrian king Assurbanipal, which probably lasted for the duration of his (Psametik's) reign, seems to have set the tone for his successors who continued to form alliances both internally and abroad.

Psametik was able to extend Egypt's influence into the Levant – and while he may not have resurrected the imperialistic glories of the New Kingdom, he maintained a form of an Egyptian "commercial monopoly" over Lebanon.[159] Psametik also installed a garrison on Elephantine, an island opposite Aswan at Egypt's southern border at Aswan and sent military expeditions into Nubia. Much like Old Kingdom rulers, Psametik I had to call on his district leaders (*nomarchs*) to gather troops for his expeditions, both against the Nubians to the South, and also against the recurring Libyan incursions from the West.[160] Increasingly, Psametik began to rely on foreign mercenaries, particularly Carian and Ionian troops, to shore up his power – a policy that was faithfully followed by his successors. Although the unreliability of mercenary soldiers became evident early on, a strong belief that their military prowess was much superior to what was available locally, kept them employed. These foreign contingents, however, were never integrated into the Egyptian army: Egyptian and Greek soldiers served under different commanders.[161]

While initially Psametik I tolerated officials who had served under the Nubians (such as Mentuemhat, the powerful Mayor of Thebes and Fourth Prophet of Amun), he gradually began appointing his own "Delta men" in key positions in Upper Egypt. For instance, one Nesaiu became mayor of two important southern cities: Edfu and el-Kab. In Middle Egypt, shipmasters who had been politically powerful under the Nubians were marginalized.[162] But perhaps Psametik's most significant appointment was that of his daughter, Nitocris, as God's Wife of Amun.

Nitocris

Assuming the official name of *Nebetneferoumout*, or "Mistress of Beauty/Perfection is Mut," Nitocris became a God's Wife of Amun in 656 BC.[163] The events surrounding

The 26th Dynasty genealogy

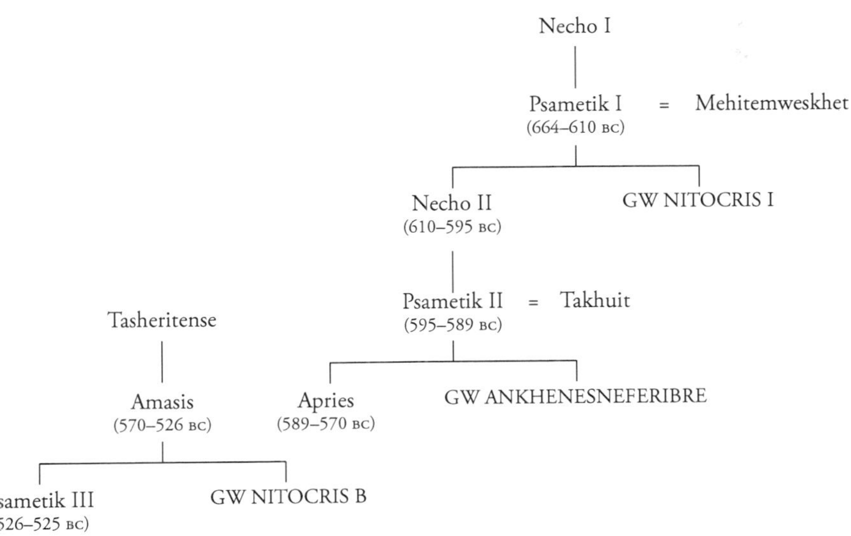

her appointment were recorded on a granite slab stela and were publicly displayed in the first court at the temple of Amun at Karnak. Known as the "Nitocris Adoption Stela," the decree starts off with Psametik's initial pronouncement of his desire to install his daughter as God's Wife (line 2).[164] Psametik's decision was made in the presence of Saite court officials, who indicated their pleasure with his decision by prostrating themselves before him, giving thanks to the King of Upper and Lower Egypt, and verbally declaring their unanimous approval of his plans (lines 5–7). The stela records the date of his speech as the twenty-eighth day of the first month of the *Akhet* season (summer) of his ninth regnal year.[165] This date coincided with March 2, 656 BC.[166] Apparently, either because Psametik lacked the political clout to initiate such an appointment, or possibly because Nitocris was too young, Psametik I could not immediately appoint his daughter to office, but had to wait nine years to bring about this monumental shift in local power.

The text also records Nitoicris's departure from her father's palace in the Delta, "clad in fine linen and adorned with new turquoise" on the twenty-eighth day of the first month of *Akhet* (line 7). Sixteen days later, she arrived at Thebes on the fourteenth day of the second month of *Akhet* (line 11), where she was greeted "with throngs of men and crowds of women standing and jubilating to meet her, surrounded by oxen, fowl, and abundant provisions, many in number" (lines 11–12).[167] But more importantly the stela details the vast estates and great quantities of daily provisions that were granted Nitocris. Psametik was not entirely responsible for provisioning his daughter. A large portion of her sizeable endowment came from independent temple estates and private individuals.[168] Psametik's pragmatism and diplomacy are most evident in his ability to induce temple personnel and private individuals alike to endow his daughter's position. But his diplomatic agility may also been in the wording of the decree itself. Instead of clearly ousting Amenirdis II from office, the text of the stela is sufficiently vague as to leave the identity of Nitocris's "adoptive mother" open to debate.[169] Caminos suggested that it was probably Amenirdis II who served as Nitocris's adoptive mother.[170] Caminos uses Psametik I's assertion in line 3, "I will not do what in fact should not be done and expel an heir from his seat … ," as a basis for inserting specific names into the text. Thus his translation of the passage in question reads: "I will give her (my daughter) to her (Taharqo's daughter) to be her eldest daughter just as she (Taharqo's daughter) was made over to the sister of her father" (line 4).[171] On the other hand, scholars such as Kitchen and Grimal have suggested that both Shepenwepet II and Amenirdis II "accepted … [Nitocris] as their successor."[172] I think that this view is probably an accurate understanding of what transpired. It is also in agreement with the stipulations of the document.

In attempting to establish his daughter's "legal" claim to succeed the Nubian princesses as the new God's Wife, Psametik had the incumbent Nubian God's Wives draw up an official transfer of title deed naming his daughter Nitocris as its beneficiary (lines 15–17).[173] The Nubian God's Wives bequeathed all their property "in country and in town" to Nitocris. Known in Egyptian as an *imyt-per* document (literally meaning "that which is in the house"), this document gave its beneficiary the right to enjoy, use, and bequeath the property named in the document.[174] In other words, it unequivocally transferred the property in question to the beneficiary. Typically, an *imyt-per* was not needed for a son to inherit his father's property, and was never used when inheritance passed to the actual "eldest son."[175] The document was needed *only* when the transaction benefited someone "other than the normal heir."[176]

The appropriation of adoption phraseology in line 4 ("I will give her (my daughter) to her … to be her eldest daughter")[177] merely reflects the need to establish Nitocris's new status as the heir to the incumbent God's Wife, thereby establishing her right of succession. The assumption of adoption phraseology was occasionally used in New Kingdom transfer of property deeds. For instance, a husband, having no children of his own, needed to "adopt" his wife as his child in order to ensure her right to inherit his property. In due course, the wife who inherited her husband's property adopted her brother in order to leave him her inherited property legally.[178] As in the case of Nitocris, the "legal fiction of adoption" was a matter of necessity.

Further underscoring the legal nature of the Nitocris Adoption Stela is the inclusion of dates and lists of witnesses in the document. Dates and a list of witnesses were two integral aspects of an *imyt-per* and as such were always recorded in *imyt-per* documents.[179] Psametik's initial pronouncement of his intention to appoint Nitocris as a God's Wife is witnessed by Saite courtiers. Once at Thebes, another group of Theban officials and clerics, "prophets, priests and friends of the temple," witnessed the transfer of property from the Nubian God's Wives to Nitocris.[180] From an ancient Egyptian legal perspective then, the Nitocris Adoption Stela, being an *imyt-per*, unequivocally established Nitocris's legal rights not only to her predecessor's property, but also to her official position.[181]

According to the stela, this transfer of property "was done in writing," further affirming the decree's legal nature. But that was not all that Nitocris received. The stela also records that the incumbent(s) proclaimed Nitocris as their successor, stating that she would be "established on our throne firmly and enduringly till the end of eternity."[182]

Monumentalized on a granite slab stela and erected and publicly displayed in the first courtyard in Karnak, the stela was visible for all to see. Public display in a temple ensured public and divine acceptance of its contents. Significantly, Psametik chose to resort to our equivalent of a civil contract to confer the office of the God's Wife on his daughter. That Psametik I would use a legal method (rather than ideological, mythological, or religious parlance) to establish his daughter's right to hold office at Thebes seems to support Spalinger's assessment of the Saite monarchy as primarily pragmatic and secular.[183] Indeed, Nitocris's appointment is probably best understood as part of Psametik I's policy of forming alliances.[184] In fact, it may be that this single act achieved the unity of Egypt under Saite hegemony. Spalinger remarked that Psametik "preferred to deal more diplomatically than militarily"[185] – and it is this tendency toward diplomacy that induced Psametik to choose a relatively peaceful method of extending his influence over the Thebaid.

Much like her predecessors, Nitocris embarked on an active building program in Thebes. At Karnak, she continued the tradition set by her Nubian and Libyan predecessors, dedicating shrines to Osiris just north of the main sanctuary and within the precinct of the temple of Monthu in North Karnak.[186] Nitocris used some of the epithets employed by the Nubians to refer to Osiris, but added her own to them. For example, one of the chapels she erected within the precinct of Monthu was dedicated to Osiris, Lord-of-Life (a Nubian epithet) to which she added *Dihebsed*, an epithet that means "he-who-grants-*sed*-festivals."[187] She also erected a columned building in the village of Malqata.[188]

Nitocris also chose to place her funerary chapel next to her predecessors' at Medinet Habu. But for some unknown reason, instead of erecting her own structure, Nitocris elected to squeeze her mortuary chapel in the narrow space available between the chapels of her Nubian predecessors (Figure 1.5).[189] To provide access to her *cella*, Nitocris also installed a second doorway into the pylon-façade of Shepenwepet's funerary chapel (Figure 1.4). When it was time to bury her own mother, Nitocris chose to erect a similar *cella* for her on the other side of Shepenwepet's *cella*. The burial of Nitoricis's mother Mehetnusekhet indicates that Nitocris was probably accompanied to Thebes by her biological mother: an indication of her tender age when she assumed office as God's Wife of Amun. Nitocirs died in 586 BC, having held office as God's Wife for sixty years.[190] She was succeeded by Ankhnesneferibre, daughter of Psametik II.

In 610 BC, Necho II (610–595 BC) succeeded Psametik as ruler of Egypt and, like his father before him, he continued to rely on mercenaries which led to disastrous results. Necho II was defeated at Megiddo and had to withdraw from the Levant. Possibly because of his repeated military defeats, Necho was vilified by his own people. In an attempt to remedy a bad military situation, Necho turned his attention to the Navy and developed Egypt's maritime connections with the Greeks.[191] Necho II was

Figure 1.5 Doorway leading to the tomb chapel of Nitocris (Photo © M. Ayad)

succeeded by Psametik II (595–589 BC), who continued his predecessor's maritime commercial activities successfully – and in 593 BC launched an attack on Nubia. The Egyptian southern border had been secure at Aswan for the first half of the dynasty. And it may be that this seemingly unprovoked attack was a diversion, launched for propagandist purposes and intended to erase the effects of Necho's repeated defeats elsewhere.[192] At any rate, several accounts of the battle, which was fought at the third cataract in Lower Nubia, were commemorated on stelae, which were erected at Karnak and at Aswan.[193] Psametik II dispatched his daughter Ankhnesneferibre to Thebes, where as heiress apparent, she became a "first prohet(ess) of Amun."

Ankhnesneferibre: the last God's Wife of Amun

Sixty years after Nitocris's appointment in 656 BC, Ankhnesneferibre, daughter of Psametik II, finally succeeded her as a God's Wife of Amun in 586 BC.[194] As "heiress apparent," Ankhnesneferibre had already acquired the title and duties of the High Priest of Amun, thus becoming the first Egyptian woman to attain this high distinction.[195] For her official, or "throne" name, Ankhnesneferibre took on *Heqatneferoumout*, or "The Female Ruler of Perfection/Beauty is Mut." Ankhnesneferibre appears opposite King Amasis (Ahmose II) in the chapel of Osiris-Wennofer-*Neb-djefa*, or "Lord of Offerings," in North Karnak and enlarged a near-by earlier chapel constructed by Nitocris.[196] Ankhnesneferibre also enlarged the chapel of Osiris-Pededankh dedicated by Shepenwepet II and Amenirdis II in North Karnak[197] and added a pro-pylon to the so-called "Edifice of the God's Wife" that Shepenwepet II erected in North Karnak. Like her adoptive mother before her, Ankhnesneferibre erected a building in the village of Malqata. Hers was a temple dedicated to Osiris Pameres, or "Osiris, who loves her."[198] Just as her predecessors erected funerary chapels at Medinet Habu, so did Ankhnesneferibre, whose chapel lay closest to the pylon-façade of Ramses III's mortuary temple at Medinet Habu.[199]

Ankhnesneferibre's tenure in office coincides with a period of intense political instability. The reign of Apries (589–570 BC) was marked by many revolts. A stela erected at Aswan records the defection of military personnel to Nubia. The reason? Growing resentment over the king's preferential treatment of the foreign contingents of his army, particularly the Greeks.[200] Possibly entertaining ambitions of westward expansion, Apries sent troops in support of a Libyan group in its war against the Greek Kingdom of Cyrene. The campaign, which was launched in 571 BC, was poorly conceived and eventually failed. The Egyptian troops, who had suffered massive losses, revolted against Apries. In the ensuing conflict, Apries relied primarily on his Greek navy to fend off the angry Egyptians. In the midst of the resulting conflict, an army general by the name of Ahmose (better known by the Hellenized version of his name: Amasis) proclaimed himself king in Sais. The rapidly succeeding events of this period possibly included an attempt on Apries' part to seize back the Egyptian throne, but the Egyptian troops rallied around Amasis and crowned him King of Egypt. One of Apries's attempts to regain the throne involved taking refuge in the Babylonian court and persuading Nebuchadnezzar to invade Egypt in order to re-instate him. If successful, the Babylonian court stood to gain enormous power and prestige in the region. Having formed an alliance with the king of Cyrene, Amasis was able to fend off the invading Babylonian troops. In the course of battle, Apries was killed.[201]

Amasis's long reign (570–526 BC) was characterized by considerable pragmatism and foresight. He instituted several judicial reforms. Greek mercenaries were relocated from their base at Pelusium, along Egypt's eastern border, to Memphis – a move that kept them closer to home, and consequently, more controllable. Amasis also established long-term alliances with Cyrene, a former foe, Lydia, and Samos and conquered Cyprus. It was during Amasis's reign that Demotic, a highly cursive script, became widely used in all of Egypt.[202] Some time during her long tenure, Ankhnesneferibre chose a successor: Nitocris, daughter of Amasis, who in due course, was named High Priest of Amun. Although the exact date of her appointment cannot be precisely determined exactly, Nitocris (B), daughter of King Amasis, seems to have assumed office as High Priest(ess) of Amun in 569 BC or shortly thereafter.[203]

The Saite dynasty finally came to an end with the short-lived reign of Psametik III (526–525 BC), which was cut short by the invading Persian troops led by Cyrus.[204] That Ankhnesneferibre survived long enough to witness the Persian conquest of Egypt in the spring of 525 BC is evident from remains at Karnak.[205] Shortly after the Persian invasion, Ankhnesneferibre died, and with her death the office of God's Wife disappeared, never to re-emerge. Her heiress-apparent never attained the status of God's Wife,[206] thus making Ankhnesneferibre the last God's Wife of Amun.

Ankhnesneferibre's sarcophagus was recovered in 1832 from a deep shaft behind Deir el-Medina. Currently housed at the British Museum (where it was assigned the object number EA 32), the lid of the sarcophagus is dominated by a near life-size figure of Ankhnesneferibre.[207] Carved in raised relief, Ankhnesneferibre wears a long, loose-fitting pleated garment. In her hands she carries a flail and a hook: shepherd's tools that came to signify the king's role as leader of his people. The royal insignia Ankhnesneferibre held in her hands may be a direct reflection of her "official" name: *Heqaneferumut* or "(female) Ruler of Perfection is Mut."

The inclusion of direct or indirect references to the goddess Mut in the names of the God's Wives of Amun, combined with the fact that to date no individuals have been identified as either the husbands or biological children of the God's Wives, led scholars to speculate widely. Two main areas of speculation clearly emerged: (1) the nature of the God's Wife role in temple ritual (which was often interpreted in sexual terms); and (2) the notion that religiously-mandated celibacy was imposed on the God's Wives of the Twenty-third to the Twenty-sixth dynasties. To address these two issues adequately and assess their validity, it is necessary to examine the scenes in which the God's Wives appear.

Amun, Mut, and the "throne names" of the God's Wives

In the period between 740–525 BC, the five women who held the title of the God's Wife of Amun all acquired "official" names upon becoming a God's Wife of Amun. The acquisition of a new, official, name was a customary feature of the Egyptian rituals of accession to the throne. But outside the royal realm, this was not a common practice. Just like a king, a God's Wife enclosed this newly acquired official name in the royal cartouche. And just as the king's throne name was placed before his given name, giving rise to the term *prenomen*, a God's Wife's newly acquired official name was also placed before her given name. The God's Wife's newly acquired official name may thus be referred to as a "*prenomen*." The more politically loaded "throne name" is intentionally avoided in this discussion. Instead, the more conservative label "official name" will be used to refer to the God's Wife *prenomen*. The official names of the five women who became God's Wives in the Libyan, Nubian, and Saite Dynasties all referred directly or implicitly to the goddess Mut, Amun's divine consort.[208] Thus, Shepenwepet I became *Khenemet-ib-Amun*, or the "One who is United with the Heart of Amun," while Amenirdis I was *Khaneferumut*, "May the Perfection of Mut appear" or the "One who appears (in) the Perfection of Mut." Shepenwepet II and Nitocris acquired similar names: *Henutneferumut* and *Nebetneferumut*, respectively. Both names mean "Mistress of Perfection/Beauty is Mut." The last God's Wife of Amun, Ankhnesneferibre, also had a similar, but more assertive name. She was *Heqatneferumut*, or "The Female Ruler of Perfection/Beauty is Mut" (see Table 1.2).

While each of these five names reflected the elevated status of the God's Wife and her intimate relationship with, and easy access to, the god Amun, the names also exhibit subtle differences. Four of the names include a direct reference to the goddess Mut, while only Shepenwepet utilized the name of Amun in her *prenomen*.

Shepenwepet I's choice of *prenomen* may have been influenced by her Libyan heritage. In the chapel of Osiris, Ruler of Eternity, Shepenwepet partners with her father Osorkon III in presenting offerings to Amun-Re, Ra-Horakhty, and Ptah. In her choice of *prenomen*, she may have been influenced by her father's devotion to Amun. Osorkon III had chosen the *prenomen* "*Step-en-Amun*" or "Chosen one of

Table 1.2 Official, or "throne," names of the God's Wives of Amun, Twenty-third to Twenty-fifth dynasty

God's Wife	*Official name*	*Translation*
Shepenwepet I	Khenemet-ib-Amun	United with the Heart of Amum
Amenirdis I	Khaneferoumout	May the Perfection (Beauty) of Mut Appear
Shepenwepet II	Henoutneferoumout	Mistress of Perfection (Beauty) is Mut
Nitocris	Nebe(t)neferoumout	Mistress of Perfection (Beauty) is Mut
Ankhnesneferibre	Heqatneferoumout	Female Ruler of Perfection (Beauty) is Mut

Amun" upon ascending to the Egyptian throne. He also added the epithet *Mery-Amun* "Beloved of Amun" to his given name.[209] Osorkon's devotion to Amun, however, was not unique to the Twenty-third dynasty. Names of Third Intermediate Period rulers exhibit a distinct bias towards Amun.[210] Similarly, kings of earlier periods of Egyptian history regularly evoked the name of Amun in both their official/throne names and given names. Much rarer in use was the verb *khnem*, "to be united with." Apart from Shepenwepet's name, the verb occurs in five other royal names only. Four of these names post-date the Twenty-third dynasty and could not therefore have inspired Shepenwepet's. Only one name predates Shepenwepet's. Once the heart-sign is removed from Shepenwepet's name, a very clear precedent emerges. Shepenwepet I's *prenomen*, *Khnemet-Ib-Amen* clearly evokes an epithet acquired by Hatshepsut. Acquired at some point in her twenty-year reign, the epithet *Khnemet-Amun*, or "United with Amun," was enclosed in the royal cartouche along with Hatshepsut's given name: var. . The epithet *khement-Amun* also regularly appears next to depictions of Hatshepsut as a king, as seen for example on the walls of the *Chapelle rouge* at Karnak.[211] In a recent article, Gay Robins suggested that Hatshepsut added this epithet to her "Son of Re" name as part of her newly formulated royal titulary. Robins noted that Hatshepsut's four other royal names each utilized Hatshepsut's feminine gender to incorporate the reference to a goddess, possibly as a word play on the feminine participle.[212] Robins further argued that since Hatshepsut's given name lacked a direct reference to a deity, it needed this additional epithet, which served to link Hatshepsut to her divine father Amun and further emphasized her intimate relationship with him.[213] Modeling her new name after Hatshepsut's was a logical thing for Shepenwepet to do. After all, Hatshepsut herself was also a God's Wife of Amun who clearly valued her role as a God's Wife and often used the title of God's Wife as her sole title.

Much like other royal personages adopting the name(s) of a predecessor or an ancestor, Shepenwepet chose to formulate her *prenomen* along the same *general* lines as Hatshepsut's epithet. Rather than assuming a name that was an identical copy of Hatshepsut's, Shepenwepet's use of a slightly different version of Hatshepsut's name was congruent with the manner in which other royals adopted the epithets of revered historical figures. Török noted that when the rulers of the Twenty-fifth dynasty adopted the names and epithets of Old Kingdom or Eighteenth dynasty rulers, they invariably used a slightly different version of the earlier epithet or name.[214] The resulting effect ensured that the new ruler would be recognized in his own right. The inspiration behind these acquired names, however, is immediately noticeable to modern scholars, and undoubtedly was also clearly visible to ancient Egyptians as well. The transparency of this kind of copying was undoubtedly intentional and was designed to clearly declare (at least the hope) that a particular king's era would emulate that of the earlier ruler(s), i.e. that it would follow policies similar to those established during the earlier reign.[215]

The absence of similar names strongly suggests that the composers of Shepenwepet I's titulary intentionally evoked an epithet of Hatshepsut's. Shepenwepet became a God's Wife of Amun at a time of weakened royal authority. What better figure to evoke than that of a female ruler who was clearly proud of her religious title as God's Wife and often used it as her sole title. At a time when the office of God's Wife was being "re-established," Shepenwepet wanted, indeed needed, to emphasize her intimate relationship with Amun. Evoking a name used by the all-powerful Hatshepsut may have served to legitimate Shepenwepet's claim to office and shore up her position as a God's Wife.

When the Nubians took over, they too manipulated the official name acquired by Amenirdis to convey a political message. Upon ascension to office, Amenirdis acquired the *prenomen Kha-neferu-mut* , also written with the variants , and .[216] Traditionally, her name has been translated as: "May the Beauty of Mut Appear,"[217] with *khai* considered a prospective verb form. Grammatically, however, the *kha* may be parsed in several different ways: *Khai* may be considered a noun, which would lend her *prenomen* to the translation rendered "The Appearance/Manifestation of Perfection is Mut"/"Mut is the Appearance/Manifestation of Perfection." *Khai* may also be considered an active participle, making the *prenomen* an adjectival phrase describing (or referring to) its holder: "She who Appears in/with the Perfection of Mut." The preposition supplied in this translation may have been omitted for space considerations.[218]

Her name may thus be translated as "May the Perfection of Mut Appear," "The Appearance/Manifestation of Perfection is Mut," or "She who Appears in Glory with the Perfection of Mut." The use of the Egyptian verb *khai* "to appear in glory" in Amenirdis's *prenomen* is quite intriguing. Once more, we find that the God's Wife's name was reflected in the epithets she used. Amenirdis chose the epithet, which may be translated as "She who Appears in Glory on the Throne of Tefnut." Amenirdis's use of several early Eighteenth dynasty titles and epithets, particularly those held by Queen Ahmose-Nefertari, clearly indicates an awareness on her part of the history of the office she was coming to. That she also intentionally evoked a link, albeit obliquely, with Hatshepsut's Golden Horus name , or "Divine of Appearances," [219] may be reasonable to conclude.

While Hatshepsut's Golden Horus name may have inspired Amenirdis's throne name, a more likely influence may be found in the names utilized by Amenirdis's immediate family members, the rulers of Egypt's Twenty-fifth dynasty. Piye initially took the Horus name of "Appearing in Glory in Napata," before changing it to "Appearing in Glory in Thebes" in, or shortly after, *c.* 728 BC.[220] Piye's two sons, Shebitqo and Taharqo, who later became the fifth and sixth rulers of the Twenty-fifth dynasty, respectively, likewise utilized that verb in their royal titulary. Shebitqo, in particular, employed several variants of the epithet "Enduring of Appearances" in both his Horus and "Two Ladies," or *Nebty*, names. Shebitqo also adopted the fuller epithets "Enduring of Appearances" as well as his father's "Appearing in Glory in Thebes" in his Horus name. Additionally, Shebitqo assumed the epithet "One Who is Caused to Appear in Truth, Beloved of the Two Lands" (which may be alternately translated as "Who Caused Maat to appear, Beloved of the Two Lands ...") in his "Two Ladies" name.[221] His successor Taharqo likewise adopted similar Horus and his Nebty names, both of which were variants on the epithet, "Exalted of Appearances." [222] *Khai* thus emerges as an element clearly favored by the Nubian rulers.

In its most basic meaning, the verb *khai* means "to appear in glory."[223] It is often said of the king upon ascension to the throne. It is also the verb used of the sun at sunrise. It is not surprising, therefore, that this verb, along with its grammatical derivates, was often used by rulers, not only of the Twenty-fifth dynasty, but also of earlier periods, who wanted to declare that their regimes commenced a new era. Tuthmosis I of the Eighteenth dynasty adopted the epithet for his "Two Ladies" name.[224] Likewise, Ramses I of the Nineteenth dynasty adopted a "Two Ladies" name which declared him "Appearing in Glory as King like Atum."[225] Indeed, as Kitchen pointed out, in their simplicity and lack of extraneous epithets, the double cartouches of Ramses I evoked those of Ahmose I, the founder of the Eighteenth dynasty.[226] Likewise, Seti I's titulary "emaphasised a glorious new beginning inspired by the Eighteenth dynasty." His Horus name declared him "appearing in Thebes," while in his Golden Horus name, Seti I was "renewing appearances." Seti's Horus name directly linked him to the "famous warrior-king, Tuthmosis III, while the other two additions were used to mark a new era."[227]

Judging by how frequently they used it in their titulary, the verb *khai* seems to have had very special connotations to the Nubian rulers of the Twenty-fifth dynasty. The Nubians portrayed/propagated themselves as restorers of Maat. Using *khai* in their royal titulary declared "the dawn of new era of order." One can even argue that the frequent use of the verb *khai* in Nubian titularies marked it as their own. Indeed, it seems that the close association of this verb with the Nubian rulers of Egypt, led the Saite rulers to avoid it altogether. By using *khai* in her *prenomen*, Amenirdis declared herself to be a member of this new order.

Furthermore, Amenirdis set herself apart from her Libyan predecessor by directly referencing the goddess Mut in her *prenomen*. Faithfully shown standing behind her husband Amun-Re, Mut was typically represented as a woman, a tight sheath dress covering her slender figure. A broad collar adorning her neck was often the only piece of jewelry worn by Mut. Mut, whose name is spelled using the hieroglyph for vulture (Gardiner sign # G14)[228] is occasionally linked with another vulture goddess: Nekhbet, the titular goddess of Upper Egypt. Like Nekhbet, Mut was represented wearing a royal crown. But while Nekhbet typically wore the White Crown of Upper Egypt, Mut was shown wearing the *peschent*, or Double Crown, of Upper and Lower Egypt.[229] Whereas Nekhbet was specifically associated with the South, Mut was a goddess of "royalty and coronation who [could] personify ... kingship."[230] It is not surprising therefore that Mut was often represented carrying the symbols of the exclusively royal *sed* festival. Just as Nekhbet was associated with Thebes (southern Heliopolis), so Mut, the mistress of *Isherou*, was associated with southern Karnak. Indeed, the southern precinct of Karnak was the domain of Mut. She was known as the "Great Mut, the mistress of *Isherou*, the mistress of the sky, the mistress of the gods." While *Isherou* could refer to the entire domain of Mut in southern Karnak, more specifically, *Isherou* was the crescent-shaped lake that dominates the landscape there. *Isherou* was also the mythic location where "lion-goddesses were appeased."[231] Mut, Amun's divine consort, was undoubtedly also his "favorite," and the one who is "united with him." In this sense, Shepenwepet's name, while directly evoking Amun's, includes an oblique reference to the goddess.

With its direct reference to the goddess Mut, Amenirdis's *prenomen* still evoked the conjugal union of Amun and Mut, but it simultaneously set her apart from Shepenwepet.

As a God's Wife, Amenirdis needed to emphasize her intimate relationship with Amun. But as a member of the new ruling house, she wanted to distance herself from her Libyan predecessor. In choosing to include Mut in her name, Amenirdis set the precedent for her successors' choice of name: the later God's Wives also incorporated the name of Mut, instead of Amun's, in their official names. It may be that Amenirdis, or her theologians, wanted to evoke the notion of Amun's and Mut's Divine union. Indeed, her successor, Shepenwepet II, appropriated the iconography of the sacred marriage, as seen on the jambs of the chapel of Osiris *Wennofer-Hery-ib-Ished*, in East Karnak.[232]

The God's Wives' official names thus seem to have been very carefully formulated. The deliberate choice of names served to proclaim their special status in relation to Amun, but it is also clear that Shepenwepet's *prenomen* included a direct reference to Hatshepsut, who was probably still quite revered as a God's Wife, if not as a ruler in her own right. Amenirdis's name, on the other hand, linked her directly to other (male) members of the dynasty, while simultaneously ushering a new political era.

2

RITES AND RITUALS

> The Egyptian temple, unlike the Greek temple or the Christian church, did not serve as a place where the believers could congregate, but was the house of the god, in which the pharaoh in his capacity as high priest, assisted by several priests, met the godhead face to face and honoured him with offerings.[1]
>
> C. J. Bleeker, *Egyptian Festivals: Enactments of Religious Renewal*, 48

> ... one, and by no means the least, of the aims of the cult is to make the earth an attractive place for the gods to live, to create in the temple a worthy residence for the god's image and a likeness of the sky, and to tend the cult image so well that it is happy to live among men.[2]
>
> Erik Hornung, *Conceptions of God in Ancient Egypt*, 229

To date, the ritualistic duties of the God's Wife of Amun have not been studied systematically. This is especially true for the 200 year period spanning dynasties Twenty-three through Twenty-six. Earlier, time-specific works, while extremely informative, do not cover the Nubian or Saite periods, focusing primarily on New Kingdom or early Third Intermediate Period evidence.[3] The material presented in this section sets about to accomplish that task. This section does not purport to be a comprehensive catalogue of *all* the iconographic scenes in which the God's Wife appear; rather, it aims to present key scenes in which the God's Wife of Amun appears performing various temple rituals, with the ultimate goal of placing the women, and the rituals they performed, within the broader religious, cultural, and historical contexts.[4]

The early occurrence of a God's Wife associated with the cult of the ithyphallic god Min has given rise to a rather sexual interpretation of the title. Despite not knowing how the sexual role of the God's Wife was translated into temple ritual, some rituals have been viewed as activities aimed at stimulating the gods sexually. This opinion is almost universally held, especially where such musical activities as shaking the sistrum are concerned.[5] This interpretation however, does not account for the role of female sistrum players in the cult of goddesses nor does it factor in scenes showing the king, or other males, holding or shaking the sistrum before various deities. In the next few pages, we will examine scenes in which the God's Wife appears with the sistrum and compare those scenes to those scenes showing the king performing the same ritual.

Entertaining the gods

Much like it is today, music was much enjoyed in ancient Egypt. In fact, the Egyptians so valued music that they envisioned a goddess, Merit, who was the deified personification of music. Merit was charged with the all-important task of "establish[ing] cosmic order by means of her song and gestures."[6] Egyptian gods, who seemed to enjoy everything that humans did, appeared to share their fondness for music as well. Even the dead god/king of the dead, Osiris, was said to have enjoyed music and dance and was credited with creating several musical instruments. Similarly, Thoth, the god of writing, invented the lyre and gave it its three strings. Thoth was also thought to have been the first "to observe the orderly arrangement of the stars and the harmony of the musical sound and their nature."[7] In general, music was thought to be an effective means of averting the gods' anger and appeasing their more dangerous aspects. This was especially true of the swooshing noise made by the sistrum and the *menat*, which was considered to have a calming effect on angry deities. Manniche suggested that chanting was punctuated by the rattling of the sistrum and the shaking of the *menat*.[8] In the Daily Temple Ritual, the chief god in a temple was awakened to the sound of chanting. As part of her service to the gods, the God's Wife is frequently shown playing the sistrum before various deities.

Playing music: shaking the sistrum

In a scene preserved on the eastern part of the Libyan façade of the Twenty-third dynasty chapel of Osiris, Ruler of Eternity, in East Karnak,[9] Shepenwepet I is shown in profile, her face turned to the left, standing before three of Egypt's national gods: Amun-Re, Ra-Horakhty, and Ptah.[10] A Ramesside hymn explains the presence of these three deities together: "Three are all gods: Amon, Ra, and Ptah. He who hides his name is Amon, he who is visible is Ra, and his body is Ptah."[11] As is typical of Egyptian art, the main figures in this scene, in this case the three national deities of Egypt, are rightward oriented.[12] Shepenwepet wears a long-sleeved, loose fitting, layered dress. A sash tied just above her natural waist gathers the dress's various layers. The dress's various layers, however, do not hide her voluptuous figure from sight. Shepenwepet also wears a broad collar and an elaborate crown that sits atop her short cropped wig. In her hands she holds two *naos*-sistra, which she shakes for the benefit of three standing deities shown facing her. The sistrum was a rattle sacred to the cow goddess Hathor, but later became associated with other gods as well.[13] Acquiring its modern name from the Greek verb *seiein* "to shake," the ancient Egyptian sistrum came in two forms: the *naos*-sistrum, whose top resembled an Egyptian sanctuary or shrine, and the loop-sistrum, whose top was arched.[14] In this scene, Shepenwepet I holds the more ancient of the two forms, the *naos*-sistrum.

Facing Shepenwepet, and closest to her, is Amun, who extends the sign of life towards her, its tip touching her hip. Amun, who is shown in profile, is represented taking a wide stride to the right. He dons his customary double-feathered crown, a curved false beard, broad collar, a pectoral, and a short kilt to which is attached a ceremonial bull's tail. A *was*-scepter held vertically in Amun's left hand separates him from Shepenwepet. In his other hand, hanging behind his back, he holds another *ankh*-sign. Behind Amun is falcon-headed Ra-Horakhty, who is represented in an identical stance to Amun's. The tip of the *ankh*-sign diagonally held in his hand touches Amun's back hand. Like Amun, Ra-Horakhty wears a broad collar, and a short kilt to which is attached the bull's tail. A solar disk rests atop his long wig. Behind Ra-Horakhty is statuesque Ptah, who is here represented standing atop a pedestal, a tight cloak completely enveloping his body. Only his *was*-scepter-grasping fists appear through a slight aperture in the upper part of his cloak.

Behind Shepenwepet is an elaborate offering table laden with all kinds of fruits, vegetables, and herbs, including lotus flowers. Four gigantic ornate bread loaves act as supports for the table. Shepenwepet seems oblivious to the table behind her. Instead, her attention is fully given to the three gods for whom she shakes the sistrum. On the other side of the table to the extreme right of the scene, a royal figure in full regalia consecrates the offerings. Shown in profile, his face turned to left, he extends a *mekes*-scepter toward the offerings. In his left hand, he carries a *hedj*-scepter and a staff.[15] He wears the White Crown of Upper Egypt and a ceremonial tripartite kilt. The inscriptions identify him as Osorkon, her father.

The offering table seems to divide the scenes in two halves. To the East (=left) of the table, the God's Wife is fully engaged in pleasing the three major, national deities of Egypt by playing music, while to the West (=right) side, the king consecrates the offerings. While both acts are performed for the benefit of the gods, it is interesting to note that the God's Wife was placed closer to the gods than the king. The proximity of the God's Wife is further highlighted by the distance that separates the king from the deities, created by placing the table between her and the king, rather than between her and the gods. The particular arrangement of this scene may be indicative that these are two separate actions shown in a ritualistic sequence, occurring one after the other.[16] Alternatively, Shepenwepet and her father may have been performing simultaneous acts of worship taking place on either side of the offering tables placed before statues of the three gods. The king, shown here standing behind the table, would in actuality be on the other side of the table, farther from the viewer.[17] Even so, placing the king behind the God's Wife emphasized her importance. Robins has aptly noted that in depictions of divine couples, "the male deity occupies the forward position and the female one the rear, irrespective of whether they are shown in temples, on royal monuments, or on private ones. So, for example, Amun precedes Mut, and Osiris precedes Isis."[18] Robins similarly pointed out that even deified Ahmose-Nefertary, despite her importance, did not "take precedence over *her son*," but was depicted sitting behind her son in group compositions.[19] Although this particular example dates to the New Kingdom, Robins points out that "rules of compositional hierarchy according to ownership and gender were almost certainly current in all periods of Pharaonic Egypt."[20]

In the same room in the chapel of Osiris, Ruler of Eternity, we find two more scenes depicting the God's Wife carrying or shaking the sistrum. On the lower register of the north wall she stands, her face, shown in profile, turned to the right to face Amun-Re. A rearing cobra at her brow, Amenirdis wears a long lappet wig surmounted by a vulture cap and two tall plumes, a loose fitting, long-sleeved, multi-layered dress, and

The sistrum, the *menat*-necklace and objects sacred to Hathor

The distinction between the two types of sistrum, *naos* or loop, is strictly based on shape. The two types share the same type of handle, which typically took the shape of a papyrus umbel. The central feature of both types of sistrum was a bi-facial Hathoric mask that attached to the top of the papyrus umbel and linked the handle to the functional top part of the sistrum. The mask adorning the sistrum, while representing a human head with cows ears, is actually that of the goddess Bat.[105] Bat may originally have been a sky goddess, whose name means "female power" or "female soul." The mask bearing her face may have been a symbol of her power, and her "ability to see before and behind."[106]

Setting the two types of sistrum apart is the shape and composition of the top part. The loop-sistrum typically comprised an arched piece of wire to which were attached three horizontal bars. Small metal disks strung through those bars would produce the distinctive rattling noise associated with the sistrum when shaken. The *naos*-sistrum is so-called because its top part took the shape of a temple's sanctuary, or *naos*. *Naos*-sistra were typically made of faience, or other such glazed material. While some scholars have maintained that this type of sistrum was "perfectly usable" despite its fragility and the "modest" quality of its sound properties, others have maintained that this type of sistrum was never intended as a musical instrument as many of the surviving examples lack the noise-producing disks. Instead, they may have been used as a votive offering.[107] In Egyptian, three words were used to refer to the sistrum: *sekhem*, *sesheshet*, and *ib*.[108] A recent study by Reynders has shown that the Egyptian word *sesheshet* was always used in the caption texts accompanying scenes of playing the sistrum, regardless of which type of sistrum was depicted in the scene. This observation has led her to conclude that the word *sesheshet* referred to the noise made by the sistrum, while *sekhem*, when applied to the sistrum, referred specifically to the incarnation or manifestation of the goddess Hathor.[109]

a shawl draped over her shoulders, whose squared edge appears next to Amenirdis's right upper arm.[21] A sash, tied at her waist, its streamers falling decoratively down the front of her dress, holds the various layers of her garment together. A broad collar, whose layered beads are clearly delineated, adorns Amenirdis's neck. In her upraised hands she carries two identical loop-sistra, their elongated loops surmounting a rounded Hathoric head. Occupying the space above the two sistra are Amenirdis's cartouche-enclosed names and titles. The inscriptions, which like Amenirdis's, are orientated toward the right, read: "The Divine Adorer *Khaneferumet*, the God's Wife Amenirdis, who appears on the throne of Tefnut."[22] In the space below Amenirdis's elbow, a caption for the scene is provided. It reads: "Shaking the sistrum before the good Lord, Amun-Re, the Great one of the gods"[23] .

Indeed, standing before her is Amun-Re, who extends an *ankh*-symbol (the key of life) to Amenirdis, the tip of its loop almost touching her nose. The *ankh*-symbol is attached to a *was*-scepter which Amun-Re holds in his right hand. Amun dons his tall-feathered crown, a false beard, a broad collar and a *naos*-shaped rectangular pendant. The top of the pendant, which is suspended on a bit of string, sits just below his broad collar. It also overlaps with the tapering shoulder straps that hold his shirt in place. A belt accentuates Amun's narrow waist while holding his kilt in place. Amun's body proportions are almost ideal. His athletic physique is not quite as heavy as that of the Nubian king officiating in another scene engraved on the same wall or some of the images characteristic of later Nubian relief carving. Traces of blue paint on his neck suggest that his body was once painted blue. Immediately in front of the tall feathers of his crown, three short columns of framed inscriptions read: "Words spoken by Amun-Re, Lord of the Thrones of the Two Lands, (O) God's Wife, Amenirdis, my heart greatly rejoices on account of this beautiful monument of yours" .[24] In his discussion of the epithet "who appears on the throne of Tefnut," Leclant interprets this and similar scenes as a "symbole très chaste de leur union."[25] According to Leclant, touching Amenirdis's nose with the *ankh*-sign is not merely symbolic of giving her life, but also indicative of theogamy, the conjugal union between Amun and Amenirdis.[26] Viewed from this perspective, playing the sistrum ceases to be a mere musical activity. It becomes an erotic activity designed to arouse the god sexually. Indeed, Leclant cites Amun's response to Amenirdis, "my heart greatly rejoices," as indicative of the pleasure that Amun derives from Amenirdis's musical activity.[27] Indeed, Amun's response is atypical. For it departs from the more usual formulaic divine response of: "To you, I have given all life and dominion, all health, all joy etc… ." However, contrary to what Leclant suggested in his article, Amun's response is *not* directly linked to Amenirdis's action in this particular scene. Rather, the text specifies the reason for Amun's joy: it was her construction of "a monument," a chapel dedicated to Osiris. At her temple at Deir el-Bahri, the same phrase accompanies a scene in which Hatshepsut drives the four calves for Amun-Min.[28]

Repeatedly, the inscriptions declare that the chapel is dedicated to Osiris. Yet, Osiris is absent from the representations found in the Nubian addition to the chapel. Instead, it is Amun who consistently appears next to Amenirdis, Shepenwepet I, and the Nubian king who presents him with *Maat*. In this particular scene, Amun is given the title of "chief of the gods," or "the great one of the gods."[29] The sign used to express "chief," *wer*, is a logogram showing a man holding a stick (Gardiner sign list # A 21). Literally meaning "the great one," Amun's epithet here was also the Egyptian designation for a (foreign) tribal ruler, where it was used with the sense of "chief" or "chieftain."[30] Although the same sign may also be read as *semsou*, the Egyptian word for "elder" or "eldest," Amun-Re does not seem to have held that particular title.[31] The inscription in the chapel of Osiris, Ruler of Eternity, declares in no uncertain terms Amun's seniority. As the "great one of the gods," Amun is acknowledged as a creator god, who existed before any of the other gods. This is particularly evident in the Theban creation myth, a version of which has survived in a Ptolemaic text known as the Khonsu Cosmogony. In this text, Amun-Re bears the title of "chief of all the gods," and is "the hidden soul" that pre-existed all the gods. There, he is also called "father of the fathers" of the primeval eight gods, who is credited with creating not only all other gods, but also Khonsu and Ptah, two creator gods in their own right.[32] Amun rejoices over the building Amenirdis erected for Osiris, because he is greater than Osiris. There is no longer any rivalry because by this time the cult of Amun had incorporated Osiris. Otto cites an interesting text dating roughly to the same time period as the chapel of Osiris, Ruler of Eternity. The text, dating to the Persian Period (525–404 BC), is an edict reportedly issued by Amun, in which he (Amun) declares the deification of Osiris as a god of the underworld, proclaims Horus heir to Osiris, and arranges for the protection of Isis. "In other words, the whole of the Osiris religion is subordinated to the protection of Amon."[33]

Despite the poor condition of the wall surface on which this scene is carved, the exceptional quality of its relief carving can still be appreciated on closer examination. Amun-Re's beard for instance is intricately braided. Similarly, the level of detail exhibited in their broad collars is exceptional. We can also see great attention to detail in the small ornamental Hathoric heads adorning the handles of the sistra in Amenirdis's hands. Not only are the eyes, nose, mouth and ears clearly carved, but also the cosmetic lines around the eyes and the brows, both executed in raised relief.

Amenirdis is also shown playing the sistrum on the façade of her funerary chapel at Medinet Habu. On the lower register of the eastern half of the pylon-façade, Amenirdis stands at the far left facing Amun-Re, "the Lord of the Thrones of the Two Lands, who is in Karnak" (Egyptian: *ipet-sout*). Standing behind Amun-Re is his divine consort the "Great Mut, the mistress of *Isherou*, the mistress of the sky, the mistress of the gods." *Isherou* was not merely the precinct of Mut in South Karnak but, more specifically, it was the crescent-shaped lake that dominates the landscape there. It was also the mythic location where "lion-goddesses were appeased."[34]

Amenirdis, her face shown in profile, turns to the right to face her divine companions. She dons a long form-fitting tight sheath dress, a broad collar, and a long lappet wig surmounted by a vulture cap and two tall plumes. A *uraeus* curls at her forehead. Amenirdis's two looped sistra occupy the space immediately in front of her face such that the loops of the sistra begin at a point parallel to her nose, their top curve aligning almost perfectly with the curvature of her head. Damage in the wall surface has caused the loss of Amenirdis's upper body, shoulders, arms and hands. The damage continues horizontally across the space between her figure and Amun's and extends to his upper body, which is mostly destroyed now along with his false beard and right shoulder. In his forward extended arm, Amun holds a *was*-scepter, while in his other hand hanging parallel to his body he grasps an *ankh*-symbol. Amun-Re wears a short kilt to which is attached a bull's tail at the back, and his tall-feathered crown. It is not clear whether he dons an upper body garment.

Mut, standing behind him, is also orientated toward the left. Mut's (and Amun's) leftward orientation is in line with Egyptian artistic convention, which dictated that deities would be shown going out of the temple. In this case, the doorway to the chapel is located in the space *behind* Mut's back. Like Amenirdis, Mut wears a vulture cap and a long sheath dress that stops mid calf. The dress is held in place by tapering shoulder straps. On her head is the crown of Upper and Lower Egypt. With the exception of her legs, Mut stands in an identical posture to Amun's, and like him, she grasps a *was*-scepter and an *ankh*-symbol. In the space between Amenirdis' slim body and Amun's *was*-scepter, a hieroglyphic text provides a caption to the scene: "She shakes the sistrum for her father, Amun-Re. She acts that she may live." The atypical ending of this brief text, "that she may live," (Egyptian: *ankh.ti*) employs a grammatical construction that is typically used in wishes.[35] It may be a scribal error. The more typical ending of the offering formula: "[for] the one who gives life" (Egyptian: *di ankh*) is the wish used after a king's name "given live." Another way of expressing the same wish was to employ the stative (Egyptian: *ankhou*), whose feminine equivalent is used here. Amun's response to her offering starts in a column of framed inscription in front of his crown and continues to the text inscribed in the space between his forward-extended leg and his *was*-scepter. The first part of the inscription reads: "Words to be spoken: To you, I have given every good and pure thing," while the second part reads: "To you I have given kingship … ." It is possible that the text was followed by a god's name,[36] but the damage to the wall makes it extremely difficult to discern any of the hieroglyphic signs. Just below Mut's hand is a similar text. It reads: "To you, I have given very many *sed* festivals." According to Te Velde, this is precisely the kind of gift that Mut regularly gives the king: "the age-span of Atum, [and] jubilee festivals (*sd*)."[37]

A similar caption accompanies a scene inscribed on the lower register of the eastern wall in Room I in the chapel of Osiris, Ruler of Eternity, in East Karnak. The scene depicts Amenirdis standing at the left before Amun-Re, "Lord of the thrones of Two Lands, who is in *Ipet-sout*" (Karnak), and Mut "the mistress of *Isherou*"[38] (Figure 2.1).

Partially framing the scene is the figure of an *ankh*-holding vulture, whose head is engraved above Amenirdis's. In the space created between the bird's horizontally spread wing and Amenirdis's head, hieroglyphic signs identify the vulture as the titular goddess of Upper Egypt "Nekhbet, mistress of southern Heliopolis." The occurrence of Nekhbet in this scene may be linked to Mut's presence in it. Both were vulture goddesses. Both were associated with the South: Nekhbet with Thebes (southern Heliopolis) and Mut, the mistress of *Isherou*, with southern Karnak. And both are represented wearing royal crowns: Nekhbet the White Crown of Upper Egypt, and Mut the *peschent*, or Double Crown, of Upper and Lower Egypt.[39] Engraved in the space behind the bird's tail and its diagonally spread wing, a single short column of unframed inscriptions reads: "She gives all life and dominion like Re forever." Also under the horizontally spread wing of Nekhbet are three unframed columns above her head. The inscriptions identify Amenirdis as the "Divine Worshipper, Khaneferumut, the God's Wife, Amenirdis, alive for ever."

Amenirdis, whose face is shown in profile, turns to the right to face Amun-Re. Wearing a short curly wig, and a loose-fitting, long-sleeved, voluminous, multi-layered dress, Amenirdis holds a *naos*-sistrum in her right hand. She does not shake the sistrum though, which rests flatly on her shoulder. Instead, she extends her left arm towards Amun, who is shown in the exact moment of placing three *ankh*-signs in her open palm. Behind Amenirdis is a short column of unframed inscriptions, which read: "Protection, life, stability, all dominion, all health, all gladness, surround <her> like Re for ever."

Figure 2.1 Chapel of Osiris, Ruler of Eternity, room I, eastern wall, lower register (Photo © M. Ayad)

Amun-Re, who turns to face Amenirdis, wears his double-feathered crown, short kilt, an upper-body garment held in place by tapering shoulder straps, and a *naos*-shaped pectoral.[40] He holds three bits of string in his left hand, from which are suspended the three *ankh*-signs that Amenirdis receives in her open hand. In his right hand, Amun holds another *ankh*-symbol, which he extends towards Amenirdis's face such that the loop that constitutes the upper part of the *ankh*-sign touches her nose. His action is symbolic of his life-giving powers. It is through this gesture that Amenirdis receives life.[41] Three short columns of texts in front of Amun-Re's crown give his titles and speech: "To you, I have given all life and dominion, happiness, and beauty and all that the gods love and live <on> forever."

Behind Amun is his divine consort Mut, who wears the double crown of Upper and Lower Egypt, a tight sheath dress and a broad collar. Mut places her hand, protectively, and affectionately, on her husband's shoulder. Her other arm hangs parallel to her body, not behind her, but in the space between her and Amun. In her right hand, she carries an *ankh*-symbol, which is modeled so that its horizontal arms form the top of the hieroglyphic sign for a festival hall (Gardiner's sign list # O 23). To this sign is attached another, similar sign (Gardiner's sign list # W 4). Composed of two signs, the lower part of this sign was the alabaster dish used in temple purification rites,

Figure 2.2 Chapel of Osiris, Ruler of Eternity, room I, eastern wall, lower register; detail (Photo © M. Ayad)

while the top part was a schematic representation of a reed hut, whose framework was supported by a central pole. The hut represented the "simplest type of a tabernacle."[42] This sign combination was used as the determinative for the word denoting the *sed* festival (Gardiner's sign list # O 23E), but when appearing on its own, it stood for the entire word denoting the *sed* festival. The entire group is followed by , the Egyptian word for "great many." The entire group in Mut's hand can thus be read as "Many *sed* festivals" (Figure 2.2).[43] It is fitting that it would be Mut, and not any other goddess, who presents Amenirdis with the jubilee signs, for she was a goddess of "royalty and coronation who [could] personify … kingship."[44]

A single column of text in front of Mut's crown reads: "Words spoken by Mut, the Great, the Mistress of Isherou." Then above Mut is the name and title of Amenirdis, probably to be taken here as a vocative: "O the God's Wife, Amenirdis." The speech is then continued in a single column of framed inscriptions engraved behind the figure of Mut: "as Eternity exists, so shall your name exist and vice-versa, enduring among the names(s) of the living. To you, I have given all life and dominion, and all stability that you may appear as a Divine Worshipper and a God's Wife upon the throne of Tefnut like Re forever."[45] A single column of texts inscribed behind Amenirdis at the far left, frames this scene:

> The God's Wife, Amenirdis, alive, she erected her monument for her father, Osiris, Ruler of Eternity. She erected for him an august temple <for> her Lord, a place for eternity through the work of knowledgeable craftsmen in a work project for eternity. She acts <for> the one who has given life.[46]

Remarkably, the scenes discussed above are the only representations showing a God's Wife shaking the sistrum that survive *in situ*. No other instances occur from the Nubian period. The extant parts of the chapels of Osiris-Wennofer-in-the-midst-of-the-Persea-Tree and Osiris-Neb-ankh, the two chapels dedicated by Shepenwepet II in East and North Karnak respectively, are devoid of scenes showing her playing the sistrum. This is not to suggest, however, that Shepenwepet was never represented taking part in such a scene. Blocks from the now-destroyed chapel of Osiris Padedankh (Osiris, the One who continuously Gives Life), also known as Osiris-Neb-djet (Osiris, Ruler of Eternity), depict Shepenwepet II playing the sistrum. Among the blocks, which are currently at the Egyptian Museum in Cairo, is a lintel (JE 39402), which is adorned with four symmetrically opposed scenes.[47] On the right-hand side is the God's Wife embraced by a deity,[48] followed by a wider scene showing Shepenwepet shaking the sistrum before Osiris, Lord of Eternity, Isis, and the deified Amenirdis. Osiris does not appear mummiform here, but rather as a healthy, muscular, well-built male, who strides forward toward Shepenwepet and holds a *was*-scepter in his hand. Between Shepenwepet and Osiris's *was*-scepter is a table of offering laden with bread, birds and vegetables. Shown in profile, Isis wearing a tight sheath dress and a long lappet wig, surmounted by a solar disk set within Hathoric horns, extends one arm forward, to touch the back of Osiris's shoulder. Isis carries an *ankh*-symbol in her other hand. Standing behind the divine couple is Amenirdis who, like Isis, wears a tight sheath dress and carries an *ankh*-symbol in her hand. Amenirdis also wears a vulture cap surmounted by two tall plumes. Clasped close to her chest is a flagellum/fly-whisk.

Two columns of framed inscriptions separate this sequence from the symmetrically opposed sequence depicted on the other half of the lintel. On the far left is King Taharqo, depicted in profile, his face turned to the right and wearing the tripartite *shendyt*-kilt and the white crown of Upper Egypt, embraced by falcon-headed Re-Horakhty. In the next scene, inscribed closer to the center of the lintel, Taharqo, similarly-attired, extends his right arm forward, while holding a *was*-scepter in his other hand. Taharqo seems to be consecrating offerings placed on the table between him and Amun. Amun is followed by falcon-headed Horsaiese, who dons the crown of Upper and Lower Egypt on his head. Deified Amenirdis brings up the rear. The scenes depicted on this lintel, along with other fragments recovered from this chapel, indicated that it was dedicated by Taharqo and Shepenwepet II.[49]

Blocks scattered in the precinct of the temple of Mut at Karnak, and in museums around the world, depict the God's Wife shaking the sistrum. The representative sample presented here, however, suffices. The God's Wife shaking of the sistrum has often been characterized as an activity aiming at sexually arousing the god for whose benefit the sistrum was shaken.[50] This interpretation, however, does not account for the presence of an offering table in the scene, nor does it take into account the numerous examples that show the king (and other males) holding or shaking the sistrum. Examples collected by F. Hesse for a recent MA thesis show that such scenes extend beyond the more commonly acknowledged Late Period examples and occur in a variety of contexts.[51]

In the Great Hypostyle Hall in the temple of Amun at Karnak, Ramses II is depicted "rattling" the sistrum before Amun-Re Kamutef and Isis (Figure 2.3).[52] The scene, which occurs on the top register of the southern half of the east wall, shows the king orientated toward the right as he faces the ithyphallic god. Between the king and the god is a long, narrow stand surmounted by a short *wesekh*-jar (Gardiner's sign list # W 10) and a lotus flower. Offering lotus flowers had become a standard practice by

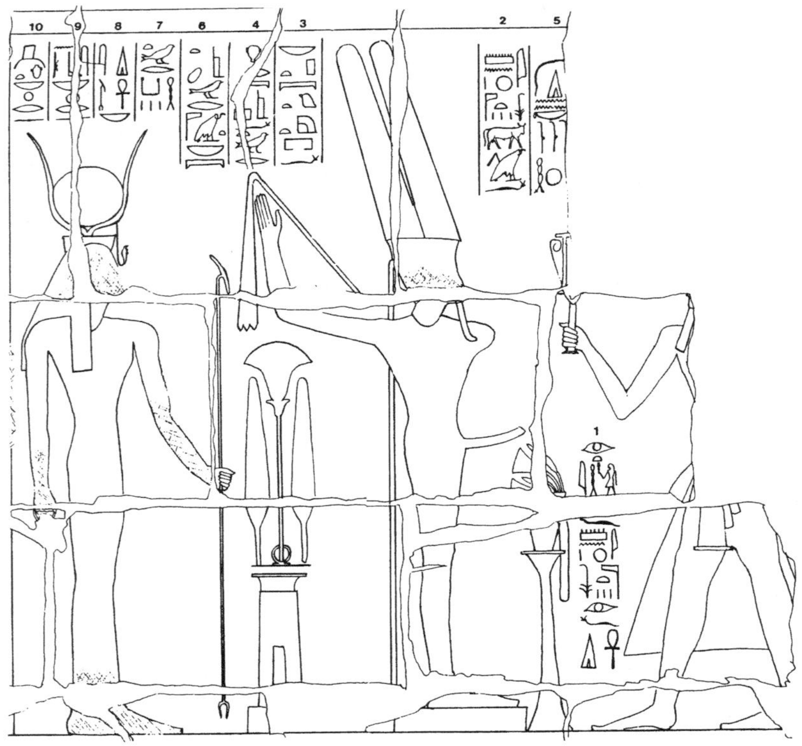

Figure 2.3 Ramses II rattling the sistrum before Amun Ka-Mutef, Karnak Hypostyle Hall (line drawing after Harold H. Nelson, *The Great Hypostyle Hall at Karnak I, Part 1 The Wall Reliefs.,* ed. William J. Murnane (Chicago, The Oriental Institute, 1981), pl. 80; reproduced with permission).

the New Kingdom.[53] At the temple of Karnak, flowers and vegetables were especially offered to the ithyphallic form of Amun-Re.[54]

The king's torso and head do not survive. Only the king's false beard, his right shoulder and arm, and his lower body are preserved. The barefoot king wears a long diaphanous skirt that extends to his mid-calf, and an elaborate apron, tied decoratively at the front. In his right hand, he clasps a *naos*-shaped sistrum, one of the volutes decorating the sistrum still visible.

Standing on a short, flat pedestal facing the king is Amun-Re Kamutef. Ithyphallic, and tightly wrapped mummy-like in a long cloak, Amun-Re Kamutef dons a tall doubled-feathered crown, a long curved beard, and brandishes a flail above his shoulder, his right arm raised squarely behind him. Amun-Re Kamutef is shown in his customary posture, carrying his regular insignia. Immediately under the god's upraised arm is a schematic representation of a temple façade topped by a lotus flower set between two tall trees (Gardiner sign list # M 1). Standing behind the temple façade is Isis, clad in a tight sheath dress. A serpent-encircled disk set within Hathoric horns atop her head, Isis wears a long lappet wig. In her right hand, she holds a *was*-scepter, while in her left hand she carries an *ankh*-symbol. While it was more customary for goddesses to hold the papyrus staff, occasionally goddesses, especially those "personifying the eye of the sun god" were also represented holding a *was*-scepter[55]

Inscribed under the king's elbow, in the space between the stand and the king's skirt, a single column of hieroglyphic text provides a caption to the scene: "Playing the sistrum <for>... his [father] Amun-Re the king of the gods. It is done <for> him who has given life." Literally, the text reads: "Performing *Ihy.t*." Ihy, whose role the king may be impersonating here, was the sistrum-shaking son of Hathor.[56] In the temple of Hatshepsut at Deir el-Bahri, Ihy appears as a naked boy sporting the side lock of youth and holding a *naos*-sistrum.[57] Although depicted on a much smaller scale than the now-erased larger figure of Hatshepsut, he precedes her as he presents an offering of wine to Hathor. The presentation is made to Hathor, who, represented in her bovine form, rests in a *per-wer* pavilion. In Egyptian, *per-wer* literally means the "great house." In essence Hatshepsut is offering to herself in this scene. For underneath the body of Hathor, she kneels in her kingly attire, her head tilted up as she feeds on the milk of this divine cow. The scene, which survives on the walls of the shrine of Hathor, thus unites Hatshepsut with her heavenly nurse.

Amun's response and name are given in two short columns of framed texts inscribed in the space in front his crown: "Words spoken: To you, I have given years of eternity, Amun-Re Kamutef." Kamutef, literally meaning the "Bull of his mother," was an aspect or epithet of Amun-Re. Although the epithet was commonly associated with Amun-Re, it is sometimes attested in connection with Min or Min-Amun-Re. First attested at Karnak during the reign of the Middle Kingdom king Senwosret I (1956–1911/10 BC), Amun-Re-Kamutef was a self-engendering deity who, by impregnating his mother, became his own father. Kamutef, "being both father and son of itself, possesses a legitimacy that is not questionable."[58] Kamutef is also known as the "bull of the Ennead," the group of nine primeval gods.[59] As Min-Kamutef, he was considered the son of Isis.[60] Seen in this context, it is understandable that Isis should appear standing protectively behind Amen-Re Kamutef in this scene.

The southern half of the east wall in the Hypostyle Hall, where this scene occurs, is dominated by offering scenes, in which Ramses II alternately offers incense, libations, wine, milk, flowers, and consecrates offerings to ithyphallic Amun-Re-Kamutef, and non-ithyphallic Amun-Re.[61] Both forms of Amun-Re were equally important and "alternated systematically on the walls of Theban temples." [62] Providing him with nourishment, the offerings energized Amun-Re and enabled him to re-enact his initial act of creation. After examining those scenes, Hesse concluded that "[a]side from the sistrum ... none of these other objects may be identified with sexuality, feminine or otherwise."[63]

In the Ptolemaic period, it became fairly common for the king to be shown playing the sistrum. Several scenes show Ptolemaic kings playing the sistrum. In the Temple of Esna, Ptolemy VI Philometer rattles the sistrum for the goddess Neith. Neith, shown in profile, her face turned to the left to face the king, dons a tight sheath dress, a broad collar, and the Red Crown of Lower Egypt. In her right hand, she holds a bow, arrows, and *was*-scepter, while in her left hand she carries an *ankh*-symbol. There, as in the scene just described above, an offering table stands between the king and the deity.[64]

Similarly, Ptolemy II offers sistra to Mut and to the lion goddess Sekhmet in the temple of Mut at Karnak (Figure 2.4).[65] In this scene, the king, shown in profile, is orientated towards the right to face the enthroned Mut.[66] He wears a broad collar and a short kilt. The wall on which the scene occurs is only partially preserved. Although the king's crown and the top part of the sistra are missing, the Hathoric face adorning the handles of his sistra is still visible. Behind the king stand a female harpist and a

Figure 2.4 King Ptolemy II shakes the sistrum before the goddess Mut, Temple of Mut at Karnak (after R. A. Schwaller de Lubicz, *The Temples of Karnak* (Rochester, VT. Inner Traditions International, 1999), pl. 430; reproduced with permission)

tambourine player. Mut, sitting on her throne, holds a papyrus-staff in her right hand. She dons a broad collar, and a tight sheath dress. Music may have been intended to appease the goddess Mut and avert her dangerous side.[67]

On the monumental gate to the temple of Montu in North Karnak, Ptolemy III or IV similarly offers both types of sistrum (the looped and the *naos*) to the goddess Mut. Offering the sistrum, however, was not limited to female deities. On the interior façade of the monumental east gate at Karnak, Ptolemy III Euergetes, wearing the royal *shendyt*-kilt and an elaborate *atef*-crown, presents a *naos*-sistrum and a *menat*-necklace to the lunar god Khonsu.[68]

Both the *menat*-necklace and the sistrum were objects sacred to the goddess Hathor, the sounds produced by the one instrument often complementing the other.[69] That this was so can be gleaned, for example, from a wall painting from the tomb of Amenemhat at Thebes (TT 82). There, a group of three musicians who stand one behind the other are shown holding the *menat*-necklace in one hand and the sistrum in the other. Manniche has remarked that the musicians are shown performing different movements: the first and the third shake the *menat*, while the middle one shakes the sistrum.[70]

On the southern half of the east wall in room I in the chapel of Osiris, Ruler-of-Eternity, Shepenwepet I stands, her face turned toward the right (= south) before Isis, who offers her the *menat*-collar and with whom she holds hands (Figure 2.5).[71] Shepenwepet wears a *uraeus*-surmounted short, curly wig. Her wig is surmounted by the Hathoric solar disk set within the double-feathers characteristic of the God's Wives' head gear. Shepenwepet wears a loose-fitting, long-sleeved, multi-layered flowing dress and a shawl over her shoulders. The many layers of her dress are gathered loosely at her waist. Beneath the layers of her loose garment, the curves of Shepenwepet's thighs are visible. A shawl draped over her left shoulder covers her upper arms. Her costume in this scene is almost identical to one worn by Amenirdis elsewhere in this room. Shepenwepet extends her right hand toward her divine companion to receive the *menat*-collar from Isis, her finger tips touching the lower edge of the collar.

The *menat*-necklace was comprised of many strands of faience beads that were connected by two strings to a counterpoise (a metal key-shaped object whose purpose was to balance, or "counterweight," the heavy weight of the necklace's many beads). The key-shaped counterpoise often served as a convenient handle from which to hold the *menat*.[72] Not a musical instrument in its own right, the multi-stranded necklace would produce a "smooth swishing" noise when shaken, as its many faience beads rubbed against one another producing a rattling noise. Both the sistrum and the *menat*-necklace were sacred to the goddess Hathor, who is often called the mistress of the *menat*.[73]

Facing Shepenwepet is Isis, who stands to the far right, at the southern end of the east wall. Her face shown in profile is turned toward the left (= north). Isis wears a form-fitting, sheath dress and a long lappet wig that reaches down to below her shoulders, and a vulture headdress, surmounted by the solar disk set within the Hathoric horns. Around her neck is a *menat*-collar, whose counter-poise can be seen hanging below her wig and filling the curved space behind the small of her back.

Figure 2.5 Chapel of Osiris, Ruler of Eternity, room I, eastern wall (after R. A. Schwaller de Lubicz, *The Temples of Karnak* (Rochester, VT. Inner Traditions International, 1999), pl. 234; reproduced with permission)

With her left hand, Isis holds the *menat*-collar away from her body, and, while it still surrounds her neck, offers it to Shepenwepet. With her other hand, she holds Shepenwepet's left hand, their two hands meeting in the triangular space created between their two bodies.

Identifying Shepenwepet and her divine consort are three columns of text inscribed in the space between her crown and Isis's. Two columns contain Shepenwepet's cartouches, while the third identify Isis as "...The Divine Mother, Mistress of Heaven." Below their joint hands is a short column of text, which reads: "To you, I have given all life and dominion, all stability, all health, all gladness, may you live forever like Re."[74] In the space behind Shepenwepet is a short column of text, which reads: "(May) all protection, life, stability, and dominion surround her like Re forever." Next to this scene, on the northern half of the upper register of the east wall is another scene depicting Shepenwepet, who is shown presenting a statuette of *Maat* to Amun-Re, "Lord of the Thrones of the Two Lands," which will be discussed in greater detail below. A single column of framed inscriptions separates the two scenes. It reads: "The Divine Worshipper, Meryt-Mut Shepenwepet, alive, chosen one of Re, the good shepherd of people, the daughter of Amun, to whom Mut gave birth."[75] In this short inscription, the goddess Mut features quite prominently: first in the epithet added to Shepenwepet's name, *Meryt-Mut*, which literally means "beloved of Mut," and later as the one who had birthed her. That Mut is repeatedly invoked in a scene that shows Shepenwepet receiving an emblem of Hathor is hardly surprising. Already by the reign of Amenhotep III (1388–1350/51 BC), the *menat*-necklace had been associated with the goddess Mut.[76]

The swooshing noise made by the sistrum and the *menat*, in particular, was especially soothing to the gods as it may have replicated the noise created by the wind going through tall papyrus stalks. Alternatively, it may have been evocative of Hathor's movement in the Delta marches.[77] The two explanations need not be mutually exclusive. In one version of the myth, Horus is nursed in the Delta marches by Hathor, who according to this particular version, had given birth to him.[78] Shaking the *menat* before the gods was thus an integral role played by musician-priestesses in the temple service. Because the *menat* often appeared in the hands of women, including temple chantresses, like the sistrum, it is often labeled as a "feminine" musical instruments. But the *menat* may also have "served a protective and regenerative function" which granted its possessor "the blessings of rebirth and eternal life."[78] These particular qualities may explain why the king is often represented receiving the *menat* from Hathor.

A scene from the tomb of King Seti I (*c.* 1290–1279/78 BC) depicts the king receiving the *menat*-necklace from "Hathor, who is in the midst of Thebes, the mistress of the West."[80] Many elements in this scene are similar to the one described above. Just as Isis holds her necklace out to Shepenwepet while holding the God's Wife's hand, so Hathor holds Seti I's hand as she offers her necklace to him. Seti I raises his hand to receive the necklace, his palm touching the outer side of the necklace. In fact, Seti seems to stand closer to Hathor than Shepenwepet to Isis.

Interpreting statements such as "pleasing" to the god as having erotic connotations seems unwarranted and rather excessive to me. [81] In the daily temple-offering ritual, female deities "everywhere received offerings of sistra or *menat* necklaces."[82] Female sistrum players (Egyptian: *sekhemyt*) are attested for the goddesses Mut and Nebet-Hetepet.[83] The Ramesside Queen Tuya, wife of King Seti I and mother of Ramses II, was a *sekhemyt*, or "sistrum player" in the cults of the goddesses Mut and Nebet-Hetepet, as well as a *menat*-bearer in the cult of Hathor.[84] As a goddess of Heliopolis, Nebet-Hetepet was associated with Hathor and Re, and in her capacity as the "mistress of the vulva" may have personified an aspect of Hathor. She was also the "female counterpart" of the creator god Atum.[85]

The sistrum as "a cult object … bearing the effigy of Hathor"[86] could also appear in the hands of male priests. In a ritual procession depicted on the walls of the temple at Medinet Habu, a priest carries a gigantic standard in the shape of a *naos*-sistrum.[87] In this particular instance, the sistrum was probably used as a standard for the goddess Hathor. Accordingly, carrying the sistrum became "an act of devotion to Hathor."[88]

A sistrum player of the god Anubis, the patron god of embalming and mummification, is also known.[89] A funerary text from the tomb of the Eleventh dynasty king Wah-ankh-Inyotef[90] expresses the deceased king's wish to play music for Hathor. His inscription reads in part:

> I am indeed the one who causes the morning awakening of the sistrum player of Hathor everyday, at whatever hour she wishes. May your heart be content with the sistrum player. May you travel in peace. May you rejoice in life and in joy with Horus who loves you, who chews on your offerings with you, who eats from your provisions with you. May you allot me to it every day. Horus, Wah'ankh, revered by Osiris, the son of Re Intef, born of Nefru.[91]

King Inyotef wanted to enlist Hathor's help in the afterlife and "felt he would win her support through the provision of not only offerings at her cult place but also the music she loved." [92] Indeed scenes showing the king shaking the sistrum come almost exclusively from an offering context. We may surmise then that shaking the sistrum was part of a larger sequence aimed at provisioning the gods with everything that sustained, entertained, or pleased them. It was even suggested that music "played a part in transmitting nourishment from food offerings to the gods ..."[93]

Likewise, the dead needed music. This need was especially celebrated during the Theben Beautiful Feast of the Valley. The Feast involved journeying to the west bank to visit the tombs of deceased relatives. Visitors often brought bouquets of flowers for presentation at the tomb and, in honor of Hathor, they shook the sistrum and the *menat* for the benefit of the deceased.[94] Often female temple musicians, singers and dancers were depicted on the tomb walls. Their instruments presented to the deceased's nostrils gave him the breath of life and imbued him with the lifetime of the gods. A song recorded in the Eighteenth dynasty tomb of Menkheperresonb, a High Priest of Amun under Tuthmosis III (1479–1425 BC) was performed by three songstresses who were depicted in his tomb shaking the sistrum and the *menat*. The song, which included praise to the king, links the two musical instruments to Amun: "To your ka! The sistra and *menats* of Amun, when the god takes his seat on the great throne of the West [at Deir el-Bahari] in great joy."[95] In this way, the sistrum seems to have become a symbol of life.[96] This association with life was not confined to the funerary contexts, but is also seen in birth houses attached to the Egyptian temples. Known by the Coptic name, *mammisi*, rituals performed in these birth houses celebrated ideas of birth and re-birth, often with music playing and singing.[97] Rebirth was the deceased's vehicle into eternal existence in the afterlife. The joy and celebration associated with birth (and consequently re-birth) may explain why Osiris, presiding over the realm of the dead, was "fond of music and dance."[98]

A text, currently in the Metropolitan Museum, New York (Pap 35.9.21), describes a new ritual for the protection of Osiris. In one part of the lengthy document, a speech by Thoth is preserved. It reads:

> I am Thoth. I repeat to you what Re has declared ... I am Thoth, master of the divine words (hieroglyphs), which put things in their (proper) place. I give

> the offerings to the gods and to the blessed dead. I am Thoth who put *Maat* in writing for the Ennead. Everything that comes out of my mouth takes on existence as (if I were) Re. I am he who cannot be driven from the sky or the earth because I know what is concealed in the sky, inaccessible on earth, and hidden in the Primeval Ocean. I am the creator of the sky, he who is at the origin of the mountains … I make the gods and men live.[99]

Associating Thoth with the cosmic role of music in the universe and crediting him with creating harmony thus takes on a different meaning.[100] Music and harmony were not attributed to a minor god, but to one who was "the creator of the sky" and who made "gods and men live."[101] Thoth's involvement in knowledge, the invention of harmony/music, and provisioning the gods helps us understand an almost mystical connection between music and offerings. Music was not only important for the gods' enjoyment and diversion, but it may have played some mystical role in transferring "nourishment from food offerings to the gods …"[102]

Seen in this context, we may surmise that shaking the sistrum was hardly an activity confined to female members of the temple hierarchy. Nor was it merely an activity designed to arouse the god sexually. Furthermore, while the king may present the sistrum to ithyphallic Amun-Re Kamutef (e.g. Ramses II at Karnak's Great Hypostyle Hall), nowhere do we find the God's Wife represented before Kamutef, or any other ithyphallic form of Amun. The only surviving association of a God's Wife with an ithyphallic god occurs in the titles of the Twenty-second dynasty princess Karomama, whose favorite title was "Divine worshipper of Amenope."[103]

While this rather conspicuous absence may be attributed to the chance accident of survival, it, nonetheless, undermines the supposed sexual interpretation of playing the sistrum. Perhaps it would be more prudent to view the ritualistic shaking of the sistrum as part of a larger sequence of activities that brought about the gods' well-being.

The various funerary and cultic references to the sistrum as a life-giving object shed a totally different light on the ritual shaking of it. The Late Period practice of writing a king's name on the sistrum was possibly an attempt to link the king, and his authority, to these life-giving and generative ideas.[104] It is such life-giving ideals that we should probably associate with representations of the God's Wife playing the sistrum before various gods.

Just as the God's Wife was able to entertain Amun with her music, so also was she capable of providing him with other means of sustenance: food, wine, milk, and *Maat*. In the next section, we will look at the God's Wife's participation in the offering ritual, both by consecrating offerings as well as by pouring libations and presenting *Maat* to the gods.

Provisioning the gods: offerings to the gods

Wine

Offering wine to the gods in the cult aimed not merely at provisioning them, but more importantly, at appeasing them and averting their potentially destructive violent aspect. Wine was offered "for the ritual assuaging of deities."[110] In the first room of the chapel of Osiris, Ruler of Eternity, in East Karnak, Amenirdis I offers wine to "Amun-Re, Lord of the thrones of the Two Lands"[111] (Figure 2.6 in the plates section). The scene, which is preserved on the north wall's top register, shows Amun striding towards Amenirdis. Represented in profile, Amun's face is turned to the left (=west) to face his companion. He wears his tall double-feathered crown, a long curved ceremonial beard, a broad collar, and a short kilt held in place by a narrow belt, to which is attached a bull's tail at the back. He also wears a tight upper-body garment that covers his abdomen and stops just under his breast. It seems to be comprised of a broad band tightly wound around his body. Two triangular knotted straps that narrow as they approach Amun's shoulders hold the garment in place. Amun carries an *ankh*-sign in his left hand, and grasps a *was*-scepter in his right hand. Traces of blue paint can still be seen on Amun's arms, legs, chest, neck, and face, as well as on his belt. Traces of yellow are found on his broad collar, probably to indicate gold, and also on his kilt. The straps were painted red.

Amenirdis, also shown in profile, her face turned toward the right (= east) to face Amun, wears a broad collar and a loose-fitting, long-sleeved, multi-layered dress, a shawl draped over her shoulders. Characteristic of Amenirdis's representation here is her especially heavy neck. This particular iconographic feature is also seen in the representation of King Shebitqo found on the lower register of the same wall (Figure 2.12), and also on the façade of the chapel.[112] On her head, Amenirdis dons a *uraeus*-surmounted short wig of tightly wound curls. Originally painted dark blue, no doubt to imitate the jet black color of her hair, currently only traces of the paint survive on the cascading layers of the wig (Figure 2.6). Quite exceptionally, she wears no other head gear. The lack of an identifying crown is quite unusual for a God's Wife, or a king, particularly when shown wearing the short wig.[113] Amenirdis's garment is similar to the one Shepenwepet wears when she is shaking the sistrum for Egypt's national deities on the opposite south wall, as well as the garment in which she received the *menat*-collar from Isis. The dress's wide balloon-like sleeves are gathered tight at her wrists, where a narrow band of cloth acts as cuffs. A sash tied at her waist gathers the dress's flowing layers. The dress's voluminous layers, however, do not hide Amenirdis's ample backside, the portrayal of which may have been intentional so as to emphasize her Nubian background. Myśliwiec has remarked that at the time this particular scene was carved, i.e. during the reign of Shebitqo, artists tended to exaggerate certain "African" features and combine them with a "sophisticated elegance" in rendering details.[114] The emphasis placed on Amenirdis's buttocks may be just such an attempt. Arms bent before her, Amenirdis I carries two round red-topped blue *nou*-jars in her hands ( ). The scene shows her in the exact moment at which she offers the jars to Amun.

In front of Amun's tall double-feathered crown and extending to the space above Amenirdis's head, seven columns of framed inscriptions tell the identities of the protagonists in this scene. Whereas Amun-Re is the "Lord of the Thrones of the Two Lands," Amenirdis is a "Divine Worshipper, who is unique on earth just as Re is [unique] in the sky, the God's Wife *Khaneferoumut*, the Divine Worshipper, Amenirdis, may she live for ever like Re." [115] Between Amenirdis and Amun's *was*-scepter, a single column of unframed inscriptions provides a caption to the scene: "Presenting wine to her father Amun-Re. It is done [for] the one who has given life."[116] Behind Amun-Re, a single column of framed inscription gives the other part of the reciprocal relationship presented in this scene: "To you, I give all life and dominion, all stability, all health, and all gladness that you may live like Re for ever and ever."[117] Behind Amenirdis, a single column of unframed inscriptions seems to contain two separate texts. Above her shoulders is the sign for "thousand" followed by a combination of two flat signs that is typically found in representations of the *sed* festival: (Gardiner's sign list # V 9) and (sign list # N 44). The latter sign was shown to represent "half a sky" symbol and was thus meant to affirm, in the context of the *sed* festival, the king's sovereignty over the extremities of the sky just as the boundary stela signs represented his dominion over the earthly realm.[118] The other text, inscribed behind Amenirdis's layered skirt is the rather formulaic: "May all protection and life surround her like Re forever." A single column of framed inscriptions separates this scene from the next, and spells out Amenirdis's motive in enlarging this chapel: "Words spoken by the Divine Worshipper, Amenirdis, may she live, may her monument be established just as the sky is established, while her name is on it <for ever> like Re." In this way, Amenirdis managed to evoke both Re's uniqueness and his endurance. The former was accomplished through a deft comparison placed before her double cartouche, while the latter was desired for both her name and the monument that bore it.

Whereas the scene just described was probably engraved shortly after the installation of Amenirdis as God's Wife when she was still very much "alive," a similar scene depicted on the pylon-façade of her funerary chapel at Medinet Habu shows her offering wine, also to Amun-Re, "the Lord of the Thrones of the Two Lands." But in this scene, which is engraved on the upper register of the eastern half of the façade, Amenirdis appears as a "deceased" person. The cartouche enclosing her name is followed by the epithet *maat kherou*. Literally translated as "true of voice," this epithet typically signifies that a person had died, stood before the divine tribunal and was found righteous, or "justified," as it is commonly rendered. Amenirdis is here represented in a purely Egyptian style, wearing the queenly vulture cap surmounted by a double-feathered crown. Other aspects of her representation here are also very traditional: the long lappet wig, the broad collar, and the tight form-fitting, sheath dress she wears. But more importantly, it is her body proportions that set the iconography of this scene apart from the earlier one preserved in the chapel of Osiris, Ruler of Eternity. Amun-Re is represented very similarly to the manner in which he is depicted in the earlier chapel. Shown in profile, his face turned to the left to face Amenirdis, he takes a stride toward her. He is similarly attired and carries the same insignia as he does in the earlier scene. As in the chapel of Osiris, Ruler of Eternity, the formulaic caption describing the scene is inscribed under Amenirdis's forward hand in the space created between Amun-Re's *was*-scepter and her figure. However,

Figure 2.7 Shepenwepet II offering wine to Osiris, chapel of Osiris-Wennofer-who-is-in-the-midst-of-the-Persea-Tree, room I, western wall (Photo © M. Ayad)

the formula used here is different from the one accompanying the earlier scene. It reads: "Presenting wine to her father Amun-Re. *She* acts [for] the one who gives life forever." Referring specifically to the officiant was characteristic of both Third Intermediate Period offering scenes and pre-Ramesside inscriptions.[119]

Also depicted in a more or less Egyptian style is Shepenwepet II offering wine to Osiris-Wennofer-who-is-in-the-midst-of-the-Persea-Tree, in the chapel named after him in East Karnak (Figure 2.7). On the west wall of the first room, Osiris, in mummiform, is shown standing on a short, flat pedestal. Fully wrapped in bandages, he faces Shepenwepet II. Although the top of his crown is missing, Osiris seems to be wearing the white crown, a rearing cobra attached to its front. He also dons a long, curved false beard. A fringed streamer coming out from under his wrappings at the back of his neck curves slightly upward before falling down parallel to his back. It stops at the horizontal line marking Osiris's bandages. Immediately under that horizontal line on the other side of his body, his wrists appear through a small aperture in his wrappings. In his clenched fists, Osiris grasps three scepters: a shepherd's crook (*heqa*-scepter), a *was*-scepter, and a flail. While the *was*-scepter is nearly of the same height as Osiris, the crook and flail, held diagonally over the *was*-scepter, are much shorter instruments, their bottom ends depicted just below Osiris's clenched fists. The flail may have been "a fly-whisk or a shepherd's whip."[120] The latter may be more likely in light of the fact that the crook was also used by shepherds. Also in his fist is an *ankh*-symbol, whose loop Osiris grasps firmly horizontally such that its end points directly toward Shepenwepet. Immediately under the *ankh*-symbol, two short columns of text, inscribed between Osiris and Shepenwepet, provide a caption to the scene: “[1]Giving wine to her father Osiris-Wen[nofer], [2]who is in the midst of the Persea tree. *She acts* [for] the one who gives life like Re for ever.” As builder of her adoptive mother’s funerary chapel, it should come as no surprise that Shepenwepet uses here the same formula inscribed on the pylon-façade of Amenirdis’s funerary chapel. She also makes a similar claim of acting for *her father*. Both God’s Wives claimed direct descent from the beneficiary of the ritual. But whereas in the representations of Amenirdis discussed above the beneficiary was Amun-Re, here it is Osiris. Behind Osiris, to the far left of the scene, is a single column of framed inscriptions stating the identity of both officiant and beneficiary. Although the first part of the inscription, along with the top row of blocks, is missing, what survives of the text reads: “the God’s Wife, the Divine Worshiper Shepenwepet, alive, the daughter of the king, the Lord of the Two Lands, the Lord or Ritual, Piye.”

Shepenwepet wears a long lappet wig, a vulture headdress, a rearing cobra on her brow where the vulture’s head would have been. Her headdress is surmounted by her customary double-feathered crown, of which only its flat base, to which the feathers were attached, survive. Behind the God’s Wife’s wig, a single column of framed texts reads: “[May she be foremost of] all living souls like Re forever.” In the space behind the God’s Wife’s back and above the smaller figure of her attendant, three short columns of framed texts identify her attendant as the: “[1]singer in the house of Amun Deisehebsed, [2] the daughter of a priest of Amun in Karnak, [3] the scribe … of the house of Amun, Nesptah, the justified ” (Figure 2.8 in the plates section). Her name, which literally translates as “The one to whom Isis grants *sed* festival(s),” may imply that Isis was associated with this all-important festival. Leclant, however, dismissed such an association on the grounds that Isis is not represented with any of the *sed*-symbols.[121]

Food

Just as the gods needed their wine, so also they required food. And, on several occasions, the God’s Wives presented food offerings to the gods and consecrated slain oxen to them. In a scene on the adjacent south wall of room I in the chapel of Osiris-Wennofer-in-the-Persea-Tree, Shepenwepet, followed by the much smaller figure of her attendant Diesehebsed, stands before an offering table. Her arm bent before her, she seems to invite her divine companions to partake of the offerings placed before them. On the other side of the table, Amun stands facing the God’s Wife. He wears his distinctive double-feathered crown, a curved false beard, a broad collar, and a *naos*-shaped pectoral hanging on a string. He also wears an upper body garment with tapering shoulder straps, and a short kilt, held in place by a belt to which is attached a bull’s tail at the back. The belt is tied in an elaborate girdle tie (known as *tyet* in Egyptian; Gardiner’s sign list # V 39).[122] Behind him stands his divine consort Mut, who places her arm affectionately around his back, her hand resting firmly on his far shoulder. Like the God’s Wife, Mut wears a tight sheath dress that stops just under her breasts. Broad tapering shoulder straps hold the dress in place. Both Mut and the

God's Wife wear the vulture headdress surmounted by a rearing cobra at the brow. But whereas the God's Wife dons her tall double-feathered crown, Mut wears the double crown of Upper and Lower Egypt. Both Amun and Mut hold *ankh*-symbols, which hang parallel to their bodies.

In a scene on the adjacent eastern wall, a God's Wife, presumably Shepenwepet II, shown in profile, her face turned to the right brandishes an *aba*-scepter, which she uses to consecrate offerings of food, incense, and four slain oxen. A rearing cobra at her brow, the God's Wife dons a wig with long lappets, the vulture headdress surmounted by a *modius*, which supports her customary tall feathers. Her slim, high-waisted body is clad in a form-fitting sheath dress that stops just under her breasts. Broad tapering shoulder straps hold the dress in place, while covering her breasts at the same time. In her outstretched hand, the God's Wife holds an *aba*-scepter firmly, while in the other hand she grasps three objects: a *menat*-neklace, a pear-shaped, piriform *hedj*-mace, and a *hetes*-scepter. The *aba*- and *hetes*-scepters were both commonly used in consecrating offerings.[123] Next to the God's Wife's upright scepter, a single column of unframed inscriptions provides a caption for her action: "Striking at the choice cut, four times."

A goose, an elongated incense burner, and choice cuts of meat along with a gigantic loaf of bread set in a stand are on the offering table. Underneath the table are four slain oxen. On the other side of the offering table are the figures of two deities: a male and a female. At the far right of the scene, and farthest from the offering table is the slim figure of a goddess, who wears a wig with long lappets, a tight sheath dress that stops just under her breasts. Her dress is held in place by two tapering shoulder straps that are knotted just below her shoulders. In her other hand, she holds an *ankh*-symbol, while suspending her other hand protectively just above her companion's shoulder, almost touching it, but not quite. In the space in front of her face, a single column of framed texts survive: "Mut/or mother, mistress of the sky, the lady ..." (Egyptian: *henout*). Closer to the offerings is the male, who, shown in profile, his head turned to the left to face the God's Wife, takes a stride forward. He wears a bag head-cloth, a long curved beard, a broad collar, an upper-body garment held in place by tapering shoulder straps, knotted just below his shoulders, and a short kilt held in place by a belt to which is attached a bull's tail at the back. In one hand he holds a *was*-scepter, and an *ankh*-symbol in the other. He has broad shoulders and muscular upper arms, thighs, and calves. The missing identifying inscriptions leave his identity open to debate as to whether he is Amun or Osiris.[124] A parallel scene, described below, convinces me that the god represented here is Osiris.

A similar, but poorly preserved, scene is found in the chapel of Osiris-Neb-ankh, where the offering scene is represented on the south wall (= left wall) of room I.[125] There, a God's Wife, presumably Shepenwepet, wearing a tight sheath dress, with a tied tapering shoulder strap, brandishes a scepter before two deities. The details of the scepter do not survive nor do the offerings that she consecrates, placed in the space between her and the two gods represented at the far right of the scene. Closer to her is Osiris, "the One who answers the downcast" (Egyptian: *pa-we[sheb]-iad*), represented in profile, his face turned to face her, and followed by his divine consort, "Isis, ... , the divine mother, mistress of ... ." Prior to the Nubian period, the epithet given to

Osiris in this scene was commonly associated with Amun, whose cult statue was often brought out during religious festivals so that people could make their supplications directly to him.[126] The same epithet was also associated with the god Ptah, who is represented in his capacity as "answerer of prayers" on the High Gate of Ramses III mortuary temple at Medinet Habu.[127] It cannot be coincidental that the lintel of the chapel is dominated by symmetrically opposed representations of Osiris and Ptah.

In this particular incarnation of his, Osiris is not represented mummiform, but rather as a striding, healthy, male, who grasps a *was*-scepter in one hand and an *ankh*-symbol in the other. Broad-shouldered and muscular, he wears a short kilt, an upper-body garment, with tapering shoulder straps, an elongated curved false beard, and a wig with a long lappet and the double-feather crown. This is the same costume Amun wears in the chapels of Osiris, Ruler of Eternity and Osiris-who-is-in-the-Midst-of-the-Persea-Tree, discussed above. But unlike Amun's *shouty*-crown, characterized by its two tall straight feathers, the crown worn by Osiris here is composed of two curved feathers, whose tops form two outward-projecting circles. The feathers frame a small solar disk set between them. This particular crown is known as the *henou*-crown.[128] In the same manner in which Osiris grasps the *was*-scepter, Isis, standing behind him, grasps a papyrus staff. Her papyrus staff alludes to writing, but also to "the document that attested [her] hegemony over the land."[129] Her papyrus staff may also refer to her role in protecting the young Horus, whom she took as a child to the Delta papyrus marches to flee from Seth. Like the God's Wife, Isis wears a sheath dress, but adds to it a broad collar. Her head, along with her face and any crowns she may have been wearing, do not survive.

Cool water/incense

In another scene from the bi-partite chapel of Osiris-Wennofer-who-is-in-the-Midst-of-the-Persea-Tree, a God's Wife, presumably Shepenwepet II, although her name does not survive, pours libations before a male deity (Figure 2.9). The scene occurs on the east wall of room II. But since the other, west and north, walls of this room no longer survive, the scene is now visible from a distance as one approaches the chapel. Remnants of the south wall are still standing, but the roof and the upper part of the walls have been destroyed. The missing parts of the wall would have included key identifying inscriptions that would have enabled us to establish the identity of the God's Wife as well as the deity represented before her, whose distinguishing headgear likewise does not survive. The god, who is shown in profile, his face turned to the right to face the God's Wife, takes a stride toward her. He wears a short kilt and an upper body garment. In his hands, he holds a *was*-scepter and an *ankh*-symbol. Her shoulders slightly stooped forward, the God's Wife wears a tight sheath dress, held in place by a single diagonal narrow shoulder strap. She wears a long lappet wig surmounted with a flat *modius*. With her two hands, she holds the neck of a libation jar from whose spout three streams of water issue. The inscription above the jar indicates that she is offering the god "cool water." In the space between the streams of water and the God's Wife's legs an inscription declares: "She acts (for) the one who gives life forever."

Figure 2.9 God's Wife pours libations, chapel of Osiris-Wennofer-who-is-in-the-Midst-of-the-Persea-Tree, room II, eastern wall (Photo © M. Ayad)

A similar scene surviving in the chapel of Osiris-*Neb-ankh* indicates that the act of pouring libations can be icongraphically combined with burning incense.[130] The scene, which is depicted on the west wall of the side room in the chapel of Osiris-Neb-ankh shows the God's Wife pouring libations with one hand, while carrying an incense burner in the other. She performs both acts for the benefit of a male mummiform deity. His figure almost completely lost now; only his hands protruding from his wrappings and clutching a *was*-scepter survive. The edge of the short flat platform on which he stands is still visible. As the scenes decorating the other walls of this chamber depict rites that have to do with the erection of the *djed*-column, an emblem of Osiris, it is most likely that the god represented here is none other than Osiris himself. The inscriptions accompanying the scene, inscribed in the space between the God's Wife's legs and the long narrow basin into which the streams of water fall, reads "cool water for her father." Next to her arm, immediately above the *ewer* (special kind of elongated vase-like jug) in her hand, is the word "incense." Both water and incense were used in purifying anything that came near the god.[131] While the use of water for cleansing purposes is clear, the use of incense merits further comment. The Egyptians believed that fragrant substances, such as olibanum pine, or terbinth resin, approximated, in the human world, the special aroma emanating from the gods. These substances, created as a result of the gods' shed tears or blood, could consequently, when burned, convey the very essence of the gods' divine nature to the object of ritual fumigations.[132] In this way, fumigating a space sanctified it, making it both suitable for and worthy of divine presence.

In both the chapel of Osiris-in-the-midst-of-the-Persea-Tree and Osiris, Lord of Life, the libations/incense scenes occur in the side room, the decoration of the main room being preserved for representations of the consecration of offerings or, as we shall see later, for the presentation of *Maat*. During the daily temple ritual, burning incense and pouring out libations marked the end of the divine meal.[133] One may surmise that a ritual sequence governed the layout of the scenes depicted in these chapels, such that the rituals depicted in those rooms took place after the events shown in the main rooms.

In a scene from the courtyard of the funerary chapel of Amenirdis, Shepwepet II offers a *hekenou*-jar to Ra-Horakhy, Isis, and deified Amenirdis.[134] The scene, which occurs on the lower register of the eastern part of the south wall of the courtyard shows Shepenwepet, standing at the far left of the scene, her face turned to the right to face her divine companions. Her slender body is clad in a tight sheath dress that stops at her mid calf. A cobra at her forehead, Shepenwepet wears an elaborately detailed vulture cap surmounted by a two tall feathers. With both arms bent before her, she offers an unguent jar to Ra-Horakhty, who stands facing her. Shepenwepet protectively holds the jar between her two hands as she tilts the smoothed-edged, rectangular container forward (Figure 2.10 in the plates section).

Standing before her is falcon-headed Re-Horakhty, who grasps a *was*-scepter in one hand and an *ankh*-symbol in the other, even as he takes a stride toward her. He wears a short kilt held in place by a belt, and an upper-body garment with two wide tapering shoulder straps. His falcon wig is decorated with carefully incised deep parallel lines. The wig is surmounted by a cobra-encircled solar disk, above which is a caption that identifies him as "Ra-Horakhty, the great god, the lord of heaven." Two short columns of framed inscriptions engraved in the space in front of the solar disk read: "[1]Words to be spoken: <I> have given to you all life and dominion, [2] Words to be spoken: <I> have given to you all health." In the space between Ra-Horakhty's scepter and Shepenwepet's slender body, just under her lower hand, an inscription reads: "Gifts of incense. She acts [for] for the one who has given life."[135]

Standing directly behind Ra-Horakhty is "the divine mother," Isis, whose narrow-waisted body is clad, like the God's Wife's, in a tight-fitting sheath dress (Figure 2.11 in the plates section). The dress, which stops just under her breasts, is held in place by curved tied straps that progressively narrow as they near her shoulders. She also wears a broad collar and a long lappet wig surmounted by a short flat platform *modius* from which sprouts a solar disk set within Hathoric horns. A great serpent curls around the disk, its body suspended on either side of the disk, with its head curling back upward in front of her brow. Isis holds a *was*-scepter in one hand and an *ankh*-symbol in the other. While it was more customary for goddesses to hold the papyrus staff, occasionally goddesses, especially those "personifying the eye of the sun god" may also be represented holding a *was*-scepter.[136] A short column of inscriptions between Ra-Horakhty and Isis gives the latter's recitation: "Words to be spoken: <I> have given to you all life and dominion."

The last figure in the scene is "the hereditary noble woman, great one of praise, the divine worshipper, Amenirdis, the justified" (Figure 2.11 in the plates section). In her right hand, Amenirdis clutches a fly-whisk, which she carries over her shoulder. The scepter is here re-imagined as a bent papyrus umbel.[137] The scepter was commonly held by royal women. In her other hand, she holds an *ankh*-symbol. Remarkably, Amenirdis makes no recitation in this scene. Instead the columns of texts between her and Isis are filled with her titles.

The offering of sacred oil or incense served several purposes. Typically aromatic, the unguents helped the deceased unite with the gods. When poured as libations, or burned before the gods, their sweet aroma ensured their good will. Oils and incense, seen as having a cleansing effect, were also connected with the idea of moral purity.[138] All three purposes may be seen in this representation. The unguent offered by Shepenwepet was partially intended for the benefit of her deceased mother, standing last in this scene, who would benefit from its cleansing effects as she prepared to unite with Osiris. Its sweet aroma, pleasing to their senses, also ensured the good will of the two divine figures standing before Amenirdis: Ra-Horakhty and Isis.

"A boon which the king gives"

In a symmetrically opposed scene on the western half of the south wall, in the courtyard of Amenirdis's funerary chapel, Shepenwepet II stands facing Atum, Wepwawet, and the justified Amenirdis. Shepenwepet is represented at the far right, her face, which is exquisitely carved, is turned to the left to face her divine companions. Much like the previous scene, Shepenwepet, here identified as a "Divine Worshipper," wears the vulture cap surmounted by two tall feathers and a form-fitting sheath dress. She stands one arm hanging behind her, parallel to her body. Damage in the wall makes it impossible to discern the posture of her other hand. Likewise, the object she offers to her divine companions does not survive, although one might interpret the small curvature surmounted by a longitudinal impression in the stone, as the top of a small statuette of the goddess *Maat*, with the distinguishing ostrich feather atop her head. A single column of unframed inscriptions starting in front of Shepenwepet's lower abdomen and extending down to her feet, provides a caption to the scene. It reads: "A boon which the king gives (Egyptian: *hetep di nesou*). She acts for the one who has given life forever." Standing closest to Shepenwepet is "the Lord of Heliopolis, the great god," Atum.

Both Atum and Wepwawet have identical postures. Left leg forward, both gods seem to take a wide stride towards Shepenwepet. In the left hand, they each grasp a *was*-scepter, and an *ankh*-symbol in the other hand. Atum wears the crown of Upper and Lower Egypt, a long, curved false beard, a broad collar and a short kilt held in place by a belt to which is attached a bull's tail at the back. He also wears an upper-body garment with tapering knotted shoulder straps. Atum's speech to her, inscribed in one column of framed inscriptions engraved in front of his crown reads: "To you, I have given all gladness."

Standing behind Atum is jackal-headed Wepwawet, who wears a pleated short kilt. Two columns of framed inscriptions engraved above Wepwawet's *was*-scepter read: "[1]Words spoken: To you, I have given all life and dominion, [2] Words spoken: To you, I have given all health." Water damage and rubbings of the wall make it extremely unclear whether he wore an upper-body garment. The same damage caused the erasure of the inscriptions above his head. Amenirdis's titles are likewise erased. Only a hacked out cartouche followed by the epithet "justified" survive. Her vulture cap surmounted by two tall feathers and the cobra at her forehead are the only discernable features of Amenirdis's costume.

The relevance of this poorly preserved scene to our discussion is that, if indeed the figure in Shepenwepet's hand is a statuette of *Maat*, then we have a clear statement here that equates the presentation of *Maat* with provisioning the gods with offerings. In the next section, we will examine this equation more closely.

Maat

The Egyptian gods did not survive on human food only. Their very existence depended on *Maat*. Egyptian religious texts are replete with statements that declare that "the gods live on *Maat*."[139] Personified as a goddess, *Maat* stood for the Egyptian concept of "world order, balance, harmony, justice and truth."[140] *Maat* was the deified concept of Order, the "just measure of things that underlies the world."[141] The gods needed to feed on *Maat* in order to maintain "the Norm, the cosmic order she represented."[142] But *Maat*, this "perfect state of things toward which one should strive" was constantly being disturbed. The act of offering *Maat* to the gods symbolized "the partnership of god and man," but also the gods' dependence on human efforts to maintain *Maat*.[143] For this reason, maintaining *Maat* was one of the king's most important functions, both on the sacral and ideological levels as well as on a more practical level. Winning wars, administering justice, and maintaining general order were some of the practical aspects of maintaining *Maat*. In temple ritual, through the symbolic act of presenting a statuette of *Maat* to the gods, the king affirmed his multi-faceted role in maintaining *Maat*.[144]

On several monuments, the God's Wives are shown presenting *Maat* to the gods.[145] In the next few pages we will look at a few key scenes that depict this rite. The material presented in the next few pages is not meant to be a comprehensive survey of all the scenes in which the God's Wives present *Maat*. But rather the scenes discussed below were selected because of their historical or cultural significance and because, in one way or another, they represent a religious, cultural, or artistic transition.

A one-line inscription on the base of a statue currently in the Louvre museum proclaims that the Twenty-second dynasty divine worshipper Maatkare presented *Maat* to Amenemope. That statue, which was discovered in the Karnak cachette in 1956–57, was dedicated by Iahentefnakht, a treasurer of Maatkare's.[146] The earliest known iconographic scene showing a God's Wife presenting *Maat* comes from the chapel of Osiris, Ruler of Eternity, in East Karnak. The scene, which is preserved on the top register of the east wall of the Nubian addition to the chapel, currently known as room I, depicts *Khnemetibamun Merymut* Shepenwepet (I) presenting *Maat* to Amun-Re "the Lord of the Thrones of the Two Lands."[147] Both god and God's Wife are represented at the same larger-than-life scale. The very top row of blocks does not survive, so it is not possible to reconstruct the titles that once stood before Shepenwepet's double cartouche.

Shown in profile, his face turned to the left to face his companion, Amun-Re takes a stride toward Shepenwepet, his right foot extended forward. Amun-Re dons a short kilt that wraps around his body and stops well above his knees. The kilt is held in place by a belt to which is attached a bull's tail at the back. The belt is tied in an elaborate girdle tie (Gardiner sign list # V 39). Amun also wears his customary two-feathered crown, a long curved false beard, a tight upper-body garment, a broad collar, and a rectangular pectoral that hangs from a bit of string that is tied behind his neck. His upper-body garment is held in place by tapering shoulder straps. The straps seem to be knotted close to Amun's clavicles. In his right hand, Amun holds a *was*-scepter, while his left hand, hanging parallel to his body, grasps an *ankh*-symbol. Amun is depicted with a rather heavy physique: broad shoulders, strong, muscular upper arms, his biceps clearly rounded, and the musculature on his legs likewise delineated. In fact, the overall impression of his physique is reminiscent of the Napatan kings. Indeed, Myśliweic has pointed out that a strong, or heavy, body build was a characteristic of the Nubian royal image.[148]

Also shown in profile, Shepenwepet's face is turned to the right to face Amun. A small statuette of the goddess *Maat* rests on her hand. Serving as a tray, her horizontally outstretched palm points toward Amun and is positioned at the same level as his shoulder. Shepenwepet wears a long body-hugging sheath dress and a broad collar. On her head, she dons a tri-partite long lappet wig, partially obscured from view by the vulture cap surmounted by a double-feathered crown. Shepenwepet's garment does not hide the curves of her body or the exaggerated protrusion of her knees. Shepenwepet I's lower body is deeply outlined, her triangular navel clearly incised inside the small curvature of her lower abdomen. Her hugely curving thighs end rather abruptly in a groove. Under Shepenwepet's left elbow, in the space between her thighs and Amun's *was*-scepter, an inscription provides a caption to the scene: "Giving *Maat* to her father Amun-Re. It is done [for] the one who has given life." This is the offering formula commonly found on Ramesside monuments. It is one of two formulaic phrases used in offering scenes. The other formula was used in pre- and post-Ramesside times.

Behind Shepenwepet, a short column of unframed inscriptions wishes her "all protection, life, stability, and dominion around her like Re forever." Single columns of framed inscriptions border this scene. Behind Amun-Re, the inscription reads: "The Divine Adorer Shepenwepet, alive, the chosen one of Re, the good shepherd of people, the daughter of Amun, whom Mut gave birth to her."[149] Inscribed behind Shepenwepet, the other column of inscriptions, with its mention of Amenirdis, seems to refer to the scene on the adjacent wall. It is completely devoted to the titles of Amenirdis. It reads: "... Amenirdis, alive, who appears with the White Crown, chosen one of Re, who has issued from his limbs, may she appear on the throne of

Tefnut like Re forever."[150] That last line of inscriptions serves as a reminder that even though it is the Shepenwepet who is depicted in this scene, the entire wall was built and decorated under the Nubians. Similarly, it should come as no surprise that Amun is depicted in a Nubian iconographic style. After all, the scene just described above, although depicting the Libyan God's Wife, was part of the decorative scheme of the *Nubian* addition to the chapel of Osiris, Ruler of Eternity.

The presentation of *Maat* is depicted two more times in the chapel of Osiris, Ruler of Eternity. Once on the lower register of the north wall of room I, where a Nubian king, probably Shebitqo presents a statuette of *Maat* to Amun-Re. The other instance, which occurs on the façade of the chapel, shows the God's Wife Amenirdis offering *Maat* to Amun. The latter scene is one of eight vignettes framing the doorway to the chapel. Each of the vignettes depicts the God's Wife, Amenirdis or Shepenwepet, before various deities. Vignettes depicting Amenirdis are engraved on the eastern jamb, while those showing Shepenwepet I are found on the western jamb.

Amenirdis presents a statuette of *Maat* to Amun-Re, "the Lord of the Thrones of the Two Lands." Shown in profile, his face turned to the left, the god is depicted proceeding out of the chapel. Amun wears the same attire he dons in the scene with Shepenwepet I in room I: the two-feathered crown, the curving false beard, the broad collar, the upper-body garment with tapering shoulder straps, and the short kilt held in place by a thick belt that ends in an elaborate girdle tie ([hieroglyph]). A bull's tail is attached to the belt at the back. Likewise, he carries the same insignia he is shown with in the previous scene: the forked *was*-scepter in his extended arm and an *ankh*-symbol clasped in the other. He also has the same heavy physique we have seen in the previous scene. In fact, his shoulders and forearms are heavier set here, while the muscles and bones of his legs and forearms are more crudely modeled in this scene. The smaller size of the scene may account for the cruder rendition of his shoulders.

Facing Amun-Re is Amenirdis who wears a broad collar and a long-sleeved, multi-layered flowing dress, very similar to the one she wore when presenting wine to him in room I. The material used for her dress was probably very fine linen; its almost transparent finery, despite the layers, does not quite hide her shapely legs, thighs, or buttocks. A sash tied underneath her breasts shapely gathers her gown, its long streamers decoratively falling down the front of her dress and reaching down almost to her feet.

Amenirdis's arms are bent before her as she holds the precious little statuette in her hands. The goddess, here represented crouching on a *nb*-basket, dons her customary ostrich feather. On her head is a long lappet wig surmounted by a vulture cap and double-feathered crown supported by a short flat platform (*modius*). With the concave hem of her garment exposing her feet and ankles, Amenirdis is barefoot and so is Amun-Re. In the space before the two tall feathers of her crown, her name and titles are given: "The Divine Worshipper, the Divine Consort/God's Consort/The One Who is United [Egyptian: *sema*] with God, Amenirdis, may she live forever." A partially preserved text inscribed in the space between her gown and Amun's scepter provides a caption to the scene: "Giving *Maat* to her lord. It (?) is done from him who has given life."[151] The hieroglyphic sign after the verb "to do" (𓁹) is missing, so it is not possible to determine whether it is the feminine of the masculine pronoun.

The reading suggested here is based on the parallel inscription accompanying the representation of Shepenwepet I presenting *Maat* in room I. Both scenes were probably engraved around the same time. It is therefore reasonable to assume that their inscriptions would be similar. A single column of framed inscriptions behind Amun-Re provides his response to her. It reads: "Words spoken: I am your [fem.] father, who created the beautiful one (or your beauty), O God's Wife, Divine Consort [Egyptian: *khnemet- netjer*], the Divine Worshipper, Amenirdis, may you live for ever."[152]

In addition to these two scenes, the presentation of *Maat* occurs a third time in the chapel of Osiris, Ruler of Eternity. The scene, which is inscribed on the lower register of the eastern part of the north wall, is immediately to the left of the doorway as one enters the chapel. It depicts a Nubian king presenting *Maat* to Amun-Re (Figure 2.12).[153] Although the king's cartouche is erased, the king's facial features convince Myśliwiec that the royal figure represented here is none other than the Nubian king Shebitqo, whose larger-than-life figure dominates the eastern part of the chapel's façade.[154] The king, shown in profile, his face turned to the right to face his divine father, receives life from Amun-Re even as he presents *Maat* to him (Figure 2.12).

It is remarkable that in the small chapel of Osiris, Ruler of Eternity, the presentation of *Maat* would be depicted in three different scenes. Of the three instances, only once is Amenirdis I shown as the officiating individual in this rite. The other two, both depicted in room I, depicted two individuals who were, technically speaking, more senior to Amenirdis: the incumbent God's Wife and the king. In both representations, King Shebitqo and Shepenwepet are represented at, or larger than, life size. Both scenes are also engraved in very close proximity to scenes that depict Amenirdis engaged in some other ritualistic activity. On the north wall, next to a representation of the king presenting *Maat* to Amun-Re, Amenirdis I is shown shaking the sistrum before the same god. The iconographic sequence depicted on the north wall of room I suggests a situation in which a more senior person supports, introduces, or otherwise sets up a protégé(e). It is almost as if the king, in participating in this ritual was not only legitimating his own power, but also Amenirdis's. Similarly, on the east wall, Shepenwepet I shown on the upper register presents *Maat* also to Amun-Re, while Amenirdis, depicted on the lower register, receives life from him. Is it possible that while Amenirdis did not present *Maat* herself in room I, she was nonetheless depicted reaping the benefits of this ritual act? Possibly.

Equally remarkable is the fact that of the three scenes depicting the presentation of *Maat*, Amenirdis's is the smallest in size, but being on the façade of the chapel, it was also the most visible. An individual approaching the chapel, may on closer examination observe, possibly in shock, the scene showing Amenirdis presenting *Maat* to Amun-Re. However, walking into the chapel, one would be immediately confronted with the larger-than-life depiction of another woman, Shepenwepet I, before Amun-Re. It is conceivable that Amenirdis, by having herself depicted offering *Maat* to Amun on the façade of the chapel, was (tentatively) proclaiming her newly established authority. While the depiction of a woman participating in this all-important ritual may have shocked Egyptian viewers, once in the chapel, an Egyptian would recognize that Amenirdis was not the first, nor the only woman, who

Figure 2.12 Nubian king presenting *Maat* to Amun-Re, chapel of Osiris, Ruler of Eternity, room I, north wall, eastern half, lower register (Photo © M. Ayad)

presented *Maat* to Amun-Re. Inside the chapel, was the larger-than-life representation of Shepenwepet I participating in this exclusively royal ritual. Similarly, the scenes on the north wall of room I depicting the king presenting *Maat* next to Amenirdis shaking the sistrum before Amun, may suggest not only the king's approval of her ritual act, but also his affirmation and support of her cultic duties.

Amenirdis is also shown presenting *Maat* on the façade of her funerary chapel at Medinet Habu. There, on the lower register of the western half of the pylon she stands at the far right of the scene. Her face, shown in profile, is turned to the left, to face Amun-Re and Hathor. All three figures in this scene are shallowly carved, with very few details given. All are thin with high, narrow waists and long slim legs. Gone are the deep furrows delineating Amun's muscles. The proportions of his body are much leaner. In identical postures, both Amun-Re and Hathor hold a *was*-scepter and an *ankh*-symbol. The scepter is held in the extended left arm, while the *ankh*-symbol hangs parallel to their bodies behind their backs. While most of Hathor's titles are erased, Amun-Re's are given as "Lord of the thrones [of the two lands] Holy-of-Place [Egyptian: *djeser-set*], the great god, Lord of Heaven/Sky." *Djeser-set* was the name of the small temple dedicated to Amun at Medinet Habu. The temple which was thought to be the mythic location of *Djeme*, the mythic mound of creation, is situated directly across from the funerary chapel of Amenirdis. Under Amun-Re's wrist, in the space between his extended forward-pacing leg and the *was*-scepter, a short column on unframed texts reads: "I give to you the kingship [Egyptian: *nsyt*] of Atum." Occupying the same spot under Hathor's hand, a similar inscription reads: "I give to you the lifetime of Re in the sky."

Amenirdis, shown in profile, has her face turned to the left to face her divine companions. She wears the long lappet wig, vulture cap and double-feathered crown characteristic of the God's Wife. Both Amenirdis and Hathor wear identical sheath dresses that stop mid-calf. In the space in front of her feathered crown, three columns of inscriptions give her titles as: "The hereditary noblewoman, great of praise, mistress of sweetness [or *iam*-scepter], sweet of love, the Divine Worshipper, the Mistress of the Two Lands, Amenirdis, justified, the King's sister of the Lord of the Two Lands [Piye], the justified, beloved of the gods." Behind Amenirdis a single column of inscriptions reads: "May the Divine Worshipper, the God's Wife Amenirdis exist at the head of all living spirits, may she appear on the seat of the place[155] of Wadjet like Re for ever." Wadjet, a cobra goddess, was one of the two titular goddesses of ancient Egypt. Along with the vulture goddess Nekhbet, Wadjet was one of the "Two Ladies" referred to in the king's *Nebty*-name. An identical inscription evoking Wadjet borders the representation, also found on the façade of Amenirdis's funerary chapel, showing Amenirdis offering wine to Amun-Re.[156]

A similar inscription also occurs in connection with another Nubian God's Wife: Shepenwepet II. The phrase, inscribed on the north wall of room I in the chapel of Osiris-Neb-ankh in North Karnak, appears above the doorway leading into chamber II. There, the context is very similar. The inscription borders an offering scene: Shepenwepet II offering milk to Wepwawet.[157] As to why Wadjet was evoked, it is not quite clear. A similar formula evokes the goddess Tefnut.[158] The formula, "who appears on the seat of Tefnut," calls upon the daughter of Re. Drawing an analogy with the royal epithet "who appears on the seat of Horus," Leclant pointed out that both Horus and Tefnut were the offspring of a supreme deity.[159] In his discussion of the occurrences of the epithet, Leclant noted a variant naming the goddess Wadjet, pointing out that the two epithets seem to be equivalent as they occasionally occur in close proximity. This is the case in the chapel of Amenirdis, where on the other half of the pylon-façade, the inscription accompanying the scene showing Amenirdis playing the sistrum names Tefnut.[160] Leclant has related the role of Tefnut as the daughter of Re to the titles held by the God's Wife, particularly, the God's Hand, to suggest a sexual interpretation for shaking the sistrum.[161] A variant occurs that omits the name of the goddess, substituting it with the determinative of a leonine goddess, and may provide a link between Wadjet and Tefnut: both goddesses could be represented as a leonine-headed female.[162]

These interpretations, however, still do not account for the appearance of Wadjet on the pylon-façade of Amenirdis. I suggest that this particular reference to Wadjet may be related to the figures shown in this scene. Associated with Lower Egypt (the North), Wadjet's main cult centers were at the ancient towns of Pe and Dep, collectively known as Buto (modern Tell el-Fara'in).[163] Hathor's main cult center was the ancient city of Memphis.[164] Hathor, shown in this scene wearing her cobra-encircled horned sun disk, was also the consort of Re, whose main cult center was Heliopolis in the North.[165] Hathor is here represented next to Amun-Re *djeser-set*, the creator god, who "opened" her to engender the Ogdoad, the set of eight primeval gods.[166] Whereas initially Hathor was linked to the god Re, by the Middle Kingdom, she was also linked to "his form as the aged Amun."[167] As a creator god, Amun-Re *djeser-set*, may be associated with "the Memphite Ptat-Tatenen."[168] Framing the scene with this inscription with its particular reference to the titular goddess of the North seems quite appropriate.

Amenirdis was not the only Nubian God's Wife to present *Maat* to Amun-Re. Her successor, Shepenwepet II is shown presenting *Maat* to Aumn-Re, "the Lord of the Thrones of the Two Lands, the Ruler of Thebes" and Mut, "the Eye of Re, the Mistress of the Sky" (Figure 2.13). The scene is inscribed on the narrow rear wall of room I in the chapel of Osiris-Neb-ankh in North Karnak.[169] Shepenwepet shown in profile, her face turned to the right to face her divine companions, stands at the far left. She wears a tight sheath dress, a broad collar and the God's Wife distinguishing headgear: the vulture headdress cap surmounted by the tall double-feathered crown. Her titles written in the space immediately before and above the double feathers name her as "the daughter of King Piye, the God's Wife Shepenwepet, alive for ever." Piye's cartouche is strategically placed in the space where Shepenwepet's *prenomen* would have been inscribed. In the space below Shepenwepet, between Amun-Re's *was*-scepter and her slim body is the offering formula. It reads: "Presenting *Maat* [to Amun-]Re. *She acts* (for) the one who has given life." Above Amun-Re's *was*-scepter is a single column of framed inscriptions, which gives his response to her cult action: "Words to be spoken: To you <I> have given all life and dominion."

Amun-Re's costume is identical to the one in which he is represented in the chapel of Osiris, Ruler of Eternity: a broad collar, a tight upper-body garment that stops just under his breast and held in place by thin tapering shoulder straps, and a short kilt with front-sloping belt to which is attached a bull's tail at the back. But here, instead of the more common girdle tie, Amun seems to have a scribal pallet tucked into his belt. Behind Amun-Re's feathers, three short framed columns indicate the identity of the now-erased figure standing behind him: "[1]Words spoken: <I> give to you … [2]Mut, the Eye of … [3]Re, the mistress of heaven." Her upper body and head are destroyed, only Mut's papyrus staff and the top of her crown survive.

The figures in this scene are crudely carved, their faces appearing fleshy with full, rounded cheeks, well-delineated full lips, extra-large eyes and prominently carved ears. Their body proportions are quite different from those seen in the Nubian section of the chapel of Osiris, Ruler of Eternity, in East Karnak. The figures here, especially Shepenwepet's, are slim with a narrow waist and an elongated torso. Shepenwepet's elongated slim torso, especially, is reminiscent of the Late Old Kingdom/First Intermediate "second style." The roundness of Amun's shoulders and the anatomical detail given to the treatment of his calves and knees are a reminder that this is a Nubian-executed carving.

Whereas in the chapel of Osiris-Wennofer-who-is-in-the-Persea-Tree, an offering of food to Amun and Mut was the most visible scene from the chapel's entrance, in the chapel of Osiris, Lord of Life, it occupies a side wall and is barely visible from the chapel's entrance. It may not be too far-fetched to suggest that, in the chapel of Osiris, Lord of Life, the presentation of *Maat*, which occupies the south wall (i.e. the wall directly opposite from the chapel's entrance) displaced the offering scene as the most prominently displayed and visible scene. Assuming such displacement was intentional and that scene placement on the chapel's various walls was deliberate, we may be seeing in this chapel a shift in emphasis regarding the source of legitimacy. In effect, in the chapel of Osiris, Lord of Life, Shepenwepet II seems to assert her legitimacy through (1) prominently depicting her presentation of *Maat* on the most easily visible wall of the chapel's inner rooms (Figure 2.13) and from (2) her depiction on the chapel's lintel and door jambs participating in rituals that mirror the king's (Figure 2.17).[170]

Figure 2.13 Shepenwepet II presents *Maat* to Aumn-Re, chapel of Osiris, Lord of Life, room I, western wall (Photo © M. Ayad)

On a small lintel in the Egyptian Museum in Cairo, Shepenwepet is also depicted offering *Maat* to Amun-Re "the Lord of the Thrones of the Two Lands."[171] There, Amun-Re is depicted seated on his throne, his face shown in profile turned to the left to face Shepenwepet. He wears his customary double-feathered crown, a false beard, a broad collar, and a shirt with tapering shoulder straps. In his forward extended arm, he holds a *was*-scepter, the base of which stops immediately above Amun-Re's feet, which rest on the base of his throne. In his other hand, he holds an *ankh*-symbol, which he extends horizontally towards the God's Wife, such that the symbol parallels Amun's thighs and ends at his knees. Shepenwepet, shown as a slender woman, her face depicted in profile turned to the right, stands facing her divine companion. She wears a vulture cap surmounted by two tall plumes, a broad collar, and a tight sheath dress. Over her back (left) shoulder, she drapes a shawl, whose horizontal flat end appears next to her left upper arm. Bordering the scene to the right and the left are single columns of framed hieroglyphic texts. The column on the right records Amun's speech: "To you, I have given all life and dominion, all health, all gladness, like Re forever," while the one behind Shepenwepet reads: "May the Divine Worshipper, Shepenwepet exist among the living spirits like Re." The latter column separates this scene from an adjacent smaller scene depicting the God's Wife embraced by the Mut. Both women are clad in tight sheath dresses and vulture caps. But while Shepenwepet dons her regular doubled-feathered crown, Mut wears the crown of Upper and Lower Egypt. Mut extends her right arm behind Shepenwepet's back, placing her grip firmly on Shepenwepet's right upper arm, while with her left hand she grasps Shepenwepet's left forearm.

Out of ten extant examples depicting a God's Wife of Amun presenting *Maat*, seven scenes were executed under Nubian patronage or during Nubian rule.[172] Five of these scenes depict either Amenirdis I, or Shepenwepet II, while the sixth, figuring Shepenwepet I, occurs on the eastern wall of the Nubian extension to the chapel of Osiris, Ruler of Eternity. The Nubians presented themselves as traditionalists, claiming the restoration of order and true Egyptian values as their motives for invading Egypt. The rather extensive depiction of the presentation of *Maat* in a transitional monument such as the chapel of Osiris, Ruler of Eternity, and later in the chapel of Osiris, Lord of Life, served as a visual reminder of their political, cultural, and religious agenda.

On the southern wall of the vestibule leading into the chapel of Amasis and Nitocris in North Karnak, we find another representation of a God's Wife offering *Maat* to Amun-Re. In this instance, Ankhnesneferibre, the last God's Wife, attended by her chief steward Sheshonq, performs the ceremony (Figure 2.14 in the plates section).[173] The top row of blocks, along with Ankhnesneferibre's titles, does not survive. But her cartouche does. As does the cartouche of her father, Psametik II, whose name is followed by the epithet "justified" (Egyptian: *maa kheru* = "true of voice"). Shown in profile, her face turned to the right, Ankhnesneferibre faces the enthroned "[Amun-]Re, the Lord of the Thrones of the Two Lands, the Great God" who reciprocates by giving her "all life and dominion." The small statuette in Ankhnesneferibre's hand, depicting *Maat* sitting on an *nb*-basket, is carefully carved, its details, e.g. the headband that holds *Maat*'s wig in place, almost impeccably preserved. Likewise, Ankhnesneferibre's face, crown and upper body are well preserved, all having been deeply cut into the stone. The cosmetic line adorning her eyes, deeply incised into the stone, extends to the side of her wig and stops at a point parallel to her ear. Ankhnesneferibre wears a broad collar and the loose-fitting long-sleeved garment, similar to those dresses worn by her predecessors in the chapel of Osiris, Ruler of Eternity. Behind her is the much smaller figure of the high steward of her estate, Sheshonq. The clean-shaven Sheshonq wears a long flaring kilt that reaches down almost to his feet. In his hand, he carries a gigantic feather which curves forward, almost touching Ankhnesneferibre's back.

Unlike the other representations of Amun-Re discussed in this section, he is here shown enthroned. He wears his customary crown, long, curved beard, and broad collar as well as the same type of upper-body garment discussed above and, as in his other representations, holds a *was*-scepter and an *ankh*-symbol. Behind Amun-Re are two standing figures. The first is that of his divine consort Mut, who wears her customary identifying headgear: the vulture cap, surmounted by the crown of Upper and Lower Egypt. She also dons a broad collar and a tight sheath dress, with tapering straps that are tied just at her shoulder. Like Amun, Mut is shown in profile, her face turned to the left. In her forward, right hand, she grasps a papyrus staff[174] that is of the same height as the *was*-scepter held by her son standing behind her. Mut, being the Eye of Re, as we have seen in the inscriptions in the chapel of Osiris-Neb-ankh, is one of the goddesses associated with the solar Eye. In her other hand, Mut holds an *ankh*-symbol, which hangs parallel to her body behind her. Behind Mut, is her son Khonsu. The inscriptions identifying him do not survive nor does his crown, with its distinguishing lunar crest. Traces of a curved line that starts somewhere near his head and ends just below his shoulder, give the impression of a falcon wig. Although typically depicted with the side-lock of youth, Khonsu could also be represented as a falcon-headed adult.[175] Perhaps not coincidentally, falcon-headed Harsiese (Horus-son-of-Isis) gives life to the king on the adjacent face of the wall (Figure 2.21b in the plates section).

The presence of the great overseer of the God's Wife's estate in this, and similar scenes, has given rise to the idea that post-Nubian rule, the power and status of the God's Wife of Amun declined.[176] This may not be necessarily so. In 1956, Paul Barguet published a short article discussing two symmetrically opposed scenes from the chapel of Amasis and Ankhnesneferibre.[177] The scenes, which will be discussed in greater detail below, depict the king and the God's Wife before various deities (Figure. 2.18 on p.79 and Figures 2.19a–b in the plates section).[178] While the king is followed by the much smaller figure of the royal *ka*, Ankhnesneferibre is followed by her majordomo, depicted at the same scale as the royal ka and appearing much smaller in size than the God's Wife. Because of the clear symmetry of the two scenes, Barguet suggested that, in this particular scene, the presence of the majordomo served in a similar capacity as that of the royal *ka* i.e. to protect and support the God's Wife in her ritualistic duty, just as the royal *ka* protected and supported the king in his priestly duty.[179]

Building houses for the gods/dedicating shrines

Provisioning the gods was not limited to providing material and immaterial food and provisions to them, but it also included building houses for them. Temples in ancient

Egypt were not places for communal worship, but they rather were the abode of the resident deity, or deities.

Performing the funerary cult of Amenirdis legitimated Shepenwepet II's status as her adoptive mother's rightful heir and successor. A major aspect of carrying out the funerary cult was the construction not only of a tomb, but also a place, a funerary temple or a chapel, where the funerary rituals could be carried out. Ever the dutiful daughter, Shepenwepet II constructed a funerary chapel for Amenirdis within the precinct of the temple of Ramses III at Medinet Habu. In an inscription on the door jamb leading into the inner chapel of Amenirdis, Shepenwepet II declared that she "built this monument of eternity for her mother."[180] Shepenwepet II also made that same declaration pictorially as well. In a scene preserved on the upper register of the south wall in the chapel's courtyard, Shepenwepet II appears next to a lion-headed female. Both Shepenwepet and her companion hold a club in one hand and a smooth, rounded pole in the other. A short looped cord holds the two poles together. The cord is tightly pulled by the two poles such that its two sides parallel each other.[181] The inscriptions next to the lion-headed goddess identify her as Sefekhet-abwy, a deity that had been associated with the goddess Seshat, "Mistress of Builders," since the time of Tuthmosis III.[182] In this name of hers, the goddess is known as the "Seven-Lady of Horns."

Shepenwepet wears a long lappet wig and a vulture cap surmounted by a *modius* and two tall plumes. Shepenwepet's cartouche and title, "Divine Adorer," are inscribed in the space in front of her double-feathered crown. Both Shepenwepet and Sefekhet-abwy are shown as slim, narrow-waisted women, who wear tight form-fitting sleeveless sheath dresses. The goddess wears a panther's skin as an over-garment. The panther's fore paws spread out over her shoulders acting more or less as straps, its head flat on her chest, just under her pendant. Forming the hem of the garment, the panther's hind paws flair out at her knees. This particular garment seems to have been made using the hides of two animals: two tails can be seen hanging down between her legs and reaching, like the sheath dress underneath, the middle of her calf. On her head, the goddess wears the symbol of Seshat: seven petals, rays, or celestial orbits, with an ecliptic or two inverted horns on top.[183]

Shepenwepet shown in profile, her face turned to the left, holds the club in her right hand and the pole in her left, just as the goddess does. The depiction of the goddess, whose rightward orientation was in line with Egyptian artistic convention, is anatomically correct: we see the back of her right hand holding the club and the inside of her left hand in which she grasps the pole. Leftward orientation, however, was quite problematic to Egyptian artists, who lacked consistency in depicting the insignia held in each hand, and sometimes erroneously attached the right arm to the left shoulder or vice verse.[184] Shepenwepet's depiction here is one such case. For while her hands are accurately depicted: the inside of her right hand holding the pole and back of her left hand grasping the pole, her left arm seems to be attached to her right shoulder. In a beautifully accurate naturalistic manner, Shepenwepet's body obscures her right arm from view, as does the left arm in hiding a portion of the club.

In this scene, Shepenwepet II and Sefekhet-abwy are partners in the ceremony of "stretching the cord" (Egyptian: *pedj-sheser*). The act of stretching the cord symbolized the surveying of the temple area. This ceremony was an integral part of the ritual sequence associated with the laying of temple foundation. In fact, often, "Stretching the Cord" pictorially summed up the act of constructing or dedicating temples.[185]

A similar scene survives in room I the chapel of Osiris, Ruler of Eternity. There, on the western part of the north wall, the God's Wife Amenirdis appears next to a human-headed goddess. Both women are clad in tight sheath dresses and each holds a club in one hand, while grasping a pole in the other. Although the name of the goddess does not survive, the distinguishing seven petals/rays and inversed horns on her head identify her as Seshat/Sefekhet-abwy (Figure 2.15). Behind the goddess a partially preserved column of inscriptions, which reads: "… which her majesty found in brick," may indicate that Amenirdis replaced an earlier mud-brick forecourt with the currently standing stone construction.[186] A single column of framed inscriptions formiing the right border of this scene. It reads: "The Divine Worshipper, the God's Wife, the God's Hand, the Great one of the *imat*-scepter, the One who fills the *wakher*-forecourt with the scent of her fragrance, Amenirdis, may she live forever, she constructed this monument for her father, Osiris, Ruler of Eternity."[187] A column of identical inscriptions mirrors this one on the other (eastern) side of the doorway. In fact, that column of inscriptions frames the scene in which the king presents *Maat* to Amun-Re (Figure 2.12). A third inscription on the façade of the chapel also pronounces Amenirdis as the builder of this chapel.[188] The three inscriptions, of course, only refer to the Nubian addition to the chapel. Still, it is quite remarkable that although it is the gigantic depiction of a Nubian king that dominates the façade of the chapel, it is the God's Wife, not the king, who is named as the "builder" of this chapel.

Another scene engraved on the upper register of the north wall shows the God's Wife in a voluminous dress standing before Amun-Re.[189] She stands at the left of the scene and turns to the right to face her divine companion. Between the god and the God's Wife is the representation of a temple (Figure 2.16). The inscription above the image of the temple indicates that she is "[presenting the temple] to her lord. It is done [for] the one who gives life and dominion like Re."[190] It has been noted above that in response to her playing the sistrum, Amun-Re declares that his "heart rejoices on account of this beautiful monument of yours."[191] Repeatedly, Amenirdis declares that "she constructed this monument for her father, Osiris, Ruler of Eternity." The emphasis placed in the inscriptions on Amenirdis's filial relationship to Osiris (in the dedicatory inscriptions) and to Amun-Re (in the offering formulae) may be an attempt to justify her assumption of the purely royal prerogative of constructing houses for the gods. Later, we see Shepenwepet brandishing a *hetes*-scepter as she consecrates a small temple in North Karnak.[192]

The inscriptions as well the pictorial record both support the idea that Amenirdis was not merely a "co-dedicator" of the chapel, but rather its true builder. The inscriptions seem to affirm the pictorial record showing the God's Wife presenting the image of a temple to Amun-Re and partnering with Seshat/Sefekhet-abwy in the rite of "stretching the cord." Typically, the king in the guise of Thoth, is Seshat's partner in this rite. But in the Twenty-fifth dynasty, we see the God's Wife performing this rite.

In the chapel of Osiris, Ruler of Eternity, the rites of "stretching the cord" and "presenting the temple to Amun" occur on the north wall of the first room, where

Figure 2.15 Amenirdis partners with the goddess Seshat in the rite of "Stretching the Cord," chapel of Osiris, Ruler of Eternity, north wall, western half, lower register (Photo © M. Ayad)

the former occurs on the lower register of the wall, west of the doorway, while the latter occurs on the upper register, east of the doorway. This room, an extension built by the Nubians, utilized the façade of the earlier construction, incorporating it as its southern wall. The Nubians neither demolished the earlier façade nor erased the scenes and inscriptions that decorated its walls.[193] In fact, Amenirdis's representation on the western half of the north wall parallels, and indeed complements, the scene depicted on the opposite south wall. There, Takeloth III of the Libyan Twenty-third dynasty is shown performing another aspect of the temple foundation ritual: the ritual consecration of the monument.[194] This scene mirrors another identical, but symmetrically opposed, scene on the eastern part of the façade showing King Osorkon III performing the same ritual. The rite is known as the *hetes*-feast, and constitutes the final phase of the temple foundation rites. This rite was necessary because building a temple did not automatically result in it becoming functional. In order for the temple to function, the resident god of a temple, or its main deity,

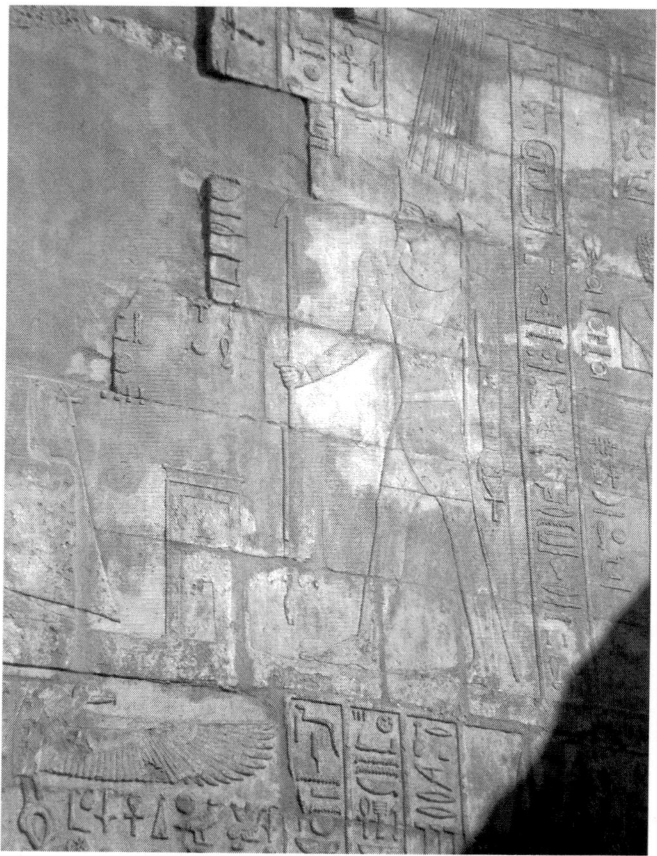

Figure 2.16 Amenirdis offers an image of a temple to Amun-Re, chapel of Osiris, Ruler of Eternity, north wall, eastern half, upper register (Photo © M. Ayad)

had to be invited to take up residence in it.[195] The king's ritual act of consecration, in effect, was an invitation for the god to inhabit the temple.[196] In this ceremony, the god was offered a special object called the *hetes*-object, which seemed "to guarantee that all the ceremonies of the cult and solemn celebrations in the newly dedicated sanctuary will be carried out according to the rules."[197] Because of the sanctity and the magnitude of these rites, only the king was allowed to perform them.[198] The scenes depicting Amenirdis "stretching the cord" and presenting a temple to Amun on the north wall, complement the act of brandishing of the *hetes*-object depicted on the opposite wall.

Partnering with the king 1: symmetrically opposed scenes

In providing for the gods

During the rest of the Twenty-fifth, and in the Twenty-sixth dynasty, the trend set by Amenirdis I in the chapel of Osiris, Ruler of Eternity was taken a step further. The God's Wives were now regularly depicted participating in rituals that not only complemented those practiced by the king, but they were also shown in scenes that mirrored the king's in his attitude, posture, and his interaction with the various deities. When depicted on architectural elements, such as door jambs and lintels, these symmetrically opposed scenes resulted in a delicately balanced compositional arrangement. Perhaps nowhere is this trend more visible than in the chapel of Osiris, Lord of Life, dedicated by Shepenwepet II and Taharqo.[199]

Above the doorway leading into the chapel of Osiris, *Neb-ankh*, or "*Lord of Life*," in North Karnak is a lintel that bears double representations of Taharqo and the God's Wife of Amun standing before various deities[200] (Figure 2.17). At the center of the lintel is a vertical cartouche enclosing the name of the chapel's inhabitant: *Osiris-*

Figure 2.17 Lintel, Chapel of Osiris, Lord of Life (Photo © M. Ayad)

neb-ankh, or Osiris, *Lord of Life*. In this chapel Osiris is also known as *Paweshebiad*, or "He Who Answers the Distressed." The cartouche, which is surmounted by a solar disk framed by two feathers, is set on a *serekh*-shaped rectangular base. Like the ancient palace-façade it resembles, eight vertical lines intersected at various intervals by horizontal dotted lines give the base the impression of recessed vertical niches. The cartouche, its base, and its feathered crown occupy the entire vertical length of the lintel from the base line up to the register line that borders the top of the scene. The cartouche also divides the lintel into two equal sections. On the right are two scenes depicting the God's Wife, while on the left, King Taharqo is shown in two scenes.

In a manner typical of Egyptian artistic convention, the deities are all depicted oriented away from the center of the lintel, such that they seem to be walking out of the chapel. On the other hand, the officiating individuals, facing the outward bound deities, seem to be walking into the chapel.[201] On the far left[202] Taharqo, barefoot and wearing the tripartite royal kilt, a broad collar and a head band/diadem and holding a *hedj*-scepter in his right hand, is embraced by falcon-headed Harsaise (Horus, Son of Isis), who grasps the king's left upper arm. In the space above his head, two columns of hieroglyphic inscriptions give Taharqo's name and identify him as a "Good God." Taharqo's face, shown in profile, turned to the right almost touches Harsiese's beak. Behind Harsiese, a single column of framed inscriptions separates this scene from the next more central episode. It reads: "Words spoken: To you, <I> have given all life and dominion, all health, all gladness, like Re for ever." In the next episode, Taharqo, similarly attired and shown in profile, his face turned to the right, wears the double crown of Upper and Lower Egypt, as he presents wine to, presumably, Osiris, although his name does not survive. A now-destroyed column of texts above his head would have given his names and titles. However, identifying Osiris are his customary regalia: the White Crown of Upper Egypt, his long curved false beard, and, most importantly, his mummy wrappings. A mummy bandage is tied around his shoulders, its loose ends falling decoratively across his body taking the shape of a baseless triangle. Osiris, who stands on a short flat pedestal, is completely cloaked. Only his hands firmly gripping his *was*-scepter appear through an opening in his cloak.

Arms bent before him and round *nou*-jars in hand, "the Son of Re" Taharqo, takes a wide stride toward Osiris. In the space under his left hand, and between his triangular jutting kilt and Osiris's *was*-scepter, a single column of unframed inscriptions provides a caption to the scene: "Presenting wine to his father. He acts <for> the one who has given life." In return Osiris declares that he has given Taharqo life and dominion. Here, the text, which is inscribed in vertical columns in the space between Taharqo's crown and Osiris's, breaks off. Behind Osiris is the slim figure of a female deity who wears a long lappet wig surmounted by a solar disk set within horns, and a long form-fitting sheath dress held in place by a diagonal shoulder strap. Although her name does not survive, she is most likely Isis. In her forward extended arm, she holds a papyrus staff while carrying an *ankh*-symbol in her other hand.

Symmetrically opposed scenes featuring the God's Wife occupy the right half of the lintel. Immediately to the right of Osiris's centrally positioned cartouche is a scene showing Shepenwepet, "[the king's daughter of] Piye" before "Ptah, Lord of Thebes," and "Hathor, who is in the midst of Thebes." Shown in profile, Shepenwepet's face is turned to the left to face her divine companions. She wears a long lappet wig surmounted by a vulture cap and two tall plumes, a broad collar and a tight sheath dress. Like Taharqo, she is barefoot, and like him, she holds round *nou*-jars in her upraised hands. An inscription below her right hand indicates that she is "presenting milk to her father. She acts <for> the one who has given life." In response, Ptah declares: "To you, I have given life and dominion." The same utterance is also made by Hathor, who stands holding a papyrus staff behind Ptah. Both inscriptions employ the grammatically correct feminine pronoun *ṯ* when addressing Shepenwepet. Hathor's representation is a mirror image of Isis's, standing in the same posture, holding the same insignia, similarly attired, and most importantly wearing the same crown: a solar disk set within Hathoric horns. Except for the pronouns employed, the framed column of inscription bordering this scene and separating it from the last episode, is identical to the one on the other side of the lintel: "Words spoken: to you [fem.] I have given all life and dominion, all health, all gladness like Re for ever."

Furthest to the right is the last scene of the lintel, in which Amenirdis is embraced by Hathor, mistress of *Iunu* (Heliopolis). Amenirdis, who is shown in profile, her face turned to the left, holds a folded *menat*-necklace in one hand, while her other hand rests on the goddess's right shoulder. In so doing, she seems to reciprocate the goddess's embrace. Further enforcing this sense of reciprocity is the placement of Hathor's hand under Amenirdis's elbow supporting it as if to aid her protégée's hand to remain securely on her shoulder. Behind Amenirdis is a single column of framed texts in which Amenirdis, justified, is wished an existence "among the living souls" that she may "appear in glory upon the throne of Wadjet." Wadjet was the titular patron goddess of Lower Egypt, and her inclusion here is understandable: the deities on this part of the lintel all have northern connection. Wadjet was similarly included in connection with the goddess Hathor, on the façade of the funerary chapel of Amenirdis discussed above.[203]

The state of the lintel's preservation is such that neither Amenirdis's nor Shepenwepet's titles survive. It is clear, however, that the figure on the far right is Amenirdis the Elder, Shepenwepet's predecessor, not her successor Amenirdis II. *Ma'a-hkeru*, the epithet placed after Amenirdis's cartouche, literally translated "True of Voice" or "justified" is placed after the names of deceased persons. Amenirdis II, daughter of Taharqo, was still alive at the time of the construction of this chapel. In fact, she survived into the reign of Taharqo's successor, Tanwetamani, and into the reign of the first Saite ruler, Psametik I, as indicated by the text of the Nitocris Adoption Stela. Line 4 of the stela indicates that Amenirdis was alive at the time of Nitocris's appointment as God's Wife in Psametik's ninth regnal year.[204]

The delicately balanced scenes show the king and the God's Wife before the mummiform gods Osiris and Ptah, respectively, and offering to two identically attired goddesses, Isis and Hathor. The different substances offered, wine and milk, while presented in identical *nou*-jars, reflect the Egyptians' simultaneous abhorrence of redundant repetitiveness and their fondness of symmetrical, balanced compositions. In daily offering ritual in the temple, wine was often presented to "certain … goddesses, such as Hathor or [other] *uraeus* divinities," while milk was most often given to "the child god."[205] In the particular arrangement found on this lintel, this does not seem to be the case. Hathor, standing demurely behind Ptah was offered milk. Indeed, the substances offered in this scene were both presented to adult male deities. One may speculate, however, that milk offered by the God's Wife, was a more "maternal," or feminine, substance. In the same way, and for the same reasons, the similarly attired goddesses, although almost identically represented, are in fact different. They are Isis and Hathor. The former was the consort of Osiris, while the latter was associated with Ptah as a Lower Egyptian deity. The choice of gods represented here is also significant. Both Osiris and Ptah are fully cloaked, their limbs hidden in their tight wrappings. Likewise, both hold a scepter. While initially Ptah's garment may not have been designed to represent mummy wrapping, his identification with the god Sokar, and later with the god Osiris, gave rise to the re-interpretation of his cloak as mummy wrappings.[206]

This wonderfully balanced lintel also illustrates the Egyptian commitment to complementary symmetry. The central two representations depict Taharqo and Shepenwepet on left and right, respectively, both arms bent, round jars in hand, before a god, represented in mummiform standing on a short, flat, pedestal and followed by his divine consort. In both scenes, the goddesses wear tight sheath dresses held in place by a triangular shoulder strap that narrows as it approaches the goddesses's shoulder. Both goddesses hold a papyrus scepter in their forward hand, and an *ankh*-symbol in the other hand, which is shown hanging parallel to their bodies and behind them. Both goddesses wear Hathor's horned disk atop their heads. Harsiese, also known as Horus the Elder, embraces the king on the far left, while his consort Hathor similarly embraces the God's Wife on the right. Yet, significantly, Hathor does not embrace Shepenwepet II, the incumbent God's Wife, but her deceased adoptive mother, Amenirdis I. It is possible that Shepenwepet, or Taharqo, still felt the need to legitimate Shepenwepet's position as God's Wife. The representation of Amenirdis next to her successor shored up the latter's authority and further consolidated her position.[207]

Remains of a nearby chapel that once lay along the route to the temple of Ptah in North Karnak similarly exhibit scenes showing the king and the God's Wife before various deities (Figure 2.18). The chapel, which was dedicated to Osiris-Wennofer-*Neb-djefa*, or "Lord of Offerings," bears the names of Amasis (Ahmose II) and Ankhnesneferibre.[208] On the jambs leading to the columned hall, scenes of the king occupy the southern (= left) jamb, while scenes of Ankhnesneferibre occupy the northern (= right) jamb.[209] Both jambs are incompletely preserved, with at least one register on the top missing. On the left jamb, the blocks that once constituted the top register (which would have been the fourth from the ground up) are still partially preserved, but none of the figures survive. On the next register, (the current top register), the king proceeds from the left. His face is shown in profile and turned to the right, the "Good God Ahmose (II) who is given life" faces the falcon-headed god Khonsu (Figure 2.19a in the plates section). A moon god, Khonsu, wears his distinctive crown: a (lunar) disk set atop a crescent. In this particular instance, a rearing cobra curls up in the middle of the disk. Khonsu wears an upper-body garment with tapering shoulder straps, and a short kilt to

Figure 2.18 Chapel of Osiris-Wennofer-*Neb-djefa* (Photo © M. Ayad)

which is attached a bull's tail at the back. Khonsu holds the king's left hand, even as he hands him over three *hed-sed* signs suspended through the loop of an *ankh*-symbol on the curved tip of a staff held in Khonsu's left hand. Behind Khonsu is the slim figure of a goddess who wears a solar disk set within Hathoric horns atop her vulture cap. She wears a long lappet wig. Her slim figure is clad in a long, tight sheath dress, held in place by one shoulder strap. In her forward extended arm, she holds a papyrus staff, while in her other hand, she holds an *ankh*-symbol. The accompanying inscriptions identify her as Hathor.

Amasis (Ahmose II) wears the double crown of Upper and Lower Egypt, a false beard, the tripartite royal kilt and an apron flanked by two rearing cobras. A bull's tail is attached to the back of his kilt. His arm is depicted across his body, and he extends his right hand forward to receive Khonsu's gift, the jubilee symbols. Extensive carving on his leg delineates the muscles around his knees and the flat surface of his bone. The sovereign is followed by the similarly-attired though much smaller figure of his *ka*. The king's *ka* wears a long lappet wig and a false beard and holds a staff in his left hand and a horizontally held *mekes*-scepter in his right. On his head is the king's Horus name: *Semen-Maat* (lit. "he who causes *Maat* to endure).

In the corresponding scene on the north (= right) jamb a falcon-headed god places the key of life at Ankhnesneferibre's nose (Figure 2.19b in the plates section).[210] The top part of the block is gone, and along with it the god's name. But he is probably Ra-Horakhty in his Theban manifestation of Monthu.[211] The double feathers behind the solar disk with its rearing cobra suggest that he is the solar incarnation of the falcon-headed god. He stands astride, his face turned to the right. He wears a short kilt, held in place by a knotted belt, and an upper-body garment that is held in place by tapering, knotted shoulder-straps. Deep vertical furrows along the god's legs exaggerate his muscular shins. The god is followed by the slim figure of a goddess, who like her counterpart on the south jamb, wears a solar disk set within Hathoric horns atop her vulture cap and long lappet wig. She is similarly attired in a long tight sheath dress held in place by a knotted tapering shoulder strap. She places her left hand protectively behind the god's shoulder while holding an *ankh*-symbol in her right hand. With the inscriptions identifying her completely gone, it is impossible to determine who she is with any degree of certainty, but her headgear suggests that she is either Isis or Hathor. And since Hathor was already represented in the corresponding scene on the left jamb, it is most likely that the goddess represented here is Isis.[212]

Shown in profile, her face turned to the left, Ankhnesneferibre extends her left hand forward to receive the life offered her. She wears the double-feathered crown, a vulture cap atop a long lappet wig. Her long-sleeved, loose gown flares out at her feet. In her right hand, she holds several insignia: a folded *menat*-necklace, and an *ankh*-symbol. Her fingers close tightly around the loop of a bigger *ankh*-symbol, which hangs from her hand. Behind her, represented at a much smaller scale is her high steward Sheshonq. Bald-headed and barefoot, Sheshonq wears a short kilt and a scarf-like band around his neck, its loose ends, of unequal lengths, falling to just below his waist. In his right hand, he holds an elongated *sekhem*-scepter. The scepter was sacred to the god Osiris in his temple at Abydos, and was often used in the consecration of offerings.[213] Sheshonq has deeply carved muscular legs.

The second register of the south jamb shows "the Son of Re, the Lord of the Two Lands, Ahmose (II), who is given life" proceeding from the left. Represented in profile, his face turned to the right, he presents *nou*-jars to ithyphallic "Amun-Re-Kamutef who is in his Sanctuary." The king wears an elaborate *atef*-crown and a short, triangular *shendyt*-kilt. Behind the king, a single short column of unframed inscriptions reads: "[May] protection and life surround him … ," while in the space immediately underneath the king's elbow, between him and his divine companion, is a cornucopia of grapes, and a lotus flower resting on a tall stand. The substance and arrangement of the offerings is very similar to those offerings placed on a tall stand between Ramses II and Amun-Re Kamutef (Figure 2.3) where the former shakes the sistrum for the latter.[214]

The god wears a double-feathered crown in which is set a solar disk, a broad collar, and a rectangular *naos*-shaped pectoral. He stands on a short flat pedestal. Vertical lines on either side of his body may indicate that his body was veiled in some way. His right arm is characteristically raised squarely behind his head, while a diagonally held fly whisk forms a triangle with the god's upraised arm. Behind Amun-Re-Kamutef is the goddess *Maat*, who is depicted as a slender human female, wearing a long, tight sheath dress, a feather and a sun disk atop her head. The inscriptions above her crown not only give her name, but also identify her as the "one who is united with Amun" (Egyptian: *khnem(et) Imen*). As we have seen above, on the façade of the chapel of Osiris, Ruler of Eternity, both Shepenwepet I and Amenirdis I use this epithet. Behind Amun-Re-Kamutef, in the space created between him and the goddess *Maat*, is the representation of a temple façade surmounted by two schematic trees that flank a central representation of an elaborate lotus flower, similar to those shown behind him when he appears before Ramses II. The bottom register of both jambs contains fecundity figures tying the emblematic plants of Upper and Lower Egypt.

In the corresponding scene on the north jamb (Figure 2. 19b in the plates section), Ankhnesnefereibre stands, her face turned to the left, one hand raised in adoration, the other carrying a small statuette of *Maat*, before "Ptah-Nun … <his?> father Atum" and Sekhmet, "the beloved of Ptah."[215] Ptah is here shown as an enshrined statue clad in a tight cap and shrouded in mummy wrapping. He wears a short false beard. His cloaked body is completely covered. Only his hands appear through a small aperture in his garment. In his clenched fists, Ptah holds an elaborate *was*-scepter in which is integrated an *ankh*-symbol and possibly a *djed*-pillar. The lioness-headed goddess raises her right hand protectively behind Ptah's shrine, while holding an *ankh*-symbol in her other hand. She wears a long tight sheath dress and a very elaborate version of the *atef*-crown. Hers seems to rest on two rearing cobras, which provide a stand for the long curved horns at the base of her crown. Two wide feathers set behind a central solar disk complete the crown.

Ankhnesneferibre's balloon-like wide sleeves fail to hide the outlines of her thin arms. In her left hand, shown in the foreground, she carries a statuette of *Maat*. Standing behind her is "the Great Overseer of the estate of the Divine Worshipper, Sheshonq." Only Sheshonq's balding head and the contours of his shoulders and upper arms are persevered. While Sheshonq's presence behind Ankhnesneferibre has been viewed as a sign of her declining power, this may not be necessarily so. In 1956, Paul Barguet published a short article discussing two symmetrically opposed scenes from the chapel of Amasis and Ankhnesneferibre.[216] In it, he argued that the much smaller figure of Ankhnesneferibre's high steward balanced the symmetrically opposed scene depicting the king's royal *ka* standing behind the sovereign (Figures 2.19a–b in the plates section). Barguet interpreted the similarity between the two scenes as suggestive of the possibility that, in relation to Ankhnesneferibre, Sheshonq functioned in a similar manner as the royal *ka*. Although Barguet admitted his lack of complete understanding of the royal *ka*'s function, he suggested that just as the royal *ka* seemed to protect and support the king in his priestly duty, so was the presence of Sheshonq's figure behind the God's Wife intended to support her in her ritualistic duty.[217]

According to Lanny Bell, the royal *ka* legitimated the king's claim to the throne.

> The king's *ka* is born with him, or rather it is created when he is conceived, perfect from the very beginning, flesh of god, and fully divine. For we see the royal *ka* depicted as his double throughout the episodes of the divine birth;

> and it accompanies him to the grave, as we see in the tombs of Amenhotep III, Tutankhamun, and Eye. The representation of this *ka* is intended as proof of his divine origins and sufficient evidence that he was predestined to rule. But he actually becomes divine only when he becomes one with the royal *ka*, when his human form is overtaken by this immortal element, which flows through his whole being and dwells in it. This happens at the climax of the coronation ceremony, when he assumes his rightful place on the "Horus-throne of the living." According to this formulation, the royal *ka* represents the "dignity" of the office of kingship, while the king is viewed as a link in the chain of divine kingship which stretches back into the very dawn of Egyptian history. As an incarnation of the royal *ka*, each king was *ex officio* a god; but the dual nature of the king is clear: embodiment of divinity while on the throne, his own mortality inexorably overtakes him.[218]

Bell further suggested that

> during the [Opet] festival, evidence that [the king] possesses the royal *ka* and that it resides in him – that he is the living royal *ka* – is displayed in the symbolic re-enactment of his divine conception and birth, his acknowledgement by Amun-Re and recognition by the Ennead, his coronation, and the proclamation of his *ka*-name.[219]

But because none of the elements enumerated by Bell are preserved in the small Osirian chapels in East and North Karnak, I believe Barguet's understanding of the role of the royal *ka* in the scene discussed above is closer to the Late Egyptian interpretation of its function.

The complementary symmetry of these scenes is not limited to their similar layout, but extends to the gods shown. Amasis stands before Amun-Kamutef. According to a Ptolemaic text dating to the reign of Ptolemy IV (221–203), Kamutef was the one "who begot his father … the creator of Ogdoad [group of eight primeval gods], the father of the fathers of the Ennead [group of nine primeval gods]."[220] The text clearly describes Kamutef as a creator god who pre-existed the two groups of primeval gods. Likewise Ptah-Nun, before whom Ankhnesneferibre stands, was "the father who begot Atum."[221] Ptah-Nun combined in his essence Nun, the personification of the primeval ocean that pre-existed creation itself and the creator god Ptah, "who conceives in his heart and creates with his tongue."[222]

Rewarded by the gods

Just as the God's Wife partnered with the king in providing the gods with offerings, so she was also rewarded by the gods, who guided her, gave her life, and protectively embraced her.

The door jambs of the chapel of Osiris, Lord of Life (*Neb-ankh-Paweshebiad*) bear symmetrically opposed scenes showing Taharqo on the left and Shepenwepet on the right being embraced by Osiris, "who answers the afflicted" and Isis "the great, the divine mother," respectively[223] (Figure 2.20a-b in the plates section). Depicted on the left jamb, Taharqo takes a wide stride to the right. He wears a tri-partite royal *shendyt*-kilt held in place by a belt to which is attached a bull's tail at the back. In his right hand, Taharqo holds a pear-shaped *hedj*-scepter and an *ankh*-symbol. But while the *ankh* hangs parallel to Taharqo's body, the scepter is held horizontally across his kilt, such that its tip aligns almost perfectly with the kilt's diagonally slanting edge. Taharqo clenches a *was*-scepter in his forward extended arm. Although his upper chest, face and most of his headgear do not survive, Taharqo seems to be wearing the crown of Upper and Lower Egypt, the tip of which can still be seen under Taharqo's cartouche. Standing next to Taharqo is the figure of the deity, probably Osiris, whose face likewise does not survive. He wears a long lappet wig surmounted by a two-feathered crown and a short kilt, held in place by a belt to which is attached a bull's tail at the back. Tucked into the belt is a scribal pallet, which may have been a different interpretation of the belt's elaborate girdle knot. Osiris places one arm behind Taharqo's back, the tips of his fingers still apparent on Taharqo's right shoulder. With his other hand, Osiris grasps Taharqo's upper arm. Taharqo and Osiris stand so close to each other that their figures overlap, Taharqo's feet obscuring Osiris's from view. Likewise, Taharqo's kilt and knee are shown in front of Osiris's. Both king and god have muscular bodies, the bones and muscles on their calves and around their knees clearly delineated. Likewise, Taharqo is shown with taut abdominal muscles. Three columns of inscriptions engraved in the space above the two figures provide their names and titles. On the right is a leftward orientated inscription that reads: "Osiris, the one who answers the aggrieved." The god's name is not actually spelled out in this inscription. Instead, an ideogram showing an enthroned deity, who extends an *ankh*-symbol toward Taharqo's titles, is provided. In the other two columns, Taharqo's names are provided. He is "the Son of Re of his (own) body, his beloved, *Khu-nefertem-re*, the King of Upper and Lower Egypt, Taharqo, given life." At the scene's upper left corner is a *shen*-holding vulture, whose spread wings frame the scene.

Represented on the right jamb, Shepenwepet stands, her face shown in profile turned to the left, next to "Isis, the Great, the Divine Mother" (Figure 2.20b in the plates section). Shepenwepet dons a tight sheath dress and a vulture cap surmounted by a *modius* from which springs a solar disk set within Hathoric horns and two tall plumes. In her left hand, hanging idly parallel to her body is a folded *menat*-necklace, while in her other, forward extended hand she holds an *ankh*-symbol. Facing Shepenwepet is Isis, who wears a tight sheath dress, a long lappet wig surmounted by a solar disk set within Hathoric horns, a *uraeus* at her brow. Isis's arms are positioned exactly like Osiris's were in relation to Taharqo: one arm gripping Shepenwepet's upper arm, while the other is wrapped protectively around her back. But whereas the figures on the left jamb overlap, the ones depicted here do not. The exception is Shepenwepet's forward extended arm, which is shown in front of Isis's upper thighs. Represented toe-to-toe, their feet touch, but do not overlap. Above their heads three columns of inscriptions provide us with their names and titles. Isis's were given above. Her mortal companion is identified as "the Divine Worshipper, the God's Wife, the God's Beloved, Shepenwepet, whose mother (was) the God's Hand Amenirdis, the justified."

The scenes represented on the two jambs, along with their accompanying inscriptions, are delicately balanced. The two deities hold the king and the God's Wife in an identical manner: one arm wrapped around behind the back, reaching for and holding the far shoulder, while the other hand firmly grasps the near upper arm. Similarly the seated god extending an *ankh*-symbol towards Taharqo's cartouche-enclosed names is balanced by the symmetrically opposed figure of a goddess who also extends an *ankh*-symbol towards the names and titles of Shepenwepet. To balance Taharqo's two cartouches, Shepenwepet includes her predecessor's as part of her own titles and epithets. Her adoptive mother's name, then, becomes part of her own filiation. Likewise, the positioning of Shepenwepet's hands mimics Taharqo's posture, and her costume and accouterments seem to be the feminine counterparts of Taharqo's. Instead of the pear-shaped *hedj*-scepter he grasps in his fist, in Shepenwepet's clenched fist is a folded *menat*-necklace.

Despite such obvious symmetry, the individuals represented in these scenes are not of equal status. Occupying the left jamb and the left half of the lintel, Taharqo's rightward orientation is congruent with his superior royal status. Gay Robins has clearly outlined that rightward orientation typically indicates the higher status of its owner as it was typically reserved for the more important figure in a scene such that the pecking order was: Gods, the Dead, men, and then women.[224] The symmetrically opposed scenes, however, are quite reminiscent of the balanced representations of Pharaonic co-regents.[225] In instances of co-regency, it is not atypical for the senior regent to have the more dominant rightward orientation.[226] Typically, such similarly balanced scenes have been taken as indicative of the equal status of the parties involved.

This representational trend continued into the Saite period, where the parallelism is clearly seen in two chapels dedicated by Ankhnesneferibre in North Karnak, the façades of the chapel of Nitocris and Amasis (later enlarged by Ankhnesneferibre), and the chapel of Ankhnesneferibre erected in North Karnak. On the door jambs of a chapel dedicated by Nitocris and Amasis, and later enlarged by Ankhnesneferibre and Psametik III, both the king and the God's Wife receive life from Amun.[227] On the left, "the king of Upper and Lower Egypt, *Ankh-ka-en-ra*, the Son of Re Psametik (III), given life for ever" stands striding towards the right. [228] Face shown in profile, Psametik turns to the right to face his divine companion, "Amun-Re the Lord of the thrones of two lands, the great god, who is in the midst of the Ennead." Psametik wears the White Crown of Upper Egypt to which is attached a *uraeus* at the front, a broad collar, and a short, narrow, kilt that stops well above his knees. The kilt is held in place by a belt to which is attached a bull's tail at the back. Down the front of the kilt is a fringed apron decorated on either side with two rearing cobras. Left foot forward, Psametik takes a stop towards Amun, who holds Psametik's left hand, the two hands meeting in the space between their kilts. The king extends his right hand forward to receive the symbol of life from Amun. Cupping his hand immediately below the horizontally carved symbol, the king's attitude gives the impression of someone who is eagerly mindful that nothing goes to waste.

The *ankh*-symbol of life is attached to a long *was*-scepter, which Amun holds diagonally across his body, such that the scepter's bottom tip parallels the bull's tail attached to the rear of Amun's kilt. Amun wears his customary doubled-plumed crown, a tall curved false beard, a broad collar, a short kilt, and an upper-body garment held in place by tapering shoulder straps. Amun's garment is similar to the one he wears in the Nubian section of the chapel of Osiris, Ruler of Eternity, and in other Nubian structures in East and North Karnak. Amun's forward foot obscures the king's from view. Amun's declares: "To you, I have given all life and dominion, and all health." A winged vulture spreads her wings above, and next to, the inscriptions giving the king's, and the god's, titles.

In a symmetrically opposed scene on the north (= right) jamb, Ankhnesneferibre receives life from "the king of the gods, the great god, the lord of heaven." Although Amun-Re's name is not mentioned in the inscriptions, his distinctive tall-feathered crown and his attire clearly identify him. Similar to his representation on the south jamb, Amun here holds a *was*-scepter to which is attached an *ankh*-symbol. Amun places the key of life close to Ankhnesneferibre's face. Ankhnesneferibre, whose face is shown in profile turned to the left to face her divine companion, wears a long tight sheath dress, anklets, a bracelet, and a broad collar around her neck. The collar seems to be tied behind her neck, its streamers falling behind Ankhnesneferibre's shoulders. A rearing cobra at her brow, Ankhnesneferibre wears a short wig surmounted by a solar disk framed by tall horns and set before two tall plumes.

Just as Psametik held the god's hand, so does Ankhnesneferibre in this scene. She, too, cups her hand as she receives the sign of life. But she seems to hold her hand closer to her body, so that her elbow dips lower than the king's. Unlike the king though, she stands with her feet close together. There is no overlap between her feet and Amun's. Instead his forward foot almost touches the tips of her toes. And whereas a vulture framed the inscriptions on the left jamb, on the right jamb a winged cobra does. Because the cobra has a vulture's wing and tail, from a distance it may be mistaken for the bird. The cobra's body emerges from underneath the folds of the anterior wing, while its tail curls along the posterior wing spread horizontally across the top of the scene. The cobra, representing Wadjet, the titular goddess of Lower Egypt, is consistently depicted on the northern pillar, as is Ankhnesneferibre. This consistency accounts for Ankhnesneferibre's (more dominant) rightward orientation on the inner phase of the pillars (see Figures 2.21a–b in the plates section). The king, along with the vulture goddess Nekhbet, consistently occupies the southern pillar in this chapel. While it may be easy to relate the depiction of the titular goddess of the Upper Egypt on the southern pillar, the king's presence on the southern pillar, especially when contrasted with Ankhnesneferibre's on the northern pillar, is not quite as easy to explain.

Amun's speech to Ankhnesneferibre is also slightly different from the one inscribed for the king. It reads: "Words spoken: To you [fem.], I have given all life and dominion, all health, and all gladness, like Re forever."

Two other symmetrically opposed scenes occur in the same chapel.[229] This time, however, they are represented with gender-specific deities. On the left jamb is Ankhnesneferibre, who receives life from Isis "the Mistress of the Ladies of the Two Lands," while on the left jamb, Psametik (III) receives life from Harsiese (Horus, Son of Isis) (Figures 2.21a–b in the plates section). In both scenes, the deities hold hands with their mortal subject even as they extend the key of life to him/her. In both scenes, divine and human are similarly attired. Both Isis and Ankhnesneferibre wear long form-fitting sheath dresses, a broad collar and a vulture cap over their long lappet wigs. Likewise, Psametik and Harsiese both don broad collars and short kilts, but no upper-body garments. The only distinguishing feature is the head gear worn by each character.

On the left (= north) jamb, Ankhnesneferibre, shown in profile, face turned to the right, dons the tall-plumed crown of the God's Wife of Amun, with its distinctive solar disk set within tall horns. Facing her, Isis wears a horned-disk Hathoric crown set atop a *modius* which surmounts her vulture cap. On the south (= right) jamb, Psametik, shown in profile, his face turned to the left wears the white crown of Upper Egypt. Facing him, falcon-headed Harsiese wears the double crown of Upper and Lower Egypt. The God's Wife and the king are shown in identical postures to the ones in which they appeared on the façade of the chapel. Similar to the representation on the façade, the god's forward foot (in this case, his left) obscures the king's forward foot. Likewise the inscriptions on the north jamb are flanked by a winged cobra, while those on the south jamb are framed by a *shen*-holding vulture. On both the eastern (outer) and western (inner) phases of the pillars, a winged vulture frames the scenes showing Psametik III receiving life from Amun-Re and Harsiese, respectively; while, in the corresponding scenes, engraved on the opposite pillar, a winged *cobra* frames the scenes of Ankhnesneferibre receiving life from Amun and Isis.

In addition to taking on specifically royal rituals, on several occasions the God's Wife of Amun appears to mirror those scenes representing the king. While from a distance, the scenes may seem identical, on closer examination, one discovers subtle variations between them. The differences were deliberate. Despite their fondness for symmetry, the Egyptians did not particularly care for redundant repetitiveness. When read together, it becomes apparent that the content of such symmetrically opposed scenes is complementary. Taharqo offers wine in the chapel of Osiris, Lord of Life, while Shepenwepet offers milk. Both substances were necessary for the sustenance of the gods. In the chapel of Ankhnesneferibre and Amasis, she presents a statuette of *Maat*, while the king presents wine to the gods. But even in almost completely perfectly symmetrically opposed scenes, such as those showing the King and the God's Wife receiving life from the gods (in the chapel of Amasis and Nitocris), the scenes are slightly varied by depicting a winged cobra instead of the vulture so that if read together, the two scenes would together convey a more comprehensive, universal message.

In addition to providing for the gods and receiving equally precious gifts from them, the God's Wife also partnered with the King in protecting the gods – or at least, the cenotaph of a particular god.

Partnering with the king 2: "for god, king, and country"

Protecting the gods

Rites of protection at the cenotaph

On a small lintel in one of three subterranean rooms in the rather enigmatic Edifice of Taharqo by the Sacred Lake, a striking scene survives. A slender, athletic-looking woman draws a long, wide-feathered arrow through a double-curved bow, as she takes aim at the last of four round targets represented at the periphery of the scene (Figure 2.22).[230] She is identified as a God's Wife in the accompanying inscriptions. Next to her is King Taharqo, the penultimate king of the Twenty-fifth dynasty, who uses his pear-headed mace as a bat with which to strike four balls. Between the archer and her partner, an acacia-surmounted mound encloses the crypt of Osiris. Together, the king and God's Wife are attempting to protect the *hen*-cenotaph of Osiris. Their actions are aimed at averting the malign forces of the universe from the god's path. The rites depicted in this scene were thus meant to assert divine, and by extension, royal dominion.

The scene occurs on a lintel embedded in the eastern wall of subterranean room E in the Edifice of Taharqo by the sacred lake at Karnak. Shown in profile, the God's Wife's face is turned to the viewer's left.[231] Right foot slightly forward, the barefoot archer takes aim at the uppermost of four doughnut-shaped targets depicted at the far left of the scene. Arrows still in place, three of the targets have been shot already. Of the original four targets, only the central two survive. The targets, which are turned to face the viewer, resemble the hieroglyphic sign for town ⊗.[232] Above the scene, five

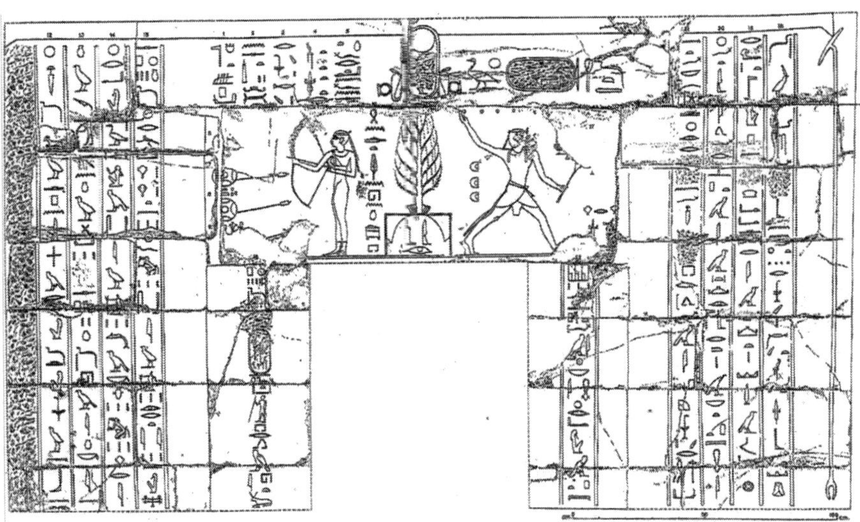

Figure 2.22 Rites of protection at the cenotaph, Edifice of Taharqo by the Sacred Lake, subterranean room E, east wall, lintel (line drawing after, after Parker *et al*, *Edifice of Taharqa by the Sacred Lake* (Providence Brown University, 1979), pl. 25; reproduced with permission)

short columns of text provide a caption for the event taking place in this scene: "[1] *The God's Wife has grasped* [2] *the bow* [3] *against the South and the North,* [4] *the West and the East* [5] *in return for what he has given her.*" The barefooted archer dons a long, form-fitting, sheath dress that falls down to her ankles. Starting just below her breast and going up and over her right shoulder, a diagonal strap holds the dress in place and a broad collar adorns her neck. She wears no other jewelry. A skull cap, secured in place by a tied ribbon, covers her hair. Of unequal lengths, the loose ends of the ribbon fall behind the God's Wife's head, brushing past her left shoulder and reaching down to her left elbow.

Behind the archer, a single column of text separates her from an acacia-surmounted mound.[233] Under the tree, a rectangular structure encloses a crypt. A hieroglyphic inscription carved within the enclosure clearly identifies the curved-topped crypt as the "mound of Osiris."[234] The group schematically represents the *hen*-cenotaph of Osiris, whose mythic location was at *Kom Djeme* on the west bank of the Nile. The small temple at Medinet Habu was thought to be a mythic location of the Mound of *Djeme*.

On the other side of the cenotaph is King Taharqo. His costume and regalia (the short tri-partite *shendyt*-kilt, the ceremonial bull's tail attached to his belt, the *ibes*-headband and the diadem on his head) clearly proclaim his status as a king of Egypt. Represented in profile, face turned to the viewer's right, the barefoot king extends his left leg forward in a wide stride.[235] Like the God's Wife, the sovereign turns away from the cenotaph. His right calf flexed, his right heel arched up above the register line with only the toes touching the ground,[236] the king is shown running towards the outer limits of the lintel. In his upraised arm, the king holds a pear-headed mace,[237] with which he strikes four balls represented above his head, one next to the other. The balls are shown at the exact moment of their release from the king's hand, his grip still cupping the fourth.[238] The sovereign takes aim at targets depicted at the far right. While the targets are not preserved, hieroglyphic texts serving as captions and engraved next to each target, relate each of the targets to a geographic designation, and accordingly, to the four cardinal points. It is toward those targets that the king seems to be running. While the king may have performed four successive runs towards each of the four cardinal points, "throwing one of the four balls in each direction,"[239] in this scene, the four runs are conflated into one. Behind the king, in the triangular space created between his upraised right arm, his flexed calf, and the acacia tree, are three D-shaped emblems. The emblems resemble similarly-shaped structures associated with the *sed* festival.[240] In scenes of the *sed* festival, similarly shaped signs symbolically marked "the extent of the king's domain"[241] and triplicate signs would appear on either side of the king.[242] It is possible that three similar symbols were depicted in the damaged area in front of the king.[243] Above the lintel, elements of Taharqo's throne name are partially preserved in a vertical cartouche, engraved directly above the central part of the scene. A pair of rearing cobras holding circular *shen*-signs flanks the cartouche. With the exception of an over-sized sun disk inscribed at the top of the cartouche, the signs inside the cartouche has been hacked out. The disk probably constituted an element of Taharqo's throne name: *Nefertum-Khu-Re*.[244] This unique scene depicts what has become known in Egyptological literature as the rites of protection at the cenotaph.

These rites were intended to avert "any malign forces from the path or procession of a god."[245] Turning their backs to the cenotaph at the center of the scene, both the king and the God's Wife are orientated toward the outer limits of the lintel. While their outward orientation may initially startle viewers, it is in fact consistent with their actions. Both the king and the God's Wife protect the cenotaph by engaging in acts of aggression: shooting arrows and batting balls. Fischer notes that while "attacking his adversary, either human or animal, the king usually faces outward from the rear of the temple (or from the longitudinal axis) as though defending the divine 'Lord of *Maat*' from the forces of chaos."[246] Likewise, both the king and the God's Wife are orientated away from the center of this scene in their efforts to defend the crypt of Osiris and combat the forces of evil.

Both the iconography and the role of the God's Wife in this scene are quite extraordinary. The equality of the scale of her representation to the king's is indicative of their similar status, but it also suggests that their respective roles in this ritual were equally important. In engaging in a rigorous, militaristic activity such as archery, she *actively* partners with the king in protecting the *ḥn*-cenotaph of Osiris.

As a deified human and the maintainer of *Maat*, the king was expected to protect the gods just as he was expected to provide for them. The God's Wife's name is omitted from the inscriptions accompanying this scene.[247] Likewise, a shortened version of her title, one that omits the name of Amun, is used. In this scene, she is not linked to her divine consort, the supreme solar deity Amun, whose name constituted an integral part of the fuller form of her title *hemet netjer en Imen* "God's Wife of Amun." In Egyptian culture, a person's name constituted an integral part of his or her personality. Such identification was so strong that carving a person's name on a statue completely transferred the whole essence of that person onto the statue and provided the person with an "alternative physical form other than the body."[248] For this reason, erasure or omission of someone's name was almost always restricted to persons who acted against *Maat*, such as Akhenaton or Hatshepsut. Clearly the God's Wife was not acting against *Maat* in this scene.

Writing about this scene in 1965, Leclant considered the symmetrical representation emblematic of the God's Wife's equal status to the king's, but he stopped short of presenting any suggestions concerning her identity.[249] During the reign of Taharqo (690–664 BC), two Nubian women held the position of God's Wife of Amun: Shepenwepet II, Taharqo's sister; and Taharqo's own daughter and appointee, Amenirdis II.[250] Of the two, Shepenwepet II seems to be the most likely candidate for the archer in this scene. She was the incumbent, while her niece, Amenirdis II, was still an "heiress apparent," who may never have attained the position of God's Wife.[251] The more senior of the two, Shepenwepet II was daughter of King Piye and, more pertinently, Taharqo's sister. In the rites depicted in this scene, the God's Wife appears as the king's peer. She is represented on the same scale as the king, and seems to be equally engaged in defending the sacred abode of Osiris. Their depiction at the same scale in parallel actions implies an equal, lateral relationship, not a hierarchical one. A lateral relationship allowed them to impersonate the roles of Shu and Tefnut who rid

Re of his enemies, the "Children of the Rebellion."[252] As his sister (Egyptian: *senet*), Shepenwepet II was also Taharqo's "(female) equal" and "(female) companion."[253] As his sister, she was on par with the king, and could thus be depicted on the same footing as him.[254] Furthermore, there is little evidence to suggest that Amenirdis II ever went beyond her status as the "heiress apparent" or "God's Wife of Amun Elect." There is hardly any mention of Amenirdis II on Theban monuments, and she may have never attained the position of God's Wife of Amun, when Nitocris was installed into office in 656 BC.[255]

The God's Wife's involvement in this scene takes on a different meaning. By aiming her arrows at the four geographic locations of the world in the Rite of Protection at the Cenotaph, the God's Wife, partnering with the king, averted danger from the Lord-of-All's way and cleared the way for him to re-establish his universal authority. Perhaps an essential question to address is why did the God's Wife, a mere mortal, assume such a prominent role in these cosmically important rites? The answer may lie in one of the most enduring of all Egyptian myths: the myth of Isis and Osiris. Isis, the loyal sister-wife sought out and collected the dismembered body of her husband, and posthumously conceived their child Horus.[256] In the rituals represented in the Edifice of Taharqo, a shortened version of the God's Wife title was used in order to allow for her full identification with the goddess Isis. For the same reason, Amun's name was suppressed. The archer had to represent the wife of the god buried in the cenotaph, Osiris. For it was only in her capacity as the Divine Consort *par excellence*, that Isis was able to fulfill her mythic role and protect his cenotaph. The omission of the God's Wife's name, and Amun's, was the result of a deliberate decision, not a matter of oversight.

"Burning fans"

A similar omission of the name of the God's Wife also occurred in the decoration of the Eighteenth dynasty chapel of Hatshepsut at Karnak. Known by its French name, Hatshepsut's *chapelle rouge*, or Red Chapel, was originally built to house the barque of Amun. Giving the chapel its color (and its name) are the red quartzite blocks that were used to construct the chapel's upper part. Black Diorite was used for the lower section of the walls.

In a series of related scenes, engraved along the inner side of the north wall of Hatshepsut's *chapelle rouge*, an un-named God's Wife partakes in the ritual burning of fans that bear the image of Egypt's enemies (Figure 2.23 in the plates section).[257] On a single block (no. 37), four vignettes arranged in two registers depict the ritual burning of fans. Proceeding from left to right, the ritual sequence begins with the scenes inscribed on the upper register and continues with the vignettes depicted on the lower register, which also proceed from left to right.[258] The first vignette shows a priestly attired, slim female wearing a tight fitting dress and a broad collar. Two shoulder straps that start just below her breasts and taper diagonally upward hold her dress in place. A belt tied around her waist is still visible, its loose ends ending in round finials, bracketing her lower abdomen and rear. Her hair is gathered closely to her skull in a fillet secured in place with a tied ribbon. The loose ends of the ribbon fall diagonally down to her shoulders. The bonnet completely covers her hair. Her face shown in profile, she turns to the left to face her male companion, who bears the title of "God's Father" (Egyptian: *it-netjer*). The God's Father's face is shown in profile, turned toward the right to face his female companion. He wears a knee-length kilt, is bare-chested, and is shown with short, cropped hair.

With the exception of their legs (hers close together while the priest takes a stride toward her), the two participants in this ritual stand in a symmetrically opposed posture. One arm passively hanging behind their bodies, both priest and priestess extend an arm horizontally forward. Clasped in the priest's right hand is a tall narrow staff that ends in an inverted triangular finial. A tall, narrow line whose end curves inward, issues from the finial. It is a torch, the curving line depicted at the top, its flame. In an attitude that mirrors her partner's, the priestess likewise extends a torch-bearing hand toward her partner. Meeting in the middle of the scene, the two torches form the focal point of the scene. A column of unframed inscriptions inscribed in the space between her shoulder and the torch, identify her as a "God's Wife" and a "God's Hand." Under the extended arms of the priest and God's Wife, two columns of unframed inscriptions provide a caption to the scene: "seizing the torch (lit flame) (and) giving <it> to the God's Wife." Indeed, because the flames of the two torches curve inward, almost touching one another, it seems that the priest is lighting her torch.

The next episode, which also occurs on the upper register, is only partially preserved.[259] Near the right edge of the block, the God's Wife, similarly attired and bearing the same titles, stands, her face shown in profile is turned to the right. Her arms hanging by her side, the God's Wife still holds the torch (whose top is now lost as the scene breaks off) diagonally downward to ignite it. An inscription that starts in the space next to her forearm, and extends to the space below her hand provides a caption to this scene. It reads: "Applying/Preparing the brazier/furnace to/with the enemy." [260] Traditionally translated as "brazier," Anthony Leahy has demonstrated that "furnace" was an equally valid, and often more suitable, translation for the Egyptian word used in this scene.[261] Unfortunately, the scene breaks off here. So it is not possible to know the shape of the vessel, basin, or furnace, in which the God's Wife supposedly dips her torch. Likewise, it is not possible to affirm whether she was accompanied by the *it-netjer* priest in this episode, or performed this aspect of the ritual on her own. Grimm suggested that it was here that the actual burning started.[262]

The third episode occurs under the first vignette, i.e. on the lower register, near the left edge of the block. There, the God's Wife appears opposite the God's Father. Both assume the same titles and attires as they did in the first episode. They also appear in an almost identical posture as they did in the first vignette: facing the God's Wife, the God's Father, who is oriented toward the right, extends his left leg forward. He extends an arm in her direction. In it, he holds a long staff with a semi-circular top. Customarily labeled a "fan," an image of a bound captive adorns the semi-circular finial. Shown in the traditional manner of a subjugated prisoner, the captive kneels, his arms attached at the elbow, are bound behind his back. The fans were presumably made of *dom*-palm, a special material that symbolized the enemies' hair.[263]

The titles of both participants are inscribed in the space created between their fans and their shoulders. She, a "God's Wife," and a "God's Hand," while he is a "God's Father." In the triangular space created under the fans is a single column of unframed inscriptions. Another, shorter, column of inscriptions engraved under the bottom end of the God's Wife's staff provides the rest of last two words of the caption "to the God's Wife." [264] Grimm suggested that this scene depicts the delivery of the fans bearing the image of Egypt's enemies.[265]

The final episode occurs on the lower register, immediately to the right of the third vignette. But there, much like the scene directly above it, only half of the scene survives. It is here in this partially preserved scene that the actual burning of the enemy's image takes place. Lacking a caption, only the titles of the officiant survive: "God's Wife" and "God's Hand." She stands, her face shown in profile is turned to the right. Just as the lower tip of the staff was visible in the second vignette, so too here an even smaller portion of the staff is preserved. The God's Wife seems to point her staff slightly upward, whereas in the second vignette, her torch pointed downward. Presumably, the God's Wife is here shown holding the fan out and into the fire in order to burn the image of the enemy. To the Egyptian mindset, burning the images of Egypt's enemies was as good as destroying them physically. Igniting the fans and the subsequent burning of the images of Egypt's enemies symbolized their "executions on earth and in the underworld."[266] Because it caused the complete destruction of the body, death by fire was reserved for the most heinous crimes, which included of course acts of rebellion both domestically and in territories conquered by the Egyptian king.[267]

Inscribed on the left edge of the adjoining block (no. 147), two columns of framed inscriptions provide a heading for the entire sequence depicted in these four vignettes. The texts, which are inscribed in retrograde, read: "[1]Going out into the forecourt (Egyptian: *wesekhet*) <in order to> perform the burning of the enemies in the midst of the forecourt. [2] Standing up behind it in order to place fire into the brazier/furnace."[268] The inscription provides a clear indication of where the ritual took place: the broad hall, or the temple's forecourt.[269]

The two-column inscription also frames a scene, depicted in two registers, of a procession of priests and priestesses.[270] On the top register, the "God's Wife," the "God's Hand," similarly attired in the tight sheath dress, belt and bonnet, and donning the same hair style, proceeds toward the right. She is one of three individuals depicted on the upper register. Ibis-headed Thoth, "lord of the Eighth nome," wearing a short kilt and holding a scroll in his left hand, leads the procession. Bringing up the rear is a slim female attendant (Egyptian: *Henoutet*), who wears a long lappet wig, a tight sheath dress and a long multi-strand necklace that almost reaches down to her waist.

The attendant's dress and hair-style are quite different from the God's Wife's. Whereas the God's Wife's hair is closely gathered and close to her skull, the attendant's hair is long and hangs loosely to below her shoulders. One cannot escape the impression that their different costumes and hair styles designated their relative temple status.

Ibis-head, Thoth also leads the procession depicted on the lower register. There, he is followed by two men. Immediately behind Thoth is a man who represented many attendants (Egyptian: *Henoutyou*). He wears a short, wrap-around kilt. Bringing up the rear of the procession is a bare-chested man who wears a triangular short kilt. Inscribed next to his shoulder is an inscription that reads: "Many Prophets" (Egyptian: *hemou netjer ashaou*). Like the person preceding him, this one also stood for many individuals. All six figures proceed to the right. As mentioned above, the accompanying inscription indicates that they are about to enter the Broad Hall (Egyptian: *wesekhet*).

Indeed, the scenes depicted on these two blocks showing the procession leading up to the actual burning of the images are part of a longer series of rituals depicted on the northern wall of Hatshepsut's sanctuary. Starting at the western side of the wall, the ritual sequence is arranged in a step-by-step, cinematographic, narration. The narrative commences with a depiction of the God's Wife leaving the palace and her entry into the temple.[271] Her face is shown in profile, and the God's Wife proceeds to the right. Emphasizing the sequential progression of the scenes is the fact that the God's Wife dons the same costume and has the same hair style throughout the entire sequence. She is shown wearing a broad collar and tight sheath dress. The same narrow belt with its rounded finials adorns her costume throughout.

The ritual burning of fans bearing the image of Egypt's enemies was aimed at protecting the gods and the entire cosmos.[272] That it was the intention here is indicated by a text preserved near the vignettes discussed above. The text, which seems to be a "formula for the ritual conjuration of the ritual destiny of affirming the triumph of the sovereign," is immediately followed by a depiction of Hatshepsut preceded by a lector priest presenting [what?] to the ithyphallic god Amun-Min. In this scene, Hatshepsut who proceeds to the right, is shown as a male king.[273]

In this way, the God's Wife is involved, once more, in a rite of cosmic magnitude. This time, however, she does not appear next to the king, but rather, next to an *it-netjer* priest or a "God's Father." *It-netjer* priests were a select subgroup of the *hem-netjer* priests, or the "Prophets."[274] The God's Fathers were typically related to the king, by blood or marriage. The title was also given to the non-royal fathers, or the fathers-in-law, of the king. Male nurses and royal tutors could also bear the title of God's Father. The cults of Amun, Min, and Ptah all employed "God's Father" priests who, much like other categories of priests, were grouped in the *phyles*. We know of a first, a second, a third *phyle*, but not a fourth.[275] The God's Wife thus appears along with the God's Fathers, prophets and the scribes of the divine books, in what essentially amounted to state-sponsored magic.[276]

And just like her colleagues, the God's Wife had to undergo a series of ritual purification rites before she could participate in the ritual burning of fans. First, before she could be admitted into the temple, the God's Wife, along with other priests, had to be ritually purified (block no. 21).[277] Next she had to be ritually bathed in the sacred lake, termed in Egyptian "the pool of cool water." That latter scene is preserved on two adjoining blocks (nos. 292 and 140).[278] Both blocks are divided into two registers. Shown in profile, her face turned to the right on the top register of block no. 292, the God's Wife stands, her feet immersed in ankle-deep water. With her back slightly bent, she leans forward. Her two arms, depicted before her bent body, seem to issue from the same shoulder. Her hair is gathered in a bonnet, held in place by a tied ribbon. It is clear that she wears a belt, its two round finials appearing on either side of her body. Her dress, however, clings very closely to her body, giving the impression that she is nude. This impression is further enforced by the absence of a hem line at her ankles. The hem line may have been assimilated into the line showing the water level at her feet.

A stream of water, represented by a wavy line above her head and in front of her body, is being poured from a jar. Issuing from a jar depicted on the adjoining block (no. 140), the same stream of water is also shown above the heads of two men who stand behind the God's Wife. Three, all male, individuals are similarly depicted on the lower register, where immediately under the God's Wife is a man assuming the same posture as the God's Wife. He wears a short kilt held in place by a belt.

To the right, two columns of framed inscriptions provide a caption to the scene. The texts, which are inscribed in retrograde, read: "Going down to be purified by the Priests/Prophets [lit. "God's servants"[, and the God's Wife, the God's Hand, in the *Qebehyt* pool, in order to proceed into the temple [lit."God's Estate"]."[279] *Qebehyt* is a term derived from the Egyptian word "to purify."[280] This latter scene indicates that the God's Wife, just like other members of the priesthood, had to undergo certain "initiation" or "induction" rites of ritual purification before she could proceed to certain parts of the temple. It is precisely this kind of washing, and the acquisition of official insignia that marks her as an "initiate" of the temple, of the same degree as a *hem-netjer* priest (traditionally translated as "prophet"). [281]

The ritual burning of fans represents the culmination of a series of rites that ultimately qualified her to participate in the ritual burning of the images of Egypt's enemies, thereby performing an act of supreme national and cosmic significance. The crux of the ritual is preserved on block no. 37, which is divided into two registers. In both the ritual burning of the fans and the lighting of the torches, she bears the titles of God's Hand as well as God's Wife.

Rites at Kom Djeme

Just as the God's Wife protected the god entombed in his cenotaph at Djeme, so also she helped clear the king's way of all harm in the rites at Djeme. While the God's Wife featured prominently opposite the king in the rites of protection at the cenotaph is depicted on the eastern wall in Taharqo's subterranean room E, she only appears as a minor figure in the "Rites at Kom Djeme," depicted on a lintel on the opposite western wall.

On the west wall in subterranean room E, a lintel above the door leading to room D depicts the primeval mound of Djeme. The Mound of Djeme was one of the mythical burial places of Osiris. Geographically, the small temple at Medinet Habu was considered to be one of several mythic locations of the Mound of Djeme. It was there that Amun-Re was brought once every ten days during the Decade Festival. Because the mound was surrounded by Nun, the primordial life-giving waters, Amun-Re's visit to this "well-spring of life," rejuvenated him and reenergized his powers.[282] In this scene, the mound is represented resting atop a pair of outstretched arms and surmounted by a falcon standing atop a lotus flower. To the left of the mound is an Anubis-fetish and a *sekhem*-scepter. Flanking the mound on the other side is a banner-carrying priest. Like the central figure of the falcon, the priest's head is turned rightward, but his torso and knees are orientated toward the left. The scene, which is poorly preserved, is an almost identical copy of an earlier scene engraved on the east wall of the inner east chamber in the chapel of Osiris, Ruler of Eternity.[283]

On either side of this central representation are two smaller scenes, each divided into three registers.[284] A single column of text separates the central scene from the two lateral ones. To the left, the top register is dominated by a representation of the king, who shown in profile, proceeds to the left carrying an Anubis emblem.[285] The king dons a *nemes*-headdress surmounted by a rearing cobra (a *uraeus*), a tunic, and a kilt to which is attached a ceremonial tail.

The barefoot sovereign is preceded by two figures represented one atop the other: a panther-skin wearing *Iunmoutef*-priest (lit. "Pillar-of-his-Mother") holding a falcon standard, and a woman who bears the titles of God's Wife and God's Hand. The priest dons a panther skin and side-lock. *Iunmoutef* priests were typically attached to the cult of *Iunmoutef*, a deity venerated in the ninth Upper Egyptian nome, whose name became associated with the priests attending his cult. In terms of attire and priestly duties, the *Iunmoutef* priest seems to have functioned quite similarly to the *sem*-priest, who, in the role of the eldest son, performed significant portions of the Opening of the Mouth ceremony, both in the royal cult at the temple and in the funerary cult.[286] *Iunmoutef*-priests also seem to have served the cult of the royal *ka*.[287]

The God's Wife wears a tight fitting bonnet, secured in place by a ribbon, and a form-fitting sheath dress. In her right hand, which is folded across her chest, she holds a palm. Her other arm hangs down by her side. Whereas the artist had to represent these two figures one atop the other, in reality, they would have walked side-by-side, with the lower figure of the priest closer to the viewer and the upper figure of the God's Wife farther from the viewer.[288]

That the priest may be understood as a personification of Horus may be gleaned from a quick analysis of the name of the deity that gave him his title. Because in Egyptian mythology the sky was personified as a woman, the goddess Nut, *Iunmoutef*'s name has been interpreted as alluding to the sky's support. More broadly, the name may be understood as "helper of his mother." The existence of the syncretic deity, Horus-*Iunmeoutef* seems to lend support to the broader interpretation of the name.[289] In this way, both priest and God's Wife seem to represent Horus and Isis, who protectively and heraldically walk before the sovereign. The king, shown here carrying the Anubis-fetish, is clearly linked to Osiris. Together, the *Iunmoutef*-priest/Horus and the God's Wife/Isis walk before the sovereign/Osiris to clear his way of all evil.

Standards, held alternately by *ankh*-signs and *was*-scepters, occupy the lower two registers. In the middle register, the standards (from left to right) are those of Wepwawet, Thoth, and Bat, the cow-headed goddess of the seventh Upper Egyptian nome, whose standard is comprised of "a pole surmounted by the fetish head of Hathor, wearing a plume." [290] Another standard of Wepwawet, also carried by an *ankh*-sign, appears in the lower register. Next, a standard of *Min-Imy-snwt* is fixed to the ground.[291] All the standards are orientated toward the left.

The vignette on the right is likewise divided into three registers. On the top and bottom registers, a female figure wearing a tight sheath dress is depicted holding a bow in her left hand and an arrow in her right. Both are shown in profile, feet together. But whereas the figure on the top faces the left, the one on the bottom is orientated toward the right. The emblems that would have adorned the head of each no longer survive. However, a parallel scene preserved in the chapel of Osiris, Ruler of Eternity, shows two similarly positioned females donning the *Imentet*-emblem atop their heads, indicating that the figure here represented the goddess of the West, whose name was *Imentet*. It has been suggested that the two females represent two statues that would have stood, facing each other, at the entrance to the chamber.[292] In the middle register is the figure of a clean shaven priest. He wears a short kilt held in place by a shoulder strap and proceeds toward the right, his head turned back to look down his outstretched arm. In his other hand, he holds a slightly bent, flexible staff that diagonally extends to the ground. The staff, which has a fan-like finial, touches the ground behind the priest's feet. The staff may actually have been a broom, with which he would sweep away his footprints.[293]

Rejuvenating the gods

The elevation of the tjest-*support*

While Isis's protective capacity is evoked in the Rites of Protection of the cenotaph, it is her revivication capabilities that are called to mind in the ritual Elevation of the *tjest*-support. Depicted on the southern wall of subterranean room E in the Edifice of Taharqo, the rite is enacted four times, for four different gods: Dedwen, Soped, Sobek, and Horus. Partnering with different priests, the God's Wife elevates each of the four gods atop a platform that resembles the hieroglyphic *tjest*-sign (Figure 2.24).[294] Represented standing, their faces shown in profile, the four deities are oriented towards the West (= the viewer's right). Dividing the episodes is a single column of descriptive texts. With the exception of the name of the god mentioned, the texts are identical. The orientation of the glyphs in the columns and lines of text below the scene suggests a right-to-left reading of this scene. The scene thus starts with the westernmost episode depicting the elevation of Dedwen and ends at the easternmost episode enacted for Horus. In each of the four instances, a single column of text points to the identity of the God's Wife. In the first two instances, she is identified as "The God's Wife of this God." The inscription is damaged in the third instance. In the fourth instance, she uses another of her religious titles: "God's Hand" in addition to "God's Wife." A different priest helps the God's Wife raise the *tjest*-support in each instance of the ritual. Precisely under the knot dissecting the *tjest*-sign, the hands of the God's Wife and the priest meet. Like the four deities, the God's Wife faces the viewer's right. She wears a tight-fitting sheath dress and a short wig secured by a knotted band that falls down and reaches below her shoulder. She is barefoot. Facing the God's Wife, the priests are orientated toward the viewer's left.[295] In Egyptian art, rightward orientation was preferred and was usually reserved for the most important figure(s) in a scene.[296]

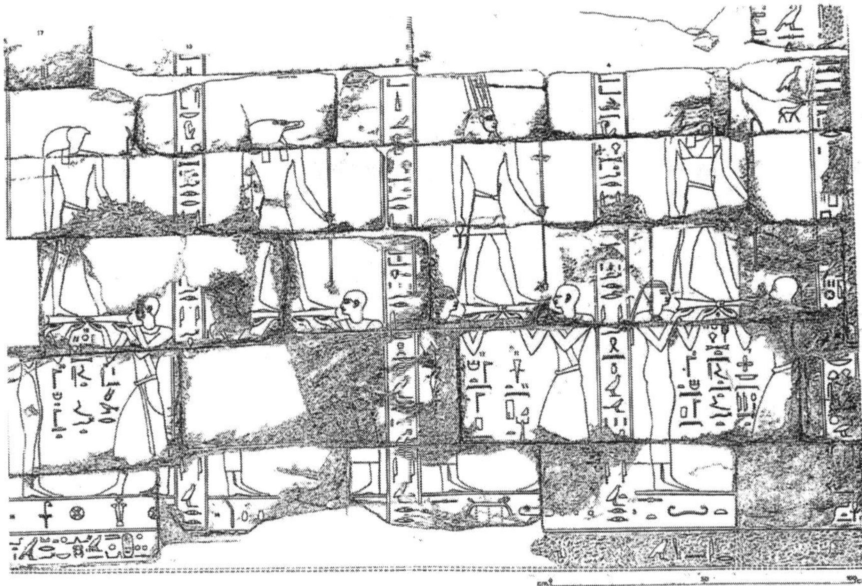

Figure 2.24 The elevation of the *tjest*-support, Edifice of Taharqo by the Sacred Lake, subterranean room E, south wall (line drawing after Parker *et al, Edifice of Taharqa by the Sacred Lake* (Providence Brown University, 1979), pl. 26; reproduced with permission)

The four gods carry identical insignia, wear similar costumes and assume the same posture. Astride atop the *tjest*-support, left leg extended forward, each of the four gods carries a *was*-scepter in the left hand, and an *ankh*-symbol in the right. They are also similarly attired. Each wears a short kilt, tied at the waist with a ceremonial tail suspended at the back of the kilt. The tail hangs vertically, parallel to their legs.

Of the four deities represented, Dedwen is the only one shown wearing an upper-body garment. Dedwen dons a tight-fitting garment that covers his chest and shoulders, its straps narrowing gradually as they near the god's neck. Although the figure of Dedwen is partially damaged (the head with its identifying gear does not survive), the accompanying texts clearly identify him by name. The texts further link Dedwen to Nubia.[297] This deity was one favored and honored by Taharqo, who (re-)dedicated the temple at Semna West to Dedwen and transferred his worship to Napata.[298] Scenes from the temple at Semna West depict Thutmose III "receiving his kingship and rule over foreign countries from Dedwen."[299] Below Dedwen's feet, the *tjest*-support is damaged at the far right (western end). The priest bears the title of "Opener of the Two Doors of the Sky" (Egyptian: *Wenenwy aawy-pet*). The "two doors of the sky" refer to the door-leaves of the shrine that house the cult statue, which may be pulled open by the highest-ranking *hem-netjer*-priest ("God's Servant"), i.e. the High Priest of Amun.[300]

The next episode is enacted for the god Soped. Shown in anthropomorphic form, Soped wears some distinctly royal headgear: the ceremonial beard and the *nemes*-headdress. The latter is the head-cloth usually worn by rulers of Egypt, but in this instance, Soped's *nemes* is surmounted by two tall feathers. In this particular enactment of the ritual, the God's Wife partners with a *smaty*-priest. The bald-headed priest wears "a long kilt and a sash across his bare chest."[301] *Smaty*-priests, the "*stolists*" of the Ptolemaic period, were responsible for dressing the god during the Daily Cult Ritual.[302] Chosen from the ranks of the *hem-netjer* priests, and having the distinguished privilege of beholding and dressing the god daily, *stolists* were among the highest ranking clergy in an Egyptian temple. This particular *smaty*-priest, is linked to the *hout-ka*, a temple that was located in the twentieth Lower Egyptian nome.[303] Indeed, the accompanying texts declare that Soped is "Lord of the East," and further associate him with Asia.[304]

Crocodile-headed Sobek is represented in the third episode of this ritual. Assuming a similar attitude and costume as the preceding two deities, he is elevated by a God's Wife and a priest. In this instance, the figures of the God's Wife and the priest are quite damaged. Only the head of the priest and the hemline of his long kilt survive, while the inscriptions identifying his rank do not. The captions link Sobek to Libya.[305]

Finally, the ritual is performed for Horus. Falcon-headed Horus assumes the same posture as the three other gods. Taharqo actively promoted the worship of Horus by dedicating temples to his cult at Buhen and Qasr Ibrim in Nubia.[306] Horus is attended by a "prophet of the *senty-wer*," a priesthood that is poorly attested and, therefore, not fully understood yet.[307] However, Goyon seems to dismiss Kees's suggestion that the *senty-wer* referred to a section at Karnak that embodied the "primeval mound of creation."[308] However, this particular interpretation of the title may actually account for the use of the God's Wife's secondary title of God's Hand, only when she is performing the ritual for Horus. According to the Heliopolitan creation myth, the creator god Atum used his hand to masturbate and thus set creation in motion. Using her title of God's Hand and associating her with a priesthood that served in that part of Karnak that symbolized the primeval mound of creation, the composers of this scene (ritualists, scribes, or iconographers) cleverly declared that of the four gods, Horus was the only true ruler of Egypt as well as a creator-god. Horus, the King of the Living, is here elevated to instill fear in Upper and Lower Egypt.[309]

The consistent presence of the God's Wife in the four episodes, as well as her identification as the "God's Wife of *This God*," led Leclant to suggest that, since the God's Wife was principally the consort of Amun, the four gods represented in these scenes must accordingly be four geographic manifestations of this supreme solar deity, who was ultimately the guarantor of (military) victory.[310] Moreover, since the four deities are clearly linked to the cardinal points, they may have represented various geographic manifestations of "the universal god Amun."[311] The ritual would thus have served to assert Amun's supreme universal authority. Amun's rule over Egypt is here symbolically represented by the presence of Horus, whose domain was Upper and Lower Egypt. Amun's authority over the entire known world was manifested in the presence of the other three deities, who each controlled regions immediately to the south, east, and west of the Egyptian border. By proclaiming the subjugation of the entire world to Amun's universal and supreme authority, the king's own dominion was guaranteed. For it is only through such universal divine rule that the king is "assured of protection."[312]

Rites of divine re-entrance

The God's Wife also features on the north wall, where she appears as part of the procession in the rites of Re-entrance of Amun-Re *djeser-aa* (lit. "he whose hand is holy") and Amen-Re *Kamutef* (lit. "the bull of his mother"). [313] At its western end, the north wall of room E is dominated by a figure of King Taharqo. Represented in profile, the rightward-orientated figure poses with his left leg slightly forward. He wears a *nemes*-headdress, a tri-partite triangular kilt to which is attached a ceremonial tail at the back, and a tight "tunic" that covers his lower torso. His right arm outstretched across his chest, the king holds a "*hetes*-object" in his right hand and carries the "ceremonial *mekes*-stick and the *hedj*-mace in his left hand.[314] Both the scale of the king's representation and his rightward orientation clearly mark him as the most important figure in this scene.[315] Five columns of text separate the king from two smaller vignettes, also depicted on the north wall. A single column of inscriptions separates the two scenes represented in the vignettes. With the exception of the deity named, the scenes are identical.

According to Goyon, the king here ritually welcomes two processions shown at the center and at the far right. The first is a procession of Amun-Re-*djeser-aa*, while the second is Amun-Re *Kamutef*. Both gods are hidden inside portable shrines, which are carried by four priests each. The shrines are rectangular, and have a curved roof that rests atop an Egyptian cavetto cornice.[316] Two carrying poles horizontally attached to the sides of the tabernacle enable four priests to carry them. By necessity the cult statues of the gods are hidden inside the tabernacle, whose sides are drawn down. Bleeker has commented on the mysterious nature of cult service, even when the service was held outside the high enclosure walls of a temple. The secrecy associated with the god's statue was especially guarded during his more public appearance in processions associated with Egyptian festivals.[317] At the head of each procession is a shrine-holding prophet (*hem*-priest). Wearing long kilts, all five individuals are similarly attired. A cloaked woman brings up the rear of the processions. She is labeled as a "God's Wife" and a "God's Hand."[318] Her cloak is long and loose and covers one of her shoulders. A long ribbon secures her hair in place. In her right hand, she carries "a palm"[319] close to her chest. She is the only woman represented in the scene.

The entire procession is oriented towards the left (= west) so that its members face a bald, clean-shaven priest, who stands at the far left of the vignette facing the procession. Shown in profile, his face turned to the right, the priest wears a long kilt and carries a *hes*-jar and an incense-burner. He seems to stand in reception of the procession of the *hn*-tabernacle, with its divine inhabitant, at its return from the west bank. Known as "the feast of the divine re-entrance," this celebration took place over a period of two days. The scepters and staffs carried by the king in this rite were typically represented in rites associated with the consecration of new temples, particularly in a rite known as "Giving the house to its lord." The ceremony, which was the final, and most important, phase of the temple foundation and consecration rituals, may have been re-enacted here to commemorate "the definitive dedication of the temple to its legitimate owner."[320]

The associated rites of "Divine Re-entrance" celebrated the return of Amun-Re from his visit to *Kom Djeme* on the west bank of Thebes. Once every ten days, during the Decade Festival, Amun-Re was brought to the small temple at Medinet Habu, the mythic location of *Kom Djeme*, where the Ogdoad, the set of eight primeval gods, were buried.[321] But *Kom Djeme* was not merely a burial ground. It was also the mythic location of the primeval mound on which the first act of creation took place. This mound was surrounded by the primordial life-giving waters, deified as the primeval god Nun. About the regenerative powers of Nun, Hornung wrote: "Regeneration is impossible in the ordered and defined world. It can happen only if what is old and worn becomes immersed in the boundless regions that surround creation – in the healing and dissolving powers of the primeval ocean Nun."[322]

Amun-Re's visit to this "well-spring of life" rejuvenated him and renewed his energies.[323] As noted above, Amun-Re *Kamutef*, was a self-generating deity. *Djeser* may be translated as "magnificent" or "exalted" but may also be used to denote "'secluded, inaccessible, hidden' so that it is the equivalent of secret."[324]

While to the modern mind, death and rejuvenation may seem like contradictory concepts, to an Egyptian they were not necessarily so. The litany of Re, essentially an elaborate hymn to the sun, explains how

> the universal god (whose visible manifestation upon earth is the solar disk) moves in a circle of perpetual ascent and descent – up to the heaven as Re, the Sun, and down to the realm of death, the Netherworld, the kingdom of Osiris. Yet in death Re gathers new strength for his resurrection, while in life he perpetually moves towards death.[325]

Bleeker drew attention to the plethora of Egyptian words "denoting the concepts: new, to renew, to be renewed, to become new, to make new, to rejuvenate, to be rejuvenated" and suggested that therein lay the key to understanding the Egyptian religious mindset.[326] He further postulated that the ancient Egyptians were

> desirous of the renewal and rejuvenation of the life of the cosmos, of the community, and the individual... . [t]his renewal had to be effected by the cultic rites, which had the power to bring about the rejuvenation and rebirth of divine life because they actualized the mythical ideas. The festivals constituted the highlights of this cultic ceremonial. Thus the ancient Egyptian festivals came to have the function of *enactments of religious renewal*.[327]

In subterranean room E, the king is shown on three of the room's four decorated walls, while the God's Wife appears on all four walls. The size and positioning of these two individuals may enable us to infer conclusions regarding the ritual sequence depicted in room E. On the lintel preserved above the doorway in the east wall, both the king and the God's Wife are represented at the same scale and appear on the same footing (Figure 2.22). As mentioned above, the king and God's Wife have complementary, *and equal*, roles in protecting the cenotaph of Osiris: she as Isis and the king as Horus, the dutiful son.[328] The protection of his father's tomb was Horus's (and consequently, the king's) ultimate duty and formed the basis for his claim to his father's throne. Protecting his father's tomb legitimated Horus's claim to his father's throne and earned him his right to succeed his deceased father. In this way, the Rites of Protection of the Cenotaph were acts that legitimated Horus's position as the King of the Living. As the living incarnation of Horus, the king could claim legitimacy through the enactment of these same acts of protection.

On the opposite, west, wall the representation preserved on the lintel leading into the innermost room of the subterranean level shows the king proceeding from the Mount of Djeme. Only the exit procession is depicted in this scene.[329] The king is preceded by the much smaller figures of a God's Wife and an *Iunmoutef*-priest, who are represented on separate register lines: the God's Wife is shown on the top register, while the priest is seen on the bottom register. The God's Wife and the priest walked ahead of the king to clear the way before him. In this way, their presence still fulfilled a protective function. The God's Wife may thus still be seen as embodying the protective function of the goddess Isis. But in this scene, it is the priest, not the king, who assumed the function of Horus. We have seen above how this priest, whose name literally means the "Pillar-of-His-Mother" came to be involved in funerary rites as the ultimate eldest son, Horus.[330] With the role of Horus now fulfilled by the priest, whose role did the king embody? I suggest that the answer to that question is: the revivified Osiris or the rejuvenated Amun. It has been noted that the main purpose of the Edifice of Taharqo by the sacred lake was to celebrate the periodic, albeit mystical, union of Amun and Re-Horakhty with Osiris.[331] Possibly because of their sanctity, the actual rites performed at Djeme are not depicted in this scene.[332] So it is not possible to know how such union of, and with, the godhead was brought about. But it seems that it was through the efficacy of these rituals that the king became identified with the re-vivified Osiris, or by extension, the new-born sun, and the rejuvenated Amun.

On the north wall, the king, represented at a heroic scale turns to the right as he welcomes two priestly processions about to re-enter the temple. The king's heroic size on the north wall contrasts sharply with his complete absence from the rituals depicted on the opposite south wall. It is not the king who elevates the four statues on the *tjest*-support, but the God's Wife, who takes as her partners several high-ranking priests (Figure 2.24). The rite was enacted four times for four different deities: Dedwen, Soped, Sobek, and Horus. The gods, whose identities are said to reflect different geographic manifestations of Amun, were each associated in the text with a distinct geographic area.[333] The king is nowhere to be seen in this ritual enactment precisely because it was there that the king was finally fully identified with the universal god: Amun, in all his geographic manifestations. The king-god unity, alluded to by Goyon and other scholars,[334] finds complete expression in the ritual elevation of the *tjest*-support. Indeed, the king's unity with the Lord of All is further emphasized by his absence. For it was through the complete convergence of god and king that the ritual elevation of the *tjest*-column proclaimed not only Amun's universal supremacy, but more importantly the king's universal authority as well. This scene thus represents the culmination of several rituals that aimed to proclaim and bring about the king's unity with the universal god Amun.

The king's authority stemmed from the king's legitimacy. In this way, the king's assumption of the role of Horus, the protector of his father and his father's tomb, in the Rites of Protection at the Cenotaph, ensured his own legitimacy. Summed-up in his throwing four balls at the four cardinal points, the king's protective function reinforced his embodiment of Horus, the King of the Living and legitimated his authority. The king was Horus on the east wall. But once his legitimacy was secured, the king's identification shifted to the more principal deity, the central beneficiary of all the rituals performed in this role. The more subsidiary role of Horus was now played by an *Iunmoutef* priest of the west wall.

The sequence of events shown in subterranean room E can thus be interpreted as follows. The rites commenced on the room's entrance, with the Rites of Protection at the Cenotaph inscribed on the lintel above the doorway leading into the room, on the eastern wall. There, the king legitimated his role by carrying out the protective duties of Horus. Next, on the opposite west wall, we see the procession proceeding out of the mount of Djeme, where the scene is similarly engraved on a lintel above a doorway leading into the adjacent room, which happens to be the innermost room of the subterranean level.

The act of legitimating protection (shown on the east wall) had to precede the rites performed at Djeme (depicted on the west wall). In the former, the king was Horus, the protector of his father; in the latter the king became, himself, the revivified Osiris and the rejuvenated creator god. The king then welcomes the returning procession (on the north wall), where his heroic size emphasizes his divine status. The king's identification with the rejuvenated Amun finds complete expression in the events depicted on the south wall, where the images of the four geographic manifestation of Amun were elevated.

In subterranean room E of the Edifice of Taharqo by the sacred lake, complementary relationships governed the layout of scenes on opposite walls, where similar themes found iconographic expression. In the four scenes depicted in underground room E of the Edifice of Taharqo, the God's Wife played a significant role in the enactment of these all-important rituals. Although her role is most pronounced on the south wall, where she appears as the main officiant in the ritual elevation of the *tjest*-support, represented on that wall, she plays the similarly important roles in the rites depicted on the east and west walls. Further, she is the only woman included in the divine processions depicted on the north wall of the same room. Throughout, the God's Wife is identified either by a shortened, more ambiguous version of her title, "God's Wife," or by the less common "God's Wife of this God." The omission of Amun's name from her titles was not only deliberate, but crucial for the proper enactment of the ritual. The God's Wife's close association with a divine spouse, especially with the faithful and loyal wife *par excellence*, Isis ensured that the actions of the God's Wife had the requisite magical potency to render them ritually effective.

Another title borne by the God's Wife in all but one of the rituals depicted in the chamber E is the title of "God's Hand." Harkening back to ancient Heliopolitan creation myth, the occurrence of this title in conjunction with Amunemipet or

Amun-kamutef, both ithyphallic, self-generating creator-god aspects of Amun of Thebes seems appropriate. During the rites at Kom Djeme, Amun of Thebes reverted to either of these forms as he visited his divine ancestors at Djeme. "God's Hand" may also be interpreted in the sense of God's instrument/or agent, especially in the contexts of burning fans bearing the images of Egypt's enemies and affirming the king's universal power.

Other rites of "royal and divine" dominion

Understandably, the Rites of Protection at the Cenotaph and the related rites of burning fans bearing the images of Egypt's enemies depicted in Hatshepsut's *chapelle rouge* have been considered part of a larger group of rituals whose aim was to assert the universal power of god, and consequently proclaim the king's own authority.[335] Collectively, those rites are known as "Rites of Royal and Divine Dominion." At least three other rituals, also known from the Twenty-fifth dynasty, served a similar purpose: the Driving of the Four Calves (Egyptian: *hout behesou*), the Consecration of *Meret*-chests, and the Elevation of the *Tjest*-column.

The first two of these rites, the ritual driving of calves and the striking of the *meret*-chests, are very closely associated, not only in temple decoration where they often appear next to each other, but also in terms of their Osirian references. Both rites occur on the southern half of the east wall in the Great Hypostyle Hall at Karnak, where Ramses II performs both rites for the benefit of Amun-Re-Kamutef. They similarly occur on adjacent walls in the courtyard of the funerary chapel of Amenirdis I at Medinet Habu. There, Shepenwepet II appears as the main officiant in the rite of the *hout-behesou*, or the ritual of Driving the Four Calves, depicted on the upper register of the eastern part of the south wall of the courtyard. On the poorly preserved adjacent east wall is the ritual presentation of the *Meret*-chests. Both rites were often performed together "during processions on the occasion of several major temple festivals."[337]

"Driving four calves"

The scene depicting the ritual driving of the four calves is found on the top register of the south wall of the courtyard, which also serves as the façade of the inner chapel. To the east of the doorway leading into the *cella* of Amenirdis, Shepenwepet II shepherds four calves driven toward three figures standing at the other end of the scene.[338] In doing so, she is taking on the traditional iconographic composition of this scene, where typically, "[t]he officiant and the divinity (or divinities) are facing each other, while the central element, in this case the four calves, is located between them." [339]

Shepenwepet is represented standing at the eastern end of the upper register of the southern wall of the courtyard (Figure 2.25 in the plates section). Her face shown in profile, Shepenwepet II is oriented toward the viewer's right (= west/the center of the wall). She dons a tight sheath, broad collar and the customary head gear of the God's Wife: the vulture headdress surmounted by two tall feathers. Slightly bent at the elbow, Shepenwepet's left arm extends forward. In her left hand, Shepenwepet holds a tall shoulder-length staff, which stands vertically parallel to Shepenwepet's body. Also in her left hand, Shepenwepet grasps the ends of four strands of rope, which coil around her hand, each terminating in a suspended *ankh*-sign. In her right hand, she holds a rod which, pointing down, slants diagonally forward toward the center of the scene. Possibly serving as a goad, the end of the rod almost touches the hind parts of the bottommost of four calves represented at the center of the scene.[340]

The ropes in Shepenwepet's hand are each attached to the second leg of each of the four calves (Figure 2.26). It is the calves that form the focal point of the scene. True to Egyptian artistic convention, the four calves, which in reality were driven side-by-side, are shown here one atop the other, the uppermost calf "being the furthest from the viewer."[341] Each calf is identified by a hieroglyphic symbol indicating its color: uppermost is the "spotted" calf (Egyptian: *saab*). Next is the white calf (Egyptian: *hedj*). The red calf (Egyptian: *desher*) follows and finally, at the bottom of the scene, or closest to the viewer, is the black calf (Egyptian: *kem*). This particular color sequence was one of two sequences found in Eighteenth dynasty representations of this ritual, where the tether was always attached to the calves' second leg.[342] Like their shepherd, the calves are orientated toward the viewer's right such that they face the three standing figures represented at the western end of the wall.

Shepenwepet drives the four calves towards those three figures. Two of the standing figures are clearly male, while the third, westernmost, figure is that of a slender female. Foremost of the three figures and closest to the calves is the god Osiris (Figure 2.26). Shown in mummiform, Osiris wears a cloak tightly wrapped around his shoulders and arms. Osiris's hands, visible through a small opening in his cloak, clutch a *was*-scepter close to his chest. On his head, Osiris dons the white crown (*hedjet*). Standing behind Osiris is Horus. Astride, and full of youthful vigor, Horus extends his right leg forward and wears the double crown of Upper and Lower Egypt. He carries a *was*-scepter in his outstretched right arm. Horus's left arm hangs down parallel to his body, his fist tightly grasping an *ankh*-sign. Attached to his kilt is a ceremonial bull's tail. Although the last figure of this triad is slightly damaged, the accompanying texts preserving most of her cartouche, indicate that the standing female is Amenirdis. The outlines of her slender body still discernible, Amenirdis stands, feet close together, behind Horus. She wears a tight sheath dress, and on her head dons the vulture headdress surmounted by two tall feathers, customary for the God's Wife. Her right arm crossed over her chest, she clasps a flail in her right hand, while her left arm hangs down parallel to her body. Deified, Amenirdis seems to replace (or possibly represent) Isis as the third member of this triad.

Occasionally, "groups of two or three divinities" were shown as beneficiaries of this ritual, e.g. the triad of Amun, Mut and Khonsu at the temple of Amun-Re at Karnak.[343] In fact, in the vast majority of scenes representing the Driving of the Four Calves indicate that the ritual was enacted for the benefit of Amun-Re, who could be shown standing or sitting on his throne. In six examples, Osiris is depicted as the beneficiary of this ritual.[344] When Horus is depicted as the main deity for whom this ritual is represented, he is shown in one of several "adult" incarnations: Horus of Buhen at Buhen, Horus of Edfu at Edfu, and Harsies at Dendera.[345] It is noteworthy that Horus was the chief residing deity at the temples at Buhen and Edfu. To the best

Figure 2.26 Shepenwepet II drives four calves before Osiris, Re-Horakhty, and deified Amenirdis, funerary chapel of Amenirdis, courtyard, southern wall, eastern half, upper register (Photo © M. Ayad)

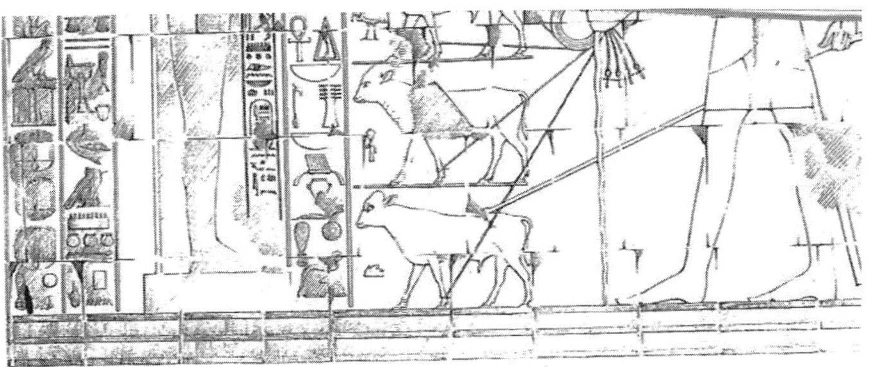

Figure 2.27 Hatshepsut drives four calves (line drawing after Edouard Naville, *The Temple of Deir el-Bahri VI Lower Terrace* (London Egypt Exploration Fund, 1908), pl. CLXI; reproduced with permission).

of my knowledge, this is the only instance where Horus and Osiris are represented together as beneficiaries of the ritual.

As represented in this scene, Shepenwepet seems to be walking into the chapel while the two gods and Amenirdis seem to be walking out of it. In this respect, Shepenwepet fully assumes the role of an officiating priest who, just like the king, would typically face the deity coming out of his shrine.[346] Accompanied by the ultimate resurrected deceased and his son, Amenirdis, the deified inhabitant of this funerary shrine is here represented coming out of her tomb-chapel. As her adopted daughter and successor, Shepenwepet takes on the role of the eldest son, who was conventionally responsible for the maintenance of his deceased father's funerary cult.

In this ritual, Shepenwepet assumes the role of the ultimate good son, who not only buried his father, but faithfully protected his tombs from the wiles of his evil uncle Seth. The caption that usually accompanies this ritual (Egyptian: *heh is*) may be interpreted as "to tread the grave" or "to seek the grave." Two verbs are commonly seen in texts accompanying this ritual: *heh* "to seek" and *houi* "to strike."[347] In an agrarian interpretation of the ritual, the calves were driven in fields in order to push newly sown seeds deeper into the ground. "Treading the grave" would thus directly link the physical movement of the calves to the notion of hiding the tomb of Osiris by stepping on it, just like they stepped on seeds.[348] "Seeking the grave," on the other hand, directly evokes the mythic role of Horus in his father's burial. After interment, Horus goes on a simulated search of his father's tomb. The search was "intended to mislead Seth and his allies, who were really seeking the tomb to violate its occupant."[349] The two interpretations do not conflict. Indeed, in essence, both interpretations lead to the conclusion that the main purpose of this ritual was the protective "concealment of the tomb of Osiris."[350] The ambiguity of the verbs used probably appealed to Egyptian ritualists, who often composed similarly multi-layered texts. Indeed, by their very ambiguity, the texts emphasize the protective role of Horus in this ritual.

In fact, it was through the fulfillment of his role in this rite that Horus, and by extension the king, was granted legitimacy as his father's rightful successor on the throne of Egypt.[351] Thus, just as Horus was responsible for ensuring a good burial for his father through enacting this ritual for his father's benefit, so Shepenwepet II performs the rite of Driving of the Four Calves for the benefit of her adoptive deceased mother, Amenirdis – and by so doing, Shepenwepet ensured her own legitimacy as her mother's successor as a God's Wife of Amun.

According to Egberts, the ritual driving of the four calves, through its agricultural aspect as well as its references to the Osirisian myth, asserted the king's dominion over all Egypt. [352] Seen in the threshing movement of the calves, the agricultural aspect of the ritual linked it to the all-important grain production process. Grain production provided the staple of the Egyptian diet: bread and beer. Bread and beer were not merely essential for private consumption, but both were used as payment in kind for services rendered to the state (such as tomb-building in the Valley of the Kings). The mythical aspect of the ritual combined two elements of the Osiris myth: the equation of Osiris with corn and the search for his tomb.

> Although the growth of vegetation is essentially a cosmic phenomenon, the cultivation of grain has important social implications. The fate of the Egyptian community depended on the success or failure of the harvest. In their own fashion, the Egyptian ritualists tried to secure the abundance of the crop. One of their devices was the driving of the calves. Viewed from a functionalist angle, this rite aimed at … the well-being of the Egyptians. [353]

Both King Taharqo and Queen Hatshepsut are represented driving the four calves. In Temple T, at Kawa, on the western wall of room H, Taharqo is depicted driving the four calves toward ram-headed Amun-Re.[354] Taharqo, who proceeds from the left, dons the Nubian skull cap surmounted by two crowned, rearing cobras. Broad-shouldered and bejeweled, Taharqo wears a falcon shirt, elaborate sandals, and a short kilt to which is attached a bull's tail at the back. An ornate panel decorates the front of his kilt, which is worn over a diaphanous longer kilt that stops at mid calf. Slanting diagonally forward is a goad, which Taharqo holds in his right hand. In his left hand he holds a shepherd's crock and grasps the loose ends of four ropes that are attached to the second leg of each of the four calves. The calves, which are represented one atop the other, are arranged in a similar order to that in which they appear in the chapel of Amenirdis: spotted, white, red, and black. Taharqo was Shepenwepet's brother and contemporary. The same order of calves is also found in a depiction of the rite in the temple of Amun-Re-Horakhte, at Karnak, where it occurs on the screen wall of the inner colonnade. In this instance, Taharqo drives the four calves towards Amun-Re, the resident deity of the temple.[355] It should come as no surprise then that the order of the calves is the same in the scenes showing Taharqo and Shepenwepet performing the *hout behesou* ritual. He is here represented driving the calves toward ram-headed Amun-Re. This particular form of Amun-Re was venerated in Napata and Temple T, where this scene is preserved, and was dedicated to him. True to the tradition of honoring the resident deity, Taharqo is shown performing the ritual Driving of the Four Calves for the benefit of Amun-Re, the Lord of Temple T.

Six times in the temple of Karnak alone, Ramses II is depicted driving the four calves. The two instances which occur in the Hypostyle Hall are found on the southern half of the east wall and the eastern half of the south wall. In both instances, the order of the calves is spotted, red, white, and black. On the east wall, Khonsu is the beneficiary of the ritual, while on the south wall, Ramses performs the ritual for ithyphallic Amun-Re.[356] The location of this latter scene on the eastern half of the south wall of the Hypostyle Hall is particularly interesting. It is conceivable that by locating her scene on the eastern half of the southern wall in the courtyard of Amenirdis's funerary chapel, Shepenwepet was trying to approximate, or even adhere to, the location of this scene in the Karnak Great Hypostyle Hall.

Ruling as "female pharaoh," Queen Hatshepsut (*c.* 1490–1469 BC) is likewise depicted driving the four calves in her funerary temple at Deir el-Bahri.[357] Proceeding to the left, she is depicted as a bare-chested male, wearing only the royal *shendyt*-kilt around her waist (Figure 2.27). Like Shepenwepet, Hatshepsut holds a goad in one hand, while in the other she grasps the loose ends of ropes tied to the second leg of each calf. The order of the calves, however, is not identical to that found in the Nubian representation of Shepenwepet II and Taharqo. While, like the Nubian scenes, the top calf is spotted and the lower one is black, the order of the middle two is reversed: the red calf appearing atop the white one in her temple at Deir el-Bahri. But perhaps more striking is Hatshepsut's male attire and stance: both contrast sharply with the depiction of Shepenwepet II, who consistently retained her feminine identity.

"Striking chests" or the presentation of meret-chests

The closely related rite of consecrating the *meret*-chests is depicted on the adjacent east wall in the court of the funerary chapel of Amenirdis I at Medinet Habu. This rite is often found on temple walls in conjunction with the Driving of the Four Calves.[358] Of the original scene depicting the consecration of the *meret*-chests in the chapel of Amenirdis, only a few columns of texts survive. The vignette itself is not preserved. The inscriptions indicate that the officiant in this rite was the "Divine Adoratrice Shepenwepet, whose mother was the Divine Adoratrice Amenirdis, the justified."[359] The caption for her actions reads: "Striking four times at the *meret*-chests … that she may act, being alive … ."[360] In this instance, Shepenwepet strikes the chests for the benefit of Osiris *khenty-imnty* ("foremost of the Westerners") and for her adoptive mother Amenirdis. Like her divine companion, Amenirdis utters a blessing/benediction for Shepenwepet's benefit. But where Osiris's speech survives almost intact ("I give to you all life and dominion; I give to you all health"), Amenirdis's speech is badly damaged, with only the words "I give to you …" surviving. Parallel scenes may allow us to reconstruct the original iconography of this scene.

Shepenwepet was likely represented standing, and shown in profile, her face would have been turned to the left. Between her and Osiris, behind whom stood deified Amenirdis, were four bandage-wrapped *meret*-chests. Shepenwepet would have held a scepter in her right hand raised high behind her head in a posture quite similar to that of the king smiting his enemies. Her left arm would have been raised, in a gesture of adoration, toward her deified mother and Osiris.[361] Behind Shepenwepet would be a group of symbols that may have included such symbols commonly found in scenes depicting the *sed* festival, such as , depicting physical earthly boundary markers or that have been recently interpreted as reflecting celestial boundaries.[362]

Forming the focal point the ritual, four *meret*-chests would have depicted at the center of the scene. Much like the calves described above, the chests would have been represented stacked one atop the other, "without overlapping."[363] While in reality the chests would have stood side by side, artistically, the top-most represented the farthest chest from the viewer, while the bottom chest was the closest to the viewer.[364] We might surmise from other examples that all four chests were identical. Of the two main types of chest "the normal bound *meret*-chest" and *naos*-shaped, the chests shown in our scene probably belonged to the former kind, the latter being "confined to the Graeco-Roman period."[365] But it is almost impossible to determine the details of the chests themselves, as the chests of the first type showed a great variety in shape and form: some were rectangular, while others, resembling "a truncated cone" were trapezoid. Within the rectangular variety, some chests had long vertical sides, while others had long horizontal sides. In some examples, *meret*-chests stood on sledges. In others, they lay squarely on the ground. Some sledges were of the flat variety, while others "turned upward at the front."[366] In the chapel of Amenirdis, the *meret*-chests probably stood on upturned sledges. Examples that pre-date our scene as well as those dating to the period immediately after the Twenty-fifth dynasty typically depict the upturned variety of sledges.[367]

Perhaps the most noticeable feature of the *meret*-chests is their binding. Although a variety of bands were used, and these were sometimes applied over the entire chest or only part of it, typically chests represented in the same scene would have the same kind of binding.[368] In the funerary chapel of Amenirdis, only the captions accompanying this scene survive. The chests are not preserved so that it is impossible to discern which type of binding decorated the chests in this scene.

The consecration of *meret*-chests is a primarily Theban rite, with Amun-Re appearing in most of the vignettes depicting it.[369] Egberts has noted that the distribution of deities "reflects in the first place the provenance of the vignettes, for the god to whom a particular temple is dedicated … figures foremost in its decoration."[370] Most vignettes depict only a single divinity as the beneficiary of this rite (e.g. Amun-Re Kamutef before Ramses II at the Karnak Hypostyle Hall). "[I]n the many vignettes featuring Amun-Re, [there is not] a clear preference for the normal or the ithyphallic form of this god."[371]

Occasionally, that deity would have a companion of the opposite sex.[372] In this respect, one might argue that Amenirdis stood for Isis in this scene. In the Ramesside tomb of Meretamun (TT 68), Osiris appears with Hathor.[373] Egberts further notes that female deities very rarely feature as the beneficiary of the consecration of the *meret*-chests. [374] In this instance, however, Amenirdis, deified, appears next to Osiris, just as she did in the Ritual Driving of the Four Calves. Her appearance next to him probably relates more to her as the deceased "owner" of the tomb-chapel for whom all the rites are enacted, rather than her substituting for his divine consort Isis. The bound chests with their elaborately wrapped bands undoubtedly "evoked the mummification of Osiris."[375]

In both the Driving of the Four Calves and the consecration of the *meret*-chests, the number four features prominently. It is the number of calves driven toward Osiris, Horus and deified Amenirdis in the former ritual, and the number of chests presented to Osiris and deified Amenirdis in the latter. A rite enacted during the festival of Min may shed light on the cosmic significance of this number. At some point during the festival, the king "orders the release of four birds. They are to proclaim to the South, North, West and East that 'just as Horus, the son of Isis and Osiris, has received the white and red crown, so has the king of Upper and Lower Egypt received the white and red crown.'" [376] Proclaiming the king's accession at, or toward, the four cardinal points ensured his universal authority. By association the number four used in both rituals also signifies the king, and the god's universal power. The same association is more explicitly stated in the Rites of Protection at the Cenotaph. For there, just as the king bats the four balls towards the four cardinal points, so the Gods' Wife directs her arrows toward four targets that symbolically stand for the four cardinal points.[377]

Through their mythical references to Osiris and their various socio-political implications, both the Driving of the Four Calves and the Presentation of the *meret*-

chests served the purpose of asserting the king's dominion, not only over all of Egypt, but universally.[378] Apart from Shepenwepet II, and with the exception of Hatshepsut, who performed these rights in her capacity as "king" of Egypt always properly attired as a king, and assuming full (masculine) costume and regalia of a king, no other female is depicted performing those two essentially royal rites. Shepenwepet's assumption of the specific iconography of these two rites may be closely related to her appearance as the beneficiary of the royal rite *par excellence*: the celebration of the *sed* festival.

Celebrating the *sed* festival

In January 1951, the *American Journal of Archaeology* published a photograph of a block recovered a year earlier during the course of excavation work conducted by the French mission in the vicinity of the Temple of Monthu in North Karnak.[379] The block depicted an enthroned figure wearing a long garment and carrying two long scepters. The garment's hem is visible a few inches above the ankles, while the forked end of one of the scepters can be seen above the rightward oriented toes of the figure. The cubic throne is set on a broad, flat base, whose sides curve downward, resembling a giant *neb*-basket.

Facing the throne is the much smaller figure of a male priest who, donning an elaborately braided side-lock and a broad collar extends his right arm toward the enthroned figure. Only his upper body is visible, his hand, curved downward, almost touches the forked end of the scepter. Above his head are three long-necked birds, which spell the Egyptian word *bau*, or "souls." In the narrow space between the priest and the throne is the figure of a bald, clean-shaven male, who like the throne's occupant, faces right. Represented at a much smaller scale than the priest, his head is depicted immediately under the priest's elbow. Like the priest, only the figure's upper body survives on this block – and like the priest, this figure too wears a broad collar. Partially visible next to the enthroned figure's knee is the lower part of a falcon, the hieroglyphic sign for "Horus."

This block was among several others recovered while clearing the six-course Ptolemaic platform that stood in front of the temple of Monthu in North Karnak.[380] Almost of equal size, the recovered blocks were all small and squarely cut.[381] Belonging primarily to two Nubian structures, Taharqo's colonnade and a building dedicated by the God's Wives Shepenwepet II and Amenirdis II, the blocks were all newly hewn under Nubian rule, none dating to earlier periods.[382]

Blocks belonging to the building of the God's Wives were exclusively recovered from the northern part of the fourth base of foundation A of the temple. Many of the blocks belonging to the God's Wives' edifice were decorated on two sides.[383] This particular feature enabled the excavators to re-assemble the recovered blocks, and drawing on parallels with other structures, to reconstruct the original plan of the building. The main door to the edifice lay along its central axis and led to a large room onto which opened two much smaller side chambers. The building was also accessible via a side door that opened onto the largest of the three rooms. Inscriptions preserved on blocks belonging to the building's façade indicate that it was a chapel dedicated to Osiris, *Pededankh*, or "Osiris, who perpetually gives life."[384]

Figure 2.6 Amenirdis offering wine to Amun-Re, Chapel of Osiris, Ruler of Eternity, room I, north wall, upper register (Photo © M. Ayad)

Figure 2.8 Shepenwepet II offering wine to Osiris, Chapel of Osiris-Wennofer-who-is-in-the-Midst-of-the-Persea-Tree, room I, western wall, detail (Photo © M. Ayad)

Figure 2.10 Shepwepet II offers a *hekenou*-jar to Ra-Horakhy, funerary chapel of Amenirdis at Medinet Habu, courtyard, south wall, eastern half, lower register (Photo © M. Ayad)

Figure 2.11 Shepwepet II offers a hekenou-jar to Ra-Horakhy, Isis and deified Amenirdis, funerary chapel of Amenirdis at Medinet Habu, courtyard, south wall, eastern half, lower register (Photo © M. Ayad)

Figure 2.14 Ankhnesneferibre offers *Maat* to Amun-Re, Mut, and Khonsu, chapel of Amasis and Nitocris, vestibule, southern wall (Photo © M. Ayad)

Figure 2.19 Chapel of Osiris-Wennofer-*Neb-djefa*, a) southern door jamb, b) northern door jamb (Photos © M. Ayad)

Figure 2.20a Taharqo embraced by Osiris, Chapel of Osiris, Lord of Life, southern door jamb (Photo © M. Ayad)

Figure 2.20b Shepenwepet embraced by Isis, Chapel of Osiris, Lord of Life, northern door jamb (Photo © M. Ayad)

Figure 2.21a Ankhnesneferibre, who receives life from Isis, Chapel of Amasis and Nitocris, room I, northern door jamb (Photo © M. Ayad)

Figure 2.21b Psametik (III) receives life from Harsiese; Chapel of Amasis and Nitocris, room I, southern door jamb (Photo © M. Ayad)

Figure 2.23 God's Wife burning fans bearing the image of Egypt's enemies; Hatshepsut's *chapelle rouge*, inner sanctuary, north wall; Karnak Open Museum (Photo © M. Ayad)

Figure 3.2 Hatshepsut's *chapelle rouge*, inner sanctuary, north wall; Karnak Open Museum (Photo © M. Ayad)

Figure 2.25 Shepenwepet II, funerary chapel of Amenirdis, courtyard; southern wall, eastern half, upper register (Photo © M. Ayad)

Figure 3.8 Amenirdis I embraced by Amun-Re, Chapel of Osiris-Wennofer-who-is-in-the-midst-of-the-Persea-tree, eastern door jamb; (Photo © M. Ayad)

Figure 3.9 Shepenwepet II embraced by Amun-Re, Chapel of Osiris-Wennofer-who-is-in-the midst-of-the-Persea-tree; western door jamb; (Photo © M. Ayad)

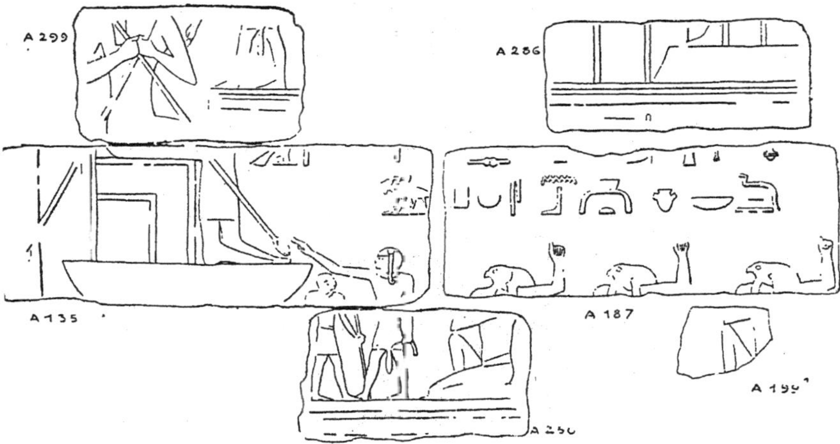

Figure 2.28 Shepenwepet II's celebration of the *sed* festival; (line drawing after Barguet and Leclant, *Karnak Nord IV*, pl CVI; reproduced with permission of the IFAO).

The building was constructed during the tenure of Shepenwepet II, who figures very prominently in its decorative scheme. The date of construction may be further defined as occurring after the death of Amenirdis I and before the adoption of Amenirdis II into office. When it does occur in this chapel, Amenirdis I's name is included only in inscriptions giving Shepenwepet's filiation, where it is always followed by the epithet *maat-kherou*, or "justified", indicating her decease prior to the building's construction and decoration. On the other hand, Amenirdis's (II) name occasionally occurs on the recovered blocks, where it is always followed by the epithet *ankh.ti*, or "alive." The building was thus probably constructed in the last few years of the Taharqo's reign (690–664 BC). Alternatively, it may have been decorated sometime during the first nine years of Psametik I's reign (664–656 BC) before the installation of Psametik's daughter as God's Wife. Nitocris was not appointed as God's Wife until Psametik's ninth regnal year.[385] It was during these turbulent years marking the transition from Nubian to Saite rule, particularly prior to Psametik I's assumption of full control of the Theban region, that the God's Wife of Amun along with Mentuemhat, the mayor of Thebes and fourth prophet of Amun, assumed effective rule of Thebes.[386]

Four engaged columns with Hathoric heads decorated the façade of the building, which was about 12 meters long and 5 meters high. The left-hand side of the façade was dominated by a larger than life representation of the God's Wife receiving life from Amun-Re, who holds the God's Wife's hand, even as he extends an *ankh*-sign to her nose. The God's Wife wears a long lappet wig surmounted by the vulture headdress and a long tight sheath dress. She is identified as Shepenwepet, "alive."[387] Blocks belonging to the left door jamb depict the God's Wife wearing a short wig surmounted by a vulture headdress, as she receives an *ankh*-sign. The figure of the deity holding the *ankh*-sign does not survive.[388] Although fewer blocks belonging to the other half of the façade survive, the decoration and inscriptions preserved on those few blocks indicate that the decoration of the façade was perfectly symmetrical.

The decorative scheme of the interior of the chapel, on the other hand, seems to have been quite complex.[389] The blocks belonging to the façade of the building were particularly useful in reconstructing the scenes of the inner wall, as almost all the blocks bore decoration on their reverse side of scenes belonging to that wall. On the reverse side of the façade, the wall to the left of the doorway was divided into three registers. It is to the middle register of that wall that the block described at the beginning of this section belongs. Other blocks belonging to the same wall enable us to determine the gender identity of the throne's occupant. The occupant's upper body is that of a woman, her breast, shown in profile, delicately curves in the space under her arm pit, her nipple touching her upper arm, partially overlapping with it. Two scepters, held in her hands, diagonally overlap across her chest. In her right hand, she holds a scepter whose forked tip is visible on the lower block. That scepter slants diagonally forward, its forked end almost touching the tip of her toes, while the tip of the other scepter can be seen behind her throne (Figure 2.28). Inscriptions preserved on other blocks belonging to the same wall clearly identify her as "the God's wife, Shepenwepet, given life, [Daughter of] the God's Hand, Amenirdis, the justified."[390] The enthroned figure is thus none other than Shepenwepet II, daughter of the Nubian king Piye of the Twenty-fifth dynasty.

Parallel representations place this scene at the center of a *sed* celebration. The throne on which Shepenwepet sits is placed on a special platform that resembles a *neb*-basket (Gardiner's sign list # V 30), but is actually a *heb*-basin (Gardiner's sign list # W 3).[391] Gardiner has suggested that this particular receptacle was characteristic of Upper Egypt.[392] Known as *sepa*, this special form of the carrying chair was characteristic of Upper Egyptian kings and, along with the platform that supports it, regularly appears in scenes depicting the *sed* celebrations.[393] A similarly set throne is seen, for example, in the festival hall erected by Thutmosis III Menkheperre at Karnak. There, wall reliefs depict Thutmosis III seated on an identical throne, which is set on a similar basket-like platform.[394] Clad in an archaic *sed* robe, Thutmosis III, like Shepenwepet, holds two diagonally crossed scepters in his clenched fists.

The other blocks recovered from the same trench enable us to identify the other figures represented in the scene. Opposite the God's Wife are two registers separated by the Egyptian sign for sky (*pet*) – the base line of the upper register ending near her elbow. On the upper level is a bare-chested male, wearing a short kilt that stops above his knees, holding a staff in his left hand, while his right hand hangs parallel to his body behind him, as he advances toward Shepenwepet. On the lower register, a similarly attired individual stands next to the *sepa* platform. Depicted on a much smaller scale than the God's Wife, like the God's Wife, he is orientated toward the right. His hair closely cropped, he wears a broad collar and a short kilt that stops well above his knees. The falcon inscribed next to Shepenwepet's knees provides a caption for this individual. He is "Horus, the Behdite." [395] Horus, the Behdite, sometimes also referred to in the literature as "Horus of Libya"[396] also appears in the fragmentary scenes depicting the *sed* celebrations of Niussere recovered from his sun temple at Abu Sir,[397] as well as those showing Thutmosis III's *sed* festival, and Osorkon II's, whose *sed* festival is depicted on the façade of his temple at Bubastis. Facing him is the slightly larger figure of a priest donning a side-lock. Clad in a panther skin, the tail of the animal hanging between his legs, this individual is a *sem*-priest or an *Iunmoutef*-priest. Both priests share the panther-skin priestly attire. They also had similar cultic duties. Assuming the role of the eldest son, the *sem*-priest performed significant portions of the Opening of the Mouth ceremony, both on cult statues in the temple, and in a funerary context.[398] *Iunmoutef*-priests were likewise funerary priests whose roles were often performed by the eldest son in the funerary cult, but an *Iunmoutef* priest seems to have had the additional responsibility of serving the cult of the royal *ka*. Indeed, Horus, as the true and ultimate supporter of his mother was also sometimes referred to as *Iunmoutef* (literally, "The-Pillar-of-His-Mother").[399] The priest extends his arm toward the God's Wife's scepter, his downward-curved palm almost touching its forked end. In so doing, his arm crosses over the smaller figure represented next to the God's Wife, his elbow above the head of the rightward-orientated male. Behind the priest are three squatting falcon-headed men, who with clenched fists pound their chests. Partially identified by the accompanying texts as the "souls of Pe," they acclaim the God's Wife, and wish her "all health and happiness for ever."[400] Above the souls of Pe, to the far right of the upper register, are two vertical poles. These poles may represent the bottom of two divine standards, which would have supported the formless skin characteristic of the god Khonsu and the emblem of Wepwawet. Similar standards may be seen in the *sed* celebration of Thutmosis III at the *Akhmenou* in Karnak.[401] As the "opener of the ways," Wepwawet was considered a guide, not just for the dead, but also in temple ritual, often acting as a master of ceremonies. He was a messenger of the gods, but also a "champion of royalty." Wepwawet's standard also came to symbolize Upper Egypt in processions.[402] The standards were posted in front of a structure, the lower part of which is still visible on the blocks. Similar structures are preserved in *sed* scenes belonging to earlier kings. The standards are found, for instance, in front of a similar structure in the *sed* scenes of the Fifth Dynasty king Niussere.

The block published in the *American Journal of Archaeology* was part of a much larger scene sequence that depicted the celebration of the *sed* festival. Indeed, the entire representation depicted on the blocks of Shepenwepet II is entirely too similar to the representations of the *sed* festivals celebrated by Tuthmosis III and Osorkon II to be anything else.

The recovery of these blocks caused an academic stir as they seemed to depict a woman, a God's Wife, celebrating the *sed* festival, the royal rite "*par excellence*."[403] Leclant gave the God's Wife a status equal to the king's, on the basis that if she enjoyed the same privilege of celebrating the *sed* festival, assuming much of the same iconography, then she must have also enjoyed the same kind of royal authority.[404] This kind of statement, however, remains largely unsubstantiated. It begs several questions. What exactly is royal authority? And how did the *sed* festival relate to it, confirm it, or renew it? Was she the first woman to celebrate the *sed* festival? If so, then what was the impetus for the celebration of the *sed* festival? And what exactly do scholars mean when they refer to the *sed* festival as a royal rite *par excellence*? How is it a royal rite? And in what respect is it special? and what does this discovery tell us, both about the celebration and about the status of the God's Wife?

Conventionally referred to as a "jubilee," or a "thirty-year" festival, Bleeker has carefully demonstrated the inaccuracy of both designations, suggesting that both were "misleading" and hindered the proper understanding of the festival.[410] In his examination of the historical evidence for the *sed* festival, however, Murnane seemed to accept the thirty-year designation unquestionably, suggesting that Hatshepsut and Osorkon II either modified or ignored the "the thirty-year principle" when celebrating their own *sed* festivals.[411] He similarly observed that Amenhotep I and Shoshenq I, who both reigned for fewer than thirty years, may have erected "Jubilee buildings before they died – if indeed they waited to observe the thirty-year term within their own reigns."[412] Bleeker further argued that the irregularity of celebrating the *sed* festival made it an inadequately random method of affirming the king's *royal*, or official, authority. Admitting that the purpose for celebrating the *sed* festival cannot be determined precisely nor can it be found "in the cycle of seasons or in the regular course of the life of the king or his people," Bleeker, nonetheless, affirms that the motivation for celebrating the *sed* festival must have been "particularly urgent," or it would not have been celebrated by kings of "such … great caliber as Sesostris III, Amenhotep III and Ramses II." [413] As for the re-affirmation and re-establishment of the king's royal authority, Bleeker suggested that the annually celebrated Min festival, precisely because of its regularity, was a more appropriate venue for that purpose.

Drawing on one of the basic meanings of the Egyptian word *sed*, Bleeker further suggested that it was, literally, a "festival of the cloth," in which the king was invested with his priestly duties, and his capacity as the ultimate high priest of Egypt renewed.[414] According to this theory, the investiture of the king's priestly authority occurred at the exact moment in which the king put on the special archaic *sed* robe. The act of donning the *sed* garment thus became the most sacral and, therefore, the most mysterious aspect of the ritual. Bleeker further argued that it was because of its special sanctity that the robing ceremony is never actually depicted among the scenes of the *sed* festival.[415] If Bleeker is correct in suggesting that the main purpose of the *sed* festival was the investiture and renewal of the king's high-priestly office, then this view would account for Shepenwepet's ability to celebrate this particularly exclusively royal festival.

Whereas the recovered blocks depicted, and belonged to, Shepenwepet II, the evidence suggests that her predecessor, her adoptive mother Amenirdis I was the first known God's Wife to *receive* the *sed* symbols. The symbols depict "two chapels placed side by side, each containing an empty throne placed on a dais with sloping sides or on the (purification) scale, which also serve as the basis of the determinative of the word 'festival' (*heb*)."[405] On at least three separate occasions, Amenirdis receives the *sed* symbols: twice from the goddess Mut and once from Thoth. She receives the *sed* symbol from the goddess Mut on the façade of her funerary chapel at Medinet Habu and in the chapel of Osiris, Ruler of Eternity, where the scene occurs on the east wall of room I.[406] The third instance also occurs in the chapel of Osiris, Ruler of Eternity (Figure 2.2). On the eastern door jamb of the chapel's entrance, Thoth is represented with Amenirdis on the bottom register. Oriented toward the left, Thoth "Lord of the Eighth nome … the great god …" is depicted coming out of the chapel. In his hand, he holds 𓁨, the hieroglyphic sign for "millions." He gives Amenirdis *sed* symbols, and addressing her, Thoth appropriately wishes Amenirdis millions of *sed* festivals.[407]

While the decorative scheme of Amenirdis's funerary chapel may have been designed and executed under Shepenwepet's direction, and may accordingly date to roughly the same general period as Shepenwepet's blocks, the representations in the chapel of Osiris, Ruler of Eternity, were executed during Amenirdis's lifetime and definitely predated Shepenwepet's blocks. Receiving *sed* symbols does not necessarily indicate that the recipient celebrated the *sed* festival.[408] Agreeing with Hornung and Steahelin, Murnane consented that

> the very common "I have given you jubilees" uttered by a divinity is a wish of sorts, frequently attested under monarchs who never celebrated a jubilee, and is rightly worthless from a historian's standpoint. Sometimes the wish is directly expressed in the god's response to the Pharaoh: thus Amun, addressing Ramses II, says, "May you celebrate Jubilees, may you repeat Jubilee(s), may you be rejuvenated like the moon." And ithyphallic Amun replies to Amenhotep III, "May you repeat millions of Jubilees."[409]

Nonetheless, it is still remarkable that a woman, a God's Wife, should be represented receiving these exclusively royal symbols. Equally remarkable is the fact that this representation dates to the Twenty-fifth dynasty, Nubian dynasty and no earlier. Indeed, it seems that this act was celebrated and that such representations were not merely symbolic.

3

AVENUES TO LEGITIMACY

> ... appearing in glory with the White Crown, the Chosen one of Re, who issued from his flesh ...
>
> Chapel of Osiris, Ruler of Eternity

Assumption of the priesthood

While Shepenwepet II's unique *sed* iconography may have signified her investiture with priestly duties, it was not until the advent of Saite rule in Egypt that a woman finally assumed the title and duties of the High Priest of Amun. In 585 BC, Ankhnesneferibre, daughter of Psametik II became the first Egyptian woman to attain the high distinction of being, formally and officially, known as the High Priest(ess) of Amun. This distinction was also shared by her heiress apparent, Nitocris (B), daughter of king Amasis, who became a High Priest(ess) of Amun in 569 BC or shortly thereafter.[1] While the Saite princesses' assumption of the priesthood represents a clear break from previous Egyptian practice, it may be understood as the culmination of a long process that had begun with the installation of Shepenwepet I, and gained momentum under Nubian rule. Indeed, the ritual scenes discussed in Part II clearly indicate that Ankhnesneferibre's appointment to the high priesthood merely gave formal expression to an already existing situation. What exactly prompted this acquiescence is not exactly clear, although an understanding of the relationship between the High Priest and the King on the one hand and the interaction of the God's Wife with the palace and the priesthood on the other may prove helpful. Indeed, the Saite princesses' assumption of the priesthood may be viewed as a direct result of the Saite rulers' "secularism;"[2] a secularism that was manifest, in part, in a marked lack of generosity towards the temple establishments.

The gradual appropriation of priestly duties

Already in the chapel of Osiris, Ruler of Eternity, the Libyan God's Wife Shepenwepet I took on the primary function of consecrating offerings to the gods. Indeed, she is represented in that chapel fifteen times – a number of depictions that surpasses

Figure 3.1 Chapel of Osiris, Ruler of Eternity, room II, western wall, lower register (line drawing © Lyla Brock)

those scenes showing either her father, the ruling king, or her brother, his co-regent.[3] That Shepenwepet would appear as the main officiant in this chapel (Figure 3.1) is particularly astounding in light of the concomitant depiction of both her father Osorkon III and her brother Takeloth III in the same chapel. As king of Upper and Lower Egypt, Osorkon III was theoretically the ultimate high priest of the land. Moreover, Takeloth III, Osorkon's co-regent, was formerly the High Priest of Amun.[4]

In effect, the representations found in the chapel of Osiris, Ruler of Eternity, propagated Shepenwepet's new role as the main cultic officiant, a role that was formerly carried out by the High priest of Amun. In his seminal study on the Third Intermediate Period, Kitchen admits that the circumstances surrounding the high priesthood of Amun "*after* the accession of Takeloth III remain a total mystery," noting a forty-year gap in which the office of High Priest of Amun remained vacant.[5] It is possible that Shepenwepet's appointment as a God's Wife was a measure intended to fill the gap caused by Takeloth III's elevation to the Egyptian throne. In the wake of civil war, leaving the high priesthood of Amun with no Theban incumbent may have been a deliberate measure designed to secure the king's position and protect his throne from the rival claims of powerful, and potentially dangerous, family members. In this way, the office of the God's Wife of Amun may have been re-introduced at this particular point in time, the Twenty-third dynasty, precisely so that it may substitute for the office of High Priest of Amun. Rather than appointing a male family member, who could potentially use his position to engender a rival dynasty, a pliable young woman posed little threat. Removing the office from the coffers of the king's chief wife and re-vamping it so that the title of God's Wife of Amun would go to a loyal royal princess was also a measure designed to keep the Theban priesthood under tight leash. A royal wife needed to be next to her husband, residing with him at his royal residence in the Delta, while a young princess, whose singlehood would ensure her total loyalty to her father, the king, could be sent to Thebes to oversee her father's interests there. Unable to produce offspring of her own, the God's Wife could not use her enormous influence to generate a rival dynastic line.[6]

The scenes preserved in the chapel of Osiris, Ruler of Eternity, suggest that Amenirdis built on the religious and ritualistic achievements of her predecessor to gain legitimacy as a God's Wife. Amenirdis took her own duties a step further. Scenes showing Amenirdis I presenting offerings to the gods abound in this chapel (for instance, her presentation of wine to Amun).[7] But, exceptionally, Amenirdis appears next to the goddess Seshat in the rite of *pedj-sesher* or "Stretching the Cord" (Figure 2.15). Oftentimes, this rite symbolically summed up the entire ritual sequence performed at the laying of a new temple foundation. Undoubtedly, this was also the case in the chapel of Osiris, Ruler of Eternity. Furthermore, on the northern wall of the first room, Amenirdis presents an image of a temple to Amun (Figure 2.16).[8] While similar scenes showing the king next to the goddess Seshat abound, never before had a women been depicted laying the temple foundation or presenting a temple to its inhabitant. Even more significantly, on the east wall of the same room, Amenirdis receives *sed* symbols from the goddess Mut (Figures 2.1, 2.2).[9] While the receipt of the *sed* symbols does not necessarily indicate a celebration of the *sed* festival, receiving those symbols had a tremendous symbolic value. Shabaqo appears on the façade of the chapel of Osiris, Ruler of Eternity, receiving *sed* symbols from Amun-Re (Figure 1. 3) as do numerous New Kingdom rulers. However, Amenirdis is the first woman known to be associated with the *sed* festival in this particular way. Unlike other women previously depicted participating in this royal festival, Amenirdis does not appear in a secondary, supportive role, next to the king as he receives those symbols. Instead, Amenirdis appears as the recipient of those highly honored symbols.

In a further progression, Amenirdis's successor Shepenwepet II seems to have celebrated the *sed* festival. In a series of blocks recovered from North Karnak, Shepenwepet II appears in several key moments of the celebration (Figure 2.28).[10] Appropriating the iconography of this exclusively royal ritual, Shepenwepet seems to have assumed the ultimate religious honor celebrated by an Egyptian king. Indeed, the power of the God's Wife of Amun peaked during the tenure of Shepenwepet II. In addition to celebrating the *sed* festival, Shepenwepet II assumed the strictly royal iconography of the ritual driving of the four calves and the consecration of the *meret*-chests.[11] Preserved on the walls of Amenirdis's funerary chapel at Medinet Habu, both rituals were enacted for the benefit of Shepenwepet's adoptive mother Amenirdis I. Shepenwepet II is also the God's Wife seen next to king Taharqo, partnering with him in the Rites of the Protection at the Cenotaph (Figure 2.22).[12]

Indeed, the rise of the priestly powers of the God's Wife of Amun coincides with a fifty-year gap during which the office of the High Priest of Amun remained vacant.[13] Further, the religious prominence of the Nubian God's Wives of Amun eclipses the earliest attested Nubian High Priest of Amun, Haremakhet who was appointed to office by his father, King Shabaqo. Neither Haremakhet, however, nor his son Harkhebit, who succeeded him to office, seems to have wielded as much power as their predecessors in office. Likewise, neither is featured prominently in the extant iconographic and textual evidence or accorded the civil and military positions occupied by their predecessors.[14] Indeed, while Harkhebit appears among a procession of priests during an oracular procession of the god Amun, administrative control of the Theban region was shared between the successive high stewards of the estate of the God's Wife, particularly Harwa and Akhmenrou, and the all-powerful mayor of Thebes, Montuemhat, while army leadership fell into the hands of Taharqo, who would later become the penultimate king of the Nubian dynasty.[15]

The exact reason that prompted Shabaqo to appoint his son to the priesthood remains unclear. Although the exact date of his appointment cannot be determined precisely, it has been suggested that Haremakhet's appointment to the priesthood may have been an attempt on Shabaqo's part to gain legitimacy in Egypt as he could not achieve the requisite legitimacy through the appointment of a God's Wife, since that position was already occupied by Amenirdis I and Shepenwepet II.[16] Haremakhet's appointment may be better viewed, however, in terms of Shabaqo's program to assume, or resurrect, older traditions. Just as moving his residence to Memphis signaled Shabaqo's desire to be viewed as an Egyptian king, so also his appointment of his son as High Priest may be considered an attempt to assert himself as a restorer of all things Egyptian. His policy seems to have worked. It is Shabaqo who appears as the first king of the Twenty-fifth dynasty in Manetho's account of Egyptian history.

The increasing religious prominence of the God's Wives may be partly attributed to their ethnic background. Scholars have noted the fragmentary nature of Libyan rule and their tendency to divide rule among semi-autonomous fiefdoms.[17] Likewise, the matriarchial tendencies of Egypt's southern neighbor have also been noted. In a recent study on the queens of Kush, Angelika Lohwasser noted the special status of the ruler's sister in choosing the rightful successor to the Nubian throne.[18] But because the exact dynamics of the king's sister's involvement in the transmission of the throne is still not quite clear, it is perhaps more prudent to look elsewhere for reasons for the unprecedented rise of the God's Wife of Amun during the Twenty-fifth dynasty.

The ritualistic elevation of the God's Wife during the Twenty-fifth dynasty may be attributed to the somewhat more egalitarian power-sharing model of the Nubian ruling house. In a recent study on the Egyptian term for "king's brother" (Egyptian: *sen nesou*), Jean Revez demonstrated that, as an official title, this term is virtually non-existent in Egyptian historical documents prior to the Twenty-fifth dynasty.[19] In his thorough study, Revez clearly showed that, as a group, the "king's brothers" are regularly attested only during the Twenty-fifth dynasty.[20] In Egyptian, the term for brother, "*sen*" may also be translated as "companion," "peer," or "equal."[21] Lateral transmission of royal power under Nubian rule is well documented. Taharqo's election decree, for instance, narrates the election of the king from among a group of his peers. Labeled the "best among his brothers," King Taharqo was, in effect, the "first among equals." It was this lateral, more egalitarian model of rule and power-sharing that allowed Shebitqo to appoint his brother as the army commander-in-chief.

> Now when His Majesty was in … (Nubia) as a recruit, a king's brother, … he came sailing northwards to … (Thebes) in the midst of the recruits for whom His Majesty, King Shebitqo, justified had sent to … (Nubia), in order that he (Taharqo) might be there with him (Shebitqo), because he (Shebitqo) loved him (Taharqo) more than all his (other) brothers.[22]
>
> (Kawa stela IV dating to Taharqo's sixth regnal year)

Ideally, the king was the commander-in-chief of the Egyptian army. By delegating military leadership to his brother, Shebitqo was, in effect, relinquishing an aspect of his royal powers. It is only under Nubian rule that we find a more lateral model of the transmission of royal power, with texts expounding on the fact that the king was "first among equals." It is conceivable that a similar power-sharing ideal applied to the Nubians' view of temple ritual. Just as the king could delegate the command of the armies to a brother, he also delegated his role in the temple to one of his sisters. In this way, that the God's Wife's receipt of *sed*-symbols and celebration of the *sed* festival occurring during the Nubian rule of Egypt can hardly be viewed as coincidental.

Saite secularism

The Saite kings' pragmatic approach to kingship and their "secular" approach to governance enabled them to take full advantage of the priestly achievements of the Nubian God's Wives of Amun and utilize their accomplishments. Instead of revoking the priestly privileges of the God's Wife, under Saite rule the God's Wife's priestly duties took on a formal expression. It is the Saites, not the Libyans nor the Nubians, who monumentalized the official decrees installing their royal princesses as God's Wives of Amun. No such decrees survive for the other God's Wives. Their formalization of the God's Wife's position is evident in their formally documenting Nitocris's appointment through an official "transfer of title" document, as well as in their bestowing the titles of the High Priest of Amun on Ankhnesneferibre, even while she was still an "heiress apparent." While the latter's elevation to office may be viewed as an official sanction of a pre-existing situation, it may also be considered a by-product of Saite secularism seen, for example, in an official negligence of the temple establishments. It has been noted that the Saite kings broke away from the tradition of bestowing large land endowments and lavishing other gifts on the temples. Spalinger noted that no offerings were made to Neith, the Saite kings' patron titular deity, after military victories.[23] Prior to Saite rule, such gifts were an almost mandatory expression of the rulers' gratitude and religiosity. It is equally important to keep in mind that, under the Saites, Thebes "was no longer the religious capital of the land."[24]

The God's Wife and initiation rites

While the Nitocris Adoption Stela had a more administrative bent to it, detailing as it did the exact amounts of provisions and agricultural lands granted Nitocris, Ankhnesneferibre's text had a distinct priestly bent to it. Compared with the courtly language of Nitocris's Adoption decree, Ankhnesnefeibre's stela seems to present her installation from the priesthood's point of view. Accordingly, it sheds more light on the process of the God's Wife's investiture with priestly authority. For example, it is clear from the Ankhnesneferibre stela that certain "initiation" rites were performed to mark the installation of a God's Wife:

> The King's daughter, first prophet Ankhnesneferibre went to the temple of Amun-Re, king of the gods, prophets, gods' fathers, *wab*-priests, lector priests, the priesthood of the temple of Amun following her, great courtiers at their head. There was performed for her every ritual of initiation of a divine adoratress of Amun into the temple by the scribe of the divine book and great *wab*-priests of this temple. There were tied for her the amulets and all the adornments of a God's Wife and divine adoratress of Amun, who appears with the two-feathered crown (on) her head as the mistress of everything which the Aten encompasses.[25]

After these initiation rites, Ankhnesneferibre's official titulary was coined. Thus, it seems that despite her position as the High Priest of Amun, Ankhnesneferibre sought to fulfill every proper aspect of ritual as she became a God's Wife of Amun.

Purification rites

While the text of the Ankhnesneferibre Adoption Stela does not elaborate on the nature of the initiation rites associated with the induction of a God's Wife, scenes preserved in Hatshepsut's *chapelle rouge* at Karnak shed some light on the type of ritual purification that a God's Wife needed to undergo in order to enter the temple.[26] Shown in profile, her face turned to the right, an unnamed God's Wife stands, her feet immersed in ankle-deep water (Figure 3.2 in the plates section).[27] Her back slightly bent, she leans forward. Her two arms, depicted before her bent body, seem to issue from the same shoulder. Her hair is gathered in a bonnet, held in place by a tied ribbon. It is clear that she wears a belt, its two round finials appearing on either side of her body. Her dress, however, clings very closely to her body, which gives the impression that she is nude. This impression is further enforced by the absence of a hem line at her ankles. The hem line may have been assimilated into the line showing the water level at her feet. Inscriptions associated with this scene indicate that the God's Wife is depicted standing in the sacred lake, termed in Egyptian "the pool of cool water," where she was ritually bathed. A stream of water, represented by a wavy line above her head and in front of her body, is being poured from a jar. Issuing from a jar depicted on the adjoining block (no. 140), the same stream of water is also shown above the heads of two men who stand behind the God's Wife.[28] To the right, two columns of framed inscriptions provide a caption to the scene. The texts, which are inscribed in retrograde, read: "Going down to be purified by the God's servants and the God's Wife, the God's Hand, in the *Qebehyt* pool, in order to enter into the temple [lit."God's Estate"]."[29] *Qebehyt* is a term derived from the Egyptian word "or purify."[30] This scene indicates that the God's Wife, just like other members of the priesthood, had to undergo certain "initiation" or "induction" rites of ritual purification before she could proceed to certain parts of the temple. It is precisely this kind of washing, as well as the acquisition of official insignia that marks her as an "initiate" of the temple, of the same degree as a *hem-netjer* priest (traditionally translated as "prophet").[31]

Priestly companions and priestly rank

Generally speaking, the scenes preserved at Hatshepsut's *chapelle rouge* indicate that already in the Eighteenth dynasty, the God's Wife enjoyed the same privileges as the members of the highest echelon of the priesthood. There, the God's Wife is consistently shown next to *hem-netjer* priests (God's Servants, or Prophets) and *it-netjer* priests (God's Father), who were themselves a select group of the *hem-netjer* priests.[32] And just as the God's Wife was shown next to those priests during the requisite purification rites, so also she appears along with two *it-netjer* priests ("God's Father"). The God's Wife, who stands behind the two priests, adores the seventeen gods of Karnak during their evening meal (Figure 3.3).[33] Shown in profile, her face is turned to the right, a broad tapering shoulder strap that starts just below her breast holds her tight sheath dress in place as she raises her arms in adoration mimicking the attitude of the two priests that accompany her. The God's Wife hair is gathered close to her skull, a band tied at the back of her head holds her bonnet in place, while the finials of a belt worn just below her waist appear on either side of her body.

Figure 3.3 Hatshepsut's *chapelle rouge*, inner sanctuary, north wall; Karnak Open Museum (Photo © M. Ayad)

A God's Wife similarly partners with a God's Father priest in the ritual burning of fans bearing the image of Egypt's enemies (Figure 2.23).[34] The ritual, designed to rid Egypt of its enemies, was considered one of a number of activities that blurred the line between religion and magic and was considered an indication of state-sponsored magic in ancient Egypt.[35] Along with an *Iunmoutef* priest (literally "the pillar of his mother"), a God's Wife clears the way before the pharaoh in the rites performed at *Djeme*.[36] This poorly attested ritual is attested twice: once in the Twenty-third dynasty chapel of Osiris, Ruler of Eternity, in East Karnak, where it occurs on the eastern/innermost wall of the inner chamber, and another along the northern wall of room E in the Edifice of Taharqo by the Sacred Lake.[37] Donning a panther skin and a youthful side-lock, *Iunmoutef* priests were typically attached to the cult of *Iunmoutef*, a deity venerated in the Ninth Upper Egyptian nome. *Iunmoutef* priests, whose title was directly derived from the deity they served, seem to have functioned very similarly to *sem*-priests in temple and funerary ritual. Assuming the role of the eldest son, a *sem*-priest performed significant portions of the Opening of the Mouth ceremony, both at the temple and in the funerary cult.[38] *Iunmoutef* priests also seem to have served the cult of the royal *ka*.[39]

In the Third Intermediate Period, the God's Wife partners with several priests. In room E of the Edifice of Taharqo by the Sacred Lake, an unidentified God's Wife partners with four different priests in the ritual Elevation of the *tjest*-column (Figure 2.24).[40] The rite, which is depicted on the southern wall of room E, is enacted four times, for four different gods: Dedwen, Soped, Sobek, and Horus. In each of the episodes, the God's Wife partners with a different priest. Thus, she appears with the "Opener of the Two Doors of the Sky" (Egyptian: *Wenenwy aawy-pet*) when elevating Dedwen, a god associated with Nubia The "two doors of the sky" referred to the door-leaves of the shrine that housed the cult statue, which would have been pulled open by the highest-ranking *hem-netjer* priest, i.e. the High Priest of Amun.[41] In the next episode, she partners with a *smaty*-priest when elevating the statue of the god Soped, a god associated with Asia. The bald-headed priest wears "a long kilt and a sash across his bare chest."[42] A *smaty*-priest (known as a "*stolist*" during the Ptolemaic period) was responsible for dressing the god during the Daily Cult Ritual.[43] Chosen from the ranks of the *hem-netjer* priests, and having the distinguished privilege of beholding, and dressing the god daily, *stolists* were among the highest ranking clergy in an Egyptian temple. This particular *smaty*-priest is linked to *hout-ka* (literally, "estate of the *ka*-spirit"), a temple that was located in the Twentieth Lower Egyptian nome.[44] Crocodile-headed Sobek is represented in the third episode of this ritual. He is elevated by a God's Wife and a priest, whose figure and titles are quite damaged. The captions link Sobek to Libya.[45] The final episode of the ritual depicts the God's Wife and a "*senty-wer*" priest elevating falcon-headed Horus. The "*senty-wer*" priesthood is poorly attested and, therefore, not fully understood.[46] While Kees suggested that the *senty-wer* referred to a section at Karnak that embodied the "primeval mound of creation," his suggestion was summarily dismissed by Goyon.[47] However, Kees's suggestion may help explain why in this particular episode, the God's Wife is also identified by her secondary title of God's Hand. Evoking the Heliopolitan creation myth,[48] this title directly links the God's Wife with a particular priesthood known for its association with the most sacred space of Karnak. This link, if deliberate, may have served to proclaim the superior status of Horus as a creator god. Indeed, the texts emphasize his more superior status by linking him to Upper and Lower Egypt.[49]

The four priests who partnered with with the God's Wife in the ritual elevation of the *tjest*-column were clearly recruited from among the highest ranking *hem-netjer* priests. Yet, their leftward orientation seems to suggest their subordinate status to the God's Wife, whose rightward orientation clearly sets her at a higher rank.

Avenues to legitimacy

Assumption of the Priesthood was just one of several strategies utilized by the God's Wives to achieve legitimacy and secure their position in power.

Shepenwepet I

We have already seen the prominence given Shepenwepet I in the scenes preserved in the chapel of Osiris, Ruler of Eternity, particularly those scenes found on the façade of the chapel. There, we find Shepenwepet standing closer to Egypt's three national deities: Amun, Ra-Horakhty, and Ptah, than her father, King Osorkon.[50] Both king and God's Wife are engaged in pleasing the gods in this scene. Carrying her sistra in hand, the God's Wife appeases the gods through playing music to them, while the king provisions them through his consecration of offerings of food. Both actions were designed to make the three gods as content as possible to live in their terrestrial man-made abode. Showing their approval, Amun and Ra-Horakhty extend life- (*ankh*-) signs toward the royal officiants, Amun's touching Shepenwepet's hip.

Whether the scene depicts two ritual actions occurring in rapid succession or represents two simultaneous ritual acts taking place on either side of the offering table, the particular arrangement of this scene is peculiar. Shepenwepet's proximity to the gods, underscored by placing the elaborate offering table behind her, rather than between her and the gods, highlights her elevated status as she seems to play a more prominent role towards the gods than her father, the king. Throughout Egyptian history, in two- or three-dimensional art, women would take a more subordinate position to the male relatives represented next to them.[51] This was true regardless of whether the woman was represented next to her father, husband, or even her son.[52] This rule, elucidated by Gay Robins, resulted in placing women behind their fathers, husbands, or sons. Appearing behind his daughter, Osorkon III occupies the more subordinate position in this scene. It was possible that this was a deliberate gesture on his part designed to indicate his support and approval of his daughter's new role in temple ritual.

The offering scene described above occurs on the top register of the eastern part of the Libyan façade. On the other side of the multi-tiered false door that dominates the decoration of the façade, two remarkable scenes survive. On the upper register, Shepenwepet is suckled by Hathor, while on the lower register Amun seems to place a crown on her head.[53] With minor variants, the scenes inscribed on the western door jamb mirror those inscribed on the eastern jamb.

Suckling scenes

Two symmetrically opposed scenes occupy the upper register of the jambs. In both scenes, Shepenwepet is shown next to a goddess who stands much taller than Shepenwepet (Figure 3.4). The goddess's right hand cups her breast, holding it firmly in place as she offers it to Shepenwepet. With her right index finger, she touches Shepenwepet's under-chin in a gesture meant to cause an infant to open her mouth to receive her mother's milk. The goddess dons an elaborate crown, a broad collar, and a tight sheath dress that stops just above her ankles. The crowns depicted in both scenes are quite similar, composed of a disk flanked by two rearing cobras and surmounted by two tall plumes. In both scenes the goddess extends an arm behind Shepenwepet's head. In her hand, she holds an *ankh*-sign. Because her palm points upward, the goddess seems to be supporting Shepenwepet's tall, elaborate crown. In both scenes, Shepenwepet wears a long flowing dress, which appears to have wide sleeves, and a very elaborate crown. With its flowing layers, Shepenwepet's dress appears quite similar to the dress she wears when shaking the sistrum before the three deities. Her attire here, though, seems longer, with the possible addition of an extra layer. A sash tied just below her breast and above her natural waist gathers the flowing layers of her dress. The long ends of the sash hang loosely in front of her dress, decoratively

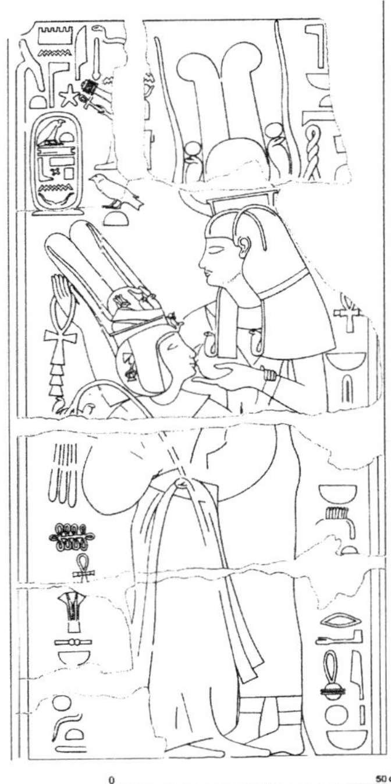

Figure 3.4 Chapel of Osiris, Ruler of Eternity, façade of Libyan chapel, door jambs, upper register (line drawing © Lyla Brock)

reaching down almost to the full length of her dress, which stops just above her ankles. On her head, Shepenwepet wears a short Nubian wig surmounted by the vulture headdress. A solar disk surmounted by two tall plumes and framed by Hathor's cow horns rest on a short, flat platform of rearing cobras, known as a *modius*. In this scene though, as in many other two-dimensional examples, the *modius* has been idealized so that the cobras are no longer visible.[54] In the space atop the *modius*, just in front of the solar disk, are the heads of two rearing cobras and a vulture. One cobra wears the crown of Upper Egypt, the other the crown of Lower Egypt, while the vulture appears to be wearing a version of the *atef*-crown on the left jamb and nothing in the corresponding scene on the right jamb. A vulture's leg is visible on the side of the wig, its claws grasping a *shen*-sign. In the hand closer to the viewer (right hand in the scene on the left; and left hand in the scene on the right), Shepenwepet holds a flagellum. The flagellum ends in three finials and is adorned with one rearing cobra on the left and two rearing cobras on the right.[55]

Scenes of a goddess suckling a king abound. For example, a limestone ostracon from Deir el-Medina depicts Seti I, wearing the blue crown, being suckled by a goddess.[56] A similar scene is engraved on the keyhole-shaped counterpoise of a *menat*-necklace of King Taharqo. A pendant worn at the back, the counterpoise balanced the considerable weight of the necklace. The scene depicts Taharqo, wearing the white crown of Upper and Lower Egypt, being suckled by a lion-headed goddess (Figure 3.5).[57] While in this example the goddess wears a long sheath dress, the king here appears in the nude. Just as the king was often depicted as an adolescent in such scenes, as seen for example on the Taharqo counterpoise, so is Shepenwepet depicted here as an adolescent girl. On the other hand, scenes showing queens or royal women

Figure 3.5 Counterpoise of King Taharqo's *menat*-necklace (reproduced with permission The Metropolitan Museum of Art, Bequest of W.Gedney Beatty, 1941 MMA 41.160.104©The Metropolitan Museum Of Art.)

represented in Shepenwepet's attitude are so rare in Egyptian art, that when they do occur, such scenes have been labeled "un-Egyptian."[58]

This rarity may be due to the special significance of receiving the milk of a goddess. In coronation rites, for instance, it was customary to depict the king being suckled by a goddess.[59] Furthermore, in a funerary context, the dead king is assimilated with a newborn through receiving the milk of a goddess. This process enables the king to live anew as a "beneficial spirit" in the afterlife. Suckling thus becomes a means of achieving resurrection.[60] Milk is also among the list of life-giving, or "vivifying," products mentioned in the Pyramid Texts (e.g. Pyr. 707 d). Protection and nutrition are also associated with milk.[61] In the Pyramid Texts, several passages discuss the suckling of the reigning king. A variety of goddesses appear in these passages. These include Isis, Nephthys, Selkit, and the goddess of el-Kab in her many forms, who was sometimes assimilated with Nut, Sekhat-Hor, or Semat-Weret (whose name literally means "Great Cow").[62] In the scenes depicted in the chapel of Osiris, Ruler of Eternity, Hathor suckles Shepenwepet on the western (= right) door jamb, while Semat-Weret appears in the corresponding scenes depicted on the opposite, eastern door jamb. The anonymous goddesses represented suckling Shepenwepet on the west wall of room II may be any of these goddess (Figure 3.1). In this poorly preserved scene, the goddess stands in a similar stance to the one preserved on the door jambs. Much taller than Shepenwepet, she turns to the right to face her young protégé. Shepenwepet still donning a short layered wig, tilts her head slightly upward to receive the goddess's nipple in her mouth. She wears a tight sheath dress, while on her head two crowns rest. Both crowns are the *peschent*: the distinctly royal crown of Upper and Lower Egypt. The crowns are arranged such that they face each other: the one on the left turned "backwards" to mirror the properly orientated crown on the right, a "unique occurrence in Egyptian iconography."[63] To the left of this vignette at the northern end of the wall, two figures stand watching this scene. Closest to Shepenwepet and her goddess is a "royal figure" holding staff and flail, followed by his wife, who likewise holds a flail.[64] The two figures are probably Shepenwepet's parents Osorkon (III) and his Chief Royal Wife, Karoatjet, named on the opposite wall (PM 13).[65] Drinking the milk of a goddess imbued a king with his divine powers.[66]

Crowning scenes

On the lower register of the door jambs leading into the original Twenty-third dynasty chapel, symmetrically opposed scenes depict Amun standing next to Shepenwepet (Figure 3.6). His face shown in profile, Amun is orientated away from doorway, so that on the western door jamb, he is orientated towards the right (= west), while on the eastern jamb, he is orientated toward the left (= east). Amun wears his customary doubled-feathered crown, a curved false beard, and a short kilt to which a bull's tail is attached at the back. Standing in a striding position, his left foot forward, Amun extends one hand behind Shepenwepet's head and places his other hand just in front of her forehead, such that the tips of his fingers almost touch the *uraeus* protruding from her diadem. On the right door jamb, an arm-band adorns his upper arm. His forward extended arm (the right in the scene on the right; and the left in the scene

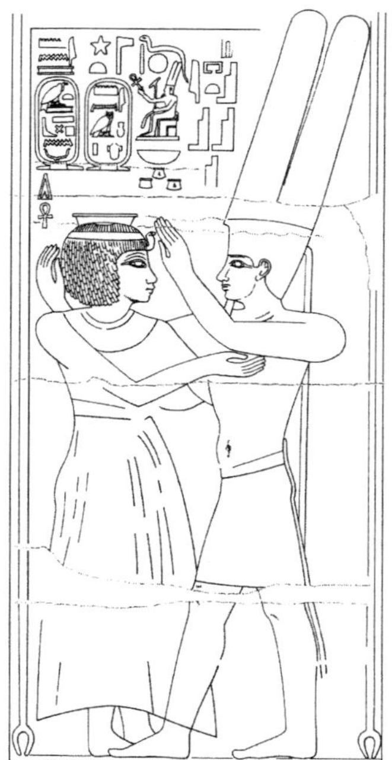

Figure 3.6 Chapel of Osiris, Ruler of Eternity, façade of Libyan chapel, door jambs, lower register (line drawing © Lyla Brock)

on the left) obscures most of his beard so that only its top part where it adjoins his chin is visible. Giving a strong impression of physical proximity, Amun's forward extended foot obscures Shepenwepet's feet from view. On the right jamb, his leg also partly obscures the hem of her dress, while on the left the hem overlaps his ankle. As is typical of Egyptian artistic conventions, the god is shown walking out of this chapel. In both representations, Shepenwepet wears a long, loose fitting, layered, dress, its multiple layers gathered by a tied sash. On the right (= western door jamb), the small bow that gathers and ties the sash is still visible. The sash appears to be very similar to one depicted in the suckling scene, its long streamer decorating the front of her dress. On both jambs, Amun is identified as "the Lord of the Thrones of the Two Lands … Karnak." The name of Amun-Re is represented as an ideogram of an enthroned god who extends an *ankh*-sign toward Shepenwepet's cartouche. *Was*-scepters frame each of the four scenes. Shepenwepet is identified as "the Divine Worshipper, Khenem(et)ibimen, Beloved of Amun, Beloved-of-Mut-Shepenwepet, given life" on the left jamb. On the right jamb, her names and epithets are identical except for the title appearing before her *prenomen*. There, she is identified as "the gift (?) of God" or possibly "the one who gives god."[67] As far as I know, this title is unattested for any other God's Wife.

The propagandistic nature of the peculiar iconographic program of the façade of the Twenty-third dynasty chapel can only be appreciated if we imagine what it must have looked like at the time its decoration was completed. An Egyptian approaching the chapel from a distance would have been immediately struck by the prominence given Shepenwepet on the façade and the frequency of her representations there. The original façade was dominated by scenes showing Shepenwepet shaking the sistrum before Amun, Re-Horakhty, and Ptah, suckled by Hathor and Semat-Weret, and crowned by Amun. To an Egyptian, these scenes would have immediately conveyed Shepenwepet's special status, not merely in temple ritual, but more importantly in relation to the gods.

Shepenwepet's striking iconography, seen especially in the scenes of suckling and crowning that decorated the jambs of the earlier structure, has led scholars to comment on the prominence given Shepenwepet in this chapel.[68] Although noting the prominence accorded Shepenwepet, Redford concluded that the chapel was erected to commemorate members of the Twenty-third dynasty. I believe that while this may have been part of the reason the chapel was built, more importantly, it served to commemorate Shepenwepet's appointment as God's Wife of Amun. Thus, scenes showing Amun and Hathor crowning and suckling her may have been placed on the jambs of the original doorway to declare her investiture with the necessary insignia and powers to perform her priestly and ritualistic duties. These scenes may thus be seen as commemorating part of an initiation ritual that marked her assumption of office as God's Wife.

An informed Egyptian would have immediately recognized that it was through the very acts represented in these scenes that the gods blessed and approved of Shepenwepet's appointment. Through the milk of a goddess, Shepenwepet was imbued with the ability to stand before the gods and consecrate their offerings. Moreover, Amun's placing of a special crown on Shepenwepet's head indicated that her appointment was not enacted by any mere mortal, but that it was the supreme deity himself who invested her with the authority to become a God's Wife. It was those very scenes that established Shepenwepet's legitimacy.

Amenirdis I

When the Nubians decided to expand the chapel of Osiris, Ruler of Eternity, they did not modify any of its original architectural elements. For instance, the *torus*-molding that decorated the corners and the external walls of the original façade is still visible. Indeed, the façade itself was incorporated into the newly constructed chamber as its southern wall. Perhaps signifying new-found prosperity, the Nubian addition, which was constructed using newly-hewn square blocks of stone, was wider than the earlier structure.[69] That the addition was constructed during the reign of Shebitqo (702–690 BC) is evident from the inscriptions preserved on the new monumental façade he erected, where his Horus name, *Djed-khaou* survives (Figure 1.3). Shebitqo's paternal uncle and predecessor, Shabaqo, had secured Nubian control of the Nile Valley up to Memphis.[70] Shebitqo was the second Nubian ruler to be in control of Egypt at least up to Memphis.[71] The chapel's enlargement was only possible after a definitive military success.

Not surprisingly, Amenirdis dominates the decorative program of the Nubian addition, where she is represented as the main officiant on all the walls of room I.

Remarkably, Amenirdis did not appropriate any of the scenes depicting Shepenwepet, nor did she erase any of her predecessor's cartouches. Instead, Amenirdis had her predecessor depicted in the scenes decorating the newly constructed walls. Shepenwepet features especially prominently on the east wall of the room added by the Nubians, where she appears in two scenes inscribed on the upper register. An epithet, "alive for ever" (Egyptian: *ankh.ti djet*), that consistently appears after Shepenwepet's cartouche-enclosed name indicates that Shepenwepet was alive and well when the Nubian annex was constructed.

Shepenwepet is shown on the top register receiving the *menat*-necklace from Isis, and offering a figurine of the goddess *Maat* to Amun (Figure 2.5).[72] Both rituals declared not only Shepenwepet's elevated status, but more importantly her role in performing the cult. *Maat*, cosmic harmony and justice, was the food which the gods desired.[73] By receiving the *menat*-necklace, an object sacred to the goddess Hathor, Shepenwepet was receiving the essential gear needed for her ritualistic role in the temple.[74] Shaking the *menat* pleased the gods. Accordingly, carrying a *menat* became an integral part of the role of musician-priestesses in the temple service. The *menat* also "served a protective and regenerative function" which granted its possessor "the blessings of rebirth and eternal life,"[75] but it is Amenirdis, not Shepenwepet, who receives life from Amun on the bottom register of the east wall (Figures 2.5 and 3.7).

The key to understanding the preservation of Shepenwepet's older scenes and her inclusion in the new decorative program thus lies in Amenirdis's need to establish her own legitimacy. Instead of erasing or appropriating any of Shepenwepet's scenes, Amenirdis sought to incorporate the entire Twenty-third dynasty façade, with its legitimating scenes, into the decorative program of the newly added chamber. In doing so, Amenirdis was claiming for herself the very same legitimacy that was bestowed on Shepenwepet in those striking scenes. By adding on, and thematically complementing the very scenes that legitimated Shepenwepet's claim to power, Amenirdis succeeded in using those very scenes with their significant ritualistic value to gain legitimacy for her own position as a God's Wife.

Just as Amenirdis, by receiving life from Amun was reaping the result of Shepenwepet's presentation of *Maat* depicted on the upper register of the east wall, in room I of the chapel of Osiris, Ruler of Eternity, so also was she able to assert her cultic authority through a similar representation showing King Shebitqo presenting *Maat* to Amun-Re on the north wall of the same room, (Figure 2.12). There, next to a representation of the king presenting *Maat* to Amun-Re, Amenirdis I is shown shaking the sistrum before the same god. The iconographic sequence depicted on the north wall of room I suggests to me a situation in which a more senior person, supports, introduces, or otherwise sets up a protégé(e). It is almost as if the king, in participating in this ritual, was not only legitimating his own power but also Amenirdis's. The sequence of scenes on the lower register of the north wall show the king presenting *Maat* next to Amenirdis, who shakes the sistrum before Amun and may suggest the king's approval of her ritual act as well as his affirmation and support of her cultic duties.[76]

Similarly, on the east wall, Shepenwepet I shown on the upper register presents *Maat*, also to Amun-Re, while Amenirdis depicted on the lower register, receives

Figure 3.7 Amenirdis receives life, chapel of Osiris, Ruler of Eternity, east wall, lower register (Photo © M. Ayad)

life from him. It is conceivable that this particular layout of scenes was intended to emphasize that although Amenirdis did not participate in the presentation of *Maat* herself, she still stood to reap the benefits of this ritual act.

At her accession to office, Amenirdis assumed several titles that were held by her immediate predecessor, Shepenwepet I. On the façade of the chapel of Osiris, Ruler of Eternity, both Amenirdis I and Shepenwepet I are given the epithet "one who is united with god" (Egyptian: *khnemet netjer*). In direct reference to one of her roles in the cult, Amenirdis also took on the epithet "she who is pleasing of hands, carrying the sistra" (Egyptian: *anet djerty kher sesheshty*), which was previously held by Shepenwepet I. Clearly aware of the history of the position of God's Wife, and its previous illustrious holders, Amenirdis evoked a direct connection with Ahmose-Nefertari, the first known woman to hold the title of God's Wife of Amun. Amenirdis was the first woman to add the title "God's Hand" to her predecessors' more commonly attested titles "God's Wife" and "Divine Adorer."[77] In doing so, Amenirdis was undoubtedly aware of the use of the title during the early part of the Eighteenth dynasty, when Queen Ahmose-Nefertari first held the title of "God's Hand." Amenirdis I also employed a variant of one of Ahmose-Nefertari's epithets: "The one who speaks and everything is done for her because of the greatness of his love for her."[78] That there was a connection with Ahmose-Nefertari and a direct evocation of her titles may be inferred from the fact that two inscribed statues of Ahmose-Nefertari were recovered from the chapel of Osiris, Ruler of Eternity, a chapel in which Amenirdis I is extensively represented.[79]

Finally, Amenirdis's ultimate claim to legitimacy came through claiming direct descent from the god Osiris. She did so on three separate occasions in the chapel of Osiris, Ruler of Eternity. On the Nubian façade of the chapel, a band of inscriptions on the bottom of the eastern jamb reads: "the great gate of the God's Wife, the Divine Worshipper, Amenirdis … beloved of her father Osiris, Ruler of Eternity."[80] Dedicatory in nature, this inscription was one of three inscriptions which mention Amenirdis's special connection to Osiris. Further asserting her Osirian pedigree is a representation of Amenirdis on the western part of the north wall in room I, where she is depicted "stretching the cord" and thereby founding this chapel for Osiris (Figure 2.15). A single column of framed inscriptions bordering the scene declares that "The Divine Worshipper, the God's Wife, the God's Hand, the Great one of the *imat*-scepter, the One who fills the *wakher*-forecourt with the scent of her fragrance, Amenirdis, may she live forever, she constructed this monument for her father, Osiris, Ruler of Eternity."[81] A column of identical text is engraved on the other (eastern) side of the doorway. In fact, that column of inscriptions frames the scene in which the king presents *Maat* to Amun-Re (Figure 2.12). The three inscriptions, of course, only refer to the Nubian addition to the chapel. But it is quite remarkable that, in the presence of a king, it is the God's Wife, not the sovereign who is named as "builder" of this chapel.[82]

Amenirdis's emphasis on her descent from Osiris is further highlighted by the complete absence of any genealogical information relating to her lineage. Leclant has remarked on the oddity of this omission, noting that neither the name of her father Kashta nor those of her biological or adoptive mothers, Pebatma and Shepenwepet I, respectively, were included in her inscriptions.[83] It is possible that the suppression of her lineage was part of a larger state-policy promoted by the Nubians aiming to establish state authority.[84] In addition to obscuring her Nubian heritage, the suppression of Amenirdis's parentage enabled her to avoid subordinating herself to Shepenwepet. As a member of the new ruling house, one of Amenirdis's objectives was to assert her primacy over her Libyan predecessor. Acknowledging that Shepenwepet was her mother (adoptive or otherwise) would have forced Amenirdis to cede primacy of representation to her, whereas in fact, she did the contrary.[85] On the Nubian façade of the chapel, in accordance with Egyptian artistic convention, the deities depicted there seem to proceed out of the chapel, their supposed divine dwelling, while the officiating individuals, in this case the two God's Wives Shepenwepet I and Amenirdis I, facing their divine companions, proceed toward the chapel's entrance.[86] Amenirdis, depicted on the eastern jamb, is orientated toward the right, while Shepenwepet appearing in complementary symmetrical scenes on the western jamb is oriented toward the left. This arrangement is quite remarkable for, in Egyptian art, "orientation to the right … establishes lateral dominance in compositions."[87] An Egyptian looking at this façade would have immediately recognized Amenirdis as the more important of the two God's Wives, her rightward orientation having established her dominance over Shepenwepet.[88] Failing to refer to Shepenwepet as "her mother" must have been the result of a deliberate decision. A mother would have occupied a more prominent position relative to her daughter.

Shepenwepet II

Shepenwepet's first claim to legitimacy came in the form of erecting a funerary chapel for Amenirdis at Medinet Habu. In his publication of the architecture of the funerary chapel of Amenirdis, Hölscher noted the existence of an "earlier crypt … exactly on the axis of the chapel."[89] He proposed that this earlier crypt indicated an earlier, different plan for the chapel of Amenirdis. He suggested that this earlier plan conformed to the plan of Shepenwepet I's earlier chapel, and that Amenirdis's chapel was likewise initially constructed of mud brick. The alterations seen in Amenirdis's crypt were probably initiated by Shepenwepet II, who also was responsible for the decision to use stone masonry in the construction of Amenirdis's chapel. That this is so, is confirmed by a band of inscriptions engraved on the inner face of the doorway leading into Amenirdis's *cella*, which declares that "Shepenwepet, daughter of Piye, built this monument of eternity for her mother Amenirdis, justified."[90] This declaration is further confirmed by the numerous scenes depicting Shepenwepet performing the funerary cult of Amenirdis, preserved both in the corridor surrounding the *cella*, and in the courtyard of the chapel. In Chapter II, we already discussed how Amenirdis, deceased and deified, appears as a beneficiary in the rites of Driving of the Four Calves and the consecration of *meret*-chests both performed by Shepenwepet (Figures 2.25 and 2.26).[91] In the Driving of the Four Calves, Shepenwepet assumes the role of the ultimate good son, who not only buried his father, but faithfully protected his tomb from the wiles of his evil uncle Seth. In fact, it was through the fulfillment of his role in this rite that Horus, and by extension the king, was granted legitimacy as his father's rightful successor on the throne of Egypt.[92] Just as Horus was responsible for ensuring a good burial for his father through enacting this ritual for his father's benefit, so also was Shepenwepet II depicted performing the rite of Driving of the Four Calves for the benefit of her adoptive mother Amenirdis – and by so doing, ensuring her own legitimacy as her mother's successor as God's Wife of Amun.

Similarly, on the outer walls of Amenirdis's *cella*, Shepenwepet is also shown pouring libations and performing various other rituals for her deceased mother. By carrying out the funerary cult of Amenirdis, Shepenwepet was laying claim to her right to succeed Amenirdis. A legal dispute from Deir el-Medina strongly suggests that providing for a father's/mother's funerary cult legitimated an heir's claim to his/her parent's property.[93] Acting as a dutiful "eldest son" thus established Shepenwepet's rights not only to Amenirdis's property, but also to her office. That this rule was equally applicable to royalty is clear from the role of the king in maintaining his deceased father's funerary cult. In fact, when a king wanted to claim legitimacy for his rule, he maintained his predecessor's funerary cult and acted as the "eldest son" in relation to his deceased predecessor even when the predecessor was not his father. For instance, the elderly courtier, Aye, established his legitimacy as Tutankhamun's successor by performing the latter's funerary cult, including performing the Opening the Mouth ritual for Tutankhamun in the tomb of Tutankhamun in the Valley of the Kings.[94]

On at least two separate occasions, Shepenwepet II used her stated relationship with Amenirdis to further legitimate her own position. The first instance occurs on the lintel of the chapel of Osiris, "Lord of Life, who answers the Afflicted" in North Karnak, while the second instance occurs on the jambs of the chapel of Osiris-Wennofer, "who is in the midst of the Persea-tree."

The lintel of the chapel of Osiris, Lord of Life bears complementary scenes, showing Shepenwepet II and King Taharqo presenting offerings to various deities (Figure 2.17).[95] To the left of a central cartouche bearing the name of the chapel's patron deity, Taharqo offers wine to mummiform Osiris and Isis, while to the right of the cartouche, Shepenwepet II offers milk to Ptah and Hathor. At the lintel's periphery, two symmetrically opposed scenes depict King Taharqo on the left embraced by Harsiese, also known as Horus the Elder, while his consort Hathor similarly embraces the God's Wife on the right. Yet, Hathor does not embrace Shepenwepet II, the incumbent God's Wife, but rather her deceased predecessor Amenirdis.[96] Reserving the central and spatially bigger space for her own use, Shepenwepet II's choice to represent her predecessor in the scenes engraved on this lintel may indicate an attempt on Shepenwepet's part to legitimate her own role as a God's Wife. It is possible that Shepenwepet, or Taharqo, still felt the need to legitimate her position as God's Wife such that the representation of Amenirdis next to her daughter was meant to shore up the latter's authority and further consolidate her position. Unfortunately, the peripheral edges of the lintel are damaged so that the titles of both women do not survive. However, the inscriptions surviving on the right jamb identify Amenirdis, not by any of her many titles, but rather as "her mother" (Egyptian: *mout.es*). There, Amenirdis's name is included as part of Shepenwepet's titulary. The jamb bears an image of Shepenwepet II embraced by Isis "the great, the divine mother" (Figure 2.20b).[97] The scene delicately mirrors a corresponding scene engraved on the left jamb, which depicts Taharqo embraced by Osiris. To balance Taharqo's two cartouches, Shepenwepet includes her predecessor's cartouche as part of her own titles and epithets. Her adoptive mother's name, then, became part of her own filiation. It should be noted though that, once more, this was a deliberate decision. Shenwepet could have included her own *prenomen* if the intention was merely to balance Taharqo's cartouches.

Divine marriage iconography

Shepenwepet's deliberate use of her mother's name and iconography is quite evident in the chapel of Osiris-Wennofer-in-the-Midst-of-the-Persea-Tree (Egyptian: *Hery-ib-pa-ished*).[98] There, in two symmetrically opposed scenes, the God's Wife embraces Amun-Re. The scenes, which occur on the door jambs leading into room I, depict Amenirdis I on the left jamb and Shepenwepet II on the right. Previously (mistakenly) identified as Amenirdis II, it is clear that the God's Wife depicted on the left jamb is Amenirdis the Elder, Shepenwepet II's adoptive mother (Figure 3.8 in the plates section).[99] Her cartouche-enclosed name is followed by the epithet "justified" (Egyptian: *maat-kherou*), indicating her decease at the time of the chapel's construction. Amenirdis II, Shepenwepet's successor, survived the entire tenure of Shepenwepet II and was still very much alive at the end of the Nubian dominion in Egypt when Psametik I installed his daughter as God's Wife.

Both God's Wives are similarly attired: tight sheath dress, broad collar, and a long lappet wig surmounted by a vulture headdress, a rearing cobra at their brows, and the two tall feathers affixed to the *modius* platform characteristic of the God's Wife headgear. Likewise, Amun appears in his customary regalia: tall double-plumed crown resting on a square platform, long curved false beard, broad collar, shirt with tapering shoulder straps, and a short kilt, held in place by a belt tied in an elaborate girdle knot. On both jambs, Amun appears to be walking out of the chapel: on the right jamb, his face shown in profile is turned to the left, while on the left jamb, he turns to the right. The God's Wives, on the other hand, in sharing an inward orientation seem to proceed towards the chapel's door.

Amenirdis I, depicted on the right, her face shown in profile turned to the left, embraces Amun-Re "the Lord of the Thrones of the Two lands." Amenirdis drapes her left arm over Amun-Re's left (far) shoulder, while with her right hand firmly clenched around her left forearm, she secures her arm in position as her palm rests flatly over Amun's chest. By contrast, Amun's arms and hands seem to be more passive. His left arm hangs behind him parallel to his body, a key of life (*ankh*-symbol) held in his hand. Amun's right arm, extended diagonally forward, overlaps Amenirdis's body, partially obscuring it. In his right hand, seen just below Amenirdis's buttocks, Amun-Re holds a bit of string from which hang three small *ankh*-signs. Amun's forward extended right leg is partially obscured by Amenirdis's shins, the tip of his right foot barely seen behind her ankles while her curvaceous thigh overlaps his kilt, obscuring its triangular pointed tip. Amun's broad shoulders and muscular upper arm overlap and obscure most of Amenirdis's upper body, his delicately curving shoulder overlapping the broad collar under her chin. Unfortunately, the condition of the stone is such that details of the faces of Amenirdis and Amun do not survive.

On the corresponding jamb, Shepenwepet's representation mirrors Amenirdis's. She is dressed similarly and stands in an identical posture to her adoptive mother's (Figure 3.9 in the plates section). But unlike her mother, whose name is followed by the epithet "justified" (Egyptian: *maat-kherou*), indicating her decease, Shepenwepet was "alive" at the time of this scene's inscription, her cartouche-enclosed name followed by "alive forever" (Egyptian: *ankh.ti djet*). Remarkably, in an act of humility, Shepenwepet ceded rightward orientation to her deceased mother.

Several details give an impression of the two figures' physical proximity: the overlapping shoulders and limbs, the touching thighs. The iconography of this scene conveys a certain and definite physical intimacy. This rare scene has one prototype. On the lower register of the southern half of the east wall in the Karnak Hypostyle Hall, the goddess Mut is depicted embracing Amun-Re (Figure 3.10). A frame surrounding the divine couple implies that their embrace took place within the confines of a shrine.[100] With her face shown in profile, turned to the left, Mut stands next to Amun-Re, her face almost touching his rightward orientated face. Like the God's Wives in the chapel of Osiris-Wennofer-who-is-in-the-Midst-of-the-Pesea-Tree, Mut wears a tight sheath dress, a long lappet wig and a vulture headdress, which is here surmounted by her distinctive crown of Upper and Lower Egypt. With her leftward orientation, Mut stands in an identical posture to Shepenwepet II's.

Like both God's Wives, she clings tightly to Amun-Re, clasping her arms around his shoulders and chest in a tight embrace. But although Amun-Re's broad shoulders obscure much of Mut's upper body from view, they are not depicted as close to each other as Amun is next to the God's Wives. For whereas in the Twenty-fifth dynasty example, the God's Wives' hips overlapped Amun's kilt, obscuring its tip from view, in the Hypostyle Hall, only Amun's feet overlap Mut's. The couples' thighs do not touch in the Nineteenth dynasty example.

The scene in the Hypostyle Hall is part of a larger sequence showing Ramses II offering incense and pouring libations before the divine couple,[101] whose embrace was hidden from public view in ancient times (Figure 3.11). Four holes drilled in the wall around Amun and Mut indicate that in antiquity the scene of their so-called "divine marriage" was veiled. While the veil may have been lifted for special occasions and on festival days, Brand suggested that this scene was covered by the clergy in an attempt to protect it, and other equally popular "icons," from the common devotional practice of "gouging at the walls."[102] Handoussa suggested that

Figure 3. 10 Divine marriage: Mut embraces Amun-Re (Photo © M. Ayad)

the embrace, which was covered in gold sheet in antiquity, took place in the divine realm. She also pointed out the deliberate use of the Egyptian verb *stj* in the captions accompanying the scene. Depending on the determinative used, this verb could mean "to burn (incense)" or "to pour (water)." It was used with the appropriate determinatives in the captions describing Ramses II's actions in this scene. With a phallic determinative, the same word could also mean "to impregnate." Handoussa suggested that the deliberate use of the verb *stj* in this scene to describe the king's ritualistic actions implied the king's divine conception and rebirth and re-affirmed the king's role in the "eternal repetition of the divine union."[103]

When appropriated by Shepenwepet II, the scene was taken out of context and utilized to proclaim her elevated status and easy access to Amun. No longer was it part of a larger ritual sequence depicting the entrance of the king into the temple.[104] Decoupled from its original context, what remained was the intimate relationship, pictorially expressed, between the supreme god and his wife. Traditionally kept out of sight, the divine embrace was now publicly displayed on the door jambs in the Twenty-fifth dynasty chapel. Substituting the goddess Mut in this divine drama, Shepenwepet II copied the scene meticulously, sharing not only Mut's costume and posture, but also her orientation. Shepenwepet's leftward orientation may have thus served a dual purpose: an exact replica of Mut's representation, while yielding the hierarchically superior rightward orientation to her deceased mother. It is possible, of course, that Shepenwepet was only concerned with the former, the latter being only a by-product of her desire to further legitimate her appropriation of the divine marriage iconography.

This particular assimilation of Mut's iconography into the representational repertoire of the God's Wife reflects an earlier assimilation by which Amenirdis and Shepenwepet incorporated Mut's name in their official "throne" names (*prenomen*).

Finally, Shepenwepet assumed for herself the iconography of the *sed* festival. Through celebrating aspects of this exclusive festival, Shepenwepet legitimated her role in the temple as the ultimate High Priest in Egypt. Shepenwepet II's extensive efforts to legitimate her position as God's Wife seem rather desperate. She adopted all known avenues to legitimacy and initiated a few of her own as well. In maintaining and officiating in the funerary cult of her deceased mother, Shepenwepet was using the time-tested ancient right of an heir, an adopted child, to inherit his father's (in this case, her mother's) property and office. Visually, she used her connection with Amenirdis, both on the lintel of the chapel of Osiris, Lord of Life, and on the door jambs at the chapel of Osiris-Wennofer-who-is-in-the-Midst-of-the-Persea-Tree to consolidate her position. On the lintel, her inclusion of her deceased mother's cartouche as part of her own titulary established her own roots and genealogy, and further legitimated her position as a God's Wife. Likewise, having her deceased mother depicted in a scene evocative of the Divine Marriage iconography further gave credence to Shepenwepet's own appropriation of the Divine Marriage iconography by which she could be depicted embracing Amun.

Figure 3.11 Karnak Hypostyle Hall, east wall, southern half, lower register (Photo © M. Ayad)

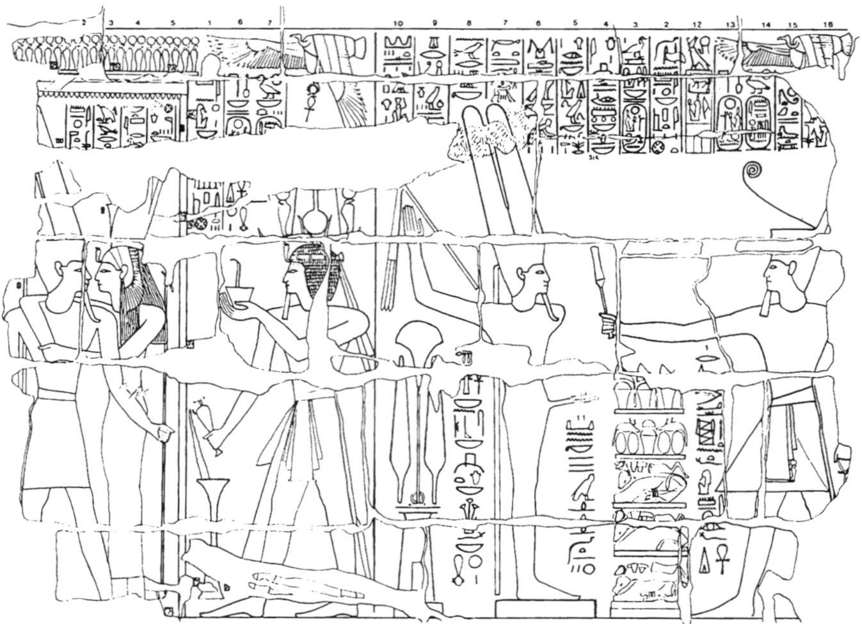

Figure 3.12 Karnak Hypostyle Hall, east wall, southern half, lower register (line drawing after Nelson, *Key Plans*, pl. 107; reproduced with permission)

Nitocris

With the dynastic change taking place during Shepenwepet's tenure in office, Psametik I sought to establish his daughter's "legal" claim to succeed the Nubian princesses as the new God's Wife. He did so by having the incumbent Nubian God's Wives Shepenwepet II and Amenirdis II draw up an official transfer of title deed naming his daughter Nitocris as beneficiary. Although undoubtedly somewhat propagandist in nature, the 'Nitocris Adoption Stela," gives us an impression of the protocol involved in the transfer of office. At Nitocris's arrival at Thebes, she is greeted by both God's Wives. Having found her pleasing and loving "her more than anything," Shepenwepet II and Amenirdis II then "made over to her [a] testament ... Their bidding was done in writing" (lines 15–17).[105] The document they drew up had two aspects to it. In the first instance, the Nubian God's Wives gave all their property "in country and in town" to Nitocris. Secondly, they officially declared her as their successor, stating that she would be "established on our throne firmly and enduringly till the end of eternity."[106] Known in Egyptian as an *imyt-per* document (literally meaning "that which is in the house"), this document gave its beneficiary the right to enjoy, use, and bequeath the property named in the document.[107] In other words, it unequivocally transferred the property in question to the beneficiary. Typically, an *imyt-per* was not needed for a son to inherit his father's property, and was never used when inheritance passed to the actual "eldest son."[108] In other words, the document was needed only when the transaction benefited someone "other than the normal heir."[109] The appropriation of adoption phraseology found in line 4 of the Adoption stela ("I will give her (my daughter) to her ... to be her eldest daughter")[110] merely reflects the need to establish Nitocris's new status as the heir to the incumbent God's Wife, thereby establishing her right of succession. The assumption of adoption phraseology was common in New Kingdom transfer of property deeds. A husband, for instance, needed to "adopt" his wife as his "eldest son" in order to ensure her right to inherit his property. In due course, the wife who had inherited her husband's property adopted her brother in order to leave him her inherited property legally.[111]

The Nitocris Adoption Stela was set up as a legal document, written, monumentalized, and publicly displayed to establish her legitimate right to become a God's Wife. Further underscoring the legal nature of the Nitocris Adoption Stela is the inclusion of dates and lists of witnesses in the document. Psametik's initial pronouncement of his desire to install his daughter as God's Wife (line 2) is dated accurately and, further, witnessed by Saite courtiers. These court officials indicated their approval and pleasure with his decision by prostrating themselves, giving thanks to the king of Upper and Lower Egypt, and finally verbally declaring their unanimous approval of his plans (lines 5–7). His speech was given on the twenty-eighth day of the first month of the *akhet* season (summer) of Psametik I's ninth regnal year, which coincided with March 2, 656 BC.[112] Nitocris's dates of departure from her father's palace in the Delta and arrival at Thebes are also meticulously noted (lines 7 and 11). She arrived at Thebes on the fourteenth day of the second month of Akhet (line 11), sixteen days after she set out from the king's residence.[113] Once there, another group of Theban officials and clerics, "prophets, priests and friends of the temple," witnessed the transfer of property from the Nubian

God's Wives to Nitocris.[114] Dates and a list of witnesses were two integral aspects of an *imyt-per* and as such were always recorded in *imyt-per* documents.[115] Monumentalized on a granite slab stela and erected and publicly displayed in the first courtyard in Karnak, the decree was then visible for all to see. Public display in a temple ensured public and divine acceptance of its contents.

From an ancient Egyptian legal perspective then, the Nitocris Adoption Stela, being an *imyt-per*, unequivocally established Nitocris's legal rights not only to her predecessor's property, but also to her new official position.[116] It is interesting to note that Psametik decided to resort to our equivalent of a civil contract to confer the office of God's Wife on his daughter. Particularly noteworthy is his use of a legal method (rather than ideological, mythological, or religious parlance) to establish his daughter's right to hold office at Thebes.

Ankhnesneferibre

Of the five God's Wives discussed in this book, Ankhnesneferibre remains exceptional. As an "heiress apparent" to Nitocris, Ankhnesneferibre was, *officially*, the High Priest of Amun (Egyptian: *hem tepy en Imen*, literally meaning "the first servant of God").[117] Nonetheless, Ankhnesneferibre still felt the need to claim her right to succeed Nitocris in the most traditional of ways: she provided her predecessor with a proper burial.

"The God's Wife Nitocris, justified, went to the sky, she was united with the sun disk, the limbs of the god [i.e. Nitocris] being merged with him who made her. Her daughter the first prophet Ankhnesneferibre, did for her everything which is done for every beneficent king" (lines 8–9).[118] In providing for her predecessor's funerary cult and burial, Ankhnesneferibre fulfilled the most basic and ancient of legitimating rites. Like Shepenwepet II before her, Ankhnesneferibre asserted her right to succeed her predecessor by assuming the role of the eldest son/daughter who performed all the necessary funerary rites for her deceased "mother." But just as Nitocris established her right to the position through a publicly displayed decree, so Ankhnesneferibre had a monument describing the circumstances surrounding her accession erected at Karnak.

In that document, Ankhnesneferibre made sure to assert her "legal entitlement" to the office by narrating the details of her adoption nine years earlier.[119] The stela conveys the impression that the event was much more subdued than her predecessor's appointment. Perhaps it was felt that there was little need for all the pomp that accompanied the installation of Nitocris sixty years earlier. Ankhnesneferibre was already in Thebes, and her decree paints events from a Theban perspective. This perhaps accounts for the "parochially Theban" concerns expressed in Ankhnesneferibre's stela.[120] Moreover, Ankhnesneferibre already occupied a position at the pinnacle of the Amun hierarchy at Karnak as the High Priest of Amun. Whether there was a need to create for her the kind of endowment created for her predecessor we will never know. But in all likelihood, there was not as much need for all the temples across the country to assert their loyalty as they had to do when Nitocris was installed. Ankhnesneferibre was a member of the ruling dynasty; a dynasty that had been in power for almost eighty years at the time of her installation as God's Wife.[121] So there may have been less of a need for all the religious establishments to demonstrate their loyalty. That Ankhnesneferibre included a detailed account of the initiation rituals involved in becoming a God's Wife on her monument may indicate her desire to assert her legitimacy in religious and ritualistic terms.

Ankhnesneferibre's pursuit of religious legitimacy may also be seen in her enlargement of the edifice built by Shepenwepet in North Karnak. In that small chapel, known by the name of its patron deity, Osiris-who-perpetually-gives-life (Egyptian: *Osiris-pa-ded-ankh*), Shepenwepet was represented celebrating aspects of the *sed* festival.[122] There, Ankhnesneferibre built a festival gateway, the inscriptions of which mention the *sed* festival and may indicate that Ankhnesneferibre celebrated the festival in her own right.[123] By enlarging this monument, Ankhnesneferibre, once more, sought to walk into the footsteps of one of her predecessors. Her addition of this gateway may have been an attempt to build on the religious legitimacy achieved by Shepenwepet II through her celebration of the *sed* festival. In this way, Ankhnesneferibre's annex would be similar in function to Amenirdis's enlargement of the chapel of Osiris, Ruler of Eternity, in East Karnak. Like Shepenwepet II before her, Ankhnesneferibre used and adapted a variety of methods to establish her legitimacy as a God's Wife.

Adoption, succession to office, and age at appointment

Amenirdis was not the only child appointed as a God's Wife. Just as the remains of Amenirdis's biological mother Pebatma were recovered at Abydos, so was Nitocris accompanied to Thebes by her mother Mehetnusekhet, a funerary chapel for whom still stands next to the God's Wives' in Medinet Habu.[124] The accompaniment of their natural mothers suggests that, at the time of their appointment to office, both Amenirdis and Nitocris were mere children, who needed maternal care when dispatched to Thebes. Crucially, the appointment of these two children as God's Wives occurred at the dangerous time of dynastic transition. It is very possible that during those times of transition, effective power remained in the hands of a few key high-ranking, male officials. Such officials included Mentuemhat, the all-powerful Mayor of Thebes, and Fourth Priest of Amun, who retained his influential position during the turbulent years of the Nubian-Saite transition; and Semtouefnakhte, a great general of the army and chief of the harbor in Middle Egypt. Both officials are named on the Nitocris Adoption Stela: the former as one of the many officials who appear to greet Nitocris, while the latter as one of two chaperones, who accompanied Nitocris on her south-bound voyage to Thebes.[125]

Indeed, since its initial publication, the Nitocris Adoption Stela has attracted much scholarly attention. And it is this single monument that gave rise to the idea that a God's Wife of the Twenty-third to the Twenty-sixth dynasties would be appointed by her father, the reigning king. The assumption has been made that this stela outlined a "protocol" for the installation of a new God's Wife;[126] a protocol that must have also been in place when other princesses of the immediately preceding dynasties were appointed into office. Thus, Piye installed his daughter Shepenwepet II as God's Wife, Kashta was the instigator of Amenirdis's appointment, and Osorkon III appointed his daughter, Shepenwepet I. However, this pattern of patriarchal appointments cannot be verified. The smaller and rather more obscure decree recording the ascension of Ankhnesneferibre clearly indicates that although she was dispatched to Thebes during the lifetime of her father, her accession to office occurred during the fourth year of her brother's reign.[127]

The complete lack of evidence for the appointment of the God's Wives prior to the Twenty-sixth dynasty leaves much to conjecture. In the case of Amenirdis, it is not clear when and how exactly Kashta would have been able to instigate her appointment. There is no evidence that Kashta ever entered Egypt. In fact, beyond the first cataract at Aswan, Kashta's name appears only in the genealogical inscriptions of his descendents. And although Kashta's name appears on Amenirdis's monuments, like other monuments bearing his name in Egypt, Kastha's name appears there as part of her filiation. An appointment by her brother, Piye, is thus far more likely. Indeed, Amenirdis seems to have held office for forty years, having survived not only her father, but also her two brothers Piye and Shabaqo. She was probably the incumbent

God's Wife when her nephew Shebitqo ascended the Egyptian throne.[128] Placing Amenirdis's appointment in her father's reign would increase her tenure by at least ten years. Although Amenirdis may have been a mere child when she assumed office as God's Wife, those ten years would unreasonably lengthen her life expectancy. It is very likely that Piye instigated his sister's appointment as God's Wife during his first campaign into Egypt, which took place sometime during his fourth regnal year (*c.* 744 BC).[129] Amenirdis, already in place when Piye launched his second military campaign into Egypt (*c.* 728 or 730 BC), would have been in a position to help garner support for her brother. Her presence in Thebes may account for the relative ease with which Piye took Thebes.[130]

Perhaps even more unclear is the identity of the instigator of Shepenwepet II's appointment into office. Three Nubian kings could have been responsible for her appointment to office: her father, King Piye, or either one of her brothers, Shebitqo or Taharqo. Her uncle Shabaqo (716–702 BC) may be safely ruled out. Shabaqo stood to gain little from the appointment of his niece. Besides, he had another important position to fill. He gave the high priesthood of Amun to his son.[131] In the chapel of Osiris, Lord of Life, Shepenwepet II appears in symmetrically opposed scenes with King Taharqo. She is likely to be the archer shown next to Taharqo in his Edifice by the Sacred Lake at Karnak. But their close association does not necessarily mean that Taharqo appointed Shepenwepet. Indeed, Shepenwepet's unprecedented equal footing with the ruling king almost implies that she was already a person of considerable political and religious clout when he came to office. It is therefore quite likely that Shepenwepet was appointed to office shortly before Taharqo's accession in 690 BC. Shebitqo, whose reign spanned the period 702–690 BC, thus emerges as the most likely candidate for the installation of Shepenwepet II. Likewise, Shepenwepet I was most likely appointed to office during the co-regency of Osorkon III and Takeloth III.[132]

Just as the Nitocris Adoption Stela formed the basis of the assumption that a God's Wife was generally appointed by her father, so it also became the most fundamental piece of evidence underlying the assumption that "adoption into office" was the customary means of succession to the office of the God's Wife of Amun. However, only the Saite God's Wives of Amun consistently maintained the fiction of referring to their predecessors as their mother(s). No such claim was ever made by Amenirids I in relation to Shepenwepet I. In the funerary chapel of Amenirdis at Medinet Habu, for instance, no reference is made of her predecessor. Instead, Amenirdis consistently refers to herself as a "royal daughter" or a "royal sister," adding the cartouche of her father or brother appropriately after each title. Nowhere in this chapel is Shepenwepet I referred to as Amenirdis's mother. Likewise, there is a conspicuous absence of any mention of Amenirdis's mother, adoptive or otherwise, in the chapel of Osiris, Ruler of Eternity.[133] Neglecting to refer to her predecessor as her "mother" would have undermined Amenirdis's claim to the office if adoption was indeed the sole mechanism universally used by these women. Such omission must have been deliberate. In the case of Amenirdis, the suppression of the names of both biological and adoptive mothers was intentional, not only to obscure her Nubian heritage, but also to distance herself from Shepenwepet I. Acknowledging that Shepenwepet was her mother, adoptive or otherwise, would have forced Amenirdis into a secondary position.[134] Acknowledging Shepenwepet I's seniority would have outright defeated the propagandist purposes of this chapel's particular iconographic program. Instead, Amenirdis asserted her divine pedigree, claiming direct descent from Osiris, the Ruler of Eternity.[135] Indeed, the name of the chapel derives from three dedicatory inscriptions, all of which were commissioned by Amenirdis and mention her name. It is equally possible though that the "language of adoption" had not yet developed.

In fact, we first see a reference to a deceased God's Wife as the incumbent's mother on the lintel and jambs, above and around the entrance to the chapel of Osiris, Lord of Life, in North Karnak. There, Shepenwepet II refers to Amenirdis as her mother and to Piye as her father. However, she does so in markedly distinct ways. On the western (rear) wall of the first room of that chapel, for instance, the titulary of Shepenwepet is given as the "God's Wife, Shepenwepet, the royal daughter [lit. the king's daughter] of Piye, justified." Using this type of filiation is very common in ancient Egyptian texts. Finding it here is, therefore, hardly surprising. The "King's mother," the "king's father," the King's son," the "King's daughter," and in the Nubian period, the "King's brother," were all common titles that were regularly used to refer to members of the royal household. Shepenwepet's filiation on the west wall thus falls well within the Egyptian norm. On the right door jamb, however, Shepenwepet's titles are given as: "God's Wife, Shepenwepet (II), her mother Amenirdis (I), justified." There, Shepenwepet defines her relationship to her predecessor in terms of how her predecessor Amenirdis relates to *her*. While all the other titles are basilio-centric, the reference to Amenirdis on this door jamb focuses on Shepenwepet and defines their relationship in terms of how Amenirdis relates to Shepenwepet. Using the more familiar "daughter of x," or "born of x" would have subordinated Shepenwepet to her deceased mother. However, the whole purpose of including Amenirdis's name was to further highlight Shepenwepet's lineage and her claim to office. Be that as it may, adoption had another aspect to it as well. Adoption, and the phraseology of mother/daughter, made the new God's Wife an heir to her predecessor. Just as the adoptee, an heir(ess), stood to gain much from the relationship, so was she also bound by duty to provide for her parent. This duty was not limited to the duration of the parent's lifetime, but was most crucial after the parent's death. It was the heiress's duty to provide for, and maintain, the funerary cult of her parent. Typically, the expense of such provision came from the heritage that the eldest son (or daughter) received.[136] In fact, a legal dispute from Deir el-Medina suggests that providing for a parent's funerary cult legitimated an heir's claim to his/her parent's property.[137] This obligation was meticulously carried out by Shepenwepet II, who monumentalized her role by erecting the funerary chapel of Amenirdis I at Medinet Habu, as an act of filial duty.

This filial duty was immediately recognized by Ankhnesneferibre, whose own adoption stela emphasized her role in burying her predecessor. The stela specifically states that "[when] the God's Wife Nitocris, justified, went to the sky, she was united with the sun disk, the limbs of god (i.e. Nitocris) being merged with him who made her, her daughter, the first prophet of Ankhnesneferibre, did for her *everything* which is done for every beneficent king."[138] In so doing, Ankhnesneferibre was laying claim to her adoptive mother's inheritance, just as King Aye legitimated his position as successor to Tutankhamun by performing the latter's funerary cult. In Tutankhamun's tomb in the Valley of the Kings (KV 62), it is the elderly King Aye, who performs the Opening of the Mouth ritual on King Tut's mummy – a role typically relegated to the eldest son.[139]

As for Amenirdis I, it is not clear whether she felt the same kind of obligation towards her predecessor, Shepenwepet I, whose own funerary chapel was destroyed in antiquity.[140] With the demolition of its walls, we will never know whether Amenirdis made such a declaration. But as noted above, Amenirdis carefully avoided referring to Shepenwepet I as her mother in the inscriptions preserved on the walls of the chapel of Osiris, Ruler of Eternity, at Karnak. It is conceivable that Amenirdis never intended to fulfill this filial obligation toward her predecessor, in life or in death. Indeed, if Hölscher's assessment regarding the destruction of Shepenwepet I's chapel in antiquity is correct, one may surmise that Amenirdis, or some later Nubian official, was responsible for the demolition of Shepenwepet I's funerary chapel.

Sexuality, celibacy and the sexual role of the God's Wife

Celibacy re-visited

The God's Wives' adoptive pattern of succession was typically viewed from the perspective that certain reproductive restrictions were imposed upon the adoptive mother and that such restrictions would have prevented her from producing offspring of her own. Often such restrictions were attributed to supposedly religiously-mandated celibacy.

Regarding the God's Wife of Amun, Sir Alan Gardiner wrote:

> From Dyn XXI onwards ... this epithet was transferred to a king's daughter who became the consecrated wife of the Theban god, and to whom human intercourse was strictly forbidden. Such a one appears to have been the earlier Makare believed to have been the daughter of the Tanite king Psunnes I; her mummy was found in the Dêr el-Bahri cache, accompanied by that of an infant which suggests that *she had died in childbirth after having offended against the rule of chastity imposed on her*."[141]

Gardiner's statement merely reflected the views commonly held regarding the imposition of celibacy on the God's Wife of Amun during the Third Intermediate Period. It was also assumed that this presumed celibacy of the God's Wife was religiously mandated. Foremost amongst the proponents of this theory was the French scholar Jean Yoyotte, who suggested that the God's Wife presided over a group of virginal celibates who were consecrated for temple service in a cloistered "celibate college of nuns."[142] Until very recently, this view was commonly held by scholars of ancient Egypt.

The argument for the celibacy of the God's Wife partially rested on the misidentification of skeletal remains found in the coffin of the Divine Worshipper Maatkare (B) of the Twenty-second dynasty. X-raying the skeletal remains found inside Maatkare's coffin revealed them to belong to her pet baboon, not to Maatkare's presumed infant child.[143] Once assumed to have died in disgrace during childbirth, it is now clear that Maatkare's pregnancy was celebrated. Definitively debunking claims that both mother and infant were "executed for the 'sacrilege' of pregnancy," it was discovered that the embalmers who worked on her mummy packed her abdomen to indicate her death at childbirth or shortly thereafter.[144] Indeed, packing Maatkare's abdomen with linen seems to indicate that Maatkare's family, like other ancient Egyptian families, valued the reproductive aspect of marriage.

Yoyotte's assumption of celibacy was not limited to the God's Wives being celibate, but extended to temple chantresses (songstresses). He based much of his argument on a misreading of a stela recovered from Abydos.[145] Yoyotte's assertions regarding the celibacy of "chantresses of the Residence of Amun" were shown to lack evidentiary support. Indeed, one such chantress had the title of *nebet per*, which literally translates to "mistress of the house", a title that was regularly held by married women.[146] Republishing the stela cited by Yoyotte, Robert Ritner demonstrated that no adoptive relationships appear among the individuals named in the text of that stela. Ritner further showed that the chantress in question had only one mother, not two as had previously been suggested by Yoyotte.[147] Ritner concluded that "[f]or the chantresses of the Residence of Amon neither religious nor political sanctions would have mandated celibacy, and evidence once cited for the supposed practice actually disproves its existence ... the 'canonical' insistence upon virginal chantresses has no justification whatsoever."[148]

In the extant iconographic record, the God's Wives of the Twenty-third to the Twenty-sixth dynasty typically appear in flowing garments that often highlighted their femininity. In other instances, they were depicted in tight, form-fitting sheath dresses that accentuated their physique. Although they were not queens in their own right, they were repeatedly shown wearing and carrying queenly regalia. In no instance did they ever deny, or try to hide, their femininity. This particular aspect of the God's Wives' iconography is particularly telling.

In various religious traditions that mandate one form or another of sexual abstinence, ascetic women typically mark their celibate state by assuming special clothing.[149] In most cases, the typically loose garments effectively hide a nun's physique and serve to obscure her gender. Buddhist nuns typically shave their head and dress very similarly to Buddhist monks, so that from a distance, Buddhist nuns are almost indistinguishable from their male counterparts.[150] Similarly, Coptic nuns typically wear the same garments as Coptic monks, but supplement their costume with three additional pieces of clothing: a *taltima*, a *mandil*, and a *tarha*. The former two are scarves while the latter is a veil worn atop the other garments. The three additional pieces are all aimed to further hide a nun's feminine curves.[151]

A few hundred years prior to the onset of the Twenty-third dynasty, Hatshepsut dressed like a man (e.g. Figure 2.27), and her scribes frequently referred to her using masculine pronouns. But Hatshepsut's assumption of male costume and regalia had everything to do with her assumption of the Egyptian throne and nothing to do with her role as a God's Wife.

The Egyptians' attitude towards marriage and sex

Generally speaking, the arguments put forth regarding the celibacy of a God's Wife, her marital status, and adoption into office, seem to equate a state of singlehood with a state of religiously mandated celibacy. Yet, there is no evidence that the ancient Egyptians viewed celibacy as a more desired state of being, achieved through – or to attain – a higher level of spirituality. Indeed, there is nothing in Egyptian religion that would encourage anyone, male or female, to go on a route of self-denial or self-mortification.

On the contrary, the Egyptians valued family life above all else, and organized their gods in nuclear family units of father, mother, and son.[152] Thus, we find Amun, Mut, and Khosu at Karnak, and Ptah, Hathor, and Nefertum at Memphis, while one of the most enduring Egyptian myths is the story of Osiris, his bereaved widow Isis, and their son Horus, who embodied the ideals of Egyptian kingship.

Indeed, it seems that coupling was the ideal state of being. In a creation myth that originated in Middle Egypt, four couples co-existed in the primeval abyss. Each couple personified the male and female aspect of "pre-creation chaos." Thus Amun and Amunet stood for hiddenness, Huh and Huhet for formlessness, Kuk and Kuket were darkness, while Nun and Naunet "were the watery abyss."[153] The female doublets in these, and other couples, were simply created by adding the appropriate grammatical ending, a "*t*" to indicate their feminine gender. Conversely, in other couples, this feminine maker was dropped to create male counterparts for prominent goddesses, e.g. Sesha, the consort of the goddess Seshat.[154]

Possibly because the Egyptians considered sex a normal part of existence, they had no qualms attributing creation to an act of masturbation in the Heliopolitan creation myth. Out of the released semen came the first divine couple: Air (male) and Moisture (female), and creation was set in motion through repeated male–female unions.[155] In this creation myth, eight of the nine primeval gods were grouped together as four couples.

Other mentions of sex in Egyptian myths include a homosexual episode in the struggle between Horus and Seth. Both gods laid claim to the throne of Egypt, while trying to discredit their rival. The episode is charged with humor and sarcasm.[156] But it also seems to imply that homosexual activity was viewed by the Egyptians as "a means of affirming one's supremacy over an inferior or subordinate; it was proof of a surplus of sexual power on the part of the active partner and a deficiency on the part of the one forced to submit."[157]

That the Egyptians recognized and valued the (re)generative powers of sexual intercourse can be detected from the fact that numerous religious, and even funerary, texts of the Old and Middle Kingdoms often include references to physical love. Identified with the god Osiris, the dead king would be resurrected through the recitation of several "spells" or "utterances." In Pyramid Texts utterance 366, the deceased's resurrection was achieved through sexual union with Isis. The spell reads: "Your sister Isis comes to you, rejoicing for love of you. You have placed her on your phallus, and your seed [i.e. semen] issues into her, she being ready like Sothis [or Sirius]."[158] Although other deities were called on to help bring about the king's resurrection, Isis's role in this process is particularly prominent. In another spell typically inscribed in the king's burial chamber, we read: "Isis, this Osiris here is your brother, whom you have made revive and live: he will live and this Unis [king's name] will live, he will not die and this Unis will not die."[159] This spell evokes Isis's role in reviving Osiris. The loyal widow roams the entire length of Egypt as she seeks to gather the various body parts of her dismembered and deceased husband. With the help of the goddess Nut, Isis managed to revive her deceased husband just long enough to conceive Horus, Osiris's rightful heir and successor.[160] Seen in this light, the explicit sexual content of PT utterance 366 refers to the life-giving, regenerative powers of Isis. Identified with Osiris, the deceased could then hope to be similarly revived.[161]

Perhaps for this reason we find numerous directives to get married in Egyptian Wisdom Literature. Indeed the first few lines of a New Kingdom text, the Instructions of Any starts with the following passage:

> Take a wife while you're young, that she may make a son for you. She should bear for you while you're youthful. It is proper to make people. Happy is the man whose people are many. He is saluted on account of his progeny.[162]

Any's directive echoes the earlier edict of Ptahhotep "to found a house, and love your wife with ardor ..."[163] It is clear from these, and similar, passages that the Egyptians encouraged marriage and viewed it as a highly desirable state of being.

Physical love was also often celebrated in Egyptian love poetry. Much like other ancient Near Eastern love poetry, Egyptian love poetry was quite sensual. For example, we read:

> I shall kiss my sister.
> She parts her lips for me.
> I am delirious
> Even without beer.[164]

And:

> Why, that girl's better than any prescription,
> ... And then when I kiss her, feel her length breast to thigh,
> ... God, what a girl, what a woman! ...[165]

Expression of desire was not limited to men. Ancient Egyptian women felt comfortable expressing their love and desire. For example, we read:

> What heaven it would be
> If my heart's own wish came true,
> ... While your arm lies gentle on my breast
> (which twists, unquiet, out of love).
> I send my stealthy wish to creep inside you
> ... My love, oh, marry! Be, in the darkness of the night,
> My lord, husband to me ... "[166]

The highly erotic nature of Egyptian love poetry suggests that the Egyptians did not have a prudish attitude towards sex. Indeed, several medical papyri document the use of contraceptives in ancient Egypt.

Contraceptives in ancient Egypt

The ancient Egyptians knew of and used contraceptives from as early as the Middle Kingdom. Contraceptive prescriptions are known from widely disparate medical papyri. Pap. Kahun, recovered near the Oasis of Fayoum in Middle Egypt, dates to the Middle Kingdom (*c.* 2040–1730 BC), while the Ramasseum medical papyri were discovered within the precinct of the funerary temple of Ramses II on the western bank of the Nile at Thebes.[167] Papyrus Ebers, Kahun, and Ramasseum IV (*c.* 1784–1662 BC), which all deal with gynecological problems, include several prescriptions for contraceptives. For example, Ebers 783 explicitly states the purpose of the prescription before providing the recipe. It reads: "Beginning of the prescriptions prepared for women/wives (*hemut*) to allow a woman (*set*) to cease conceiving (*iur*) for one year, two years or three years," then proceeds to give the recipe in detail: *qaa* part of acacia (*djaret*), dates; grind with one hem (450 ml) of honey, lint is moistened with it and placed in her flesh (*iuf*)."[168]

Most contraceptives were applied topically by women who would place the concoctions in the vagina (Egyptian: *kat*) or "at the mouth of the uterus."[169] Some ingredients are known to have had spermicidal effect (such as honey) while some of the active ingredients of the herbs used in these concoctions can still be found in other ancient and medieval contraceptive recipes and even in modern day laboratory-produced contraceptives.[170] A seemingly popular recipe (mentioned in Ramesseum IV (C, 2–3) and Kahun 21) had crocodile excrement as one of its main ingredients. This particular ingredient led to wide speculation that some of these recipes worked by virtue of their deterrent effect.[171] Although most of these prescriptions involved topical application, oral contraceptives were also known from the Nineteenth dynasty onward (*c.* 1320–1200 BC), when they are first mentioned in the Berlin Medical Papyrus.[172] Access to these contraceptives seems not to have been restricted in ancient Egypt. But even if such knowledge was privileged, by virtue of their status both in the temple and as members of the ruling families, the God's Wives would have had access to the most privileged, or restricted knowledge. Thus to equate a state of singlehood with celibacy seems to be both unnecessary and unwarranted.

Prohibitions against sexual activity in ancient Egypt

Prohibitions against sexual activity focused primarily on consorting with alien women or committing adultery. For example, a passage from the Middle Kingdom Instructions of Ptahhotep reads:

> If you want friendship to endure in a house which you enter, as a master, brother, or friend, in whatever place you enter, beware of approaching the women! Unhappy is the place where it is done … . A short moment like a dream, then death comes for having known them… .[173]

While a passage from the Instructions of Any reads:

> Beware of a woman who is a stranger,
> One not known in her town:
> Don't stare at her when she goes by,
> Do not know her carnally.
> …
> I am pretty, she tells you daily,
> When she has no witnesses;
> She is ready to ensnare you,
> A great deadly crime when it is heard.[174]

Another prohibition had to do with having intercourse within the temple. Indeed, sexual activity within the temple was strictly forbidden. In Chapter 125 of the Book of the Dead (BD), also known as the "declaration of innocence," the deceased had to recite a series of acts which they did *not* commit. The recitation ensured their worthiness of achieving the afterlife. In one section of BD 125, we read: "I have not committed adultery in the sacred places of my city god."[175] Herodotus confirmed this prohibition and observed that the Egyptians "make it a matter of religious observance not to have intercourse with a woman in temples nor to enter a temple without washing after being with a woman … the Egyptians in this and in all other matters are exceeding[ly] strict against the desecration of their temples" (Book II, 64).[176] In the hot climate of Egypt, washing was good hygienic practice. The prohibition was not a pronouncement against sexual activity *per se*, but rather a ban concerning committing the act in sacred space. It should come as little surprise therefore that there is no evidence of temple prostitution in ancient Egypt. Another rationale for this prohibition is the general modesty of Egyptians. Indeed, while they enjoyed conjugal activity and celebrated the generative powers of sexual intercourse, they seem to have considered sex more of a private matter to be conducted indoors.[177]

Prohibitions were primarily directed against sexual activity that violated a friend's trust, or took place within sacred space. That latter prohibition may serve to debunk the idea that a God's Wife had a specifically sexual role in the temple.

The God's Wife's sexual role and her association with ithyphallic gods

Despite never defining how such a role played out in temple ritual, references to the God's Wife's "sexual role" may be found in current scholarship. For example, Gay Robins writes that the God's Wife was "probably responsible for rituals meant to stimulate the god sexually," although she admits that it is not clear how such a role "translated into temple cult."[178] Foremost among the often-"sexualized" rituals is playing music to the gods. But as we have seen above, the king may shake the sistrum before male and female deities and often received the *menat*-necklace from female goddesses. It has been shown that the former was part of a larger sequence of rituals designed for the enjoyment of the gods. Similarly, we have seen that none of the rituals that feature the God's Wife have remotely sexual connotations.

Moreover, while the title of God's Wife may have been associated with the ithyphallic god Min in the First Intermediate Period,[179] remarkably, with only one exception, there is no evidence linking the God's Wives to Min or any other ithyphallic deities. The exception is the title of a Divine Adorer of the Twenty-second dynasty: Karomama's. A statuette of Karomama lists her title as: the "Divine Adorer of the Amenope (in Egyptian: *douat netjer en Imen-opet*). Amenope, an ithyphallic form of Amun, was believed to reside in the temple of Luxor, whose name in Egyptian may be translated as the "Southern Harem." Karomama's title probably indicates that her responsibilities were most closely associated with the cult of this particular god.[180] Be that as it may, the fact is that there are no extant iconographic scenes that show any of the God's Wives of the Twenty-third to the Twenty-sixth dynasty next to Min or any other ithyphallic deities. Min's erect state was not considered "indecent." Min's erection denoted his fecundity and self-generating, creative powers.[181] Mythically, Min did not need a wife – and consequently, there was no need to depict a woman next to him. Similarly absent are representations of the dwarf god Bes, a house-hold deity, whose presence was noted in scenes "where physical love [was] celebrated."[182]

Although the door jambs of the chapel of Osiris-Wennofer-in-the-Midst-of-the-Persea-Tree are adorned with depictions of Amenirdis I (justified), and Shepenwepet II embracing the god, Amun, we have seen above how those scenes were part of a larger propagandist scheme aimed at legitimating Shepenwepet II into office.[183] Holding tight to Amun, Shepenwepet II appropriated the iconography of "divine marriage" to further assimilate with the goddess Mut.

The noticeable longevity of the God's Wives' tenure in office combined with the fact that no biological children are attested for any of the five women who held office between *c.* 740 and 525 BC indicate that they probably never bore children. As to whether they engaged in sexual relations, that's anybody's guess, and remains a private matter that becomes increasingly irrelevant in view of the political advantages gained by having a single, possibly sterile God's Wife in place. The God's Wives' singlehood may be best understood as a function of the economically advantageous aspects of adoption and the political climate prevalent during those turbulent times. Any restrictions placed on their reproductive rights may be best viewed from a political perspective: a childless God's Wife could not use her enormous power and influence to engender a rival dynasty.

EPILOGUE

The end of the God's Wife as an institution

It has been noted above that the office of God's Wife disappeared at the death of Ankhnesneferibre shortly after the Persian conquest of Egypt. This abrupt disappearance may be more directly related to the manner in which Persian women were socialized in the Achaemenid court than to the internal dynamics of Theban theocracy. In order for the office to have survived under Persian rule one of two courses of action could have been followed: (1) Nitocris B would attain *and* retain the office of God's Wife or (2) one of Darius I's own daughters would get appointed to office.[1] That Nitocris B could no longer hold office under Persian rule was a direct outcome of Achaemenid state policy, which prescribed the addition of "a layer of … [Persian] officials above the top layer of Egyptian officials …."[2] An Egyptian native could not retain a position of supreme economic or political significance. The office of God's Wife was no exception.

In following the precedent set by his Libyan, Nubian and Saite predecessors, Darius I could arguably have gained control over the Theban area in a peaceful manner. He would also have remained faithful to his own state policy. Several factors, however, contributed to the Persians' reluctance to send an unmarried royal daughter to reside in Thebes and control the vast wealth of the Amun Temple. In the Achaemenid court, the royal daughters functioned primarily as "pawns in the king's marriage policy."[3] They were not expected, nor were they trained, to hold a position of such economic independence. Archaeologically, the royal daughters are invisible.[4] Similarly, of all the classes of Persian society, only women are not represented in the palace reliefs of Persepolis.[5] The textual evidence is equally silent on "mortal women." Even when a royal daughter and mother could provide her son with his only link to the founder of the dynasty, her father, his accession record would avoid any mention of her.[6]

In the absence of archaeological, iconographic, and textual evidence, it seems logical to assume that Achaemenid royal women were not allowed the freedom and status exercised by Egyptian women. In the Achaemenid court, marriage alliances of royal daughters, not their singlehood, better achieved the royal agenda. Such alliances were manipulated to serve the double purpose of ensuring the loyalty of Persian nobles *and* limiting "the number of families marrying into the royal family."[7] For this reason, Achaemenid royal daughters were allowed to wed only members of the Persian nobility. It was not until Alexander the Great swept through the Persian territories that Darius III was forced to offer his daughter in marriage to a non-Persian, Alexander himself.[8] This offer stemmed from an extreme political circumstance. It was only under such extreme political conditions that Achaemenid royal daughters broke away from their traditions. That the situation in Egypt never compelled them to break away from their prescribed cultural traditions can be attributed to the Persians' superior military prowess and their effective administration of their vast empire. At no point did the Egyptian situation constitute one of the extreme circumstances that would require employing equally extreme measures.

The political and economic factors that necessitated the use of this political device under Nubian and Saite rule were eliminated by the advent of Persian rule in Egypt. The Persians' military advantage, their efficient administration of the provinces, including Egypt, and the tight control they kept over their vast empire shielded Achaemenid daughters from the need to break away from their cultural traditions. It might be argued then that it is precisely because of the elevated status attained by the God's Wives during the Twenty-fifth and Twenty-sixth dynasties that the office of God's Wife of Amun disappeared. A Persian princess could not fulfill such a role. The office of God's Wife of Amun had always been used as a vehicle for retaining or transmitting royal political power; once the political need for it was eliminated, the office disappeared.

In accounting for the disappearance of the office of the God's Wife shortly after the end of the Saite period, I have based my analysis on the assumption that the women who held this office during the Libyan, Nubian and Saite dynasties were single. To date, there is no evidence, textual, pictorial or archaeological that any of the five women who became God's Wives during the Libyan through Saite periods had husbands or gave birth to natural children. For several reasons, I have avoided the term "*celibate*," preferring the term "*single*." This choice arises from a conviction that (1) religiously mandated celibacy was *not* part of the ancient Egyptian religious tradition; (2) singlehood does not necessarily imply celibacy, especially in view of the fact there is documented evidence that the ancient Egyptians knew of, and used, contraceptives and abortifacients from as early as the Middle Kingdom. Finally, the single status of the God's Wives of that period was politically motivated.

The legacy of the God's Wives of Amun

Perhaps the most lasting legacy of the God's Wives is their contribution to Egyptian temple architecture. In the funerary chapel of Amenirdis at Medinet Habu, for instance, is the earliest known occurrence of an inner sanctuary surrounded by a corridor; a feature that becomes a standard element of later temple architecture.[9]

That the Nubian God's Wives remained very prominent figures in Nubian history is evident from King Aspelta's account of his ancestry, in which he mentions no fewer than six Divine Worshippers. Living some two hundred years after the Nubians left Egypt, Aspelta may have been metaphorically referring to the God's Wives as his mothers. He may have had an adoptive relationship in mind, when he had his inscription penned. Alternatively, it is possible that he traced his ancestry through a female line descendent from Amenirdis II. Such a female line could have resulted from a marital union that Amenirdis II embarked on after being ousted from her Theban position. It is conceivable though that this female line resulted from a sequence of adoptions that originated in "a second postulated adoption of Amenirdis II, of purely Napatan character." [10]

But perhaps the God's Wives' most lasting influence may be seen in the titles and epithets born by the Ptolemaic queens of Egypt. Indeed, it seems that the Ptolemaic queens borrowed most extensively from the titularies of the Nubian God's Wives.[11] Four Ptolemaic queens, for instance, employed the title "female Horus" (Egyptian: *heret*), frequently used by Shepenwepet II. Queen Arsinoe II, in particular, seems to have adopted several of the God's Wives' titles and epithets. She was a "Mistress of Appearances" (Egyptian: *nebet khaou*), a title borne by the Twenty-second dynasty God's Wife, Karomama. Like Ankhnesneferibre before her, Arsinoe II bore the title of "female governor" (Egyptian: *haty-aa*), and set the precedent for her successors by using another of Ankhnesneferibre's titles: *heqat*, or "female ruler."[12] Indeed, Arsinoe II, often considered "exceptional," a "pioneer for later queens," and a "role model for the dynasty," took the drastic measure of proclaiming herself a goddess.[13] Perhaps signifying her new status, Arsinoe II took the epithet, "Lady of all that the sun disk encircles," (Egyptian: *henout shen neb en iten*);[14] an epithet frequently born by both Amenirdis I and Ankhnesneferibre, and one that indicates the universality of her reach. As a pioneer of the Ptolemaic dynasty, Arsinoe II was the first queen to adopt characteristically Egyptian elements in her iconography. The double *uraeus*, for instance, appears on her statues.[15] The titles adopted by Arsinoe II also strongly evoke earlier Egyptian titles.[16] Arsinoe II's *prenomen*, *khenmet-ib-en-Maat*, or "She who is united with the Heart of Maat," for instance, is very similar to Shepenwepet I's *prenomen*, which in turn was a variant of Hatshepsut's throne name.[17] The three names are part of a handful of names that employ the rather rare element: *khnem*, or "united."

Although no evidence survives to indicate that the Ptolemaic princesses were indoctrinated in the history of Egypt, it is conceivable that the Ptolemaic queens' heavy borrowing from earlier Egyptian tradition was an attempt to legitimate their rule in Egypt by actively seeking a link with prominent female figures from the Egyptian past.

NOTES

INTRODUCTION

1 Erik Hornung, *Conceptions of God in Ancinet Egypt: The One and the Many*. Trans. John Baines (Ithaca: Cornell University Press, 1982), 60.
2 Donald B. Redford, *From Slave to Pharaoh: The Black Experience of Ancient Egypt* (Baltimore: Johns Hopkins University Press, 2003), 60, 72; Redford, D. B., *Pharaonic King-Lists, Annals and Day Books: A Contribution to the Study of the Egyptian Sense of History*. SSEA Publication III (Mississauga: Benben Publications, 1986), xiii–xiv.

1 THE HISTORICAL SETTING

1 A. H. Gardiner, *Egyptian Grammar: Being an Introduction to the Study of Hieroglyphs*. Third Edition, Revised (Oxford: Griffith Institute, 1957), 502.
2 Erik Hornung, *Conceptions of God in Ancient Egypt: The One and the Many*. Trans. John Baines (Ithaca: Cornell University Press, 1982), 38.
3 Hornung, *Conceptions of God*, 36.
4 Gardiner, *Egyptian Grammar*, 502.
5 Hornung, *Conceptions of God*, 38.
6 Gardiner, *Egyptian Grammar*, 492.
7 Ibid, 487.
8 Raymond O. Faulkner, *Concise Dictionary of Middle Egyptian* (Oxford: Griffith Institute, 1962), 310; and Gardiner, *Egyptian Grammar*, 487.
9 See, for example, A. M. Blackman, "On the Position of Women in Ancient Egyptian Hierarchy" *JEA* 7 (1921): 8–30 at 12–13; M. Gitton, *Les divines épouses de la 18e dynastie* (Paris: Les Belles-Lettres, 1984), 6; Gay Robins, *Women in Ancient Egypt* (Cambridge, Mass.: Harvard University Press, 1993), 149 and 153; and Lana Troy, *Patterns of Queenship in Ancient Egyptian Myth and History*. Uppsala Studies in Ancient Mediterranean Civilizations 14 (Uppsala, 1986), 91–92 and 94–96.
10 Betsy Bryan, "Property and the God's Wives of Amun" in *Women and Property;*, eds. D. Lyons and R. Westbrook (Harvard University: Center for Hellenic Studies, 2005): 1–15, at 2 and 5.
11 See Leonard H. Lesko, "Ancient Egyptian Cosmogonies and Cosmology" in *Religion in Ancient Egypt: Gods, Myth, and Religious Practice*, ed. Byron E. Shafer (Ithaca: Cornell University Press, 1991), 91–93, for a concise summary of this creation myth; and Hornung, *Conceptions of God*, 66–67, and 86, for a discussion of Atum's name.
12 Lesko, "Egyptian Cosmogonies," 93.
13 M. Gitton and J. Leclant, "Gottesgemahlin," *LÄ* II, 793, n.13–14; and Gitton, *Les divines épouses*, 5–6.
14 Hornung, *Conceptions of God*, 57–60.

15 H. G. Fischer, "Egyptian Women in the Old Kingdom and the Heracleopolitan Period," in *Women's Earliest Records from Ancient Egypt and Western Asia: Proceedings of the Conference on Women in the Ancient Near East,*, ed. B. S. Lesko (Atlanta: Scholars Press, 1989), 19; Gitton, *Les divines épouses*, 5.
16 Naguib Kanawati, *The Rock Tombs of El-Hawawish* 3 (Sydney: Macquarie Ancient History Association, 1982), 33–35 and Figure 26.
17 Ibid, 33; see William A. Ward, *Essays on Feminine Titles of the Middle Kingdom and Related Subjects* (Beirut: American University of Beirut, 1986), 14 and 18–19, for these two titles.
18 Ward, *Essays on Feminine Titles*, 19.
19 Ibid, 22 and 27–28.
20 Ibrahim Harari, "Nature de la Stèle de donation de function du roi Ahmôsis à la reine Ahmès-Nefertari," *ASAE* 56 (1959): 139–201.
21 See M. Gitton, *L'épouse du dieu Ahmes Néfertary: Documents sur sa vie et son culte posthume* (Paris: Les Belles-Lettres, 1975); Gitton, *Les divines épouses,* 21–23.
22 Hermann Kees, "Das Gottesweib Ahmes-Nefertari als Amonspriester," *Orientalia* 23 (1954), 57–63; and Michel Gitton, "La Résiliation d'une fonction religieuse: nouvelle interpétation de la stèle de donation d'Ahmès-Néfertary," *BIFAO* 76 (1976): 65–89.
23 Bryan, "Property and the God's Wives of Amun," at 6–7; see also comments by Bernadette Menu in "Women and Business Life in the First Millennium B.C." in *Women's Earliest Records*, 193–212.
24 Robins, *Women in Ancient Egypt*, 152.
25 Gay Robins, "The God's Wife of Amun in the 18th Dynasty in Egypt" in *Images of Women in Antiquity*, eds. A. Cameron and A. Kuhrt (London: Routledge, 1983), 65–78, at 70.
26 Bryan, "Property and the God's Wives of Amun," 6–7.
27 Troy, *Patterns of Queenship*, 171 and 188; Luc Gosselin, *Les Divines épouses d'Amon dans l'Égypte de la XIXe à la XXIe dynastie* (Paris: Cybele, 2007), 252.
28 Troy, *Patterns of Queenship*, 97–99.
29 M.-A. Bonhême, *Pharaon: Les secrets du pouvoir* (Paris: Armand Colin, 1988), 80–85.
30 For Hatshepsut's cycle, see PM II, 348–49; for Amenhotep III's copy, see PM II, 326–27.
31 John Baines, "The Dawn of the Amarna Age," in *Amenhotep III: Perspectives on His Reign*, eds. David O'Connor and Eric H. Cline (Ann Arbor: University of Michigan Press, 2001), 292.
32 William J. Murnane, *Texts from the Amarna Period in Egypt* (Altanta: Scholars Press), 1995, 22–27; Dimitri Meeks and Christine Favard-Meeks, *Daily Life of the Egyptian Gods*. Trans. G. M. Goshgarian (Ithaca: Cornell University Press, 1996), 59 and 121–22.
33 "Three stories of Wonder," in Miriam Lichtheim, *Ancient Egyptian Literature I: The Old and Middle Kingdoms* (Berkeley: University of California Press, 1973), 215–222, particularly 220–221.
34 Helmut Brunner, *Die Geburt des Gottkönigs des Neuen Reiches* I (Mainz, Wiesbaden, 1961), 60–62.
35 Betsy Bryan, "Antecedents to Amenhotep III," in *Amenhotep III: Perspectives on His Reign*, eds. David O'Connor and Eric H. Cline (Ann Arbor: University of Michigan Press, 2001), 29.
36 Ibid, 61.
37 W. Raymond Johnson, "Monuments and Monumental Art under Amenhotep III: Evolution and Meaning," in *Amenhotep III: Perspectives on His Reign*, eds. David O'Connor and Eric H. Cline (Ann Arbor: University of Michigan Press, 2001), 87.
38 Robins, "God's Wife of Amun," 70.
39 Troy, *Patterns of Queenship*, 97–99.
40 Erik Hornung, *History of Ancient Egypt,* trans. D. Lorton (Ithaca: Cornell University Press, 1999), 122; and Nicolas Grimal, *A History of Ancient Egypt*, trans. I. Shaw (Oxford: Blackwell, 1992), 288–290.
41 The Epigraphic Survey, *The Temple of Khonsu* I: *Scenes of King Herihor in the Court,* OIP 100 (Chicago: The Oriental Institute of the University of Chicago, 1979).

42 See Miriam Lichtheim, *Ancient Egyptian Literature* II: *The New Kingdom* (Berkeley: University of California Press, 1976), 224–30, for a translation of the report.
43 R. Krauss, "Isis," *LÄ* III, 203–4; T. B. Bács, "A Note on the Divine Adoratrix Isis, Daughter of Ramesses VI," *GM* 148 (1995): 7–11, at 10.
44 Gosselin, *Divines épouses: XIXe à la XXIe dynastie*, 206–7 and 257. See Part III below for a discussion of issues pertaining to the celibacy of the God's Wife.
45 J. Černý, "Queen Ēse of the Twentieth Dynasty and Her Mother," *JEA* 44 (1958): 31–37; and Gosselin, *Divines épouses: XIXe à la XXIe dynastie*, 148–54.
46 R. Krauss, "Isis," *LÄ* III, 203–4. The very few surviving documents seem to indicate that this is the case. Another, unknown wife of Ramses III, held the title of God's Wife, but she was not a Divine Adoratrice. See C. E. Sander-Hansen, *Das Gottesweib des Amun* (Copenhagen: Ejnar Munksgaard, 1940), 7; Gitton and Leclant, "Gottesgemahlin," *LÄ* II, 803. Cf. Troy, *Patterns of Queenship*, 171 and 188. See also J. Černý, "Queen Ēse," 32 and 35–36; Gosselin, *Divines épouses: XIXe à la XXIe dynastie*, 193–208.
47 Gosselin, *Divines épouses: XIXe à la XXIe dynastie*, 258.
48 Not to be confused with the wife of Pinudjem I.
49 Cf. Troy, *Patterns of Queenship*, 173–74 and 188; Gitton and Leclant, "Gottesgemahlin," *LÄ* II, 803–4.
50 Gosselin, *Divines épouses: XIXe à la XXIe dynastie*, 213–50, especially p. 237.
51 Ibid, 223.
52 Cf. Troy, *Patterns of Queenship*, 177, 188.
53 Gosselin, *Divines épouses: XIXe à la XXIe dynastie*, 260; Gitton and Leclant, *LÄ* II, 800.
54 The political situation in Egypt is vividly described in Piye's victory stela (CG 48862), which remains one of the major sources of information on Egypt at the time. K. A. Kitchen, *Third Intermediate Period in Egypt (1100–650 BC),* (Warminster: Aris & Phillips, 1995), 136–37, bases much of his analysis on this period on Piye's stela. See Miriam Lichtheim, *Ancient Egyptian Literature* III: *The Late Period* (Berkeley: University of California Press, 1980), 68–80 for a translation of the stela.
55 Richard Fazzini distinguishes these four administrative centers from various other principalities in Fazzini, *Egypt: Dynasty XXII–XXV* (Leiden and New York, E. J. Brill, 1988), 3.
56 Anthony Leahy, "The Libyan Period in Egypt: An Essay in Interpretation," *Libyan Studies* 16 (1985): 51–65, at 59.
57 Robert Ritner, "Fragmentation and Re-integration in the Third Intermediate Period," 9 (forthcoming)
58 B. Trigger, *Nubia under the Pharaohs* (London: Thames and Hudson, 1976), 139.
59 L. Török, *The Kingdom of Kush: Handbook of the Napatan – Meroitic Civilization* (Leiden: Brill, 1997), 144.
60 Trigger, *Nubia*, 140.
61 Ibid, 139.
62 David Aston and John H. Taylor, "The Family of Takeloth III and the 'Theban' Twenty-third Dynasty," in Libya and Egypt (c. 1300–750 BC),, ed. Anthony Leahy (London: School of Oriental and African Studies, 1990), 131–54, at 147–48; see also D. Aston, "Two Osiris Figures of the Third Intermediate Period," *JEA* 77 (1991): 99–101; see also Jean Yoyotte, "Des lions et des chats: Contribution à la prosopographie de l'époque libyenne," *RdÉ* 39 (1988): 169–70.
63 Török, *Kingdom of Kush*, 144, especially the temple of Khnum at Elephantine.
64 L. Török in *Fontes Historiae Nubiorum: Textual Sources for the History of the Middle Nile Region between the Eighth Century BC and the Sixth Century AD*. Vol 1: *From the Eighth to the Mid-Fifth Century BC*, eds. T. Eide, T. Hägg, R. H. Pierce, and L. Török (Bergen: University of Bergen, Department of Classics, 1994), 41. Henceforth cited as *FHN*.
65 L. Török, *FHN*, 42.

66 Kitchen, *Third Intermediate Period*, 149–51; D. Dunham and M. F. Laming Macadam, "Names and Relationships of The Royal Family of Napata," *JEA* 35 (1949): 139–49, esp. pp. 141 and 149.
67 See E. R. Russmann, "Egypt and the Kushites: Dynasty XXV," in *Africa and Africans in Antiquity*,, ed. E. M. Yamauchi (East Lansing: Michigan State University Press, 2001), 116.
68 Jean Leclant, "Kashta, Pharaon, en Egypte," *ZÄS* 90 (1963): 74–81, at 74–75.
69 A photograph of the stela is published in Leclant, "Kashta," 75. A translation and commentary of the stela may be found in R. Pierce and L. Török, *FHN*, 45–47.
70 Kitchen, *Third Intermediate Period*, 151.
71 Török, *Kingdom of Kush*, 155.
72 Ibid, 155.
73 Cf. L. Bell, "The New Kingdom 'Divine' Temple: The Example of Luxor," in *Temples of Ancient Egypt*,, ed. B. E. Shafer (Ithaca: Cornell University Press, 1997), 157–76, for the *Opet*-festival as a celebration legitimating kingship.
74 Kitchen, *Third Intermediate Period*, 231; Richard A. Parker, "King Py, a Historical Problem," *ZÄS* 93 (1966): 111–114; Török, *Kingdom of Kush*, 155, dates the campaign to 728 BC; it is elsewhere dated to 730 BC, e.g., in Russmann, "Egypt and the Kushites," 117.
75 Lichtheim, *Ancient Egyptian Literature* III, 68–80; R. H. Pierce, "Great Triumphal Stela of Piye, Year 21" in *FNH*, 62–113; and N.-C. Grimal, *Étude sur la propagande royale égyptienne I: La stèle triomphale de Pi(ankh)y au Musée du Caire (JE 48862 et 47086–47089)*. Mémoires publiés par les membres de l'institut français d'archéologie orientale du Caire 105 (Cairo: IFAO, 1981).
76 Pierce, "Great Triumphal Stela," 77.
77 Ibid, 89–98.
78 Török, *Kingdom of Kush*, 163; and Török, "Piye (Piankhy, Py). Titles" in *FNH*, 51–52.
79 Russmann, "Egypt and the Kushites," 117.
80 L. Török, "Shabaqo. Evidence for Reign. Regnal years," in *FHN*, 121–23.
81 Fazzini, *Dynasty XXII–XXV*, 3.
82 W. G. Waddell, *Manetho* (Cambridge, Mass.: Harvard University Press, 1940), 168–69.
83 Russmann, "Egypt and the Kushites," 117–18.
84 R. H. Pierce, "Commemorative scarab of Shabaqo," in *FHN*, 123–125 at 124.
85 Török, *Kingdom of Kush*, 166.
86 Ibid, 167.
87 Russmann, "Egypt and the Kushites," 118.
88 Ibid, 118.
89 Török, *Kingdom of Kush*, 167.
90 Ibid, 168.
91 Kitchen, *Third Intermediate Period*, 201 and 382. The hiatus lasted from *c.* 754 to 704 BC (ibid., 480). See also H. Kees, *Die Hohenpriester des Amun Von Karnak von Herihor bis zum Ende der Äthiopenzeit. Probleme der Ägyptologie* 4 (Leiden: E.J. Brill, 1964), 163–69; and G. Vittmann, *Priester und Beamte in Theben der Spätzeit.* BÄ 1 (Vienna: Veröffentlichungen der Institut für Afrikanistik und Ägyptologie der Universität Wien, 1978), 61–63.
92 See Török, *Kingdom of Kush*, 168, for the suggestion that Shabako's appointment of his son was directly related to his inability to achieve the needed legitimacy through the appointment of a God's Wife, since that position was already occupied by Amenirdis I and Shepenwepet II.
93 Russmann, "Egypt and the Kushites," 118; Manetho, *Aegyptiaca*. Trans. W. G. Waddell (Cambridge, Mass.: Harvard University Press, 1940), 166–69.
94 L. Török, "Shebitqo. Evidence for reign. Regnal years," in *FHN*, 127–29; Russmann, "Egypt and the Kushites," 118.
95 Russmann, "Egypt and the Kushites," 118.

96 Török, *Kingdom of Kush*, 170, citing Kawa III, line 9, and Kawa V, line 14.
97 Pierce, "Stela of Taharqo on the high Nile in Year 6 from Kawa (Kawa V)" in *FHN*, 145–55, at 153–54.
98 Török, *Kingdom of Kush*, 170, citing Kawa V, line 17.
99 Török, *Kingdom of Kush*, 171.
100 Jean Leclant, *Recherches sur les monuments thébains de la XXVe dynastie dite éthiopienne*. Bd'É 36 (Cairo: IFAO, 1965), 56–58.
101 Russmann, "Egypt and the Kushites," 119.
102 Török, *Kingdom of Kush*, 174; Russmann, "Egypt and the Kushites," 119.
103 Russmann, "Egypt and the Kushites," 119.
104 L. Török, "Tanutamani. Evidence for reign. Regnal years," in *FHN*, 191–93, at 192.
105 Ibid,192.
106 Kitchen, *Third Intermediate Period*, 172.
107 Ibid, 172–73.
108 Ibid, 399 and Leclant, *Monuments thébains*, 352.
109 Regnal dates for Osorkon III follow Kitchen, *Third Intermediate Period*, 349.
110 For a discussion of the God's Wives' singlehood/celibacy, see Chapter 3.
111 Legrain, "Osiris-Hiq-Djeto," 131; PM II, 206 (13). On the title Lord of Ritual (Egyptian: *neb ir khet*), see Caroyln Routledge, *Ancient Egyptian Ritual Practice: ir-xt and nt-a* (Ph.D. dissertation, University of Toronto, 2001), and idem, "Did Women 'Do Things' in Ancient Egypt?" in *Sex and Gender in Ancient Egypt,*, ed. Carolyn Graves-Brown (Swansea: The Classical Press of Wales, 2008), 157–77, especially pp. 161–64.
112 Kitchen, *Third Intermediate Period*, 352, and genealogical table on p. 476.
113 Ibid, 201, 359.
114 See Uvo Hölscher, *The Excavations of Medinet Habu. Volume V: The Post-Ramesside Remains* (Chicago: University of Chicago Press, 1954), 17–20.
115 Ibid, 18.
116 PM II, 205–206; see also Georges Legrain, "Le temple et les chapelles d'Osiris à Karnak I: Le temple d'Osiris-Hiq-Djeto," *RT* 22 (1900): 125–36, and 146–49; and Donald B. Redford, "An Interim Report on the Second Season of Work at the Temple of Osiris, Ruler of Eternity, Karnak," *JEA* 59 (1973): 16–30, at 20.
117 Kitchen, *Third Intermediate Period*, 151, n. 289; A. Lohwasser, "Queenship in Kush: Status, Role, and Ideology of Royal Women," *JARCE* 38 (2001): 61–76, at 69; Grimal, *History of Ancient Egypt*, 335.
118 Sander-Hansen, *Gottesweib*, 9. See also Kitchen, *Third Intermediate Period*, 149–50 and 478.
119 Kitchen, *Third Intermediate Period*, 359.
120 Anthony Leahy, "The Adoption of Ankhnesneferibre at Karnak," *JEA* 82 (1996): 145–65, at 162. See also Anthony Leahy, "Kushite Monuments at Abydos," in *The Unbroken Reed: Studies in the Culture and Heritage of Ancient Egypt in Honour of A. F. Shore*. Occasional Publication 11,, eds. C. Eyre, A. Leahy, and L. M. Leahy (London: Egypt Exploration Society, 1994), 182–87; Stephen Wenig, "Pabatma-Pekereslo-Pekar-tor: Ein Beitrag zur Frühgeschichte der Kuschiten," *Meroitica* 12 (1990): 333–52, at 345.
121 For a description of the Nubian addition, see Leclant, *Monuments thébains*, 47–54.
122 For a more detailed description of the layout and content of the vignettes depicting the God's Wives Amenirdis I and Shepenwepet on the façade of this chapel, see Mariam F. Ayad, "The Transition from Libyan to Nubian Rule: The Role of the God's Wife of Amun" in *The Libyan Period in Egypt: Historical and Chronological Problems of the Third Intermediate Period*, eds. Gerard P. F. Broekman, R. J. Demarée and Olaf E. Kaper (Leiden: The Netherlands Institute for the Near East, 2008), 29–49, especially 38–40.
123 Leclant, *Monuments thébains*, 369, n.2; and *idem*, "Gotteshand," *LÄ* II, 813; see also Mariam F. Ayad, "The Funerary Texts of Amenirdis I: Analysis of their Layout and Purpose," (Ph.D. diss., Brown University, 2003), 14 and 20–21.

124 Ayad, "Funerary Texts of Amenirdis I," 20; for statues of Ahmose-Nefertari, see Legrain, "Osiris-Hiq-Djeto," 135.

125 The epithet is inscribed on the back pillar of the Amenirdis alabaster statue in the Cairo museum. See K. Jansen-Winkeln, "Amenirdis und Harwa," *DE* 35 (1996): 39–48, at 40. See also Gitton, *Ahmes Néfertary*, 100, for Ahmos-Nefertari's similar epithet *ḏd.s ḫt nbt ir.tw n.s*. For a fuller discussion of the epithets, see Ayad, "The Funerary Texts of Amenirdis I," 20–21.

126 Kitchen, *Third Intermediate Period*, 386–87.

127 PM II, 194–95; Leclant, *Monuments thébains*, 23–36; Georges Legrain, "Le temple et les chapelles d'Osiris à Karnak III: La chapelle d'Osiris, Maître de la Vie ( )," *RT* 24 (1902): 208–14; Leclant, Jean. "Osiris *p3-wšb-i3d*," in *Ägyptologische Studien herausgegeben von O. Firchow* (Berlin: Akademie Verlag, 1955), 197–204.

128 PM II, 202–203; Leclant, *Monuments thébains*, 41–47; Donald B. Redford, "New Light on Temple J at Karnak," *Orientalia* 55 (1986): 1–15.

129 PM II, 5–13 and plan ii for the ramp where blocks belonging to this chapel were recovered; Leclant, *Monuments thébains*, 379–81; Barguet and Leclant, *Karnak Nord* III, 109–28.

130 Hölscher, *Excavation* V, 22.

131 See Hölscher, *Excavation* V, 22.

132 Contra Grimal, *History of Egypt*, 344, who assigns Amenirdis I's chapel to Shabaqo's reign. Regnal dates are based on Kitchen, *Third Intermediate Period*, 154 and 378–79.

133 Ayad, "Funerary Texts of Amenirdis I," 46–71.

134 Hölscher, *Excavation* V, 20.

135 IHölscher, *Excavation* V, 22; Arnold, *Temples*, 49.

136 Hölscher, *Excavation* V, 22.

137 G. Daressy, "Inscriptions de la chapelle d'Amenirtis à Médinet-Habou," *RT* 23 (1901): 4–18.

138 For Amenirdis's selection of the Opening of the Mouth scenes, see Mariam F. Ayad, "The Selection and Layout of the Opening of the Mouth Scenes in the Chapel of Amenirdis I at Medinet Habu," *Journal of the American Research Center in Egypt* 41 (2004):113–134; for her selections from the Pyramid Texts, see Mariam F. Ayad, "Some Remarks on the Pyramid Texts Inscribed in the Chapel of Amenirdis I at Medinet Habu" in *Essays Presented to Leonard H. Lesko upon his Retirement from the Wilbour Chair of Egyptology at Brown University, June 2005*, eds. Stephen E. Thompson and Peter Der Manuelian (Providence: Brown University, Department of Egyptology and Ancient Western Asian Studies, 2008), 1–13; and "The Pyramid Texts of Amenirdis I: Selection and Layout" in *Journal of the American Research Center in Egypt* 44 (2007): (71–92).

139 B. J. Kemp, *Ancient Egypt: Anatomy of a Civilization* (London and New York: Routledge, 1993), 92–98; for the use of the tent shrine in the temple complex of Djoser, particularly "temple T," see J.-P. Lauer, *La Pyramide à Degrés: L'architecture* I: *Texte* (Cairo: IFAO, 1936), 149–52.

140 The superstructures of the royal tombs at Tanis and the chapel of Shepenwepet I were built of mud brick. Cf. R. Stadelmann, "Das Grab im Tempelhof: Der Typus des Königsgrabes in der Spätzeit," *MDAIK* 27 (1971): 111–23.

141 Arnold, *Temples*, 49.

142 See Hölscher, *Excavation* V, 22 for remarks on the structural changes of the chapel of Amenirdis I and the argument that it was originally a mud brick structure; and ibid., 18–20, for the mud brick funerary chapel of Shepenwepet I. See also Redford, "Osiris, Ruler of Eternity," 19, for coincidence of the switch from mud brick to stone masonry in this chapel with the dynastic change from the Twenty-third to the Twenty-fifth dynasty.

143 Hölscher, *Medinet Habu* V, 23–26, and Figure 29.

144 Kitchen, *Third Intermediate Period*, 480.

145 Leclant, *Monuments thébains*, 363–367.

146 Kitchen, *Third Intermediate Period*, 403–4.

147 D. Dunham and F. Laming McAdam, "Names and Relationships of the Royal Family of Napata," *JEA* 35 (1949): 139–49, at 141 note 1.
148 Hölscher, *Medinet Habu* V, 23 and PM II, 478.
149 L. Habachi, "Mentuhotep, the Vizier and Son-in-Law of Taharqa" in E. Endesfelder *et al.* (eds) *Ägypten und Kusch: Schriften zur Geschichte und Kulture des Altes Orients* (Berlin, 1977), 165–70.
150 R. Morkot, "Kingship and Kinship in the Empire of Kush" in *Studien zum antiken Sudan: Akten der 7. Internationalen Tagung für meroitishtische Forschungen von 14. bis 19. September 1992 in Gosen bei Berlin*, ed. Steffen Wenig (Wiesbaden: Harrassowitz Verlag, 1999), 179–229, at 197.
151 Leclant, *Monuments thébains*, 364–65.
152 See A. Dodson, "The Problem of Amenirdis II and the Heirs to the Office of God's Wife of Amun during the Twenty-sixth Dynasty," *JEA* 88 (2002): 179–86, for the suggestion that there was a Shepenwepet III who may have succeeded Nitocris and held office before the ascension of Ankhnesneferibre.
153 Erhart Graefe, "Nochmals zum Gebrauch des Titels *dwꜣt-nṯr* in der Spätzeit" *JEA* 89 (2003): 246–47.
154 See p. 139 below.
155 For the scene depicted in the Red Chapel of Hatshepsut, see pp. 172–79; for the God's Hand performing the sacred rites at Kom Djeme, see p. 181 below; for her role in the ritual elevation of the *tjest*-column, see pp. 184–88, especially p. 187 below.
156 For the jambs bearing Shepenwepet's titles and filiation, see p. 158 below; for the blocks bearing scenes from the *sed* festival, see p. 214 below.
157 Anthony Spalinger, "The Concept of the Monarchy during the Saite Epoch – and Essay of Synthesis," *Orientalia* 47 (1978): 12–36, at 14.
158 Amélie Kuhrt, *The Ancient Near East* II (London: Routledge, 1995), 637.
159 Spalinger, "The Concept of Monarchy," 16.
160 Spalinger, "The Concept of Monarchy," 15, and Kitchen, *Third Intermediate Period*, 405–6.
161 Spalinger, "The Concept of Monarchy," 19; and Kuhrt 640.
162 Kitchen, *Third Intermediate Period*, 405 and Spalinger, "The Concept of Monarchy," 18.
163 A. B. Lloyd, "The Late Period," in *Ancient Egypt: A Social History*, 335; Kitchen, *Third Intermediate Period*, 403–5.
164 Ricardo A. Caminos, "The Nitocris Adoption Stela," *JEA* 50 (1964): 71–101, at 74.
165 ibid., 74 and 81.
166 ibid., 81.
167 ibid., 74.
168 ibid., 75, and 100–101.
169 ibid., 78.
170 ibid., 79.
171 ibid., 74.
172 Kitchen, *Third Intermediate Period*, 404; Grimal, *History of Ancient Egypt*, 354.
173 Caminos, "The Nitocris Adoption Stela," 75.
174 Tom Logan, "The *Jmyt-pr* Document: Form, Function, and Significance," *JARCE* 37 (2000): 49–73, at 70.
175 ibid., 71.
176 Logan, "The *Imyt-pr* Document," 67.
177 Caminos, "The Nitocris Adoption Stela," 74.
178 Alan H. Gardiner, "Adoption Extraordinary," *JEA* 26 (1940): 23–29, especially 23–24; C. J. Eyre, "The Adoption Papyrus in Social Contex,t" *JEA* 78 (1992): 207–21; S. Allam, "A new look at the Adoption Papyrus (reconsidered)," *JEA* 76 (1990): 189–91.
179 Logan, "The *Imyt-pr* Document," 71.
180 Caminos, "The Nitocris Adoption Stela," 75 and 87.
181 Bryan, "Property and the God's Wife," 11.

182 Lines 16–17 of the decree. See Caminos, "The Nitocris Adoption Stela," 75.
183 Spalinger, "Concept of Monarchy," 17, 26, 29, 30.
184 ibid., 14.
185 ibid., 16.
186 PM II, plan iv [3].
187 PM II, 13–14; Louis A. Christophe, *Karnak-Nord* III: *(1945–1949)*. Fouilles de l'Institut Français du Caire XXIII (Cairo: IFAO, 1951), 29–48.
188 PM II, 19–20; Christophe, *Karnak-Nord* III, 97–112.
189 Hölscher, *Medinet Habu* V, 24, and Figure 29.
190 Alan H. Gardiner, *Egypt of the Pharaohs: An Introduction* (Oxford: Clarendon Press, 1961), 354; Lloyd, "The Late Period," 303; Leahy, "Adoption of Ankhnesneferibre," 160.
191 Spalinger, "The Concept of Monarchy," 20 and Kuhrt 640–41.
192 Spalinger, "The Concept of Monarchy," 21–23.
193 Kuhrt, 642.
194 Gardiner, *Egypt of the Pharaohs*, 354; Lloyd, "The Late Period," 303; Leahy, "Adoption of Ankhnesneferibre": 160.
195 Gardiner, *Egypt of the Pharaohs*, 354; Leahy, "Adoption of Ankhnesneferibre," 146 and 158. Leahy indicates that, on her adoption stela, Ankhnesneferibre is referred to as first prophet of Amun, *hem netjer tepy en Imen*, *before* her formal "accession ceremony" (line 8 of the stela). Apparently she held the title of high priest of Amun as an "adopted daughter of Nitocris I." The stela was first published in 1904 by G. Maspero, "Deux Monuments de la Princesse Ankhnasnofiribri," *ASAE* 5 (1904): 84–92.
196 For the chapel of Osiris-Wennofer-Neb-djefa, see PM II, 193–94 and xx. For the additions Ankhnesneferibre made to her adoptive mother's chapel, see PM II, 192–93. Scenes engraved on the walls of these two chapels are discussed in detail in Part II.
197 PM II, 5–6; Barguet and Leclant, *Karnak-Nord* III, 128–31.
198 PM II, 19; Christophe, *Karnak-Nord* III, 19–23.
199 Hölscher, *Medinet Habu* V, 28.
200 Kuhrt, 642–43 and Spalinger, "The Concept of Monarchy," 25.
201 Kuhrt, 644–45 and Spalinger, "The Concept of Monarchy," 25–26.
202 Spalinger, "The Concept of Monarchy," 27 and Kuhrt, 636.
203 Anthony Leahy, "The Earliest Dated Monument of Amasis and the End of the Reign of Apries," *JEA* 74 (1988): 197–8; and *idem*, "Adoption of Ankhnesneferibre," 158.
204 Kuhrt, 646.
205 H. de Meulenaere, "La famille du roi Amasis," *JEA* 54 (1968): 187; see also P. Barguet, *Le temple d'Amon-Re à Karnak: Essai d'exégèse* (Cairo: IFAO, 1962), 6 and 14, where her name is associated with Psametik III's.
206 Leahy, "Adoption of Ankhnesneferibre," 162. For Nitocris B as High Priest of Amun, see Vittmann, *Priester und Beamte*, 63. Note that here only the date of her appointment is given.
207 Initially published by C. E. Sander-Hanssen, *Die religiösen Texte auf dem Sarg der Anchnesneferibre, neu herausgegeben und erklärt* (Copenhagen: Levin & Munksgaard, 1936), the sarcophagus of Ankhnesneferibre most recently appeared in Nigel C. Strudwich, *Masterpieces of Ancient Egypt* (London: Trustees of the British Museum, 2006), 276–77.
208 Excluded from this list are Amenirdis II and Nitocris B as they each attained the status of "heiress apparent," but in all likelihood, never assumed the title of God's Wife of Amun.
209 Jürgen von Beckerath, *Handbuch der ägyptischen Königsnamen* (Berlin: Deutscher Kunstverlag, 1984), 264–65, no. 4.
210 *Setep-en-Amen* was part of the *prenomen* of Amenemope (ibid., 254 no. 4), Siamun (ibid., 254 no. 6), and the High Priest of Amun Pinudjem I (ibid., 255 no. 1) of the Twenty-first dynasty, as well as Sheshonq I (ibid., 257 no. 1), Osorkon II (ibid., 259 no. 5), and Sheshonq III (ibid., 260 no. 7) of the Twenty-second dynasty. In addition to Osorkon III, two other Twenty-third dynasty rulers incorporated *Setep-en-Amen* in their throne names:

Pedubaste (ibid., 264 no. 1) and Rudamun (ibid., 266 no. 6). *Mery-Amen* was an epithet commonly added to the birth names of almost all the rules of dynasties XXI–XXIII (see von Beckerath, 253–54, no. 1; ibid., 254, no. 6; ibid., 255, no. 1; ibid., 257, no. 1; ibid., 258, no. 2; ibid., 259–260, no. 6; ibid., 260, no. 7; ibid., 261, no. 8; ibid., 261, no. 9; ibid., 262, no. 10; ibid., 263, no. 5; ibid., 264, nos. 1–3; ibid., 265, nos. 4–5; ibid., 266, nos. 6–7).

211 Von Beckerath, *Königsnamen*, 226, no. 5. For the epithet occurring before Hatshepsut's name as a God's Wife, see for example, the inscription on a Kohl jar included in the exhibition catalogue: *Hatshepsut from Queen to Pharaoh,*, ed. C. Roehrig (New York: Metropolitan Museum of Art, 2005), 143.

212 Robins, "The Names of Hatshepsut as King," 103 and 107–108; Beckerath, *Königsnamen*, 226, no. 5.

213 Robins, "The Names of Hatshepsut as King," 107.

214 Török, *The Kingdom of Kush*, 200–201, 207, where he notes that from "Shabaqo onwards, the continuity of the Kushite dynasty is repeated stressed. Titles without exact Egyptian models or parallels repeatedly occur in titularies, and they testify to a traditional procedure in which a titulary was, as a whole, created as an individual proclamation. The maintenance of this procedure is also attested by the fact that there is no Kushite titulary which would in its entirety correspond to an Egyptian titulary."

215 Török, *The Kingdom of Kush*, 197, 200–201.

216 Von Beckerath, *Königsnamen*, 271–272.

217 Kitchen, *Third Intermediate Period*, 359.

218 A case for omitting the preposition in royal names was made in reference to the omission of the preposition *mi* "like" from the throne names of Tuthmosis III and Ramses II in John Bennett, "The Meaning of the Royal Nomen and *Prenomen*," *JEA* 206–207.

219 Von Beckerath, *Königsnamen*, 226, no. 5.

220 Török, *Kingdom of Kush*, 200. Piye's earlier Horus name is not included in Von Beckerath, *Königsnamen*, 269, no. 3.

221 Von Beckerath, *Königsnamen*, 270, no. 5; Török, *Kingdom of Kush*, 201.

222 Von Beckerath, *Königsnamen*, 271, no. 6; Török, *Kingdom of Kush*, 201.

223 Rainer Hanning, *Grosses Handwörterbuch Ägyptisch–Deutsch. Die Sprache der Pharaonen (2800–950 v. Chr.)* (Mainz: Verlag Philipp von Zabern, 1995), 586–87; Faulkner, *Concise Dictionary*, 185; Donald B. Redford, "*ḫꜥy* and Its Derivatives," in *Studies in the History and Chronology of the Eighteenth Dynasty* (Toronto: University of Toronto Press, 1967), 3–27; Margit Schunck, *Untersuchungen zum Wortstamm ḫꜥ* (Bonn: Dr. Rudolf Habelt GMBH, 1985).

224 K. A. Kitchen, "The Titularies of the Ramesside Kings as Expression of Their Ideal Kingship" *ASAE* 71 (1987): 131–141, at 131–32.

225 Von Beckerath, *Königsnamen*, 234, no. 1.

226 Kitchen, "The Titularies of the Ramesside Kings," 132; For the names of Seti I, see Von Beckerath, *Königsnamen*, 234, no. 2.

227 Kitchen, "The Titularies of the Ramesside Kings," 132–33.

228 Gardiner, *Egyptian Grammar*, 469.

229 H. te Velde, "Towards a minimal definition of the goddess Mut," *Ex Oriente Lux* no. 26 (1979–1980): 3–9, at 6. See also *ibid.*, 4, where Te Velde further explores the connection between Nekhbet and Mut.

230 Ibid., 6.

231 Ibid., 3–9, at 7.

232 See chapter III below for a detailed discussion of this scene.

2 RITES AND RITUALS

1 C. J. Bleeker, *Egyptian Festivals: Enactments of Religious Renewal*. Studies in the History of Religions, Supplement to Numen 13 (Leiden: Brill, 1967), 48.
2 Hornung, *Conceptions of God in Ancient Egypt*, 229.
3 Cf. Michel Gitton, "Le rôle de la femme dans le clergé d'Amon à la 18e dynastie," *BSFE* 75 (1976): 31–46, which focuses on Eighteenth dynasty evidence; and S-A. Naguib, *Le clergé féminin d'Amon thébain à la 21e dynastie* (Leuven: Uitgevery Peeters en Department Oriëntalistiek, 1990), 211–24, which examines the Twenty-first dynasty evidence for women in temple hierarchy. A welcome addition to recent scholarship is Luc Gosselin's *Les divines épouses d'Amon dans l'Egypte de la XIXeme à la XXIeme dynastie* (Paris: Cybele, 2007).
4 Ingrid Stoeper's PhD dissertation, "De Bouwactiviteit van de Godsgemalinnen van Amon van de 25e en 26e Dynastie" (Gent, 1997), which has yet to be published, catalogued the iconographic scenes in which the God's Wives appear.
5 Robins, *Women in Ancient Egypt*, 153 and 156, Troy, *Patterns of Queenship*, 91–92.
6 Lise Manniche, *Music and Musicians in Ancient Egypt* (London: British Museum, 1991), 57.
7 Manniche, *Music and Musicians*, 57, quoting Diodorus.
8 Manniche, *Music and Musicians*, 63–65.
9 PM II, 205 (9); Legrain, "Osiris-Hiq-Djeto," 129. D. B. Redford, "An Interim Report on the Second Season of Work at the Temple of Osiris, Ruler of Eternity, Karnak" *JEA* 59 (1973): 16–30, at 21 and pl. 20. A line drawing of the scene was also published in Redford, *From Slave to Pharaoh*, Fig. 16.
10 See David P. Silverman "Divinity and Deity in Ancient Egypt," in *Religion in Ancient Egypt: Gods, Myth, and Religious Practice*, ed. Byron E. Shafer (Ithaca: Cornell University Press, 1991), 33; and Leonard H. Lesko, "Egyptian Cosmogonies," 111.
11 Eberhard Otto, *Ancient Egyptian Art: The Cults of Osiris and Amon*. Trans. Kate Bosse-Griffiths (New York: Thames and Hudson, 1967), 52 and 123.
12 H. Schäffer, *Principles of Egyptian Art*, ed. E. Brunner-Traut. Trans. John Baines (Oxford: Griffith Institute, 2002), 205.
13 Manniche, *Music and Musicians*, 63.
14 Ibid., 62; Christiane Ziegler, "Sistrum," *LÄ* V, 959–963; Marleen Reynders, "Names and Types of the Egyptian Sistrum," in *Acts of the Seventh International Congress of Egyptologists*, ed. C. J. Eyre (Leuven: Peeters, 1998), 945–55.
15 Geoffrey Graham, "Insignias" in *The Oxford Encyclopedia of Ancient Egypt* I, ed. Donald B. Redford (Oxford: Oxford University Press, 2001), 163–67.
16 See Schäffer, *Principles of Egyptian Art*, 227–30.
17 As suggested by Professor A. Niwinski in a personal communication on October 27, 2007. See also Schäffer, *Principles of Egyptian Art*, 172–73, for non-overlapping juxtaposed figures represented one behind the other when in actuality they would be *next to* one another. This was also a typical way of depicting couples seated next to each other: the wife is almost always shown seated behind her husband, and consequently, farther from the table of offerings and the viewer. See Schäffer, *Principles of Egyptian Art*, 173–77.
18 Gay Robins, "Some Principles of Compositional Dominance and Gender Hierarchy in Egyptian Art," *JARCE* 31 (1994): 33–40, at 36.
19 Ibid., 36; emphasis mine.
20 Ibid., 38.
21 Amenirdis's shawl is similar to the one depicted in Gillian Vogelsang-Eastwood, *Pharaonic Egyptian Clothing* (Leiden: E. J. Brill, 1993), 158, Fig. 9.2.
22 Hieroglyphic text based on personal photographs taken at the wall in 2003 and 2007. The texts were also published in Legrain, "Osiris-Hiq-Djeto," 127.
23 Hieroglyphic text based on personal photographs taken at the wall in 2003 and 2007; it was also published in Legrain, "Osiris-Hiq-Djeto," 127.

24 Hieroglyphic text based on personal photographs taken at the wall in 2007; it was also published in Legrain, "Osiris-Hiq-Djeto," 127.
25 Jean Leclant, "Tefnout et les Divines Adoratrices thébaines," *MDAIK* 15 (1957):166–71, at 170.
26 Leclant, "Tefnout," 170, n. 5.
27 Ibid., 170.
28 Edouard Naville, *The Temple of Deir el-Bahri* VI: *Lower Terrace* (London: Egypt Exploration Fund, 1908), 7 and pl. CLXII. See pp. 103–108 below for a discussion of the ritual driving of the four calves.
29 Christian Leitz, *Lexikon der Ägyptischen Götter und Götterbezeichnungen* I. Orientalia Lovaniensia Analecta 110 (Leuven: Peeters, 2002), 313–15.
30 Faulkner, *Concise Dictionary*, 64.
31 Ibid., 229. However, Amun is not listed as having the epithet "*ser*" in Leitz, *Lexikon der Ägyptischen Götter* I.
32 Leonard H. Lesko, "Ancient Egyptian Cosmogonies," 105–6; and Richard A. Parker and Leonard H. Lesko, "The Khonsu Cosmogony," in *Pyramid Studies and Other Essays Presented to I. E. S. Edwards,*, ed. John Baines *et al.*, Occasional Publications 7. London: Egypt Exploration Society, 1988, 168–75.
33 Otto, *The Cults of Osiris and Amon*, 124.
34 Te Velde, "A Minimal Definition of Mut," 7.
35 James P. Allen, *Middle Egyptian: An Introduction to the Language and Culture of Hieroglyphs* (Cambridge: Cambridge University Press, 2000), 217.
36 As is the case in the corresponding inscription accompanying the presentation of *Maat*, discussed below on pp. 119–135.
37 Te Velde, "A Minimal Definition of Mut," 6.
38 Ibid., 7.
39 Te Velde, "A Minimal Definition of Mut," 6; See also ibid., 4, where he further explores the connection between Nekhbet and Mut.
40 Amun is similarly attired in the representations on the upper register.
41 In its symbolism the gesture is similar to Michelangelo's depiction of God extending a life-giving finger towards Adam on the ceiling of the Sistine chapel.
42 Bleeker, *Egyptian Festivals*, 27; Gardiner, *Egyptian Grammar*, 528.
43 Te Velde, "A Minimal Definition of Mut," 6.
44 Te Velde, "A Minimal Definition of Mut," 6.
45 Legrain, "Osiris-Hiq-Djeto," 127.
46 Legrain, "Osiris-Hiq-Djeto," 127.
47 Jean Leclant, *Monuments thébains*, 101, pl. LXIII, A.
48 The top part of the scene was destroyed, so it is not possible to determine the identity of this god, but Leclant (*Monuments thébains*, 101) suggests it was Amun.
49 Ibid., 100, pl. LXIII B.
50 E.g., Leclant, "Tefnout," 170.
51 Flora Hesse, "The Iconography and Use of the Sistrum in the Pharaonic Period," (University of Memphis, M.A. thesis, 2007), Ch. 6. See Leclant, "Tefnout," 170, n. 7 for the assertion "Le rite des sitres, qui semble surtout feminin … sauf à l'époque tardive…"
52 Harold H. Nelson, *The Great Hypostyle Hall at Karnak* I, Part 1: *The Wall Reliefs.*, ed. William J. Murnane (Chicago: The Oriental Institute, 1981), pl. 80.
53 E. Brunner-Traut, "Lotos," *LÄ* III, 1094.
54 Meeks and Favard-Meeks, *Daily Life of the Egyptian Gods*, 128.
55 Graham, "Insignias," 166.
56 Leitz, *Lexikon der Ägyptischen Götter* I, 542–48.
57 Edouard Naville, *The Temple of Deir el-Bahri* III: *Shrine of Hathor and the Southern Hall of Offerings* (London: Egypt Exploration Fund, 1901), 5 and pl. CIV.
58 Claude Traunecker, "Kamutef," in *The Oxford Encyclopedia of Ancient Egypt* II (Oxford University Press, 2001), 221.

59 Herbert Jacobsohn, "Kamutef," *LÄ* III 308–9.
60 Traunecker, "Kamutef," 221.
61 Nelson, *Great Hypostyle Hall*, pl. 260.
62 Traunecker, "Kamutef," 222.
63 Hesse, "The Iconography of the Sistrum," 51.
64 See Serge Sauneron, *Le Temple d'Esna* (Cairo: IFAO, 1963), 32–34.
65 Manniche, *Music and Musicians*, 66.
66 R. A. Schwaller de Lubicz, *The Temples of Karnak* (Rochester, Vt.: Inner Traditions International, 1999), pl. 430; Te Velde, H. "Mut, the Eye of Re," in *Akten des vierten internationalen Ägyptologen Kongresses München 1985* III, ed. S. Schoske (Hamburg: Helmut Buske, 1989), 395–403, at 397.
67 Serge Sauneron, "Les Inscriptions Ptolemaiques du Temple de Mout a Karnak," *BIFAO* 45 (1968): 45–52.
68 Schwaller de Lubicz, *Temples of Karnak*, pl. 277.
69 Manniche, *Music and Musicians*, 63.
70 Ibid., 64.
71 Scene description based on the photographs published in Schwaller de Lubicz, *Temples of Karnak*, pl. 234.
72 Manniche, *Music and Musicians*, 63; Cyril Aldred, *Jewels of the Pharaohs: Egyptian Jewelry of the Dynastic Period* (London: Thames and Hudson, 1978), 18.
73 François Dumas, "Les objets sacrés de la déesse Hathor à Dendara," *Rd'É* 22 (1970): 63–78, at 66–67; and Schafik Allam, *Beiträge zum Hathorkult (bis zum Ende des Mittleren Reiches)*, MÄS 4 (Berlin: Verlag Bruno Hessling, 1963), 125–29.
74 Legrain, "Osiris-Hiq-Djeto," 128.
75 Ibid., 128.
76 Barbara S. Lesko, *The Great Goddesses of Egypt* (Norman: University of Oklahoma Press, 1999),143.
77 Ibid., 100.
78 Ibid., 107, citing a text from the temple of Hatshepsut at Deir el-Bahri published in Naville, *Temple of Deir el-Bahri* III, 4.
79 A. K. Capel and G. E. Markoe (eds), *Mistress of the House, Mistress of Heaven* (New York: Hudson Hill Press, 1996), 136.
80 The scene was included as Fig. 34 in Bonhême, *Pharaon: Les secrets du pouvoir*, 125. It appeared more recently in Christiane Ziegler, *The Louvre: Egyptian Antiquities* (Paris: Editions Scala, 1990), 55–56; and more recently in Jaromir Malek, *Egypt: 4000 Years of Art* (London: Phaidon, 2003), 220.
81 See for example Jean Leclant, "Tefnut et les Divines Adoratrices," 170; and Troy, Patterns of Queenship, 92–99, particularly p. 92 ff. for her discussion of the erotic component of the "Hathoric renewal."
82 Meeks and Favard-Meeks, *Daily Life of the Egyptian Gods*, 128.
83 Troy, *Patterns of Queenship*, 190.
84 Ibid., 168 and 190.
85 Barbara S. Lesko, *Great Goddesses*, 270.
86 Manniche, *Music and Musicians*, 62.
87 Reynders, "Names and Types of the Sistrum," 951, Fig. 2.
88 Manniche, *Music and Musicians*, 57.
89 Ibid., 63.
90 Although the exact regnal dates of King Inyotef Wah-ankh are not precisely known, he ruled some time between 2160 and 2025 BC.
91 Quoted in Barbara S. Lesko, *Great Goddesses*, 100.
92 Barbara Lesko, *Great Goddesses*, 100.
93 Manniche, *Music and Musicians*, 115.
94 Ibid., 70–71.
95 Ibid., 72.

96 Ibid., 63.
97 Ibid., 68.
98 Ibid., 57.
99 Jean-Claude Goyon, "Textes Mythologiques II. Les revelations du mystère des quatre boules" *BIFAO* 75 (1975): 349–399, at 376, quoted in Meeks and Favard-Meeks, *Daily Life of the Egyptian Gods*, 100–101.
100 Manniche, *Music and Musicians*, 57.
101 Meeks and Favard-Meeks, *Daily Life of the Egyptian Gods*, 101.
102 Manniche, *Music and Musicians*, 115.
103 See p. 10 above. The title occurs on the bottom of a votive statue of the goddess *Maat* dedicated by one of her officials. See Helen Jacquet-Gordon, "A Statuette of Ma'et and the Identity of the Divine Adoratress Karomama," *ZÄS* 94 (1967): 86–93, at 86–87.
104 Manniche, *Music and Musicians*, 68.
105 H. G. Fischer, "The Cult and Nome of the Goddess Bat," *JARCE* 1 (1962): 7–18.
106 Barbara Lesko, *Great Goddesses*, 23.
107 Cf. Manniche, *Music and Musicians*, 63 and Reynders, 945.
108 Ziegler,"Sistrum," *LÄ* V, 959.
109 Reynders, "Names and Types of the Sistrum," 947 and 950.
110 Hornung, *Conceptions of God in Ancient Egypt*, 205.
111 Hieroglyphic texts is based on Legrain, "Osiris-Hiq-Djeto," 127 and personal photographs taken at the wall in 2003.
112 Karol Myśliwiec, *Royal Portraiture Dynasty XXI-XXX* (Mainz am Rhein: Phillip Zabern, 1988), 39.
113 Ibid., 90.
114 Ibid., 45.
115 Legrain, "Osiris-Hiq-Djeto," 127.
116 *Rdit ỉrp n ỉt.s ỉmn-rˁ ỉr.f ˁnḫ ḏt.* This Ramesside form of the offering formula is discussed in Emily Teeter, *The Presentation of Maat: Ritual and Legitimacy in Ancient Egypt* (Chicago: Oriental Institute of the University of Chicago, 1997), 77. It is one of two variants of the formula that occurs on the chapels of the God's Wives.
117 Legrain, "Osiris-Hiq-Djeto," 127.
118 A. J. Spencer, "Two Hieroglyphs and Their Relation to the Sed-Festival," *JEA* 64 (1978): 52–55, at 54.
119 Teeter, *Presentation of Maat*, 77.
120 J. Gwyn Griffiths, "Osiris" in *The Oxford Encyclopedia of Ancient Egypt* I, ed. D. B. Redford (Oxford: Oxford University Press), 615–19, at 615.
121 Leclant, *Monuments thébains*, 287.
122 Gardiner, *Egyptian Grammar*, 548.
123 Graham, "Insignias," 165.
124 Because he interpreted the name of the goddess standing next to him as Mut, Legrain suggested that the god represented here was Amun. Leclant, on the other hand, suggested it was Osiris. See Leclant, *Monuments thébains*, 45.
125 PM II, 194 (3); see Leclant, *Monuments thébains*, 30, for a line drawing of this scene.
126 Leclant, *Monuments thébains*, 272; and *idem*, "Osiris *p3-wšb-ỉ3d*," 203–4; and Otto, *The Cults of Osiris and Amon*, 127.
127 Barbara S. Lekso, *Great Goddesses*, 233.
128 Leclant, "Osiris *p3-wšb-ỉ3d*," 199; see Katja Goebs, "Crowns," in *The Oxford Encyclopedia of Ancient Egypt* I, ed. D. B. Redford (Oxford: Oxford University Press, 2001), 321–26, at 324, who points out that the flat crown worn by Amun, which resembles the base of the Red Crown, may also be called *henou*.
129 Meeks and Favard-Meeks, *Daily Life of the Egyptian Gods*, 59.
130 See Leclant, *Monuments thébains*, 34–35, where a line drawing of this scene may be found.

131 Meeks and Favard-Meeks, *Daily Life of the Egyptian Gods*, 127; see also A. M Blackman, "The Significance of Incense and Libations in Funerary and Temple Ritual," *ZÄS* 50 (1912) 69–75.
132 Meeks and Favard-Meeks, *Daily Life of the Egyptian Gods*, 59 and 70.
133 Ibid., 127.
134 The identification of the jar carried by Shepenwepet II as a *hekenou*-jar is based on the figure in E. V. Pischikova, "Representations of Ritual and Symbolic Objects in Late XXVth Dynasty and Saite Private Tombs," *JARCE* 31 (1994): 63–77, at 67.
135 Although the signs are badly damaged the reading suggested here is based on traces of the Egyptian words *nḏ-ḥr sntr* (?).
136 Graham, "Insignias," 166.
137 Ibid., 165; see also Cyril Aldred, *Akhenaton and Nefertiti* (London: Thames and Hudson, 1973), 115 for an Amarna royal woman, probably Queen Tiye, carrying the same scepter.
138 Pischikova, "Representations of Ritual and Symbolic Objects," 68.
139 Hornung, *Conceptions of God in Ancient Egypt*, 214, citing coffin texts spells CT II, 35g and CT VII, 468e.
140 Silverman, "Divinity and Deities," 34; and W. Helck, "Maat" *LÄ* III, 1110–19.
141 Hornung, *Conceptions of God in Ancient Egypt*, 213.
142 Meeks and Favard-Meeks, *Daily Life of the Egyptian Gods*, 66.
143 Hornung, *Conceptions of God in Ancient Egypt*, 213 and 215.
144 Bonhême, *Pharaon: Les secrets du pouvoir*, 132–35.
145 See Teeter, *Presentation of Maat*, 113–115 for a comprehensive list of all the scenes in which the God's Wives of the Third Intermediate Period present *Maat* to Amun-Re.
146 Jacquet-Gordon, "A Statuette of Ma'et and the Identity of Karomama," 86–87.
147 PM II, 205 (6) I.1. See also Teeter, *Presentation of Maat*, 113; and Leclant, *Monuments thébains*, 53, for a brief description of the scene.
148 Myśliwiec, *Royal Portraiture Dynasty XXI-XXX*, 34–36.
149 See Legrain, "Osiris-Hiq-Djeto," 128; Leclant, *Monuments thébains*, 53, n. 2.
150 See Legrain, "Osiris-Hiq-Djeto," 128.
151 The scene is briefly described in Leclant, *Monuments thébains*, 51, and Legrain, "Osiris-Hiq-Djeto," 126, who misread the "*nḥ*" sign as a "*k*."
152 Hieroglyphic text is based on Legrain, "Osiris-Hiq-Djeto," 127 and personal photographs taken at the wall in 2007.
153 See Legrain, "Osiris-Hiq-Djeto," 127; Leclant, *Monuments thébains*, 52.
154 Myśliwiec, *Royal Portraiture Dynasty XXI-XXX*, 38.
155 Dittography, probably due to a scribal error.
156 See pp. 53–54 above.
157 See Leclant, *Monuments thébains*, 32, for a line drawing of the scene.
158 Troy, *Patterns of Queenship*, 182.
159 Leclant, "Tefnout," 166.
160 See pp. 39–40 above.
161 Leclant, "Tefnout," 168–70.
162 Ibid., 167, n. 2 and n. 5.
163 Barbara Lesko, *Great Goddesses*, 69–71.
164 Allam, *Hathorkult*, 3–22.
165 Ibid., 113–16.
166 Leonard H. Lesko, "Ancient Egyptian Cosmogonies," 106.
167 Barbara Lesko, *Great Goddesses*, 100.
168 Otto, *The Cults of Osiris and Amon*, 123.
169 See Leclant, *Monuments thébains*, 31, for a line drawing of this scene.
170 For a detailed description of the parallel representation of the King and God's Wife on the lintel and door jambs leading into the chapel of Osiris, *Neb-ankh*, see pp. 75–78 below.
171 Paul Barguet and Jean Leclant, *Karnak-Nord* III *(1949–1951)* (Cairo: IFAO, 1954), Fig. 121.

172 Teeter, *Presentation of Maat*, 113–15.
173 PM II, 192.
174 Graham, "Insignias," 166.
175 Helmut Brunner, "Chons" *LÄ* I, 960–63; Jennifer Houser-Wegner, "Khonsu," in *The Oxford Encyclopedia of Ancient Egypt* II, ed. D. B. Redford (Oxford: Oxford University Press, 2001), 233.
176 See for example, Teeter, *Presentation of Maat*, 13, who picks up a suggestion made by Leclant in *Monuments thébains*, 365.
177 Paul Barguet, "Un aspect religieux du grand-majordome de la divine adoratrice," *BSFE* no. 20 (Feb. 1956): 7–9.
178 See pp. 78–82 below.
179 Barguet, "Un aspect religieux du grand-majordome," 9.
180 See pp. 19–21 above and Ayad, "Funerary Texts of Amenirdis," 55.
181 M. Isler, "An Ancient Method of Finding and Extending Direction," *JARCE* 26 (1989): 191–206, at 203.
182 G. A. Wainwright "Seshat and the Pharaoh," *JEA* 26 (1940): 30–40, at 30, where he cites PT § 616 in which Nephthys is identified with Seshat.
183 See Wainwright "Seshat and the Pharaoh," 33 for the identification of the object(s) comprising the head dress of this goddess; see also Park, "Stretching of the Cord," 841 for the view that the seven objects shown on the Seshat's headdress refer to "the orbital paths of the seven easily observed planets following the ecliptic."
184 Schäffer, *Principles of Egyptian Art*, 301; and Goyon's remarks on the depiction of the leftward-oriented archer in Parker *et al.*, *The Edifice of Taharqa by the Sacred Lake*. Brown Egyotological Studies 8 (Providence: Brown University Press, 1979), 61.
185 A. Badawy, *History of Egyptian Architecture* (Los Angeles: University of California Press, 1968), 63; R. Park, "Stretching of the Cord" in *Proceedings of the Seventh International Congress of Egyptologists. Cambridge, 3–9 September 1995*,, ed. C. Eyre (Leuven: Utigeverij Peeters, 1998), 839–48.
186 Reford, "Ruler of Eternity," 17, 19; Legrain, "Osiris-Hiq-Djeto," 126.
187 The inscription was also published in Legrain, "Osiris-Hiq-Djeto," 126; and her titles were included in Troy, *Patters of Queenship*, 184 and 189.
188 See Legrain, "Osiris-Hiq-Djeto," 126; Leclant, *Monuments thébains*, 54.
189 See Legrain, "Osiris-Hiq-Djeto," 127; Leclant, *Monuments thébains*, 52.
190 See Legrain, "Osiris-Hiq-Djeto," 127.
191 See p. 38 above.
192 Leclant, *Monuments thébains*, 379: "Dans l'édifice reconstitué des Divine Adoratrice de Karnak-Nord, Chepenoupet II brandit le *ḥts* en compagnie du prêtre Iounmutef, puis renverse les godets, avec la légende caratéristique: 'Ofrir (l'oie)' Accompagnée du 'prêtre-lecteur' et de 'l'ami unique', elle s'avance, tenant de la main gauche un sceptre et de la droite de *ḥts*, horizontalement; un taureau se trouve scarifié; un prêtre 'sem', coiffé de la boucle tombante et tenant droit le bâton de consécration, pronounce la formule rituelle 'Parole à dire: qu'il n'entende pas'."
193 For a discussion on the ideological incorporation of the Libyan decorative scheme into the Nubian iconographic cycle as a means of legitimating Amenirdis's position as a God's Wife, see pp. 129–131 below.
194 Legrain, "Osiris-Hiq-Djeto," 128; and Redford, "Osiris, Ruler of Eternity," Figure 3 on p. 23.
195 Meeks and Favard-Meeks, *Daily Life of the Egyptian Gods*, 125.
196 Parker *et al.*, *Edifice of Taharqa*, 55.
197 Ibid., 56, no. 9.
198 Bonhême, *Pharaon: Les secrets du pouvoir*, 140–44.
199 PM II, 194–95; Leclant, *Monuments thébains*, 23–36; Georges Legrain, "Le temple et les chapelles d'Osiris à Karnak III: La chapelle d'Osiris, Maître de la Vie ( )," *RT* 24 (1902): 208–14.

200 PM II, 194 (2); see also Leclant, *Monuments thébains*, 28, for a line drawing of the scenes on the lintel; and Legrain, "Maître de la Vie", 209–210 for the texts inscribed on the lintel.
201 Lanny Bell, "The New Kingdom 'Divine Temple': The Example of Luxor," in *Temples of Ancient Egypt*,, ed. B. E. Shafer (Ithaca: Cornell University Press, 1997), 163, who writes "Conventionally in Egyptian art, a deity is represented as looking out from the shrine in which he resides ... , and the king is shown facing the deity and, therefore, that shrine." Bell here cites Dieter Arnold, *Wandrelief und Raumfunktion in ägyptischen Templen des Neuen Reiches*. MÄS 2 (Berlin: Bruno Hessling, 1962), 128.
202 Left and right with respect to the viewer.
203 See pp. 66–67 above
204 Caminos, "Nitocris Adoption Stela," 74.
205 Meeks and Favard-Meeks, *Daily Life of the Egyptian Gods*, 128.
206 Adolf Erman, *Die Religion der Ägypter* (Berlin: De Gruyter, 1934), 25–27; Hermann Te Velde, "Ptah" *LÄ* III, 1177–1180; Van Dijk, Jacobus, "Ptah" in *The Oxford Encyclopedia of Ancient Egypt* III, ed. D. B. Redford Oxford: Oxford University Press, 2001, 74–76; Edward Brovarski, "Sokar," *LÄ* V, 1055–1174; Catherine Graindorge, "Sokar," in *The Oxford Encyclopedia of Ancient Egypt* III, ed. D. B. Redford (Oxford: Oxford University Press, 2001), 305–7.
207 See p. 134 below.
208 PM II, 193–94.
209 PM II, 193 (1).
210 PM II, 193 (1).
211 So PM II, 193 (1).
212 So PM II, 193 (1).
213 Graham, "Insignias," 165.
214 See pp 45–46 above.
215 PM II, 193 (1)
216 Barguet, "Un aspect religieux du grand-majordome," 7–9.
217 Ibid., 9.
218 Lanny Bell, "Luxor Temple and the Cult of the Royal Ka," *JNES* 44 (1985): 251–94, at 258.
219 Ibid., 289.
220 Marianne Doresse, "Le dieu voilé dans sa châsse," *Rd'É* 25 (1973): 92–135, at 130–31; *idem.*, "Le dieu voilé dans sa châsse," *Rd'É* 23 (1971): 113–136, at 120–21; and Dirk Van der Plas, "The Veiled Image of Amenapet" in *Effigies Dei: Essays on the History of Religions*, ed. D. Van der Plas. (Leiden E. J. Brill, 1987), 1–12, at 3.
221 This is the Memphite conception of creation, which is preserved on the Shabaka stone published in James H. Breastead, "The Philosophy of a Memphite Priest," *ZÄS* 39 (1901): 39–54; trans. John A. Wilson, *ANET*, 4–6.
222 Leonard H. Lesko, "Ancient Egyptian Cosmogonies," 96.
223 PM II, 194 (2); see also Leclant, *Monuments thébains*, 28, for a line drawing of the scenes on the jambs; and Legrain, "Maître de la Vie", 210, for a partial publication of the texts inscribed on the jambs.
224 Robins, "Compositional Dominance and Gender Hierarchy," 33 and 36.
225 William J. Murnane, *Ancient Egyptian Co-regencies*. SAOC 40 (Chicago: The Oriental Institute, 1977), 200, 202–4.
226 As seen, for example, in the balanced and parallel representations of the Libyan kings Osorkon III and Takeloth III in the chapel of Osiris, Ruler of Eternity.
227 PM II, 192 (1, a–b).
228 Jürgen von Beckerath, *Handbuch der ägyptischen Königsnamen* (Berlin: Deutscher Kunstverlag, 1984), 112.
229 PM II, 192 (1, d–e).

230 Parker *et al.*, pl. 25; and M. Ayad, "On the Identity and Role of the God's Wife of Amun in Rites of Royal and Divine Dominion," *JSSEA* 34 (2007): 1–13.
231 Schäffer, *Principles of Egyptian Art*, 302, for the suggestion that this was also how an Egyptian would have "distributed right and left."
232 Gardiner, *Egyptian Grammar*, 498. The similarity stems from the cross created on the surface of the target by the four curved arches that originate, and end, at the perimeter of each target. However, the cross depicted on these targets is less angular than the one formed by the crossroads of Gardiner sign list O 49.
233 The text identifies the tree as a *šndt n hnw* or "a Nile Acacia tree." See Faulkner, *Concise Dictionary*, 270.
234 Although the M 18 sign is used here (a combination of the reed leaf and the walking legs), this is probably a misspelling of *iʿt*, the word for "mound", rather than the verb to "come." See Faulkner, *Concise Dictionary*, 7 for *i3t* and 10 for *ii*. See also Parker *et al. Edifice of Taharqa*, 64 n. 32. Cf. WB I, 26.
235 Left and right with respect to the viewer.
236 Schäffer, *Egyptian Art*, 16: "… Egyptian art indicates even a very swift running pace merely by showing a longer stride with raised back heels and front toes placed on the ground."
237 Probably a periform, *hedj*-mace, T3. Gardiner, *Egyptian Grammar*, 510.
238 Parker *et al.*, *Edifice of Taharqa*, 62 and pl. 25; Leclant, *Monuments thébains*, pl. xlvii; and Fazzini, *Dynasty XXII-XXV*, 23 and pl. xxvi.
239 Parker *et al.*, *Edifice of Taharqa*, 62.
240 Ibid., 62 and pl. 25.
241 Spencer, "Two Enigmatic Hieroglyphs," 55.
242 Ibid., 52.
243 Parker *et al.*, *Edifice of Taharqa*, 62, n. 15.
244 See *FHN*, 129–30; and Kitchen, *Third Intermediate Period*, 388.
245 Fazzini, *Dynasty XXII–XXV*, 23. See also M. Étienne, *Heka: Magie et envoûtement dans l'Égypte ancienne* (Paris: Réunion des Musées Nationaux, 2000), 36–39, for the casting of the four balls as an Osirian rite.
246 H. G. Fischer, *Orientation of Hieroglyphs* – Part 1*: Reversals* (New York: The Metropolitan Museum of Art, 1977), 46.
247 Parker *et al.*, *Edifice of Taharqa*, 61, n. 2 and 80.
248 Allen, *Middle Egyptian*, 81.
249 Leclant, *Monuments thébains*, 379.
250 Regnal Dates for Taharqo follow Kitchen, *Third Intermediate Period*, 387.
251 Ibid., 387 and 391.
252 Parker *et al.*, *Edifice of Taharqa*, 61–62 and pl. 25, coll. 14–15.
253 See Faulkner, *Concise Dictionary*, 230, for *sen* as "equal."
254 Jean Revez, "The Metaphorical Use of the Kingship Term *sn* 'Brother'," *JARCE* 40 (2003): 123–31, at 127; and ibid., 124, where he points out that, from the Eighteenth dynasty onwards, a wife (*ḥmt*) was generally referred to as *snt* "sister," and further that, the plural *snw* "brothers" "can refer to people of equal status."
255 See pp. 21–22 and p. 25 above; Leclant, *Monuments thébains*, 365–67; Kitchen, *Third Intermediate Period*, 403–4, and n. 945. See also Ricardo Caminos, "The Nitocris Adoption Stela," *JEA* 50 (1964): 71–101, at 78.
256 Convenient summaries of this myth may be found in Leonard H. Lesko, "Ancient Egyptian Cosmogonies," 92–93; and in Meeks and Favard-Meeks, *Daily Life of the Egyptian Gods*, 165–66.
257 Franck Burgos and Francois Larché, *La Chapelle Rouge: Le sanctuaire de barque d'Hatshepsout*. Volume I: *Fac-similés et photographies des scènes* (Paris : Éditions Recherches sur les Civilisations, 2006), 213; The scene is also discussed in Robins, *Women in Ancient Egypt*, 112, where it appears as Fig. 41; Gitton, "Le rôle des femmes," 40–41; Naguib, *Clergé féminin*, 215–17.

258 Alfred Grimm, "Feind-Bilder und Bilderverbrennung: Ein Brandopfer zur rituellen Feindvernichtung in einer Festdarstellung der 'Chapelle Rouge,'" *VA* 4 (1988): 207–14, at 211.
259 Grimm, "Feind-Bilder," 211.
260 Burgos and Larché, *Chapelle Rouge,* 213, block no. 37.
261 For "brazier," see Faulkner, *Concise Dictionary*, 48; for "furnace," see Anthony Leahy, "Death by Fire in Ancient Egypt," *JESHO* 27 (1984): 199–206, at 202; see also Rainer Hanning, *Großes Handwörterbuch: Ägyptisch–Deutsch (2800–950 v.Chr.)* (Mainz am Rhein: Verlag Phillip von Zabern, 1995), 157.
262 Grimm, "Feind-Bilder," 211.
263 R. K. Ritner, *The Mechanics of Ancient Egyptian Magical Practice*. SAOC 54 (Chicago: University of Chicago Press, 1993), 210.
264 Burgos and Larché, *Chapelle Rouge,* 213, block no. 37.
265 Grimm, "Feind-Bilder," 212.
266 Ritner, *Mechanics of Magical Practice*, 158.
267 Leahy, "Death by fire," 201–2.
268 Grimm, "Feind-Bilder," 209, translates the last word in this inscription as "fire-victim."
269 Patricia Spencer, *The Egyptian Temple: A Lexicographical Study* (London: Kegan Paul, 1984), 88.
270 Burgos and Larché, *Chapelle Rouge,* 213, block no. 147; Grimm, "Feind-Bilder," 212.
271 Ibid., 212, block no. 21.
272 Ritner, *Mechanics of Magical Practice*, 207–12.
273 Burgos and Larché, *Chapelle Rouge,* 213.
274 John Gee, "Prophets, Initiation and the Egyptian Temple," *JSSEA* 31 (2004): 97–107, at 100.
275 Labib Habachi, "Gottesvater," *LÄ* II, 825–26.
276 This was hinted at, but not explicitly stated, in Ritner, *Mechanics of Magical Practice*, 210.
277 Burgos and Larché, *Chapelle Rouge*, 212, block no. 21.
278 Burgos and Larché, *Chapelle Rouge*, 216, block nos. 292 and 140.
279 Ibid.
280 Faulkner, *Concise Dictionary* 277.
281 Gee, "Prophets, Initiation and the Egyptian Temple," 102.
282 Fazzini, *Dynasty XXII–XXV*, 22; and Kathlyn Cooney, "The Edifice of Taharqa by the Sacred Lake: Ritual Function and the Rule of the King," *JARCE* 37 (2000): 15–47, at 34–36.
283 Legrain, "Osiris-Hiq-Djeto,' 133.
284 Parker *et al.*, *Edifice of Taharqa*, 49, pl. 22.
285 Ibid.
286 Hermann te Velde, "Iunmutef," *LÄ* III 212–213.
287 Bell, "Cult of the Royal *Ka*," 260.
288 Schäffer, *Principles of Egyptian Art*, 189–90, 198.
289 Hermann te Velde, "Iunmutef" *LÄ* III, 212–213.
290 Parker *et al.*, *Edifice of Taharqa*, 49, pl. 22; Fischer, "The Cult and Nome of Bat," 7–18.
291 Parker *et al.*, *Edifice of Taharqa*, 49, pl. 22.
292 Ibid., 51.
293 Ibid., 50.
294 Sign no. S 24, a "girdle knot " See Gardiner, *Egyptian Grammar*, 506.
295 Parker *et al.*, *Edifice of Taharqa*, 65 and pl. 26.
296 Robins, "Compositional Dominance and Gender Hierarchy," 33.
297 Parker *et al.*, *Edifice of Taharqa*, 67 and pl. 26, col. 5: "Beware, Nubia."
298 Török, *Kingdom of Kush*, 176 and n. 333.
299 Ibid.
300 Serge Sauneron, *The Priests of Ancient Egypt*. Trans. David Lorton (Ithaca: Cornell University Press, 2000), 59; Parker *et al.*, *Edifice of Taharqa*, 67, n. 24.

301 Parker *et al.*, *Edifice of Taharqa*, 66 and pl. 26.
302 Sauneron, *Priests of Egypt*, 60; Günther Vittmann, "Stolist," *LÄ* VI, 63–66; Edward Brovarski, "Templepersonal," *LÄ* VI, 388; Parker *et al.*, *Edifice of Taharqa*, 67, n. 31 cite a *smaty*-priest of Soped at Saft el-Henneh.
303 Parker *et al.*, *Edifice of Taharqa*, 67, n. 32 citing Gauthier, *D. G.* III, 135; and *ibid.*, pl. 26, col. 11.
304 Parker *et al.*, *Edifice of Taharqa*, 67 and pl. 26, col. 8. Col. 10 reads: "Beware, Asia …"
305 Ibid., 68 and pl. 26; Leclant, *Monuments thébaines*, pl xlviii.
306 Török, *Kingdom of Kush*, 176.
307 Parker *et al.*, *Edifice of Taharqa*, 68, n. 39.
308 Ibid.; H. Kees, *Das Priestertum in Ägyptischen Staat von Neuen Reich bis zur Spätzeit. Probleme der Ägyptologie* I. Leiden: Brill, 1953, 209–10; Ét. Drioton, "Deux Statues Naophores consacrées à Apis," *ASAE* 41 (1941): 21–35, at 24; Louis-A. Christophe, "Les Divinités du papyrus Harris I et leurs epithets," *ASAE* 54 (1956): 345–89, at 361, n. 1.
309 Parker *et al.*, *Edifice of Taharqa*, 68 and pl. 26.
310 Leclant, *Monuments thébains*, 299 and pl. xlviii.
311 Parker *et al.*, *Edifice of Taharqa*, 69.
312 Ibid., 69.
313 Parker *et al.*, *Edifice of Taharqa*, 55–60, pl. 24; Cooney, "The Edifice of Taharqa: Ritual Function," 28.
314 Parker *et al.*, *Edifice of Taharqa*, 55.
315 See Fischer, *Orientation of Hieroglyphs*, 6–7, for the rightward orientation of principal figures; and R. H. Wilkinson, *Magic and Symbol in Egyptian Art* (London: Thames and Hudson Ltd., 1994), 39–42, for the significance of the king's "massive" scale of representation.
316 Parker *et al.*, *Edifice of Taharqa*, 57.
317 Bleeker, *Egyptian Festivals*, 48.
318 Cf. coll. 13 and 35 in Parker *et al.*, *Edifice of Taharqa*, pl, 24.
319 Parker *et al.*, *Edifice of Taharqa*, 57–58, where her wig is described as "archaic;" her attire a "coat-dress."
320 Parker *et al.*, *Edifice of Taharqa*, 55; and Cooney, "The Edifice of Taharqa: Ritual Function," 28.
321 Leonard H. Lesko, "Ancient Egyptian Cosmogonies," 106.
322 Hornung, *Conceptions of God in Ancient Egypt*, 161.
323 Fazzini, *Dynasty XXII-XXV*, 22; and Cooney, "The Edifice of Taharqa: Ritual Function," 34–36.
324 Bleeker, *Egyptian Festivals*, 45, quoting S. Morenz, *Ägyptische Religion*, 93 and 105.
325 Alexander Piankoff, *Litany of Re* (New York: Bollingen Foundation, 1964), 10 quoted in Bleeker, *Egyptian Festivals*, 118.
326 Ibid., 21.
327 Ibid., 22.
328 See pp. 89–90 above.
329 Fazzini, *Dynasty XXII-XXV*, 23.
330 See n. 287 on p. 95 above.
331 Goyon, "An Interpretation of the Edifice," in Parker *et al.*, *Edifice of Taharqa*, 81.
332 Similar to the argument make by Bleeker (in *Egyptian Festivals*, 123) regarding the *sed*-festival.
333 See pp. 96–99 above.
334 Goyon, "An Interpretation of the Edifice," in Parker *et al.*, *Edifice of Taharqa*, 81 and 84; Fazzini, *Dynasty XXII-XXV*, 22.
335 Goyon, "Interpretation of the Edifice," in Parker *et al.*, *Edifice of Taharqa*, 84.
336 See note 1 above.

337 A. Egberts, *In Quest of Meaning: A Study of the Ancient Egyptian Rites of Consecrating the Meret-chests and Driving the Calves* (Leiden: Nederlands Instituut voor het Nabije Oosten, 1995), 440.
338 Ibid., 246 and pl. 120; and A. M. Blackman and H. W. Fairman, "The Significance of the Ceremony *ḥwt bḥsw* in the Temple of Horus at Edfu," *JEA* 35 (1949): 98–112, and *idem*, *JEA* 36 (1950), 63–81.
339 Egberts, *In Quest of Meaning*, 249.
340 Ibid., 250.
341 Egberts, *In Quest of Meaning*, 255; Schäfer, *Principles of Egyptian Art*, 186–88, 190.
342 Egberts, *In Quest of Meaning*, 256.
343 Ibid., 254, n. 24, "Examples of three gods are B.a-XIX.6-Ka.1 (Amun-Re, Mut, and Khonsu), and B.a-XXVII.2-Hi.1 (Amun-Re of Hibis, Wepwawet, and Hathor of Medjed)."
344 Egberts, *In Quest of Meaning*, 254–55.
345 Egberts, *In Quest of Meaning*, 255.
346 Bell, "The New Kingdom 'Divine Temple,'", 163: "Conventionally in Egyptian art, a deity is represented as looking out from the shrine in which he resides … , and the king is shown facing the deity and, therefore, that shrine." Bell cites Dieter Arnold, *Wandrelief und Raumfunktion in ägyptischen Tempeln des Neuen Reiches*. MÄS 2 (Berlin: Bruno Hessling, 1962), 128.
347 Egberts, *In Quest of Meaning*, 354. See also WB III, 46–48 for *hwi*; and WB III, 151–52 for *hh*.
348 Egberts, *In Quest of Meaning*, 354; Goyon, *Rituels Funéraires*, 58, n. 2; Blackman and Fairman, "The Significance of the Ceremony *ḥwt bḥsw* 2" (1950): 78–79.
349 Egberts, *In Quest of Meaning*, 356.
350 Ibid., 355–56.
351 Ibid., 362.
352 Ibid., 436–41.
353 Ibid., 372.
354 M. F. Laming Macadam, *The Temples of Kawa* II: *History and Archaeology of the Site* (London: Oxford University Press, 1955), pl. xxii-a.
355 Egberts, *In Quest of Meaning*, 232; Jean Leclant, "La colonnade éthiopienne à l'est de la grande enceinte d'Amon à Karnak," *BIFAO* 53 (1953) : 113–72, at 138, Fig. 9; *idem*, *Monuments thébains*, pl. xxv-b.
356 Egberts, *In Quest of Meaning*, 226–27 and 272–78; Nelson, *Great Hypostyle Hall*, pl. 259 for a general view of the south wall.
357 Edouard Naville, *The Temple of Deir el-Bahri* VI: *Lower Terrace* (London: Egypt Exploration Fund, 1908), 5, pl. CLXI.
358 See Egberts, *In Quest of Meaning*, pl. 73 and p.. 46, 171 for the texts accompanying this scene.
359 A transcription along with a translation of the texts accompanying this scene may be found in Egberts, *In Quest of Meaning*, 171 and pl. 73.
360 Ibid., 171 and pl. 73.
361 See Egberts, *In Quest of Meaning*, 54 for a description of the act of the consecration of the *meret*-chest.
362 Ibid., 64; see also Spencer, "Two Enigmatic Hieroglyphs," 52–55.
363 Egberts, *In Quest of Meaning*, 67.
364 Egberts, *In Quest of Meaning*, 67 (citing Schäfer, *Principles of Egyptian Art*, 196–204).
365 Egberts, *In Quest of Meaning*, 68.
366 Ibid., 68.
367 Ibid., n. 29 lists a Twentieth dynasty example from Medinet Habu a (A.a XX.2-MH.2) as well as a Twenty-seventh dynasty example from the temple of Amen at Hibis (A.a-XXVII.2-Hi.1), both depicting *meret*-chests on up-turned sledges.
368 Egberts, *In Quest of Meaning*, 69.

369 Ibid., 66.
370 Ibid., 66.
371 Ibid., 66.
372 Ibid., 65.
373 Ibid., 43; PM I, 766; KRI II, 294: 13–15.
374 Ibid., 66.
375 Ibid., 356.
376 Bleeker, *Egyptian Festivals*, 112.
377 See pp. 87–90 above.
378 Egberts, *In Quest of Meaning*, 436–41.
379 Ann Perkins, "Archaeological News," *American Journal of Archaeology* 55.1 (1951): 81–100, at 82.
380 For the position of the ramp relative to the temple, see PM II, plans ii and iii.
381 Barguet and Leclant, *Karnak Nord* III, 109.
382 Perkins, "Archaeological News," 81; and Barguet and Leclant, *Karnak Nord III*, 109.
383 Ibid.
384 Ibid., 111.
385 See p. 24 above.
386 Barguet and Leclant, *Karnak Nord* III, 127.
387 Ibid., 111, Fig. 118
388 Ibid., Figs. 118 and 120.
389 Ibid., 110.
390 Ibid., 116, and pl. CVI, block no. A 209.
391 Gardiner, *Egyptian Grammar*, 525 and 527.
392 A. H. Gardiner, "Horus the Behdite," *JEA* 30 (1944): 23–60, at 33.
393 Hanning, *Großes Handwörterbuch*, 692; Schwaller du Lubicz, *Temples of Karnak*, 832, n. 25.
394 Schwaller du Lubicz, *Temples of Karnak*, pl. 201.
395 Barguet and Leclant, *Karnak Nord* III, 114.
396 Leclant, *Monuments thébains*, 381.
397 A. H. Gardiner, "Horus the Behdite," *JEA* 30 (1944): 23–60, at 32–33.
398 Hermann te Velde, "Iunmutef," *LÄ* III, 212–213.
399 Edmund S. Meltzer, "Horus," in *The Oxford Encyclopedia of Ancient Egypt* II, ed. D. B. Redford (Oxford: Oxford University Press, 2001), 119–122, at 120.
400 Barguet and Leclant, *Karnak Nord* III, 114–15 and pl. CIV, blocks no. A 135 and A 187.
401 Schwaller du Lubicz, *Temples of Karnak*, 632.
402 Erhart Graefe, "Upaut," LÄ VI, 862–64; Jennifer Houser-Wegner, "Wepwawet," in *The Oxford Encyclopedia of Ancient Egypt* III, ed. D. B. Redford (Oxford: Oxford University Press, 2001), 496–97.
403 Leclant, *Monuments thébains*, 379.
404 Ibid., 381.
405 Bleeker, *Egyptian Festivals*, 98.
406 See pp. 40–43 above.
407 Legrain, "Osiris-Hiq-Djeto," 126; and Leclant, *Monuments thébains*, 51 (5).
408 Bleeker, *Egyptian Festivals*, 98.
409 William J. Murnane, "The Sed Festival: A Problem in Historical Methods," *MDAIK* 37 (1981): 369–76, at 375.
410 Bleeker, *Egyptian Festivals*, 113.
411 Murnane, "Sed Festival," 373.
412 Ibid., 374.
413 Bleeker, *Egyptian Festivals*, 122.
414 Ibid., 120–22.
415 Ibid., 123.

3 AVENUES TO LEGITIMACY

1 Leahy, "Earliest Dated Monument of Amasis," 197–8; and ibid., "Adoption of Ankhnesneferibre," 158; Vittmann, *Priester und Beamte*, 63.
2 Spalinger, "The Concept of Monarchy," 17 and 29.
3 Redford, "Osiris, Ruler of Eternity," 21.
4 Kitchen, *Third Intermediate Period*, 96 352–53 and 356–58.
5 Ibid., 201.
6 See pp. 146–52 below for a discussion of the celibacy of the God Wife.
7 See pp. 52–53 above.
8 See pp. 71–74 above.
9 See pp. 40–43, p.114 above.
10 See pp. 110–115 above.
11 See pp. 103–110 above.
12 See pp. 87–90 above.
13 Kitchen, *Third Intermediate Period*, 201 and 382. The hiatus lasted from *c.* 754 to 704 BC (ibid., 480). See also H. Kees, *Die Hohenpriester des Amun Von Karnak von Herihor bis zum Ende der Äthiopenzeit. Probleme der Ägyptologie* 4 (Leiden: E. J. Brill, 1964), 163–69; and G. Vittmann, *Priester und Beamte in Theben der Spätzeit.* BÄ 1 (Vienna: Veröffentlichungen der Institut für Afrikanistik und Ägyptologie der Universität Wien, 1978), 61–63.
14 Kitchen, *Third Intermediate Period*, 201.
15 Ibid., xli, 157–58, 160–61 383–86.
16 See Török, *Kingdom of Kush*, 168.
17 Fazzini, *Dynasty XXII–XXV*, 2; David O'Connor, "New Kingdom and Third Intermediate Period," in B. G. Trigger *et al.*, *Ancient Egypt: A Social History* (Cambridge: Cambridge University Press), 235–241.
18 Lohwasser, "Queenship in Kush," 64.
19 Jean Revez, "Frère du roi: l'évolution du role du frère du roi dons les modalités successorales en Égypte ancienne." Unpublished PhD dissertation, Université de Paris-IV Sorbonne, 1999.
20 Revez, "Metaphorical use of *sn*," 131.
21 Faulkner, *Concise Dictionary*, 230.
22 Pierce, "Stela of Taharqo from year 6 from Kawa (Kawa III)," in *FHN*, 135–43, at 138–39.
23 Spalinger, "The Concept of Monarchy" 17.
24 Ibid., 32.
25 Lines 9–13 of the Ankhnesneferibre Stela; Leahy, "The Adoption of Ankhnesneferibre," 148.
26 Burgos and Larché, *Chapelle Rouge*, 216, Block no. 21.
27 Ibid., Block no. 292.
28 Ibid., Block nos. 292 and 140.
29 Ibid.
30 Faulkner, *Concise Dictionary*, 277.
31 Gee, "Prophets, Initiation and the Egyptian Temple," 102.
32 Ibid., 100.
33 Robins, *Women in Ancient Egypt*, 151, citing Gitton, "Le rôle des femmes," 39–40 and Figure 4.
34 See pp. 90–94 above.
35 Ritner, *Mechanics of Magical Practice*, 204–14.
36 See pp. 94–96 above.
37 Parker *et al.*, *Edifice of Taharqa*, pls. 22–23.
38 Hermann te Velde, "Iunmutef," *LÄ* III, 212–213.
39 Bell, "Cult of the Royal *Ka*," 260.

40 Parker *et al.*, *Edifice of Taharqa*, pl. 26; see pp. 96–99 above.
41 Sauneron, *The Priests of Ancient Egypt*, 59; Parker *et al.*, *Edifice of Taharqa*, 67, n. 24.
42 Parker *et al.*, *Edifice of Taharqa*, 66 and pl. 26.
43 Sauneron, *Priests of Egypt*, 60; Günther Vittmann, "Stolist," *LÄ* VI, 63–66; Edward Brovarski, "Templepersonal," *LÄ* VI, 388; Parker *et al.*, *Edifice of Taharqa*, 67, n. 31 cite a *smaty*-priest of Soped at Saft el-Henneh.
44 Parker *et al.*, *Edifice of Taharqa*, 67, n. 32 citing Gauthier, *D. G.* III, 135; and *ibid.*, pl. 26, col. 11.
45 Parker *et al.*, *Edifice of Taharqa*, 68 and pl. 26; and Leclant, *Monuments thébains*, pl. xlviii.
46 Parker *et al.*, *Edifice of Taharqa*, 68, n. 39.
47 Ibid.; Kees, *Priestertum*, 209–10; Drioton, "Deux Statues Naophores," 24; Christophe, "Les Divinités du papyrus Harris," 361, n. 1; Sethe, *Thebanische Tempeleinscriften*, 89: text 104 (b).
48 See p. 5 above.
49 Parker *et al.*, *Edifice of Taharqa*, 68 and pl. 26.
50 See pp. 35–36 above.
51 Robins, "Principles of Compositional Dominance and Gender Hierarchy," 38; see also p. 36 above.
52 Robins, "Principles of Compositional Dominance and Gender Hierarchy," 36.
53 Schwaller de Lubicz, *Temples of Karnak*, pl. 235. A discussion of the scenes also appears in Redford, "Osiris, Ruler of Eternity," 21 and Fazzini, *Egypt: Dynasty XXII-XXV*, 20–21.
54 See, for example, Capel and Markoe, *Mistress of the House, Mistress of the Heaven*, 130, for a votive limestone stela with Taweret and Mut in which Mut's head, represented in profile turned to the left, is adorned with "a flat *modius* crown." Sculpture in the round often provides greater detail and illumines two-dimensional art. See ibid., 125–27 (cat. nos. 57 and 59c) for statues of Isis (winged with Osiris or nursing Horus, respectively) wearing such a *modius*.
55 Graham, "Insignias," 163–67
56 The 31.2 cm high and 18 cm ostracon is currently at the Cleveland Museum of Art and is included in Capel and Markoe, *Mistress of the House, Mistress of the Heaven*, 117–18 as cat. no. 50.
57 MMA 41.160.104 (H. 9.7 cm; W. 4.5 cm; Th. 0.8 cm).
58 I. Hofmann, *Studien zum meroitischen Königtum* (Brussels: Foundation Reine Elisabeth, 1971), 37–38.
59 Bonhême, *Pharaon*, 85–92, especially 85–86; and J. Leclant, "The Suckling of Pharaoh as a Part of the Coronation Rites in Ancient Egypt. Le rôle de l'allaitement dans le cérémonial pharaonique du couronnement" in *Proceedings of the IX th International Congress for the History of Religion, Tokyo 1958* (published 1960), 135–45.
60 Jean Leclant, "Le rôle du lait et de l'allaitement d'après les textes des pyramides," *JNES* 10 (1951): 123–27 at 125.
61 Leclant, "Le rôle du lait et de l'allaitement," 127.
62 Ibid., 23.
63 Redford, "Osiris, Ruler of Eternity," 23; Legrain, "Osiris-Hiq-Djeto," 131.
64 Redford, "Osiris, Ruler of Eternity," 23.
65 Legrain, "Osiris-Hiq-Djeto, 131.
66 Bonhême, *Pharaon: les secrets du pouvoir*, 85–92.
67 I am most grateful to Lyla Brock for generously supplying me with her unpublished line drawings of the scenes engraved on the door jambs.
68 See, for example, Redford, "Interim Report," 21–22; Fazzini, *Egypt: Dynasty XXII-XXV*, 20–21.
69 Reford, "Interim Report," 19. Although the room's dimensions are not specifically mentioned in the text, the chapel's plan, which is drawn to scale in ibid., 18, Figure 2, clearly indicate the wider dimensions of the Nubian addition.
70 Kitchen, *Third Intermediate Period*, 378–380; Eide *et al.*, *FHN* 1, 123–25.

71 Kitchen, *Third Intermediate Period*, 383–87; Eide *et al.*, *FHN*, 125–29.
72 For the rite of the receiving the *menat*-necklace, see pp. 47–49 above; for offering *Maat*, see pp. 61–63 above.
73 Hornung, *Conceptions of God in Ancient Egypt*, 214, citing coffin texts spells CT II, 35g and CT VII, 468e.
74 Capel and Markoe, *Mistress of the House, Mistress of the Heaven*, 100.
75 Ibid., 136.
76 See pp. 37–39 above.
77 Leclant, *Monuments thébains*, 369, n. 2; and *idem*, "Gotteshand," *LÄ* II, 813.
78 The epithet is inscribed on the back pillar of Amenirdis's alabaster statue in the Cairo museum. See Jansen-Winkeln, "Amenirdis und Harwa," 40. See also Gitton, *Ahmes Néfertary*, 100, for Ahmose-Nefertari's similar epithet.
79 Legrain, " Osiris-Hiq-Djeto," 135.
80 Ibid., 126; Leclant, *Monuments thébains*, 54.
81 See pp. 72–73 above. The inscription was also published in Legrain, "Osiris-Hiq-Djeto," 126; and her titles were included in Troy, *Patterns of Queenship*, 184 and 189.
82 See pp. 72–73 above.
83 Leclant, *Monuments thébains*, 53: "Les liens de parenté d' Aménirdis I ne sont pas indiqués dans les parties subsistantes, ni avec son père Kachta l'Ethiopien, ni avec sa mère adoptive, Chepenoupet I, la fille d'Osorkon III, devant laquelle elle a pleine préséance."
84 Robert K. Ritner "Fragmentation and Re-integration in the Third Intermediate Period," in *The Libyan Period in Egypt: Historical and Chronological Problems of the Third Intermediate Period*, eds. Gerard P. F. Broekman, R. J. Demarée and Olaf E. Kaper (Leiden: The Netherlands Institute for the Near East, In Press).
85 Ayad, "The Transition from Libyan to Nubian Rule," 48–49.
86 Dieter Arnold, *Wandrelief und Raumfunction in aegyptischen Templen des N.R.* MÄS 2 (Berlin: Bruno Hessling, 1962), 128; Fischer, *Orientation of Hieroglyphs*, 41; Bell, "The New Kingdom 'Divine Temple,'" 127–84.
87 Robins, "Principles of Compositional Dominance and Gender Hierarchy," 36.
88 Ayad, "Transition from Libyan to Nubian Rule," 46–47.
89 Hölscher, *Excavations* V, 22.
90 Ibid., 20; see pp. 19–21 above.
91 See pp. 103–108 above, for the Driving of the Four Calves, and pp. 108–110 for the consecration of the *meret*-chests.
92 Egberts, *In Quest of Meaning*, 362.
93 Jac. J. Janssen and P. W. Pestman, "Burial and Inheritance in the Community of the Necropolis Workmen at Thebes (Pap. Boulaq X and O. Petrie 16)" *Journal of the Economic and Social History of the Orient* 11.2 (1968): 137–170, at 140; Eyre, "The Adoption Papyrus," 215; see Logan, "The *Imyt-pr* Document," 68, for the rites to inherit an administrative or religious office, as part of a deceased father's legacy.
94 Horst Beinlich and Mohamed Saleh, *Corpus der hieroglyphischen Inschriften aus dem Grab des Tutanchamun* (Oxford: Griffith Institute, 1989), 1–2; and William J. Murnane, *Texts from the Amarna Period in Egypt*. Society for Biblical Literature. Writings from the Ancient World 5. (Atlanta: Scholars Press, 1995), 224.
95 See pp. 75–86 above.
96 Mistakenly identified as Amenirdis II in PM II, 194 (2).
97 See pp 82–84 above. PM II, 194 (2); see also Leclant, *Monuments thébains*, 28, for a line drawing of the scenes on the jambs; and Legrain, "Maître de la Vie," 210, for a partial publication of the texts inscribed on the jambs.
98 PM II, 203–204; and Leclant, *Monuments thébains*, 41–47.
99 The God's Wife on the left jamb is mistakenly identified as Amenirdis II in PM II, 202; and Tohfa Handoussa, "The Rebirth of Ramses II in the Hypostyle Hall of Karnak," in *Hommages à Fayza Haikal*. Bd'É138 (Cairo: IFAO, 2003), 107–10, at 109.

100 Peter Brand, "Veils, Votives, and Marginalia: The Use of Sacred Space at Karnak and Luxor" in P. F. Dorman and B. M. Bryan (eds.), *Sacred Space and Sacred Functions in Ancient Thebes*. Occasional Proceedings of the Theban Workshop. SAOC 61. Chicago: Oriental Institute, 2007), 51–83, at 62.
101 See Nelson, *Great Hypostyle Hall*, pl. 107, for a line drawing of the scene.
102 Brand, "Veils, Votives, and Marginalia," 62 and 65.
103 Handoussa, "The Rebirth of Ramses II," 109.
104 Ibid.; see Nelson, *Great Hypostyle Hall*, pl. 260, for the other reliefs surrounding this scene on the southern part of the east wall.
105 Caminos, "The Nitocris Adoption Stela," 75.
106 Lines 16–17 of the decree. See Caminos, "The Nitocris Adoption Stela," 75.
107 Logan, "The *Imyt-pr* Document," 70.
108 Ibid., 71.
109 Ibid., 67.
110 Caminos, "The Nitocris Adoption Stela," 74.
111 A. H. Gardiner, "Adoption Extraordinary," *JEA* 26 (1940): 23–29; Eyre, "The Adoption Papyrus," 207–21.
112 Caminos, "The Nitocris Adoption Stela," 81.
113 Ibid., 74.
114 Ibid., 75 and 87.
115 Logan, "The *Imyt-pr* Document," 71.
116 Bryan, "Property and the God's Wife," 11.
117 Line 5 of her adoption stela. See Leahy, "Adoption of Ankhnesneferibre," 157–58; and Vitmann, *Priester und Beamte*, 63.
118 Leahy, "The Adoption of Ankhnesneferibre," 148.
119 Ibid., 156.
120 Ibid., 157.
121 Ibid.
122 See pp. 110–115 above.
123 Barguet and Leclant, *Karnak-Nord*, 128–31.
124 See pp. 37 and 54 above.
125 Lines 9 and 21 of the Nitocris Adoption Stela. See Caminos, "Nitocris Adoption Stela," 74–5.
126 Török, *The Kingdom of Kush*, 148–150. In so doing, he follows the assumption put forward by H. von Zeissl, *Äthiopen und Assyrer in Ägypten: Beiträge zur Geschichte der ägyptischen "Spätzeit"* (Glückstadt: J. J. Augustin, 1955), 68, and accepted by Gardiner, *Egypt of the Pharaohs*, 343.
127 Leahy, "Adoption Stela," 148 and 155.
128 Kitchen, *Third Intermediate Period*, 478 and 480.
129 Ibid., 359; and Ayad, "Funerary Texts of Amenirdis I," 20.
130 See p. 12 above.
131 See p. 14 above.
132 See pp. 15–16 above.
133 Leclant, *Monuments thébains*, 53: "Les liens de parenté d' Aménirdis I ne sont pas indiqués dans les parties subsistantes, ni avec son père Kachta l'Ethiopien, ni avec sa mére adoptive, Chepenoupet I, la fille d'Osorkon III, devant laquelle elle a pleine préséance."
134 See Robins, "Compositional Dominance and Gender Hierarchy in Egyptian Art," 34 for the assertion that most often, even when a mother is represented with her son, he ,still takes lateral precedence. The exceptions mostly occur when "the mother is in fact the wife of the owner of the monument and forms a couple with him. The son and all offspring are normally conceived as subsidiary figures that are placed after both parents."
135 Legrain, "Osiris-Hiq-Djeto," 126; Leclant, *Monuments thébains*, 54. PM 205, (4): left jamb, bottom.
136 Eyre, "The Adoption Papyrus," 215.

137 Jac. J. Janssen and P. W. Pestman, "Burial and Inheritance in the Community of the Necropolis Workmen at Thebes (Pap. Boulaq X and O. Petrie 16," *Journal of the Economic and Social History of the Orient* 11.2 (1968): 137–70.
138 Lines 8–9; emphasis mine. See Leahy, "The Adoption of Ankhnesneferibre," 148.
139 Murnane, *Texts from the Amarna Period*, 224; Beinlich and Saleh, *Tutanchamun*, 1–2.
140 See p. 36 above.
141 Gardiner, *Egypt of the Pharaohs*, 343; emphasis mine.
142 Jean Yoyotte, "Les vierges consacrées d'Amon thébain," *CRAIBL* 1961 (1962): 43–52.
143 James E. Harris and Kent R. Weeks, *X-Raying the Pharaohs* (New York: Charles Schribner's Sons, 1973), 173–75; also cited in Robert K. Ritner, "Fictive Adoptions," *GM* 164 (1998): 85–90, at 90, n. 40.
144 Harris and Weeks, *X-Raying the Pharaohs*, 174, cited by Ritner, "Fictive Adoptions," 90, n. 40.
145 Ritner, "Fictive Adoptions," 86.
146 Ibid., 88–89.
147 Ibid., 87.
148 Ibid., 90.
149 See, for example, Elizabeth Abbott, *A History of Celibacy* (New York: Scribner, 2000), 169, for the distinctive red garb of Hindu ascetics, which is "reminiscent of the costume of criminals."
150 Abbott, *A History of Celibacy*, 177.
151 Pieternella van Doorn-Harder, *Contemporary Coptic Nuns* (Columbia: University of South Carolina Press, 1995), 99.
152 Traunecker, *The Gods of Egypt*, 57.
153 Lesko, "Egyptian cosmogonies," 94–95
154 Traunecker, *The Gods of Egypt*, 57.
155 See pp. 9–10 above.
156 Miriam Lichtheim, *Ancient Egyptian Literature* II: *The New Kingdom* (Berkeley: University of California Press, 1976), 214–23, especially pp. 219–20; Meeks and Favard-Meeks, *Daily Life of the Egyptian Gods*, 68–69.
157 Meeks and Favard-Meeks, *Daily Life of the Egyptian Gods*, 69.
158 R. O. Faulkner, *The Ancient Egyptian Pyramid Texts* (Oxford: Clarendon Press, 1969), 120.
159 James P. Allen, *The Ancient Egyptian Pyramid Texts* (Atlanta: Society of Biblical Literature, 2005), 35.
160 Lesko, "Egyptian Cosmogonies," 91–92; and Meeks and Favard-Meeks, *Daily Life of the Egyptian Gods*, 31, 142, and 165–66.
161 Meeks and Favard-Meeks, *Daily Life of the Egyptian Gods*, 142 and 166.
162 Émile Sauys, *La sagesse d'Ani: Texte, traduction et commentaire*, Acta Orientalia 2 (Rome: Pontificio Istituto Biblico, 1935) 13–14. A full translation of the instructions may be found in Miriam Lichtheim, *Ancient Egyptian Literature* II: *The New Kingdom* (Berkeley: University of California Press, 1976), 135–46, at 136.
163 Z. Žába, *Les Maximes de Ptahhotep* (Prague: Éditions de l'académie tchécoslovaque des sciences, 1956), 41–42; see also Lichtheim, *Ancient Egyptian Literature* I, 69.
164 Barbara Hughes Fowler, *Love Lyrics of Ancient Egypt* (Chapel Hill: University of North Carolina Press, 1994), 37.
165 John L. Foster, *Love Songs of the New Kingdom* (Austin: University of Texas Press, 1974), 58–61.
166 Ibid., 107.
167 John F. Nunn, *Ancient Egyptian Medicine* (London: British Museum Press, 1996), 34.
168 Ibid., 196.
169 Ibid.
170 John M. Riddle, *Contraception and Abortion from the Ancient World to the Renaissance* (Cambridge, Mass: Harvard University Press, 1992), 69–72.
171 Nunn, *Ancient Egyptian Medicine*, 196.

172 Riddle, *Contraception and Abortion from the Ancient World*, 72.
173 Papyrus Prisse 9, 8–12. See Žába, *Les Maximes de Ptahhotep*, 37–38; see Georg Möller, *Hieratische Lesestücke für den Akademischen Gebrauch* I (Leipzig: J.C. Hinrichs'sche Buchhandlung, 1927), 2, for a fascimile of the original hieratic text; and Lichtheim, *Ancient Egyptian Literature* I, 61–80, at 68, for a translation of this passage.
174 Sauys, *La sagesse d'Ani*, 29–32; Lichtheim, *Ancient Egyptian Literature* II, 137.
175 Papyrus of Nu, cited in Lise Manniche, *Sexual Life in Ancient Egypt* (London: Kegan Paul, 2002), 10.
176 *Herodotus: Books* I–II. Trans. A. D. Godley (Cambridge, Mass: Harvard University Press, 1920), 350–51.
177 Manniche, *Sexual Life*, 8–9.
178 Robins, *Women in Ancient Egypt*, 153.
179 See p. 4 above.
180 See p. 10 above and Gosselin, *Divines épouses: XIXe à XXIe dynastie*, 260.
181 Manniche, *Sexual Life*, 33.
182 Ibid., 35.
183 See pp. 135–39 above.

EPILOGUE

1 M. Ayad, "Some Thoughts on the Disappearance of the God's Wife," *JSSEA* 28 (2001): 1–14.
2 J. H. Johnson, "The Persians and the Continuity of Egyptian Culture," in *Achaemenid History VIII: Continuity and Change. Proceedings of the Last Achaemenid Workshop, April 6–8, 1990. Ann Arbor, Michigan*,, eds. H. Sancisi-Weerdenburg, A. Kuhrt, and M. Cool Root (Leiden: Nederlands Instituut voor het Nabije Oosten, 1994), 150.
3 M. Brosius, *Women in Ancient Persia 559–331 BC* (Oxford: Clarendon Press, 1996), 189.
4 With no tombs of their own, it has been suggested that the royal daughters were buried within the cists of their fathers. See M. Cool Root, *King and Kingship in Achaemenid Art*, 72, for the funerary complexes of Darius I and his successors at Naqshi Rustam/Persepolis. See Maria Brosius, *Women in Ancient Persia: 559–331 BC* (Oxford: Clarendon Press, 1996), 102, for the suggestion that these women may have been buried with their husbands.
5 M. Cool Root, "The Persepolis Perplex: Some Prospects Born of Retrospect" in *Ancient Persia: Art of an Empire*, 5. Their absence, however, has been explained as an extension of the Assyrian custom of not depicting women (Spycket, "Women in Persian Art," 43). It remains, nonetheless, indicative of their status in society.
6 E.g. Xerxes, whose accession record does not include any reference to his mother Atossa, despite her being the daughter of Cyrus, the founder of the dynasty. See Sancisi-Weerdenburg, "Exit Atossa: Images of Women in Greek Historiography on Persia," in *Images of Women in Antiquity*, 25–26.
7 Brosius, *Women in Persia*, 194.
8 Ibid., 76.
9 See p. 19 above.
10 Al-Rayah, "Napatan Kingdom," 117.
11 Sally-Ann Ashton, *The Last Queens of Egypt* (London: Pearson, 2003), 11.
12 Troy, *Patterns of Queenship*, 196–97.
13 Ashton, *Last Queens of Egypt*, 57 and 97, 99.
14 Troy, *Patterns of Queenship*, 196.
15 Ashton, *Last Queens of Egypt*, 97–98 and 102.
16 Ibid., 105.
17 Von Beckerath, *Königsnamen*, 287, no. 2a; see pp. 29–31 above for Shepenwepet's name.

BIBLIOGRAPHY

Abbott, Elizabeth. *A History of Celibacy*. New York: Scribner, 2000.

Aldred, Cyril. *Akhenaton and Nefertiti*. London: Thames and Hudson, 1973.

——. *Jewels of the Pharaohs: Egyptian Jewelry of the Dynastic Period*. London: Thames and Hudson, 1978.

Allam, Schafik. *Beiträge zum Hathorkult (bis zum Ende des Mittleren Reiches)*. MÄS 4. Berlin: Verlag Bruno Hessling, 1963.

——. "Quelques aspects du marriage dans l'Égypte ancienne," *JEA* 67 (1981): 116–35.

——. "A New Look at the Adoption Papyrus (reconsidered)," *JEA* 76 (1990): 189–191.

Allen, James P. *Middle Egyptian: An Introduction to the Language and Culture of Hieroglyphs*. Cambridge: Cambridge University Press, 2000.

——. *The Ancient Egyptian Pyramid Texts*. Atlanta: Society of Biblical Literature, 2005.

Al-Rayah, S. "The Napatan Kingdom (c. 860 BC–310 BC)," PhD University of Liverpool, 1981.

Arnold, Dieter. *Wandrelief und Raumfunktion in ägyptischen Templen des Neuen Reiches*. MÄS 2, Berlin: Bruno Hessling, 1962.

——. *Temples of the Last Pharaohs*. New York and Oxford: Oxford University Press, 1999.

Ashton, Sally-Ann. *The Last Queens of Egypt*. London: Pearson, 2003.

Aston, David. "Two Osiris Figures of the Third Intermediate Period," *JEA* 77 (1991): 99–101.

—— and Taylor, John H. "The Family of Takeloth III and the 'Theban' Twenty-third Dynasty," in: *Libya and Egypt (c.1300–750 BC)*, ed. Anthony Leahy. London: School of Oriental and African Studies, 1990, 131–54.

Ayad, Mariam. "Some Thoughts on the Disappearance of the Office of God's Wife of Amun," *JSSEA* 28 (2001): 1–14.

——. "The Funerary Texts of Amenirdis I: Analysis of their Layout and Purpose," Providence: Brown University, 2003. Unpublished Ph.D. dissertation.

——. "Towards an Edition of the Chapel of Amenirdis I at Medinet Habu," in: *Nubian Studies 1998: Proceedings of the Ninth Conference of the International Society of Nubian Studies. August 21–26, 1998, Boston, Massachusetts*, ed. T. Kendall. Boston, 2004, 214–22.

——. "La sposa divina, la divina Adoratrice e il Clero di Amon durante la XXV dinastia," in: *L'enigma di Harwa alla scoperta di un capolavoro del Rinascimento Egizio*, eds. S. Einaudi and F. Tiradritti. Turin, 2004, 107–127.

——. "The Selection and Layout of the Opening of the Mouth Scenes in the Chapel of Amenirdis I at Medinet Habu," *JARCE* 41 (2004): 113–34.

——. "Towards a Better Understanding of the 'Opening of the Mouth Ritual,'" in: *Proceedings of the Ninth International Congress of Egyptologists, Grenoble, 6–12 September 2004*, eds. J-C Goyon and C. Cardin. Orientalia Lovaniensia Analecta 150. Leuven: Peeters, 2007, 109–116.

——. "On the Identity and Role of the God's Wife of Amun in Rites of Royal and Divine Dominion," *JSSEA* 34 (2007): 1–13.

——. "Some Remarks on the Pyramid Texts Inscribed in the Chapel of Amenirdis I at Medinet Habu," in: *Egypt and Beyond: Essays Presented to Leonard H. Lesko upon his Retirement from the Wilbour Chair of Egyptology at Brown University, June 2005*, eds. Stephen E. Thompson and Peter Der Manuelian. Providence: Brown University, Department of Egyptology and Ancient Western Asian Studies, 2008, 1–13.

——. "The Transition from Libyan to Nubian Rule: The Role of the God's Wife of Amun," in: *The Libyan Period in Egypt: Historical and Chronological Problems of the Third Intermediate Period*, eds. Gerard P. F. Broekman, R. J. Demarée and Olaf E. Kaper. Leiden: The Netherlands Institute for the Near East, 2008, 29–49.

Bács, T. B. "A Note on the Divine Adoratrix Isis, Daughter of Ramesses VI," *GM* 148 (1995): 7–11.

Badawy, A. *History of Egyptian Architecture.* Los Angeles: University of California Press, 1968.

Baines, John. "Kingship, Definition of Culture, and Legitimation," in: *Ancient Egyptian Kingship*, eds. David P. Silverman and David O'Connor. Leiden: E. J. Brill, 1995, 3–48.

—— and Jaromir Malek. *Atlas of Ancient Egypt.* Rev, ed. Cairo: American University in Cairo Press, 2005.

Barguet, Paul. "Un aspect religieux du grand-majordome de la divine adoratrice," *BSFE* no. 20 (1956): 7–9.

——. *Le temple d'Amon-Re à Karnak: Essai d'exégèse*. Cairo: IFAO, 1962.

Barguet, Paul and Leclant, Jean. *Karnak-Nord* IV: *(1949–1951)*. Fouilles de l'Institut Français du Caire. Cairo: IFAO, 1954.

Beckerath, Jürgen von. *Handbuch der ägyptischen Königsnamen*. München: Deutscher Kunstverlag, 1984.

——. "Sobeknofru," in: *LÄ* V (1984), 1050–51.

Beinlich, Horst and Mohamed Saleh. *Corpus der hieroglyphischen Inschriften aus dem Grab des Tutanchamun*. Oxford: Griffith Institute, 1989.

Bell, Lanny. "Luxor Temple and the Cult of the Royal Ka," *JNES* 44 (1985): 251–94.

——. "The New Kingdom 'Divine Temple': The Example of Luxor," in: *Temples of Ancient Egypt*, ed. B. E. Shafer. Ithaca: Cornell University Press, 1997, 127–84.

Bennet, John. "The Meaning of the Royal Nomen and Prenomen" *JEA* 51 (1965): 206–7.

Bierbrier, M. L. *The Late New Kingdom in Egypt (1300–664 BC)*. Warminster: Aris & Phillips, 1975.

Bietak, M. *Chronologie der Nubischen C-Gruppe: ein Beitrag zur Fühgeschichte unternubiens zwischen 2200 und 1550 vor chr.* Vienna: Herman Böhlaus, 1968.

Blackman, A. M. "The Significance of Incense and Libations in Funerary and Temple Ritual," *ZÄS* 50 (1912): 69–75.

—— and Fairman, H. W. "The Significance of the Ceremony *ḥwt bḥsw* in the Temple of Horus at Edfu," *JEA* 35 (1949): 98–112.

—— and Fairman, H. W. "The Significance of the Ceremony *ḥwt bḥsw* in the Temple of Horus at Edfu," *JEA* 36 (1950): 63–81.

Bleeker, C. J. *Egyptian Festivals: Enactments of Religious Renewal.* Studies in the History of Religions, Supplement to Numen 13. Leiden: Brill, 1967.

Bonhême, Marie-Ange. *Les noms royaux dans l'égypte de la troisième période intermédiaire. BdÉ* 98. Cairo: IFAO, 1987.

——. *Pharaon: Les secrets du pouvoir.* Paris: Armand Colin, 1988.

——. "Kingship," in: *Oxford Encyclopedia of Ancient Egypt*, ed. D. B. Redford. Oxford: Oxford University Press, 2001, 238–45.

Bonnet, Hans. *Reallexikon der ägyptischen Religionsgeschichte.* Berlin: Walter de Gruyter & Co, 1952.

——. *Reallexikon der ägyptischen Religionsgeschichte*, Berlin: 2000.

Brand, Peter. "Veils, Votives, and Marginalia: The Use of Sacred Space at Karnak and Luxor," in: P. F. Dorman and B. M. Bryan, *Sacred Space and Sacred Functions in Ancient Thebes.* Occasional Proceedings of the Theban Workshop SAOC 61. Chicago: Oriental Institute, 2007, 51–83.

Breastead, James H. "The Philosophy of a Memphite Priest," *ZÄS* 39 (1901): 39–54.

Broekman, Gerard P. F. "The Nile Level Records of the Twenty-second and Twenty-third dynasties in Karnak: A Reconsideration of their Chronological Order," *JEA* 88 (2002): 163–78.

Brosius, Maria. *Women in Ancient Persia 559–331 BC.* Oxford: Clarendon Press, 1996.

Brovarski, Edward. "Templepersonal," *LÄ* VI, 388.

——. "Sokar," *LÄ* V, 1055–1174.

Brown, Peter. *"The Body and Society:" Men, Women, and Sexual Renunciation in Early Christianity.* New York: Columbia University Press, 1988.

Brunner, Helmut. *Die Geburt des Gottkönigs des Neuen Reiches* I. Mainz, Wiesbaden, 1961.

——. "Chons," *LÄ* I, 960–63B.

Brunner-Traut, E. "Lotos," *LÄ* III, 1094.

Bryan, Betsy, "In Women, Good and Bad Fortune Are on Earth: Status and Roles of Women in Egyptian Culture," in: *Mistress of the House, Mistress of Heaven,* eds. A. K. Capel and G. E. Markoe. New York: Hudson Hill Press, 1996, 25–46.

——. "Property and the God's Wives of Amun," in: *Women and Property,* eds. D. Lyons and R. Westbrook. Harvard University: Center for Hellenic Studies, 2005, 1–15.

Burgos, Franck and F. Larché, *La Chapelle Rouge: Le sanctuaire de barque d'Hatshepsout.* Volume I: *Fac-similés et photographies des scènes.* Paris: Éditions Recherches sur les Civilisations, 2006.

Caminos, Ricardo A. "The Nitocris Adoption Stela," *JEA* 50 (1964): 71–101.

Capel, Anne K. and Glenn E. Markoe (eds.) *Mistress of the House, Mistress of the Heaven: Women in Ancient Egypt.* New York: Hudson Hills Press, 1996.

Černý, J. "Queen Ēse of the Twentieth Dynasty and Her Mother," *JEA* 44 (1958): 31–37.

Christophe, Louis A. *Karnak-Nord* III: *(1945–1949).* Fouilles de l'Institut Français du Caire XXIII. Cairo: IFAO, 1951.

——. "La Double datation du Ouadi Gassous," *BIE* 35 (1953): 141–52.
——. "Les trois derniers grands majordomes de la XXVIe dynastie," *ASAE* 54 (1956): 83–100.
——. "Les Divinités du papyrus Harris I et leurs epithets," *ASAE* 54 (1956): 345–89.
Collier, S. "The Crowns of Pharaoh: Their Development and Significance in Ancient Egyptian Kingship," (PhD diss., UCLA, 1996).
Cool Root, M. *King and Kingship in Achaemenid Art: Essays on the Creation of an Iconography of Empire*. Acta Iranica. Troisième Série: Textes et Mémoires IX. Leiden: E. J. Brill, 1979.
——. "The Persepolis Perplex: Some Prospects Born of Retrospect," in: *Ancient Persia: Art of an Empire*, ed. D. Schmandt-Besserat. Malibu: Undena Press, 1980, 5–13.
Cooney, Kathlyn. "The Edifice of Taharqa by the Sacred Lake: Ritual Function and the Rule of the King," *JARCE* 37 (2000): 15–47.
Cruz-Uribe, Eugene. "A New Look at the Adoption Papyrus," *JEA* 74 (1988): 220–23.
Daressy, Georges. "Le chapelle d'Amenirtis," *RT* 23 (1901): 4–18.
Dieleman, Jacco. *Priests, Tongues and Rites: The London-Leiden Magical Manuscripts and Translation in Egyptian Ritual (100–300 CE)*. Religions in the Graeco-Roman World 153. Leiden: Brill, 2005.
Dils, Peter. "Wine for Pouring and Purification in Ancient Egypt," in: *Ritual and Sacrifice in the Ancient Near East: Proceedings of the International Conference Organized by the Katholieke Universiteit Leuven from the 17th to the 20th of April 1991*, ed. J. Quaegebeur. Orientalis Lovaniensia Analecta 55 (Leuven: Peeters, 1993), 107–23.
Dodson, Aidan. "The Problem of Amenirdis II and the Heirs to the Office of God's Wife of Amun during the Twenty-sixth Dynasty," *JEA* 88 (2002): 179–86.
Doresse, Marianne. "Le dieu voilé dans sa châsse," *Rd'É* 23 (1971): 113–136.
——. "Le dieu voilé dans sa châsse et la fête du début de la décade," *Rd'É* 25 (1973): 92–135.
——. "Le dieu voile dans sa châsse et la fête du début de la décade," *Rd'É* 25 (1979): 36–65.
Dorman, Peter F. and Bryan, Betsy M. (eds.) *Sacred Space and Sacred Function in Ancient Thebes*. SAOC 61. Chicago: Oriental Institute of the University of Chicago, 2007.
Drioton, E. "Deux Statues Naophores consacrées à Apis," *ASAE* 41 (1941): 21–35.
Dumas, François. "Les objets sacrés de la déesse Hathor à Dendara," *Rd'É* 22 (1970): 63–78.
Dunham, Dows and M. F. Laming Macadam. "Names and Relationships of the Royal Family of Napata," *JEA* 35 (1949): 139–49.
Dunn, Marilyn. *The Emergence of Monasticism: From the Desert Fathers to the Early Middle Ages*. Oxford: Blackwell, 2003.
Egberts, Arno. *In Quest of Meaning: A Study of the Ancient Egyptian Rites of Consecrating the Meret-Chests and Driving the Calves*. Leiden: Nederlands Instituut voor Het Nabije Oosten, 1995.
Eide, T. Hägg, R. H. Pierce, and L. Török. *Fontes Historiae Nubiorum: Textual Sources for the History of the Middle Nile Region between the Eighth Century BC and the Sixth Century AD*. Vol 1: *From the Eighth to the Mid-Fifth Century BC*. Bergen: University of Bergen, Department of Classics, 1994.

Epigraphic Survey. *The Temple of Khonsu* I: *Scenes of King Herihor in the Court*. OIP 100. Chicago: The Oriental Institute of the University of Chicago, 1979.

Erman, Adolf. *Die Religion der Ägypter*. Berlin: Der Gruyter, 1934 and 1978.

Erman, Adolf and H. Grapow. *Wörterbuch der ägyptischen Sprache* I-IV. Leipzig: J. C. Hinrichs'sche Buchhanlung, 1926–1950.

Étienne, M. *Heka: Magie et envoûtement dans l'Égypte ancienne*. Paris: Réunion des Musées Nationaux, 2000.

Eyre, C. J. "The Adoption Papyrus in Social Context," *JEA* 78 (1992): 207–21.

Fairman, H. W. "The Kingship Rituals of Egypt," in: *Myth, Ritual, and Kingship*, ed. Samuel H. Hooke. Oxford: Clarendon Press, 1958, 74–104.

Faulkner, R. O. *A Concise Dictionary of Middle Egyptian*. Oxford: Griffith Institute, 1961.

——. *The Ancient Egyptian Pyramid Texts*. Oxford: Clarendon Press, 1969.

Fazzini, Richard. *Egypt: Dynasty XXII–XXV*. Leiden: E. J. Brill, 1988.

Finnestad, Ragnhild Bierre. "Temples of the Ptolemaic and Roman Periods: Ancient Traditions in New Contexts," in: *Temples of Ancient Egypt*, ed. B. E. Shafer. Ithaca: Cornell University Press, 1997, 185–237.

Fischer, H. G. "The Cult and Nome of the Goddess Bat," *JARCE* 1 (1962): 7–18.

——. *The Orientation of Hieroglyphs* – Part 1: *Reversals*. New York: Metropolitan Museum of Art, 1977.

——. "On Some Reinterpretations of Royal Names," *GM* 108 (1989): 21–29.

Foster, John L. *Love Songs of the New Kingdom*. Austin: University of Texas Press, 1974.

Fowler, Barbara Hughes. *Love Lyrics of Ancient Egypt*. Chapel Hill: University of North Carolina Press, 1994.

Frandsen, Paul. "Trade and Cult," in: *The Religion of the Ancient Egyptians: Cognitive Structures and Popular Expression*, ed. Gertie Englund. Uppsala: Acta Universitatis Upsalieneis, 1987, 95–108.

Gabra, S. *Rapport sur les fouilles d'Hermoupolis ouest*. Cairo: IFAO, 1941.

Gardiner, Alan H. "Adoption Extraordinary," *JEA* 26 (1940): 23–29.

——. "Horus, the Behdite," *JEA* 30 (1944): 23–60.

——. *Egyptian Grammar*. Third Edition. Oxford: Griffith Institute, 1957.

——. *Egypt of the Pharaohs: An Introduction*. Oxford: Oxford University Press, 1964.

Gardiner, Alan H. and T. Eric Peet. *The Inscriptions of the Sinai*. London: Egypt Exploration Society. 1952–1955.

Gee, John. "Prophets, Initiation and the Egyptian Temple," *JSSEA* 31 (2004): 97–107.

Gillan, Robin. "Sokebneferu," in: *The Oxford Encyclopedia of Ancient Egypt*, ed. D. B. Redford. Oxford: Oxford University Press, 2001, 301.

Gitton, Michel. *L'épouse de dieu Ahmes Néfertary*. Paris: Belles-Lettres, 1975.

——. "Le rôle de la femme dans le clergé d'Amon à la 18e dynastie," *BSFE* 75 (1976): 31–46.

——. "La résiliation d'une fonction religieuse: nouvelle interpretation de la stèle de donation d'Ahmès Néfertary," *BIFAO* 76 (1976): 65–89.

——. *Les divines épouses de la 18e dynastie*. Paris: Belles-Lettres, 1984.

Gitton, Michel and Leclant, Jean. "Gottesgemahlin," *LÄ* II, 792–812.

Godley, A. D. (trans.). *Herodotus: Books I–II*. Loeb Classical Library 117. Cambridge, Mass: Harvard University Press, 1920

Goebs, Katja. "Crowns," in: *The Oxford Encyclopedia of Ancient Egypt* I, ed. D. B. Redford. Oxford: Oxford University Press, 2001, 321–26.

Gosselin, Luc. *Les Divines épouses d'Amon dans l'Égypte de la XIXe à la XXIe dynastie.* Études et Mémoires no. 6, Paris: Cybele, 2007.

Goyon, Jean-Claude. "Textes Mythologiques II. 'Les revelations du mystère des quatre boules,'" *BIFAO* 75 (1975): 349–99.

Graefe, Erhart. *Untersuchungen zur Verwaltung und Geschichte der Institution der Gottesgemahlin des Amun von Beginn des neuen Reiches bis zur Spätzeit.* Wiesbaden: Otto Harrasssowitz, 1981.

——. "Upaut," LÄ VI, 862–64.

——. "Der autobiographische Text des Ibi, Obervermögensverwalter der Gottesgemahlin Nitocris, auf Kairo (JE 36158)," *MDAIK* 50 (1994): 85–99.

——. "Die Adoption ins Amt der *ḥswt njwt ẖnw ni imnw* und der *šmswt dw3t-nṯr* (zu Ritner Artikel in GM 164, 1998, 85 ff)," *GM* 166 (1998): 109–12.

——. "Nochmals zum Gebrauch des Titels *dw3t-nṯr* in der Spätzeit," *JEA* 89 (2003): 246–47.

Graham, Geoffrey. "Insignias," in: *The Oxford Encyclopedia of Ancient Egypt,* ed. Donald B. Redford. Oxford: Oxford University Press, 2001, 163–67.

Graindorge, Catherine. "Sokar," in: *The Oxford Encyclopedia of Ancient Egypt* III, ed. D. B. Redford. Oxford: Oxford University Press, 2001, 305–307.

Graves-Brown, Carolyn (ed.). *Sex and Gender in Ancient Egypt.* Swansea: The Classical Press of Wales, 2008.

Griffiths, J. Gwyn. "Osiris," in: *The Oxford Encyclopedia of Ancient Egypt* I, ed. D. B. Redford. Oxford: Oxford University Press, 615–19.

Grimal, N.-C. *Étude sur la propagande royale égyptienne* I: *La stèle triomphale de Pi(ankh)y au Musée du Caire (JE 48862 et 47086–47089).* Mémoires publiés par les membres de l'institut français d'archéologie orientale du Caire 105 Cairo: IFAO, 1981.

——. *Les termes de la propagande royale égyptienne: de la XIX*[e] *dynastie à la conquête d'Alexandre.* Paris: Imprimerie Nationale, 1986.

——. *A History of Ancient Egypt,* trans. I. Shaw. Oxford: Blackwell, 1992.

Grimm, Alfred. "Feind-Bilder und Bilderverbrennung: Ein Brandopfer zur rituellen Feindvernichtung in einer Festdarstellung der 'Chapelle Rouge,'" *VA* 4 (1988): 207–14.

Gundlach, Rolf. "Temples," in: *The Oxford Encyclopedia of Ancient Egypt,* ed. D. B. Redford. Oxford: Oxford University Press, 2001, 363–79.

Habachi, Labib. "Mentuhotep, the Vizier and Son-in-Law of Taharqa," in: E. Endesfelder *et al.* (eds) *Ägypten und Kusch: Schriften zur Geschichte und Kulture des Alten Orients.* Berlin: Adademie-Verlag, 1977, 165–70.

——. "Gottesvater," *LÄ* II, 825–26.

Handoussa, Tohfa. "The Rebirth of Ramses II in the Hypostyle Hall of Karnak," in: *Hommages à Fayza Haikal.* Bd'É 138, eds. N. Grimal, A. Kamel, and C.-M. Sheikholeslami. Cairo: IFAO, 2003.

Hanning, Rainer. *Großes Handwörterbuch: Ägyptisch–Deutsch (2800–950 v.Chr.).* Mainz am Rhein: Verlag Phillip von Zabern, 1995.

——. *Ägyptisches Wörterbuch I: Altes Reich und Erste Zwichenzeit.* Mainz am Rhein: Verlag Phillip von Zabern, 2003.

Harari, Ibrahim. "Nature de la Stèle de donation de function du roi Ahmôsis à la reine Ahmès-Nefertari," *ASAE* 56 (1959): 139–201.

Harris, James E. and Weeks, Kent R. *X-Raying the Pharaohs.* New York: Charles Schribner's Sons, 1973.

Helck, W. "Maat," *LÄ* III, 1110–19.

Hesse, Flora B. "The Iconography and Use of the Sistrum in the Pharaonic Period." University of Memphis, 2007. Unpublished M.A. thesis.

Hofmann, I. *Studien zum meroitischen Königtum.* Monographies Reine Elisabeth 2. Brussels: Foundation Reine Elisabeth, 1971.

Hölscher, Uvo. *Excavation Medinet Habu* V*: the Post-Ramesside Remains.* Chicago: Oriental Institute of the University of Chicago, 1954.

Hornung, Erik. *Conceptions of God in Ancient Egypt: the One and the Many.* Trans. John Baines. Ithaca: Cornell University Press, 1982.

——. *History of Ancient Egypt.* Trans. David Lorton. Edinburgh: Edinburgh University Press, 1999.

Houser-Wegner, Jennifer. "Khonsu," in: *The Oxford Encyclopedia of Ancient Egypt* II, ed. D. B. Redford. Oxford: Oxford University Press, 2001, 233.

——. "Wepwawet," in: *The Oxford Encyclopedia of Ancient Egypt* III, ed. D. B. Redford. Oxford: Oxford University Press, 2001, 496–97.

Hunter, David G. *Marriage, Celibacy, and Heresy in Ancient Christianity.* Oxford: Oxford University Press, 2007.

Isler, M. "An Ancient Method of Finding and Extending Direction," *JARCE* 26 (1989): 191–206.

Iversen, Erik. "Reflections on Some Ancient Egyptian Royal Names," in: *Pyramid Studies Presented to I. E. S. Edwards* London: Egypt Exploration Society, 1988, 78–88.

Jacobsohn, Herbert. "Kamutef," *LÄ* III 308–9.

Jacquet-Gordon, Helen. "A Statuette of Ma'et and the Identity of the Divine Adoratress Karomama," *ZÄS* 94 (1967): 86–93.

Jansen-Winkeln, Karl. "Amenirdis und Harwa," *DE* 35 (1996): 39–48.

Janssen, Jac J. and Janssen, Rosalind M. *Getting Old in Ancient Egypt.* London: The Rubicon Press, 1996.

Janssen, Jac. J. and Pestman, P. W. "Burial and Inheritance in the Community of the Necropolis Workmen at Thebes (Pap. Boulaq X and O. Petrie 16," *JESHO* 11.2 (1968): 137–170.

Johnson, Janet H. "The Persians and the Continuity of Egyptian Culture," in: *Achaemenid History VIII: Continuity and Change. Proceedings of the Last Achaemenid Workshop, April 6–8, 1990. Ann Arbor, Michigan*, eds. H. Sancisi-Weerdenburg, A. Kuhrt, and M. Cool Root. Leiden: Nederlands Instituut voor het Nabije Oosten, 1994, 49–59.

Johnson, Janet H. "The Demotic Chronicle as a Statement of a Theory of Kingship," *JSSEA* 13 (1983): 61–72.

Kanawati, Naguib. *The Rock Tomb of El-Hawawish* 3. Sydney: Macquarie Ancient History Association, 1982.

Kaplony, Peter. "Königstitulatur" *LÄ*, 641–59.

Kees, Hermann. *Das Priestertum im Ägyptischen Staat vom neuen Reich zur Spätzeit. Probleme der Ägyptologie* 1. Leiden and Köln: E. J. Brill, 1953.

——. "Das Gottesweib Ahmes-Nefertari als Amonspriester," *Orientalia* 23 (1954): 57–63.

——. *Die Hohenpriester des Amun Von Karnak von Herihor bis zum Ende der Äthiopenzeit. Probleme der Ägyptologie* 4. Leiden: E. J. Brill, 1964.

Kemp, Barry J. *Ancient Egypt: Anatomy of a Civilization*. London and New York: Routledge, 1993.

Kientz, F. K. *Die politische Geschichte Ägyptens vom 7. bis zum 4. Jahrhundert vor der Zeitwende*. Berlin: Akademie Verlag, 1953.

Kitchen, K. A. "The Titularies of the Ramesside Kings as Expression of Their Ideal Kingship," *ASAE* 71 (1987): 131–41.

——. *Third Intermediate Period in Egypt (1100–650 BC)*. Warminster: Aris & Phillips, 1995.

——. "Pharaoh Ramesses II and His Times," in: *Civilizations of the Ancient Near East* IV, ed. J. Sasson. New York: Hendrickson Publishers, 2001, 763–74.

——. "Ramses V–XI," *LÄ* V, 124–29.

Krauss, R. "Isis," *LÄ* III, 203–4.

Kruchten, Jean-Marie. *Les annales des prêtres de Karnak (XXI–XXIIImes Dynasties) et autres textes contemporains relatifs a l'initiation des prêtres d'Amon*. Orientalia Lovaniesia Analecta 32. Leuven: Departement Oriëntalistiek, 1989.

Kuhrt, Amélie. *The Ancient Near East II*. London: Routledge, 1995.

Kurth, Dieter. "A World Order in Stone – The Late temples," in: *Egypt: The World of the Pharaohs*, eds. Regine Schulz and Mattias Seidel. Köln: Könemann, 1998.

Lacau, Pierre, and Chevier, Henri. *Une chapelle d'Hatshepsout à Karnak* I. Cairo: IFAO, 1977.

Laming Macadam, M. F. *The Temples of Kawa* II: *History and Archaeology of the Site*. London: Oxford University Press, 1955.

Lauer, J.-P. *La Pyramide à Degrés: L'architecture I: Texte*. Cairo: IFAO, 1936.

Leahy, Anthony. "Death by Fire in Ancient Egypt," *JESHO* 27 (1984): 199–206.

——. "The Libyan Period in Egypt: An Essay in Interpretation," *Libyan Studies* 16 (1985): 51–65.

——. "More Light on a Saite Official of the God's Wife of Amun," *JEA* 74 (1988): 236–39.

——. "The Earliest Dated Monument of Amasis and the End of the Reign of Apries," *JEA* 74 (1988): 197–8.

—— (ed.). *Libya and Egypt (c.1300–750 BC)*. London: School of Oriental and African Studies, 1990.

——. "Appendix: The Twenty-third Dynasty," in: *Libya and Egypt (c.1300–750 BC)*, ed. A. Leah. London: School of Oriental and African Studies, 1990, 177–200.

——. "Abydos in the Libyan Period," in: *Libya and Egypt (c.1300–750 BC)*, ed. A. Leah. London: School of Oriental and African Studies, 1990, 155–176.

——. "Kushite Monuments at Abydos," in: *The Unbroken Reed: Studies in the Culture and Heritage of Ancient Egypt in Honour of A. F. Shore*. Occasional Publication 11, eds. C. Eyre, A. Leahy, and L. M. Leahy. London: Egypt Exploration Society, 1994, 182–87.

——. "The Adoption of Ankhnesneferibre at Karnak," *JEA* 82 (1996): 145–65.

Leclant, Jean. "Quelques données nouvelles sur l'édifice dit de Tahaqa", près de la sacre à Karnak," *BIFAO* 49 (1950): 181–95.

——. "Le rôle du lait et de l'allaitement d'après les textes des pyramides," *JNES* 10 (1951): 123–27.

——. "La colonnade éthiopienne à l'est de la grande enceinte d'Amon à Karnak," *BIFAO* 53 (1953): 113–72.

——. "Osiris *pꜣ-wšb-iꜣd*," in: *Ägyptologische Studien herausgegeben von O. Firchow*. Berlin: Akademie Verlag, 1955, 197–204.

——. "Tefnout et les Divines Adoratrices thébaines," *MDAIK* 15 (1957): 166–71.

——. "The Suckling of Pharaoh as a Part of the Coronation Rites in Ancient Egypt. Le rôle de l'allaitement dans le cérémonial pharaonique du couronnement," in: *Proceedings of the IXth International Congress for the History of Religion*. Tokyo 1958 (published 1960), 135–45.

——. "Kashta, Pharaon, en Egypte," *ZÄS* 90 (1963): 74–81.

——. *Recherches sur les monuments thébains de la XXVe dynastie dite éthiopienne.* Bd'É 36. Cairo: IFAO, 1965.

——. "Un manche de sistre au nom de Shabataka," in: *Pyramid Studies and Other Essays Presented to I. E. S. Edwards*. Edited by John Baines, T. G. H. James, Anthony Leahy and A. F. Shore. London: The Egypt Exploration Society, 1988, 152–53.

——. "Achamonrau," *LÄ* I, 52–52.

Leclère, François and Laurent Coulon. "La nécropole osirienne de la 'Grande Place' à Karnak. Fouilles dans le secteur Nord-est du Temple d'Amon," in: *Proceedings of the Seventh International Congress of Egyptologists. Cambridge, 3–9 September 1995*, ed. C. Eyre. Leuven: Utigeverij Peeters, 1998, 649–59.

Lefkowitz, Mary R. "Influential Women," in: *Images of Women in Antiquity*, eds. Averil Cameron and Amélie Kuhrt. London: Routledge, 1983 and 1993, 49–63.

Legrain, Georges. "Le temple et les chapelles d'Osiris à Karnak I: Le temple d'Osiris-Hiq-Djeto ," *RT* 22 (1900): 125–36, 146–49.

———. "Le temple et les chapelles d'Osiris à Karnak III: La chapelle d'Osiris, Maître de la Vie ," *RT* 24 (1902): 208–14.

Leitz, Christian. *Lexikon der Ägyptischen Götter und Götterbezeichnungen* I. *Orientalia Lovaniensia Analecta* 110. Leuven: Peeters, 2002.

———. *Lexikon der Ägyptischen Götter und Götterbezeichnungen* VIII: *Regiter. Orientalia Lovaniensia Analecta* 128. Leuven: Peeters, 2003.

Leprohon, Ronald J. "The Programmatic Use of the Royal Titulary in the Twelfth Dynasty," *JARCE* 33 (1996): 165–71.

——. "Royal Ideology and State Administration in Pharaonic Egypt," in: *Civilizations of the Ancient Near East* I, ed. J. Sasson. New York: Hendrickson Publishers, 2001, 273–87.

Lesko, Barbara S. (ed.). *Women's Earliest Records from Ancient Egypt and Western Asia: Proceedings of the Conference on Women in the Ancient Near East. Brown University, Providence, Rhode Island November 5–7, 1987*. Atlanta: Scholars Press, 1989.

——. *The Great Goddesses of Egypt*. Norman: University of Oklahoma Press, 1999.

Lesko, Leonard H. "Ancient Egyptian Cosmogonies and Cosmology," in: *Religion in Ancient Egypt: Gods, Myth, and Religious Practice*, ed. Byron E. Shafer. Ithaca: Cornell University Press, 1991, 88–122.

Lichtheim, Miriam. "The High Steward Akhmenru," *JNES* 7 (1948): 163–79.

——. *Ancient Egyptian Literature* Vols. I–III. Berkeley: University of California Press, 1973–81.

Lloyd, Alan. "The Late Period," in B. G. Trigger, B. J. Kemp, D. O'Connor, and A. B. Lloyd, *Ancient Egypt: A Social History.* Cambridge: Cambridge University Press, 1983.

Logan, Tom. "The *Jmyt-pr* Document: Form, Function, and Significance," *JARCE* 37 (2000): 49–73.

Lohwasser, Angelika. *Die königlichen Frauen im antiken Reich von Kusch: 25. Dynastie bis zur Zeit des Nastasen. Meroitica* 19. Wiesbaden: Harrassawitz Verlag, 2001.

——. "Queenship in Kush: Status, Role, and Ideology of Royal Women," *JARCE* 38 (2001): 61–76.

Malek, Jaromir. *Egypt: 4000 Years of Art*. London: Phaidon Press, 2003.

Malinine, I. M. "L'expression désignant l'enfant adoptif en égyptien," in: *Comptes Rendus du Groupe Linguistique d'Études Chamito-Sémitique (GLECS)* VI: *Années 1951–1954*. Paris: École Pratique des Hautes- Études, 1952, 13–15.

Manniche, Lise. *Music and Musicians in Ancient Egypt*. London: British Museum Press, 1991.

——. *Sexual Life in Ancient Egypt*. London: Kegan Paul, 2002.

Manuelian, Peter der. "An Essay in Document Transmission: *Nj-k3-ʿnh* and the earliest *hrw-rnpt*," *JNES* 45 (1986): 1–18.

——. *Living in the Past: Studies in Archaism of the Egyptian Twenty-Sixth Dynasty*. London and New York: Kegan Paul International, 1994.

Martin, G. T. *The Memphite Tomb of Horemheb, Commander-in-Chief of Tutankhamūn* I: *The reliefs, inscriptions, and commentary*. Excavation Memoir 55. London: Egypt Exploration Society, 1989.

——. *The Hidden Tombs of Memphis: New Discoveries from the Time of Tutankhamun and Ramesses the Great*. London: Thames and Hudson, 1991.

——. *The Tomb of Tia and Tia: A Royal Monument of the Ramesside Period in the Memphite Necropolis*. Excavation Memoir 58. London: Egypt Exploration Society, 1997.

Maspero, G. "Deux Monuments de la Princesse Ankhnasnofiribri," *ASAE* 5 (1904): 84–92.

Matta, Girgis and George R. Hughes. *The Demotic Legal Code of Hermopolis West*. Biliothèque d'Étude 45. Cairo: Institut Français d'Archéologie Orientale, 1975.

Mausse, Marcel. *The Gift: The Form and Reason for Exchange in Archaic Societies*. Trans. W. D. Halls. London: Routledge, 1990.

Meeks, Dimitri. *Année Lexicographique: Egypte ancienne*. 3 vols. Paris: 1980–1982.

Meeks, Dimitri and C. Favard-Meeks. *Daily Life of the Egyptian Gods*. Trans. G. M. Goshgarian. Ithaca: Cornell University Press, 1996.

Meltzer, Edmund S. "Horus," in: *The Oxford Encyclopedia of Ancient Egypt* II, ed. D. B. Redford. Oxford: Oxford University Press, 2001, 119–122.

Menu, Bernadette. "Women and Business Life in the First Millennium B.C.," in: *Women's Earliest Records*, 193–212.

de Meulenaere, H. *Le Surnom Egyptien à la Basse Epoque*. Istanbul: Nederlands Historisch-Archaeologicsch Institut in het Nabije Oosten, 1966.

——. "La famille du roi Amasis," *JEA* 54 (1968): 183–87.

Möller, Georg. *Hieratische Lesestücke für den Akademischen Gebrauch* I. Leipzig: J. C. Hinrichs'sche Buchhandlung, 1927.

Monnet, Janine. "Un monument de la corégence des divines adoratrices Nitocris et Ankhenesneferibré," *Revue d'Égyptologie* 10 (1955): 37–47.

Morenz, S. *Ägyptische Religion*. Trans. Ann E. Keep. London: Methuen & Co Ltd, 1960.

Morkot, Robert. "Kingship and Kinship in the Empire of Kush," in: *Studien zum antiken Sudan: Akten der 7. Internationalen Tagung für meroitishtische Forschungen von 14. bis 19. September 1992 in Gosen bei Berlin*, ed. Steffen Wenig. Wiesbaden: Harrassowitz Verlag, 1999, 179–229.

——. *The Black Pharaohs*. London: The Rubicon Press, 2000.

Murnane, William J. *Ancient Egyptian Co-regencies*. SAOC 40. Chicago: The Oriental Institute, 1977.

——. "The Sed Festival: A Problem in Historical Methods," *MDAIK* 37 (1981): 369–76.

——. *Texts from the Amarna Period in Egypt*. Atlanta: Scholars Press, 1995.

Murray, Margaret A. *Index of Names and Titles of the Old Kingdom*. London: Kegan Paul, 2004.

Myśliwiec, K. *Eighteenth Dynasty before the Amarna Period*. Iconography of Religions XVI, 5. Leiden: E. J. Brill, 1985.

——. *Royal Portraiture Dynasty XXI–XXX*. Mainz am Rhein: Phillip Zabern, 1988.

——. *The Twilight of Ancient Egypt*. Ithaca: Cornell University Press, 2000.

——. "Atum," in: *The Oxford Encyclopedia of Ancient Egypt*, ed. D. B. Redford. Oxford: Oxford University Press, 2001, 158–60.

Naguib, Saphinaz-Amal. *Le clergé féminin d'Amon thébain à la 21e dynastie*. Leuven: Uitgevery Peeters en Department Oriëntalistiek, 1990.

Naville, E. *The Temple of Deir el-Bahri* I: *North-western end of the Upper Platform*. London: Egypt Exploration Fund, 1894.

——. *The Temple of Deir el-Bahri* II: *Northern half of the Middle Platform*. London: Egypt Exploration Fund, 1896.

——. *The Temple of Deir el-Bahri* III: *End of the Northern half and the Southern half of the Middle Platform*. London: Egypt Exploration Fund, 1898.

——. *The Temple of Deir el-Bahri* IV: *Shrine of Hathor and the Southern Hall of Offerings*. London: Egypt Exploration Fund, 1901.

——. *The Temple of Deir el-Bahri* VI: *Lower Terrace*. London: Egypt Exploration Fund, 1908.

Nelson, Harold H. *The Great Hypostyle Hall at Karnak*, Vol. 1, Part 1: *The Wall Reliefs*. Edited by William J. Murnane. Chicago: The Oriental Institute, 1981.

Niwinski, A. "The Solar-Osirian Unity as Principle of the Theology of the 'State of Amun,' in Thebes in the 21st Dynasty." *Jaarbericht von het Vooraziatisch-Egyptisch Genootschap Ex Oriente Lux* 30 (1987–1988): 89–107.

Nunn, John F. *Ancient Egyptian Medicine*. London: British Museum Press, 1996.

O'Connor, David. "The New Kingdom and Third Intermediate Period," in: B. G. Trigger, B. J. Kemp, D. O'Connor, and A. B. Lloyd, *Ancient Egypt: A Social History*. Cambridge: Cambridge University Press, 1983.

O'Connor, David and Eric H. Cline (eds.). *Amenhotep III: Perspectives on His Reign*. Ann Arbor: University of Michigan Press, 2001.

Onstine, Suzanne Lynn. *The Role of the Chantress (Šmꜥyt) in Ancient Egypt*. BAR International Series 1401. Oxford: Archaeopress, 2005.

Osing, Jürgen. *Der Tempel Sethos' I in Gurna: Die Reliefs und Inschriften* I. Mainz am Rhein: Philipp von Zabern, 1977.

Otto, Eberhard. *Ancient Egyptian Art: The Cults of Osiris and Amon*. Trans. Kate Bosse-Griffiths. New York: Thames and Hudson, 1967.

——. "Amun," *LÄ* I, 237–48.

Quirke, Stephen. *The Cult of Re: Sun-Worship in Ancient Egypt*. New York: Thames and Hudson, 2001.

Park, R. "Stretching of the Cord," in: *Proceedings of the Seventh International Congress of Egyptologists. Cambridge, 3–9 September 1995*, ed. C. Eyre. Leuven: Utigeverij Peeters, 1998, 839–48.

Parker, Richard A. "King Py, a Historical Problem," *ZÄS* 93 (1966): 111–14.

Parker, Richard A., J. Leclant, and J-C. Goyon. *The Edifice of Taharqa by the Sacred Lake of Karnak*. Brown Egyptological Studies 8. Providence: Brown University Press, 1979.

Parker, Richard A. and Lesko, Leonard H. "The Khonsu Cosmogony," in: *Pyramid Studies and Other Essays Presented to I. E. S. Edwards*, ed. John Baines *et al.*, Occasional Publications 7. London: Egypt Exploration Society, 1988, 168–75.

Peden, Alex J. "Ramesses VI," in: *The Oxford Encyclopedia of Ancient Egypt* III, ed. D. B. Redford Oxford: Oxford University Press, 2001, 120.

——. "Ramesses IX," in: *The Oxford Encyclopedia of Ancient Egypt* III, ed. D. B. Redford. Oxford: Oxford University Press, 2001, 121.

Perkins, Ann. "Archaeological News," *AJA* 55.1 (1951): 81–100.

Piankoff, Alexander. *Litany of Re*. New York: Bollingen Foundation, 1964.

Pischikova, E. V. "Representations of Ritual and Symbolic Objects in Late XXVth Dynasty and Saite Private Tombs," *JARCE* 31 (1994): 63–77.

Porter, Bertha and Moss, Rosalind. *Topographical Bibliography of Ancient Egyptian Hieroglyphic Texts, Reliefs, and Paintings*. II. *Theban Temples*. Oxford: Clarendon Press, 1972.

Ranke, H. *Die ägyptischen Personennamen*. 3 vols. Glückstadt: J. J. Augustin, 1935, 1949, 1977.

Redford, Donald B. *Studies in the History and Chronology of the Eighteenth Dynasty: Seven Studies*. Toronto: University of Toronto, 1967.

——. "An Interim Report on the Second Season of Work at the Temple of Osiris, Ruler of Eternity, Karnak," *JEA* 59 (1973): 16–30.

——. *Pharaonic King-Lists, Annals and Day Books: A Contribution to the Study of the Egyptian Sense of History*. SSEA Publication IV. Mississauga: Benben Publications, 1986.

——. "New Light on Temple J at Karnak," *Orientalia* 55 (1986): 1–15.

——. *Egypt, Canaan and Israel in Ancient Times*. Cairo: American University in Cairo Press, 1993.

——. *From Slave to Pharaoh*: *The Black Experience of Ancient Egypt*. Baltimore: Johns Hopkins University Press, 2003.

Revez, Jean. "Frère du roi: l'évolution du rôle du frère du roi dons les modalités successorales en Égypte ancienne." Unpublished PhD dissertation, Université de Paris-IV Sorbonne, 1999.

——. "The Use of the Kingship Term *sn* 'Brother'," *JARCE* 40 (2003): 123–31.

Reynders, Marleen. "Names and Types of the Egyptian Sistrum," in: *Acts of the Seventh International Congress of Egyptologists*, ed. C. J. Eyre. Leuven: Peeters, 1998, 945–55.

Riddle, John M. *Contraception and Abortion from the Ancient World to the Renaissance*. Cambridge, Mass: Harvard University Press, 1992.

Ritner, Robert K. *The Mechanics of Ancient Egyptian Magical Practice*. Studies in Ancient Oriental Civilization 54. Chicago: Oriental Institute Publications, 1993.

——. "Fictive Adoptions or Celibate Priestesses?" *GM* 164 (1998): 85–90.

——. "An Oblique Reference to the Expelled High Priest Osorkon?" in: *Gold of Praise: Studies on Ancient Egypt in Honor of Edward F. Wente*, eds. E. Teeter and J. A. Larson. SAOC 58 Chicago: Oriental Institute of the University of Chicago, 1999, 351–80.

——. "Libyan vs. Nubian as the Ideal Egyptian," in: *Egypt and Beyond: Essay Presented to Leonard H. Lesko upon His Retirement from the Wilbour Chair of*

Egyptology at Brown University. June 2005, eds. Stephen E. Thompson and Peter Der Manuelian. Providence: Department of Egyptology and Ancient Western Asian Studies, Brown University, 2008, 305–14.

——. "Fragmentation and Re-integration in the Third Intermediate Period," in: *The Libyan Period in Egypt: Historical and Chronological Problems of the Third Intermediate Period*, eds. Gerard P. F. Broekman, R. J. Demarée and Olaf E. Kaper. Leiden: The Netherlands Institute for the Near East. In press.

Robins, Gay. *Women in Ancient Egypt*. London: British Museum Press, 1993.

——. "The God's Wife of Amun in the 18th Dynasty in Egypt," in: *Images of Women in Antiquity*, eds. Averil Cameron and Amélie Kuhrt. London: Routledge, 1983 and 1993, 65–78.

——. "Some Principles of Compositional Dominance and Gender Hierarchy in Egyptian Art," *JARCE* 31 (1994): 33–40.

——. "The Names of Hatshepsut as King," *JEA* 85 (1999): 103–13.

Roeder, Günther. *Statuen Ägyptischer Königinnen im Anschluss an den Torso Amon-Erdas II in Sydney untersucht*. Leipzig: J. C. Hinrichs'sche Buchhandlung, 1932.

Roehrig, Catharine H. *Hatshepsut from Queen to Pharaoh*. New York: Metropolitan Museum of Art, 2005.

Roth, Ann Macy. "The Absent Spouse: Patterns and Taboos in Egyptian Tomb Decoration," *JARCE* 36 (1999): 37–53.

Routledge, Carolyn. "*Ancient Egyptian Ritual Practice: Ir-xt and nt-a*," PhD dissertation, University of Toronto, 2001.

——. "Did Women 'Do Things' in Ancient Egypt?," in *Sex and Gender in Ancient Egypt*, ed. Carolyn Graves-Brown. Swansea: The Classical Press of Wales, 2008, 157–77.

Russmann, Edna R. *The Representation of the King in the XXVth Dynasty*. Bruxelles and Brooklyn: Monographies reine Élisabeth, 1974.

——. *Eternal Egypt: Masterpieces of Ancient Art from the British Museum*. London: British Museum Press, 2001.

——. "Egypt and the Kushites: Dynasty XXV," in: *Africa and Africans in Antiquity*, ed. E. M. Yamauchi. East Lansing: Michigan State University Press, 2001.

Saleh, Heidi. *Investigating Ethnic and Gender Identities as Expressed on Wooden Funerary Stelae from the Libyan Period (c. 1069–715 BCE) in Egypt*. Bar International Series 1734. Oxford: Archaeopress, 2007.

Sancisi-Weerdenburg, H. "Exit Atossa: Images of Women in Greek Historiography on Persia," in: *Images of Women in Antiquity*, eds. Averil Cameron and Amélie Kuhrt. London: Routledge, 1993, 20–33.

Sander-Hansen, C. E. *Die religiösen Texte auf dem Sarg der Anchnesneferibre, neu herausgegeben und erklärt*. Copenhagen: Levin & Munksgaard, 1936.

——. *Das Gottesweib Des Amun*. Copenhagen: Ejnar Munksgaard, 1940.

Sauneron, Serge. *Le Temple D'Esna*. Cairo: IFAO, 1963.

——. "Les Inscriptions Ptolemaiques du Temple de Mout a Karnak," *BIE* 45 (1968): 45–52.

——. *La Porte ptolémaïque de l'enciente de Mout à Karnak*. MIFAO 107. Cairo: IFAO, 1983.

——. *The Priests of Ancient Egypt*. Trans. David Lorton. Ithaca: Cornell University Press, 2000.

—— and Jean Yoyotte. "La campagne nubienne de Psammétique II et sa signification historique," *BIFAO* 50 (1952): 157–207.

Säve-Söderbergh, T. "Aniba," *LÄ* I, 272.

Schäffer, Heinrich. *Principles of Egyptian Art*, ed. Emma Brunner-Traut. Trans. J. Baines. Oxford: Griffith Institute, 2002.

Schneider, Thomas. *Lexikon der Pharaonen: Die altägyptischen Könige von der Frühzeit bis zur Römerherrschaft*. Düsseldorf Zürich: Artemis & Winkler, 1997.

Schulenburg, Jane Tibbetts. *Forgetful of Their Sex: Female Sanctity and Society ca. 500–1100*. Chicago: University of Chicago Press, 1998.

Schunk, Margit. *Untersuchungen zum Worststamm ḫꜥ*. Bonn: Dr. Rudolf Habelt GMBH, 1985.

Schwaller de Lubicz, R. A. *The Temples of Karnak*. Rochester, Vt.: Inner Traditions International, 1999.

Sethe, Kurt. *Urkunden der 18. dynastie: historische-biografische Urkunden*. Berlin: Akademie Verlag, 1927–30.

——. *Thebanische Templeinscriften aus griechisch-römischer Ziet*. Berlin: Akademie Verlag, 1957.

Shafer, Byron E. (ed.). *Religion in Ancient Egypt: Gods, Myths, and Personal Practice*. Ithaca: Cornell University Press, 1991.

Sieber, Elizabeth. "Assimilating the Past – The Art of the Late Period," in: *Egypt: The World of the Pharaohs*, eds. Regine Schulz and Mattias Seidel. Köln: Könemann, 1998.

Silverman, David P. "Divinity and Deity in Ancient Egypt," in: *Religion in Ancient Egypt: Gods, Myth, and Religious Practice*, ed. Byron E. Shafer. Ithaca: Cornell University Press, 1991, 7–87.

——. "The Nature of Egyptian Kingship," in: *Ancient Egyptian Kingship*, eds. David P. Silverman and David O'Connor. Leiden: E. J. Brill, 1995, 49–91.

Spalinger, Anthony. "The Concept of the Monarchy during the Saite Epoch – an Essay of Synthesis," *Orientalia* 47 (1978): 12–36

Spencer, A. J. "Two Enigmatic Hieroglyphs and Their Relation to the Sed-festival," *JEA* 64 (1978): 52–55.

——. *Death in Ancient Egypt*. London: Penguin, 1982.

Spencer, Patricia. *The Egyptian Temple: A Lexicographical Study*. London: Kegan Paul, 1984.

Stadelmann, Rainer. "Das Grab im Tempelhof: Der Typus des Königsgrabes in der Spätzeit," *MDAIK* 27 (1971): 111–23.

Stoeper, Ingrid. "De Bouwactiviteit van de Godsgemalinnen van Amon van de 25e en 26e Dynastie." Unpublished dissertation, Gent, 1997.

Strudwick, Nigel. *Masterpieces of Ancient Egypt*. London: Trustees of the British Museum, 2006.

Suys, E. *La sagesse d'Ani: Texte, traduction et commentaire*. Analecta Orientalia 11. Rome, 1935.

Te Velde, Hermann. "Towards a Minimal Definition of the Goddess Mut," *Ex Oriente Lux* no. 26 (1979–1980) Leiden, 1980, 3–9.

——. "Mut, the Eye of Re," in: *Akten des vierten internationalen Ägyptologen Kongresses München 1985* III, ed. Sylvia Schoske. Hamburg: Helmut Buske, 1989, 395–403.

——. "Iunmutef," *LÄ* III, 212–13.

——. "Ptah," *LÄ* IV, 1177–80.

Teeter, Emily. *The Presentation of Maat: Ritual and Legitimacy in Ancient Egypt*. SAOC 57. Chicago: Oriental Institute of the University of Chicago, 1997.

——. "Celibacy and Adoption among Gods' Wives of Amun and Singers in the Temple of Amun: Re-examination of the Evidence," in: *Gold of Praise: Studies on Ancient Egypt in Honor of Edward F. Wente*, eds. E. Teeter and J. A. Larson. SAOC 58. Chicago: Oriental Institute of the University of Chicago, 1999, 405–14.

——. *Ancient Egypt: Treasures from the Collection of the Oriental Institute, University of Chicago*. Chicago: Oriental Institute, 2003.

Thompson, Stephen E. and der Manuelian, Peter (eds). *Egypt and Beyond: Essays Presented to Leonard H. Lesko upon his Retirement from the Wilbour Chair of Egyptology at Brown University. June 2005*. Providence, RI: Department of Egyptology and Ancient Western Asian Studies, Brown University, 2008.

Török, L. *The Kingdom of Kush: Handbook of the Napatan-Meroitic Civilization.* Leiden: Brill, 1997.

Traunecker, Claude. *The Gods of Egypt*. Trans. D. Lorton. Ithaca: Cornell University Press, 2001.

——. "Kamutef," in: *The Oxford Encyclopedia of Ancient Egypt* II. Oxford: Oxford University Press, 2001, 221–22.

Trigger, Bruce. *Nubia under the Pharaohs*. London: Thames and Hudson, 1976.

Trigger, Bruce, B. J. Kemp, D. O'Connor, and A. B. Lloyd. *Ancient Egypt: A Social History*. Cambridge: Cambridge University Press, 1983.

Troy, Lana. *Patterns of Queenship in Ancient Egyptian Myth and History*. Uppsala Studies in Ancient Mediterranean Civilizations 14. Uppsala: Almqvist & Wiksell International, 1986.

Van der Plas, Dirk. "The Veiled Image of Amenapet," in: *Effigies Dei: Essays on the History of Religions. Studies in the History of Religions* 51, ed. D. Van der Plas. Leiden: E. J. Brill, 1987, 1–12.

Van Dijk, Jacobus, "Ptah," in: *The Oxford Encyclopedia of Ancient Egypt* III, ed. D. B. Redford. Oxford: Oxford University Press, 2001, 74–76.

Van Doorn-Harder, Pieternella. *Contemporary Coptic Nuns*. Columbia: University of South Carolina Press, 1995.

Vandier, Jacques. "L'intronisation de Nitocris," *ZÄS* 99 (1972): 29–33.

Varille, Alexander. *Karnak* I. Fouilles de l'Institut Français du Caire XIX. Cairo: IFAO, 1943.

Verhoeven, Ursula. "Tefnut," *LÄ* VI, 269–304.

Vittmann, Günther. *Priester und Beamte im Theben der Spätzeit*. Beiträge zur Ägyptologie 1. Vienna: Afro-Pub, 1978.

——. "Stolist," *LÄ* VI, 63–66.

Vogelsang-Eastwood, Gillian. *Pharaonic Egyptian Clothing*. Leiden: E. J. Brill, 1993.

Waddell, W. G. *Manetho*. Cambridge, Mass.: Harvard University Press, 1940.

Wainwright, G. A. "Seshat and the Pharaoh," *JEA* 26 (1940): 30–40.

Ward, William A. *Essays on Feminine Titles of the Middle Kingdom and Related Subjects*. Beirut: American University of Beirut, 1986.

Watson, Philip J. *Costume of Ancient Egypt*. London: Batsford Ltd, 1987.

Wenig, Stephen. "Pabatma-Pekereslo-Pekar-tor: Ein Beitrag zur Frühgeschichte der Kuschiten," in: *Meroitica* 12 (1990): 333–52.

Wildung, Dietrich. *Sudan: Ancient Kingdoms of The Nile*. Paris and New York: Flammarion, 1997.

Wilkinson, R. H. *Magic and Symbol in Egyptian Art*. London: Thames and Hudson Ltd., 1994.

Wilson, John. A. "Myths, Epics, and Legends," in: *Ancient Near Eastern Texts Relating to the Old Testament*, ed. James B. Pritchard. Princeton: Princeton University Press, 1969, 3–36.

Yamauchi, E.. M. (ed.). *Africa and Africans in Antiquity*. East Lansing: Michigan State University Press, 2001.

Yoyotte, Jean. "Les vierges consacrées d'Amon thébain," *CRAIBL* 1961 (1962): 43–52.

——. "Des lions et des chats: Contribution à la prosopographie de l'époque libyenne," *RdÉ* 39 (1988): 169–70.

Žába, Z. *Les Maximes de Ptahhotep*. Prague: Éditions de l'académie tchécoslovaque des sciences, 1956.

Zeissl, H. von. *Äthiopen und Assyrer in Ägypten: Beiträge zur Geschichte der ägyptischen "Spätzeit."* Glückstadt: J.J. Augustin, 1955.

Ziegler, Christiane. "Sistrum," *LÄ* V, 959–963.

Zivie, C. *Le Temple de Deir Chelouit* I–III. Cairo: IFAO, 1982–1986.

INDEX

Bold page numbers indicate illustrations

Achaemenid court and state policy 153–4
Ahmose (c.1552–1527 BC) 4, 6
Ahmose II *see* Amasis
Ahmose-Nefertari 4, 6, 19, 131; donation stela 4, 6
Ahhotep, Queen 4
Alara, Nubian ruler (c.780–760 BC) 11
Amasis, Saite ruler (570–526 BC) 27–8, 78–82
Amenirdis I, God's Wife 16, 18, 19, 22, 53; appointment of 142–4; chapel builder 72, **73**, 74, 132, (colour plates 2.12, 2.15); dates and affiliation 22; descent from Osiris 132, 144; divine marriage 135; "driving four calves" 104, **105**, 106; embraced by Amun-Re 135 (colour plate 3.8); funerary chapel 19–21, **20**, 39, 53, 59, 60, 65, 103–6, 104, **105**, 106, 114–15, 118, 133, 143, 154; "God's Hand" 22; "justified" 134, 135, 77, 78, 111, 60, (colour plates 2.11, 3.8); legitimacy 118, 130–2; *meret* chests 108, 109; names and titles 19, 29, 31, 32–3, 53, 62–3, 66, 72, 131, 132; Nubian features 52, 62, 63, **65**; offering wine to Amun 52, 53–4, (colour plate 2.6); offers temple image to Amun-Re 72, **74**, 118; presenting *Maat* 63–4, 64–7; receiving life from Amun 40–1, **48**, 130, **131**; relationship to Amun-Re 38, 39, 40, 41, **41**, 135; relationship to Mut 39–43; relationship to Shepenwepet I 132; representations of 52, 53, 129–133, (colour plate 2.6); *sed* celebration/symbols 40, **41**, 42, **42**, 114–15, 118; shaking sistrum before the gods 37–43, 130; status relative to the king 118; "stretching the cord" with Seshat 72, **73**, 74, 118, 132; and Wadjet 66–7, 77
Amenirdis II, possible God's Wife 21, 24, 77, 89, 90, 111, 134; daughter of Taharqo 89; "God's Hand" 21
Amun *see* Amun-Re
Amun-Re: creator god 38–9, 46; crowning Shepenwepet I 127–9, **128**; "driving four calves" 104, 107; giving life 84–5; giving life to Amenirdis I 40–1, **48**, 130, **131**; *Kom Djeme* 94–5, 100; Mut, divine marriage with 134–8, **136**, **138**; offerings of food 55–6; official names 29–31; receiving *Maat* 62, 63–4, 65–6, 67, **68**, 69; relationship to the God's Wife 38; relationship to Nubian Royalty 38–9; relationship to Osiris 38–9; representations of 35–6, 39, 41, 52, 53, 55–6, 67, 70, 135, (colour plate 2.6); titles 53
Amun-Re-Kamutef 44–6, **44**, 51, 80–1, 82, 103
Ankhnesneferibre, last God's Wife of Amun 2, 22, 26, 27–8, 116, 140–1; Adoption Stela 2, 121, 140; and Amasis 78–82; dates and affiliation 22; enlargment of chapels 27, 141; heiress apparent to Nitocris 140; High Priest of Amun 27, 116, 120, 121, 140; high steward of 70, 80; initiation 120–1; legitimating rites 140–1, 145; offering *Maat* to Amun-Re 69–70; rewarded by Amun-Re 84–6; rewarded by Isis 85–6; sarcophagus 28
Apries, Saite ruler (589–570 BC) 27
Atum, creator god 60–1, 98

Barguet, Paul 70, 81
Bell, Lanny 81–2
Bleeker, C.J. 99, 100, 114

Brand, P. 136
Bryan, Betsy 6

Caminos, R.A. 24
chapels: of the God's Wife of Amun at Karnak 2, **2**; of Nitocris and Amasis 84–6, *see also* Amenirdis I, funerary chapel; Osiris, chapels; Shepenwepet I, funerary chapel
Chief Royal Wife 6, 16, 117, 127
contraceptives in ancient Egypt 150–1

Dedwen 96, 97
'Divine Adorer' 3, 10, 19, 152
divine marriage iconography 134–8, **136**, **138**
'Divine Worshipper' 15
Djeme *see Kom Djeme*
Dodson, Aidan 21
Donation Stela of Ahmose-Nefertari 4, 6
"driving four calves" 103–8, **105**

Egberts, A. 106, 109
Egypt: Assyrian domination 2; Libyan period 10–11; New Kingdom 4, 5, 6, 8; Nineteenth Dynasty 6; Nubian "rule" 11–15, 16, 118–20; Saite rule 22–3, 26–7; Third Intermediate Period 9–10, 15; Twentieth Dynasty 8, 9; Twenty-first Dynasty 9, 10; Twenty-second Dynasty 10; Twenty-third Dynasty 15; Twenty-fifth Dynasty 13, 31, 115; genealogy 12 Twenty-sixth Dynasty,genealogy 23
elevation of the *tjest*-support ritual 96–9, **97**, 101–2

Fischer, H.G. 89
funerary cult 71, 144
four, significance of number 109

Gardiner, Alan H. 112, 146
goddesses suckling king and Shepenwepet I 124–7, **125**, **126**
"God's Hand" 3, 10, 19, 91, 92, 94, 95, 96, 99, 131; heiress apparent 21–2; Horus connection 98; ithyphallic connection 102–3; sexual role 4
the God's Wife, historical development of title 1–4, 6, 8–10, 119
the God's Wife of Amun; adoption 142–5; appointment of 142–3; associated titles 3–4, 6, 9, 10, 16, 131, 155; burning fans ritual 90–4, 123, (colour plate 2.23); celibacy 146–7, 152; child appointees 142; dates and affiliation **22**; divine marriage iconography 134–8, **136**, **138**; *elevation of the* tjest-*support* ritual 96–9, **97**, 101–2, 123; the end of the institution 28, 153–4; high steward of 70, 80, 118–19; iconography and femininity 147; initiation rites 120–1; Isis role 101, 102; legacy of 154–5; names omitted in ritual 89, 90, 102; Nubian incumbants 20, 21, 120; offerings to the gods 52–60; official names 29–33, **29**; political appoinment 6, 117, 142; pouring libations 57, **58**; power and status 36, 70, 84, 89, 93, 113, 118, 119, 124; presenting *Maat* 61–9, 69; priestly function and privileges 91–4, 96–9, **97**, 101–2, 116, 118, 122–4, **122**; purification rites 121, 93–4 (colour plate 3.2); re-establishment of office 31; *sed* celebration 112–15; sexual role 151–2; single status 9, 154, *see also* Amenirdis I; Amenirdis II; Ankhnesneferibre; "God's Hand"; Nitocris; Shepenwepet I; Shepenwepet II
the God's Wife of Amun, and the king; complimentarity 86, 102; lateral relationship **87**, 89–90, 100; rejuvenating the gods 96–103; "rites at Kom Djeme" 94–6; rites of divine re-entrance 99–103; rites of protection at the cenotaph 87–90, **87**; symmetrical presentation 75–8, **75**, 78–82, 82–6, (colour plates 20a and 20b)
the God's Wives' edifice, *sed* celebration 110–15
Gosselin, Luc 9
Goyon, J-C. 98, 99, 101, 123
Graefe, Erhart 21–2
Grimal, N.-C. 24
Grimm, A. 91

Habachi, Labib 21
Handoussa, T. 136–7
Harsiese 76, 78, 85, 134
Hathor 45, 67, 77, 79, 130; *menat* and sistrum 47, 49, 50; receiving *Maat* 65–6; symmetrical presentation 77–8, 134
Hatshepsut 4, 6, 45, 93; *chapelle rouge* 22, 30, 90–4, 103, 121, 122, **122**, (colour plate 2.23); "driving four calves" **105**, 107–8; male attire **105**, 147; official names 30–1; Queen (c. 1490–1469 BC) 107; *sed* festival 114
Heliopolitan creation myth 5, 98, 102, 123, 148

Hesse, F. 44, 46
High Priest of Amun 8, 9, 14, 118, 143
High Steward of God's Wife 70, 80, 118–19
Hölscher, Uvo 20, 133, 145
Hornung, E. 100, 115
Horus: the Behdite 112; creator god 124; "driving four calves" 104, **105**, 106; king identifies with 101–2; official names 31–2; rejuvenating ritual 96, 98; and Taharqo 98
Hyksos 6
Hypostyle Hall at Karnak 103, 135–7

incense offering 58–60
Isis 44–5; embraces Shepenwepet II 82, 83, 134, (colour plate 2.20b); giving life to Ankhnesneferibre 85–6; the God's Wife 101, 102; offers *menat* to Shepenwepet I 47–8, 130; and Osiris 148–9; protection at the cenotaph 90; representation of 57, 59–60, (colour plate 2.11); *sed* symbols 55; symmetrical presentation 76–8, 80
Isis, daughter of Ramses VI 9, 15; first single God's Wife 9, 15
Isis, name of Ramesside God's Wives 9
Iunmoutef-priest 101, 102, 113, 123

ka 79, 81–2, 113
Kamutef 45
Karnak: chapels of God's Wife of Amun 2, **2**; Great Hypostyle Hall (Ramses II) 103, 135–7; temple of Khonsu 9, *see also* chapels
Karoajet, Chief Royal Wife of Osorkon III 16, 127
Karomama Merytmut, God's Wife 10, 51, 152
Kashta, Nubian ruler (c.760–747 BC) 11–12, 16, 142
Kees, H. 98, 123
Khonsu 78–9, 107, 113
Khonsu Cosmogony 38
Kitchen, K.A. 24, 117
Kom Djeme 94–5, 98, 100, 102

Leahy, Anthony 10, 91
Leclant, Jean 21, 38, 66, 89, 98, 113, 132
Lohwasser, Angelika 119

Maat 51, 60, 61, 89, 130; goddess 81; presented by the God's Wives 61–9; presented by kings 63, 64, **65**
Maatkare, Divine Worshipper 22nd Dynasty 10, 61, 146

Manetho 13, 119
Manniche, Lise 35, 47
marriage and sex, Egyptian attitude 147–50
Maspero, G. 12
Mehetnusekhet, mother of Nitocris 21, 26, 142
menat necklace and collar 47–9, 50
Mentuemhat, Mayor of Thebes 111, 119, 142
meret chests, consecration of 108–10
Min 45; association with God's Wife 4, 34, 152; festival 114
Morkot, R. 21
mortuary and cultic architecture (Egypt) 20–1
Murnane, W.J. 114, 115
music for the gods 35, 50–1, 152, *see also* *menat*; sistrum
Mut 28; divine marriage with Amun-Re 134–8, **136**, **138**; and God's Wife 137; offered sistra 46–7, **46**; relationship with Amenirdis I 42–3, **42**; relationship to Shepenwepet II 137; representations of 39–40, 41–2, 55–6, 69, 70; significance of name 29, 31, 32–3
Mysliwiec, K. 52, 62, 64
myths: divine conception of king 7–8; Heliopolitan creation myth 5; Isis and Osiris 148–9

Nebet-Hetepet 49
Necho II, Saite ruler (610–595 BC) 26–7
Neferure, God's Wife 6
Nekhbet 32, 40
Nitocris (B) daughter of Amasis 28, 90; High Priest of Amun 28, 116
Nitocris, daughter of Psametik I and God's Wife of Amun 15, 21, 22, 23–6, 90, 111, 139–40; building program 25–6, **26**; child appointee 142; "Nitocris Adoption Stela" 2, 24–5, 77, 120, 139–40, 142, 143; official names 29
Nubian 'God's Wives' 24, 25, 154–5
Nubians in Egypt 11–15, 32, 69, 129; power-sharing model 119–20
Nun, regenerative powers 100

offerings to the gods; food 55–7; incense 58–60; libations 57–8, 59; wine 52–5
Osiris: "driving four calves" 104, **105**, 106; embraces Taharqo 82–3, 84; libations to 58; mystical union with Amun

and Re-Horakhty 101; relationship to Amun-Re 38–9, 56–7; representations of 43, 54–5, **54**, 56–7, 76; shrines 25; symmetrical representation 76–8
Osiris, chapels 22, 38, 43, 59; *Heqa Djet* 19; *Neb-ankh* or " Lord of Life" 19, 22, 43, 56, 58, 59, 66, 68, 75–8, **75**, 82–4, 134, 137; "Osiris-who-perpetually-gives-life" 141; *Wennofer-in-the-Persea-Tree* or "Ruler of Eternity" 16, **17**, **18**, 22, 35–9, 40, **41**, **42**, 47, **48**, 52, 54–55, 57, **58**, 61–2, 114–115, 116, **117**, 118, 123, 124–6, 127–9, **128**, 129–132, 134–5, 143, 152 (colour plate 2.6); *Wennofer-Nebdjefa* or "Lord of Offerings" 43, 78–82, 137, (colour plates 2.19 a and b)
Osorkon II, *sed* festivals 114
Osorkon III (c. 777–740 BC) 15, 16, 36, 117, 127; official names 29–30
Otto, E. 39

Pamiu, Viceroy of Kush 11
Panehsy, Viceroy of Kush 8–9, 11
partnering with king *see* symmetrical presentation
Persian conquest of Egypt 153–4
Piye, Nubian ruler (747–716 BC) 12–13, 16, 31, 142, 143
protection at the cenotaph, rites 87–90, **87**, 101
Psametik I(664–656 BC), Saite Dynasty 15, 22–3, 24, 111, 139
Psametik II (595–589 BC) 26, 27, 69
Psametik III (526–525 BC), rewarded by Amun-Re and Harsiese 84–6
Ptah 36, 76–7, 78, 81
Ptah-Nun 82
Ptolemaic Queens of Egypt 155
Pyramid Texts 14–19, 127
Ra-Horakhty 36, 59
Ramses II (c.1279–1213 BC): divine marriage 136; "driving four calves" 107; sistrum 44–6, **44**
Ramses VI 9
Ramses IX (c.1127–1108 BC) 8, 9
Ramses XI (c.1104–1075 BC) 8, 9
Reynders, M. 37
Ritner, Robert 10
Robins, Gay 30, 36, 84, 124, 151
Russmann, E.R. 11

Saite dynasty (26th Dynasty) 2, 13, 15, 22–3, 26–8, 116; God's Wives 120, 143
sed celebration 110–15
Sefekh-Abwy 71–2
Shabaqo, Nubian ruler (c.716–702 BC) 13–14, 16; King of Egypt 118, 119, 129, 143
Shebitqo, Nubian ruler (702–690 BC) 119, 129, 143; legitimacy of regime 130; presenting *Maat* to Amun-Re **65**, 130, 132; representation 52, 64, **65**; royal titles 31–2
Shepenwepet I, Libyan God's Wife of Amun 15–16, 22, 62; apparent role with sistrum 35–6; appointment to office 143; crowning scenes 127–9, **128**; dates and affiliation 22; "Divine Adorer" 62; exceptional proximity to gods 124; funerary chapel 16, **17**, 26; legitimacy 128–9, 130; *menat* necklace and collar 47–9, 130; offering food to Amun 55–6; official names 29–31, 33; political appointment 117; presenting *Maat* to Amun-Re 62, 65, 130, (colour plate 2.5); priestly duties 116–17, **117**; relationship to Amenirdis I 132, 144, 145; relationship to Isis 47–8, 130; suckled by Hathor 124–7, **125**; titles 128, 131
Shepenwepet II, Nubian God's Wife of Amun 19–21, 22, 24, 89; Amenirdis funerary cult and chapel 19–21, 43, 71–2, 133, 137, 144, 145; appointment to office 143; assertion of legitimacy 68, **75**, 78, 106, 133, 152; "Divine Adorer" 71; divine marriage iconography 134–8, **136**, **138**, 152; "Divine Worshipper" 60; "driving four calves" 103–6, **105**, 133; elevated status 137; embraced by Amun-Re 135, (colour plate 3.9); embraced by Isis 82, 83, 134, (colour plate 2.20b); "God's Hand" 22; and king Taharqo **87**, 118; offering incense 59, (colour plate 2.10); offering milk to Wepwawet 66; offerings to Osiris 54–5, **54**, 57, (colour plate 2.8); official names 29; playing the sistrum 43; presentation of *meret* chests 108; presenting *Maat* to Amum-Re 67, **68**, 69; priestly function and privileges 116, 137; and Ptah 76–7; relationship to Amenirdis I 133–5, 137; relationship to Mut 137; royal iconography 110, 118; *sed* celebration 22, 111, **111**, 112, 114–15, 116, 118, 137; "stretching the cord" with Sefekh-Abwy 71–2; symmetrical representation with Taharqo 75–8, **75**, 134

Sheshonq 70, 80
Shoshenq I 114
sistrum 34–51; associated with Bat and Hathor 37; the God's Wife shaking 35, 43, 44, 51; Ptolemaic kings 46–7, **46**; rattling, Ramses II 44–6, **44**; sexual interpretation 38, 44, 46, 51, 66
Smendes (1075–1044 BC) 9
Sobek 96, 98
Soped 96, 97–8
Spalinger, Anthony 25, 120
suckling by the gods 124–7, **125**
symmetrical representation, king and God's Wife 75–8, **75**, 134; Amasis and Ankhnesneferibre 78–82; Saite period 84–6; Taharqo and Shepenwepet II 75–8, 82–4, 87–90, 134

Taharqo, Nubian ruler and King of Egypt(690–664 BC) 14–15, 19, 31, 32, 43, 119, 143; "driving four calves" 107; Edifice of Taharqo 22, 87–8, **87**, 90, 94–103, 123; embraced by Osiris 82–3, 84; and Osiris 76; promotion of Horus 98; rewarded by gods 82–4, (colour plates 20 a and b); rites of protection 87–8; symmetrical representation with Shepenwepet II 75–8, 82–4, 87–90, 134; unity with gods/legitimacy 101–2, 106
Takeloth III (c.754–734 BC) 16, 117
Tanwetamani, last Kushite ruler 15
Tausret, Queen regnant (c.1209–1200 BC) God's Wife 6
Te Velde, H. 40
Tefnut 66
temple foundation rites 73–4
Thoth 51, 92
Török, L. 30

Viceroy of Kush 8–9, 11

Wadjet 66–7, 77
Wenou-Min 4
Wepwawet 60, 61, 113

Yoyotte, Jean 146–7

An environmentally friendly book printed and bound in England by www.printondemand-worldwide.com

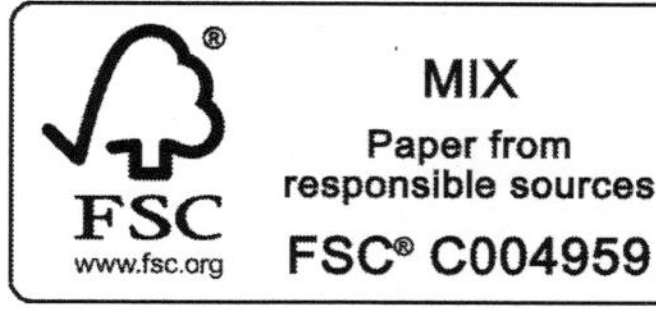

This book is made entirely of chain-of-custody materials; FSC materials for the cover and PEFC materials for the text pages.

#0304 - 020113 - C8 - 234/156/12 - PB